God and World in the Old Testament

Terence E. Fretheim

God and World in the Old Testament

A Relational Theology of Creation

Abingdon Press
Nashville

GOD AND WORLD IN THE OLD TESTAMENT
A RELATIONAL THEOLOGY OF CREATION

This book is printed on acid-free paper.

Library of Congress Cataloging-in-Publication Data

Fretheim, Terence E.
God and world in the Old Testament : a relational theology of creation / Terence E. Fretheim.
p. cm.
Includes bibliographical references and indexes.
ISBN 0-687-34296-1 (binding: adhesive, perfect : alk. paper)
1. Creation—Biblical teaching. 2. Bible. O.T.—Theology. 3. Bible. O.T.—Criticism, interpretation, etc. I. Title.

BS1199.C73F74 2005
231.7'65—dc22
ISBN 13: 978-0-687-34296-9 2004020007

Chapter 5 is adapted from "Law in the Service of Life: A Dynamic Understanding of Law in Deuteronomy" by Terence E. Fretheim, first published in *A God So Near: Essays on Old Testament Theology in Honor of Patrick D. Miller*, edited by Brent A. Strawn and Nancy R. Bowen; Winona Lake, Indiana: Eisenbrauns, 2003.

Portions of chapter 6 are adapted from "The Character of God in Jeremiah" by Terence E. Fretheim, first published in *Character and Scripture: Moral Formation, Community and Biblical Interpretation* edited by William P. Brown. Copyright © 2002 by the Wm. B. Eerdmans Publishing Company.

Portions of chapter 6 are adapted from "The Earth Story in Jeremiah 12" by Terence E. Fretheim, first published in *Readings from the Perspective of Earth* edited by Norman C. Habel. Copyright © 2000 by the Sheffield Academic Press. Reprinted by permission of The Continuum International Publishing Group.

Chapter 7 is an adaptation of "God in the Book of Job" by Terence E. Fretheim, first published in *Currents in Theology and Mission* (1999): 85-93.

Continued on page 398.

08 09 10 11 12 13 14—10 9 8 7 6 5 4

MANUFACTURED IN THE UNITED STATES OF AMERICA

Contents

FOREWORD

Creation has been a career-long concern of mine. My very first book was a study of Genesis 1–11; more than a decade ago the preparation of my NIB commentary on Genesis solidified that interest; and several articles along the way have sought to draw out that conversation. I have noted along the way that creation was a sorely neglected theme in Old Testament studies. Yet, it took some time before I fully realized that creation is a much more fundamental substratum of Old Testament theological reflection than most scholars imagine. And so I have thought it especially important to move beyond the creation accounts and seek to discern the depth and breadth of creational thought across the canon. Many more texts and traditions could have been drawn into the conversation, but I must leave that task for others to pursue.

This volume would not have been completed without the help of many persons. I wish to express my appreciation to students at Luther Seminary, who have interacted over the years with this material in earlier forms. Gratitude is also due to several colleagues—Paul Sponheim, Diane Jacobson, and Frederick Gaiser—who read all or portions of this material along the way. I am also grateful to the administration and board of directors of Luther Seminary for granting a leave of absence in order to complete this work. The encouragement of editors at Abingdon Press—Greg Glover and Kathy Armistead especially—has been invaluable.

A special thanksgiving is extended to my wife, Faith, for her unfailing support along the way. I dedicate this volume to our three grandchildren—Kelly, Shannon, and Emre—wonderful creations who came to life over the course of time that this book was written. Thanks be to God.

Terence E. Fretheim

INTRODUCTION

The importance of creation has often been underestimated by church and academy. Indeed, we can speak of the "marginalization of creation" in biblical and theological study over the course of much of the twentieth century (and before).[1] Only in the last generation or so have significant efforts been made to recover a proper role for creation in biblical-theological reflection. The purpose of this volume is to contribute to this emerging conversation from an Old Testament theological perspective.

The causes of the marginalization of creation are many and complex. Certainly and most basically, an anthropocentrism has been at work in pervasive ways. Also, often cited are various cultural-social-political realities. Such an influence can be observed in the 1936 seminal article on creation by Gerhard von Rad, which at least in part reflects those theological efforts concerned to respond to "natural" emphases of national socialism in Germany. This article, with its subordination of creation to redemption, has been remarkably generative of further reflection on creation in the Old Testament, both positively and negatively.[2] But the factors contributing to the neglect of creation among biblical scholars have been much more wide-ranging than the key factors that grounded von Rad's concern. One could cite the following trajectories of reflection that have diminished the place of creation:

(1) a focus on history, particularly salvation history, at the expense of nature; indeed, creation has been seen as being in the service of *Israel's* history;[3]
(2) the association of creation with the cosmologies of Canaanite and other ancient Near Eastern religions, often negatively perceived to be syncretistic "nature religions" and hence at odds with Israel's most basic theological commitments;

(3) a relinquishment of the study of nature to the scientists, not least in view of the controversies generated by creationists;
(4) various theological perspectives (from deism to radical transcendence to absolute sovereignty) that remove God from too close a brush with the continuing life of the created order, raising questions as to whether God was actually engaged with life in the real world;[4]
(5) an existentialism that tends to see all of reality from the perspective of human existence;
(6) a political theology centered on the liberation of the human to the neglect of the nonhuman;
(7) a theology of the word where preaching and the administration of the sacraments are so sharply focused on the human and the salvation of the human;
(8) an emphasis on the spiritual and otherworldly dimensions of religious life to the neglect of the bodily and earthly dimensions of spirituality;
(9) various end-of-the-world scenarios, wherein God is soon going to blow everything up anyway, so why bother to care for creation;
(10) the diminishment of the importance of the Old Testament in the teaching and preaching of the church;
(11) an evident patriarchalism in biblical interpretation that occasioned a stress on interventionist, virile modes of understanding God's "mighty acts," to the neglect of the more feminine themes of creation and blessing.[5]

When these wide-ranging factors are so enumerated, it is evident that the "forces" arrayed against a careful attention to matters of creation have been considerable.

From another perspective, our time has also seen the (re)emergence of romantic views of the nonhuman world, wherein a valuing and respect for the natural order has morphed into a deep protectiveness that suggests that nature is unable to care for itself; indeed, nature may even be approached as "victim." In such cases, the proper human approach has too often become a virtual worship of the natural order, too commonly accompanied by a point of view that gives human beings no special place among God's creatures. In view of these differing perspectives, Northrop

Frye has charted the task well: "to steer some sort of middle course between the Gnostic contempt for nature and the pagan adoration of it."[6]

That a concern for creational matters has intensified over recent years cannot be credited to the church or to the theological disciplines to any great extent. Chiefly responsible for this salutary development has probably been the emergence of an ecological consciousness, deeply set within increasing numbers of individual psyches, with an expanding societal concern. Though such a focus has too often been motivated solely or primarily by a concern for the future of the human race, the environmental benefits should not be downplayed. Other factors are certainly important, such as a greater appreciation of the value of ancient Near Eastern creation thought; an openness to a greater range of texts that have to do with creation (not just originating creation), especially Wisdom literature; the welcome expansion of the conversation between science and religion; an increased awareness of the global scale of environmental issues; and an intensified sense of the deep relatedness and interdependence of all creatures.[7]

Yet, even with this broader cultural commitment, the importance of creation theology in theological reflection has been slow to take hold, not least in the biblical disciplines.[8] One can survey recent Old Testament theologies, such as those of Brevard S. Childs,[9] Horst Dietrich Preuss,[10] Bernhard W. Anderson,[11] and Erhard Gerstenberger,[12] and it becomes evident that creation theology is given less than a central place. Walter Brueggemann's *Theology of the Old Testament* may be considered near a midpoint to where we ought eventually to be.[13] John Goldingay's *Old Testament Theology* also represents a shift in emphasis, primarily because he takes the biblical narrative sequence seriously and begins his projected three-volume work with a significant exposition of the creation accounts and related creation texts.[14] Rolf Rendtorff makes an obvious but neglected point: "The Hebrew Bible begins with creation. Old Testament Theologies usually do not. How is that? The answer is obvious: because of the theology of the respective authors of Old Testament theologies."[15] We will engage aspects of these discussions as we proceed.

At the same time, it must be said that over the course of the last generation several important biblical-theological developments have enabled creation to assume a more prominent (and rightful!) place in Old Testament theology. Indeed, there has been a veritable rush on books and articles dealing with creation in the Hebrew Bible. Among the scholars that especially deserve mention are: Claus Westermann,[16]

H. H. Schmid,[17] Rolf P. Knierim,[18] Odil Hannes Steck,[19] Bernhard W. Anderson,[20] Jon D. Levenson,[21] James Barr,[22] Ronald A. Simkins,[23] Leo G. Perdue,[24] William P. Brown,[25] Karl Löning and Erich Zenger,[26] Stefan Paas,[27] W. Randall Garr,[28] and *The Earth Bible* series, edited by Norman C. Habel.[29] We will seek to integrate their insights regarding creation as we move through the discussion. While we will be focusing on this Old Testament conversation, it should be noted that there has also been a flood of work on issues of ecotheology and ecopractice across all disciplines; many such volumes include discussions and essays on matters relating to Old Testament texts.[30] In addition, the increasing number of books and articles on creation by systematic theologians will be important for our conversation.[31]

As a way of beginning, I briefly lift up the work of three of these scholars whose work has been especially important in charting a new course for the Old Testament understanding of creation.

Claus Westermann's studies have been significant in giving creation a stature in its own right.[32] Working with von Rad's perspectives, and against them,[33] he carves out an important niche of creational reflection, particularly with respect to the category of blessing, wherein God is active in the ebb and flow of everyday life. At the same time, he will also make claims that seem to subordinate creation to salvation history: "the history established by God's saving deed was expanded to include the beginning of everything that happens."[34] Westermann might have recognized more clearly that blessing could be considered under a category such as continuous creation (e.g., Psalm 104).[35] In addition, Westermann claims that the creation accounts do not have an interest in historical origins (whether interpreted as an act of salvation or in other terms); rather, they are a witness to God's *ongoing* creative work in every present moment. These accounts are understood in terms of ritual actualization in which the word about creation is recited in worship and the Creator is praised as the source of a lively word for ongoing life (and not as a source for intellectual probing). Insufficiently recognized by Westermann is the distinction between viewing the creation accounts as historical and as a story of the past.[36] Moreover, for Westermann, creation is not a matter of belief ("creation faith") but is an *assumption* held by all peoples in that time (cf. Paul in Acts 17:25-28). Yet, he might have made a cleaner distinction between an assumption that the world had been created by a deity and a *belief* in the God of Israel (rather than another deity) as the one who has created the world.[37]

Even more important for these newer developments is the work of H. H. Schmid,[38] "perhaps the most powerful treatment in the recovery of creation as a proper dimension of Israel's faith."[39] He strongly emphasizes creation (rather than, say, covenant) as a comprehensive theological horizon or framework within which Israel's most basic theological themes are developed and its historical experiences articulated. Attending to the understanding of creation in surrounding cultures, with which Israel positively but not uncritically engaged, Schmid shows that creation in Israel is understood in terms of both origination and continuing order. But, it is the latter that he lifts up for special attention. He specifies that *sedeqah*, "righteousness" (similar to the Egyptian *ma'at*), refers to a harmonious world order built by God into the very infrastructure of creation. So, wherever righteousness is practiced by human beings in the sociopolitical spheres, that act is in tune with the creation, and it fosters the proper integration of social and cosmic orders.[40] When humans do not so practice righteousness, adverse effects are felt across all created spheres. And so, for the Old Testament, matters such as justice, politics, and nature are interrelated as "aspects of one comprehensive order of creation."[41] This framework of a comprehensive world order, "a universal righteousness," is of decisive import for the shaping of the moral life. William P. Brown in *Ethos of the Cosmos* takes his lead from such a perspective and focuses on the power of the creation traditions in "forming the moral identity of communities of faith."[42]

Rolf Knierim has been especially helpful in pointing out that the way in which the interpreter works with creation has immense implications for the way in which one thinks about the God of the Bible.

> Yahweh is not the God of creation because he is the God of the humans or of human history. He is the God of the humans and of human history because He is the God of creation. . . . The most universal aspect of Yahweh's dominion is not human history. It is the creation and sustenance of the world. This aspect is at the same time the most fundamental because creation does not depend on history or existence, but history and existence depend on and are measured against creation.[43]

Creation exists quite apart from the history of the human.

> If Yahweh is not . . . the God of all reality, he cannot be the one and only God because he is not God universal. Yahweh may be Israel's God

> in oneness and exclusivity, but if he is not Israel's God because he is first of all God of all reality and of all humanity, he is a nationalistic deity or an individualistic idol, one among others, actually a no-god. Without the critical notion of universality, the affirmation of Yahweh's oneness and exclusivity does not substantiate the affirmation of his true deity.[44]

Such an analysis would support the following claims. God is the God of the entire cosmos; God has to do with every creature, and every creature has to do with God, whether they recognize it or not. God's work in the world must be viewed in and through *a universal frame of reference*. That the Bible begins with Genesis, not Exodus, with creation, not redemption, is of immeasurable importance for understanding all that follows.[45] At least from the perspective of the present shape of the biblical witness, creation is as basic and integral to Israelite faith and its confession as is the first article of the creed to Christians.

The Origins of Israel's Creation Faith

The above reflections prompt a discussion regarding the origins of Israel's creation faith.[46] Only a brief survey is possible here; various dimensions of this conversation will be evident throughout the volume. Where did Israel get its understanding of God as Creator? When was creation integrated into Israel's theological perspective and its confession of faith in God? The texts do not speak clearly to such issues; interpreters must draw inferences from various sources, and scholarly opinions have varied considerably—dating from early in Israel's life to late. In thinking through such questions, interpreters must be careful not to limit the presence of creation faith to contexts that use certain words or phrases (e.g., *bārā'*, "create").[47] Moreover, the definition the interpreter gives to creation will also affect the response to these issues. If, for example, creation is understood only in terms of the creation accounts and their echoes, or only in terms of the physical universe, the search for origins will be (too) narrowly conceived.[48] Among the several possibilities, I take note of a few matters.

More generally, without a special concern for dating, James Barr helpfully speaks of Israel's understanding of creation as deriving from "Israel's own knowledge and experience of the world."[49] Barr points especially to two dimensions of experience:

(1) Ancient accounts of the beginning of the world inherited from Israel's environment, Mesopotamian accounts especially. The correspondences that exist between the biblical accounts and ancient Near Eastern creation texts show the extent to which Israel's understandings of creation are informed by nonsalvific traditions and themes and preceded Israel's salvific confessions.[50] If these understandings were present in that world generally, it is likely that they were current also in Israel. At the same time, there is no evidence to suggest a direct dependence. (2) Israel's own reflections on issues that arose from within the community, including priestly concerns for boundaries and separations as well as wisdom interests in observations made of the world.[51]

To these important observations one might add Israel's own experience of creation itself; these people lived close to the ground, if you will, and the natural world filled their lives. Creation was a lively reality for them prior to the development of specific ideas about creation. It would seem likely in view of this experience that the God in whom they believed (whether monotheism or its predecessors) was linked to creation as a matter of course. Given the fact that the texts often speak of such everyday realities as family and clan, the birth and growth of children, homes and fields, wild and domestic animals, and weather with its effects for good or ill, it may be that "blessing" was a basic and early understanding of Israel's God as Creator.[52]

Yet, the question remains as to the point at which this experience and Israel's reflections upon it drew creation into its most basic confession of faith or was integrated with other key dimensions of the faith. It has probably been most common to suggest that Israel's experience of redemption in the exodus events constituted the initial core of its faith, into which various other dimensions of the faith were grafted over time (such as creation).[53] To put it too baldly: Yahweh is redeemer, therefore Yahweh must be creator. An inference is then often drawn; namely, creation was theologically dependent upon redemption, or even subordinated to redemption, in Israel's reflection and witness. The absence of reference to God as Creator in the early historical credos (e.g., Deut 26:5-9; Josh 24:2-13), but its presence in later recitals (e.g., Neh 9:6-37), has been cited as evidence.

This perspective has not been sustained, however, except in the weakened sense that Israel's redemptive (and other historical) experience helped nuance its already existent confession of God as Creator. Aside from difficulties associated with the dating of the credos, a close examination of early texts that speak of the exodus redemption (e.g., Exodus 15) shows that they are permeated with creation talk, in terms of structure, vocabulary, and theme. God's work in creation is the *assumption* for the interpretation of these constitutive events, providing the basic categories and interpretive clues as to what God is about. It is the Creator God who is understood to be the redeemer of Israel from Egypt.[54] This suggests that considerable theological reflection regarding God as Creator was a significant part of Israel's confession from an early, though uncertain, time.[55] Rolf Rendtorff speaks to the point in a general way: "faith in God the Creator was perceived and experienced as the all-embracing framework, as the fundamental, all-underlying *premise* for *any* talk about God, the world, Israel, and the individual."[56]

In a major study, Stefan Paas reflects on the chronological issue through an analysis of earlier prophetic texts, namely, Amos, Hosea, and Isaiah. In addition, Paas engages in considerable effort to show that Ugaritic and Egyptian influence on early Israel included dimensions of creation thought (both originating and continuing creation). He believes the evidence shows that theological perspectives regarding creation can be tracked back into the early monarchial period at least.[57] Paas's work supports an understanding that Israel's confession of God as Creator was relatively early. Studies of other texts (e.g., Genesis 1–2) and traditions (e.g., Royal-Zion) with a view to the question of origins and growth of creation thought in Israel would need to be pursued to fill out this picture.[58] Given the general truth in the phrase *lex orandi lex credendi* that worship shapes belief, it seems likely that the regular round of worship from early times would have honed for Israel the belief in God as Creator.

An Overview

This volume is a theological study of creation in the Old Testament. More particularly, it is an effort to develop a relational theology of creation. It will be shaped most fundamentally by my conviction that Israel's understanding of God has decisively shaped its reflections about creation. God and creation must be considered together, because again and again the texts keep them together. I make no claims that a theological approach is the only legitimate way of working with the texts that speak of creation. Literary and sociohistorical studies will continue to be very important, and it will be evident that I have been dependent upon such work throughout.

My task in this volume is not to review every Old Testament text that speaks of creation. Given my comprehensive definition of creation (see ch. 1), a full theological study of creation in the Hebrew Bible would be a multivolume work. My objective is to work theologically through several key texts on creation in the hopes that such reflections will foster still more theological reflection, both in the academy and in religious communities. Even more, I hope that these reflections will be of help to those who are working through pressing issues in our time, especially those having to do with the environment and the interface of religion and science.

The overall plan for this volume is relatively straightforward, with a focus on specific texts that center on creation. In chapter 1, key theological perspectives will set the stage for the rest of the volume, including what is meant by the word *creation*, the importance of relationality in thinking through biblical understandings of creation, and issues of divine presence in creation. Chapters 2–5 will work through the Torah's presentation of creation: the creation accounts (I work with the present form of the text), Genesis 3–11, Israel's foundation narratives (Genesis 12–50; Exodus) and the relationship of creation and law. I move in chapter 6 to a consideration of creation in the prophets, working especially with issues of the relationship of creation and judgment (in general terms and with texts from Amos and Jeremiah) as well as creation and salvation (primarily Isaiah 40–55). In chapter 7, especially pertinent texts from the Wisdom literature will be explored (especially Proverbs 8 and Job 38–41). In chapter 8, I lift up a key dimension of creation in the book of Psalms, especially the praise of nature. The concluding chapter will seek to bring together some key points regarding a relational model of creation and the vocation of human and nonhuman.

Chapter One

Theological Perspectives

In this chapter I will explore several fundamental issues necessary in any theological interpretation of creation in the Old Testament. They include the language of creation, what is meant by the word *creation*, the importance of relationality in thinking through biblical understandings of creation, and issues of divine presence in creation.

Language of Creation

A remarkable number of Hebrew words are used with reference to creation, with God as subject: *bārā'* ("create," Gen 1:27); *'āsāh* ("make," Gen 1:26); *pā'al* ("make," Prov 16:4); *yāṣar* ("form," Isa 43:1); *bānāh* ("build," Amos 9:6); *qānāh* ("create," Gen 14:19); *kûn* ("establish," Ps 93:1); *yāsad* ("found," Zech 12:1); *nāṭāh* ("stretch out," Isa 51:13); *yālad* ("bring forth," Ps 90:2); *ḥûl* ("birth," Deut 32:18).[1] The list could be extended; see also the "Modes of Creation" in the next chapter. The sheer number of words indicates that Israel's thought about creation was wide-ranging and complex.[2]

In delineating the various metaphors associated with God as Creator, Ronald A. Simkins distinguishes between "internal" metaphors, associated with birth and plant growth, and "external" metaphors, associated with order and differentiation.[3]

The internal metaphors include the divine shaping of an individual in the womb of the mother: "the Lord . . . formed me in the womb" (Isa 49:5; cf. Jer 1:5).[4] This language is extended in some texts to refer to the creation of Israel as a people, with more explicit maternal images for God (e.g., Isa 44:2; cf. Ps 22:9-11; Num 11:11-12; Deut 32:18). Given the correlation of the womb and the (depths of the) earth, the image of God as a potter working with clay is sometimes associated with the womb imagery for individuals (Job 10:8-11; Ps 139:13-15; cf. Gen 2:7) and more generally for the people (Isa 45:9-12; cf. 29:15-16; 64:8; Jer 18:2-6). Birthing metaphors are also used for the new creation of God's people (Isa 42:14; 49:14-15, 20-21). Remarkably, birthing language is also used for God's creation of the nonhuman creatures (e.g., Job 38:8-9, 28-30; Ps 90:2; Prov 8:24-25).[5]

Images of creation associated with agricultural life, especially planting, are parallel with the birthing metaphors: plants sprouting from the ground and persons birthed from the womb (cf. Ps 139:13-15, where "womb" is imaged as "the depths of the earth"; Isa 44:2-4, where womb and plant growth are correlated). God causes the grass and plants to grow (Ps 104:14-16). God also plants Israel as a vintner would plant a vineyard and care for its growth (Isa 5:1-2; 27:2-6; Jer 2:21; Hos 10:1; Ps 80:8-9, 14-15). Botanical imagery is also used for the new creation that God will bring forth (Isa 45:8); Israel will once again be "planted" in the land (Amos 9:15; Jer 1:10) and they

> shall take root,
> Israel shall blossom and put forth shoots,
> and fill the whole world with fruit. (Isa 27:6; cf. Hos 14:5-7)[6]

More external metaphors of creation include those that depict God as designer and builder of buildings, though the more basic metaphor may be that of God as artisan.[7] God is the one who has laid the foundations of the earth and the cornerstone (Isa 48:13; 51:13; cf. Job 38:4-6; Ps 104:5) and builds the chambers of the heavens (Amos 9:6). Images of ordering, gathering, and the establishing of boundaries are also used (Job 38:8-11; Ps 33:7; 74:17; 104:6-8). In addition, metaphors of conflict against chaotic forces and the establishment of boundaries are used in some texts (Ps 74:12-17; cf. 77:16-20; 89:9-13; Isa 51:9-11).[8]

Given the fact that metaphors drawn from human work and life processes can be used for God's creative activity, continuities with human creativity are genuine; God's creative work is not absolutely unparalleled among the creatures.[9] This is to recognize the yes and the no in every metaphor used of God. That metaphors drawn from plant life can also be used indicates some continuities between God's work and the work of the nonhuman creatures (already in Gen 1:11-13, 20, 24).

Explicit creational interests occur in every corner of the Old Testament, including in every major tradition, from early to late, including the priestly, Exodus, Sinai, Royal-Zion, and prophetic traditions, and in numerous echoes and allusions. They also occur in most types of literature: poetry and prose, laments and hymns of praise, narratives and Wisdom poems, prophetic oracles and apocalyptic visions. But no doctrinal treatises or theological essays can be found, so concrete is the interest in creation (Prov 8:22-31 may be an exception). More particularly, one could speak of the presence of these interests in creation accounts, individual laws, and theophanic texts, whether theophanies of the warrior (primarily) or theophanies of the word.[10] Some scholars have thought the creation materials to be associated especially with a chaos-creation tradition, within which God once vanquished chaos, but not finally, and so a potential conflict between chaotic elements and God's creational designs is present.[11] This pervasiveness of such creational interests in the Old Testament is, in part, due to the fact that they were current in the literature of the larger region and Israel participated in this cultural reality (see "Excursus" in the next chapter).

The rhetorical strategies used by the authors in presenting creational material vary, and our closer look at the texts will reveal several. Questions to be raised in a consideration of this issue include: How does creation material function as proclamation to a given audience (e.g., the exiles)?[12] Is it used to convict or warn, to comfort or reassure? Is it used to tell a story of the past or characterize the "way things are"? Is it used to support a theological argument or religious claim? Is it used to exalt the Creator, or to bring honor to the creatures? These issues will emerge from time to time in what follows.

To What Does *Creation* Refer?

Does the Old Testament present a unified understanding of creation? Most scholars would deny this to be the case, illustrated by, say, the differences between the creation accounts (Gen 1:1–2:4*a*; 2:4*b*–3:25). Yet, are these differences fundamental or are they more incidental, due to angles of vision in view of differing literary and historical contexts?

Creation is a theme that pervades the biblical narrative, but what the word *creation* entails is not immediately evident. By way of an initial summary: because creation in the Old Testament is a *theological* category, it is not to be equated with *nature* or *world*.[13] To speak of "creation" is to state that the cosmos does not simply exist; it was *created* by God. More particularly, as outlined below, the creative activity of God includes the work of originating, continuing, and completing creation. The word *creation* can also be used for the *result* of such creative activity, but not in the sense of a finished product, given the reality of continuing creation. Creation also includes the activity of creatures (human and nonhuman) in and through which God works to create in ever new ways.

Many scholars, implicitly or explicitly, disagree with such comprehensive understandings of creation. Indeed, it is common to understand the word *creation* solely in terms of beginnings, the origination of the cosmos; God's work as Creator is restricted to what God does in the Genesis creation accounts and their scriptural echoes. Dennis J. McCarthy, for example, reflects such an opinion when he states that "creation" in a "technical meaning" has to do with the "absolute beginning of our world."[14] In this connection, the language of "creation" is sometimes limited to that which is created "out of nothing" and hence everything since "the beginning" is only a working with what already exists, a "rearrangement" of what has already been created. While a few texts do understand creation as origination "out of nothing" (2 Macc 7:28; Rom 4:17; Heb 11:3), these passages do not thereby exclude a broader meaning for the word *creation*.[15] Or, from another angle, Claus Westermann is among those who object to the notion of *creatio continua*, preferring blessing instead, that is, providence rather than ongoing creating.[16] Several recent efforts from biblical-theological and systematic perspectives push strongly in this direction.[17]

I want to claim that God's work as Creator cannot be so confined; "creation" is not simply viewed as a matter of origination or a divine activity chronologically set only "in the beginning." Ben C. Ollenburger correctly states: "To demand of 'creation' that it refer only to absolute beginnings . . . is virtually to deny the possibility of speaking of creation with respect to the Bible."[18] Ollenburger goes on to insist that what is entailed in the word *creation* should be determined by scriptural usage and not prior assumptions about its meaning; the most basic argument for a more comprehensive understanding of creation is the Old Testament's own testimony. If readers have in mind only issues of origination, then the texts are relatively infrequent, at least in any explicit sense. On the other hand, if a broader understanding of creation is being used, the number of texts increases significantly.[19]

The Old Testament does in fact use the language of creation for divine activity that is other than God's originating work (e.g., Ps 104:30, "when you send forth your spirit, they are created"). Indeed, the verb *bārā'*, "create," so central to speaking of creation in Genesis 1, is used more often elsewhere in the Old Testament (especially in the Prophets) for God's continuing creative activity in and through the historical process, especially in Isaiah 40–55 (e.g., Isa 45:8; 54:16).[20] While creation does entail "making something that was not there before," such an understanding does not necessarily entail creating "out of nothing." God's creating in Genesis 1, for example, includes ordering that which already exists (e.g., the earth of 1:2 only "appears" in 1:9). Indeed, only a few activities of God specifically named in Genesis 1 can be considered "out of nothing."[21] Such ordering activity would result in something genuinely new (a "first coming into being"), and hence properly termed "creation."

This biblical picture is in tune with recent science/theology discussions regarding epigenesis, that is, the continued emergence of new forms of reality at various stages in the history of nature.[22] To call something "new" is to speak of "the coming-to-be of things," and the language of "creation" fits such realities.[23] Because God is involved it is possible, indeed important, to speak of something genuinely "new" coming into being through time and space. God works creatively with already existing realities to bring about newness. This understanding also entails the idea that the present (and future) is not wholly determined by the past; God does bring the "new" into existence. Beyond God's work as sole Creator, certainly the central reality in thinking about creation, God also creates in and through creaturely activity.[24] And so, for example, human beings have been given creative capacities to work with already existing "stuff" not unlike what God does in Genesis 1–2; the creativity of the human creature is such that genuinely new realities are regularly brought into being.[25]

In view of these reflections, I speak of creation as having three interrelated points of reference: the beginning and the end of the world and the times in between.[26]

1. Originating Creation. God is the *ultimate* source of the creation. Most fundamentally, creation is an act of God whereby "heaven and earth" are originally brought into being, understood both in terms of "out of nothing" and ordering. The creation accounts in Genesis 1–2 are the primary witness to this creative activity, though "out of nothing" is on the edges of the text. Several other texts witness to this originating creative action of God (Psalms 33; 104; Wis 9:1-2; Heb 11:3). Still others link Wisdom and the Logos to this creative act (Prov 8:22-31; John 1:1-5).[27]

Several scholars believe that the creation accounts speak not of a past creative act but of an ongoing creative action of God that gives life to every creature. From this perspective, Genesis 1–2 have to do "with the subsistence of the world and of mankind, not with the intellectual question of the origin."[28] But Bernhard W. Anderson rightly responds that, though Gen 1:1 is grammatically ambiguous, it has to do with "the origination of all things."[29] At the same time, it seems more accurate to claim that Genesis 1 deals with matters regarding origination, but without making claims regarding "all things." As we have noted, genuine newness is more broadly conceived than describing that which takes place in the beginning. But Genesis 1–2 does refer to a *temporal* beginning; it tells a genuine story of the past, quite apart from issues of "history."[30]

Expanding the discussion, creation is often associated only or primarily with the origins of the *physical* universe. But it is imperative to think about creation in the Old Testament more broadly. Various texts associate God's creative activity with other orders of life: social (e.g., the family), cultural (including religious), and national order. Certain of these realities are evident already in Genesis 1–2. For example, the luminaries are created with worship life in view ("times and seasons"; 1:14-18), and the day of rest is certainly linked in some way with later sabbatical practices (2:1-3).[31] That the man leaves his parents to cling to his wife (2:24) roots later matters regarding social order within creation as well. Or, moving beyond the creation accounts, God's creative work has to do not only with God's ongoing work in the *physical* world but also with such realities as the ordering of families and nations, including cities (e.g., Genesis 10–11; note the emphasis on "families"), as well as the development of various arts and sciences (Gen 4:17-24). Also to be included is the development of new law in view of new times and places (Gen 9:1-7), already grounded in creation (1:28; 2:16-17).[32] Moreover, texts such as Exod 15:1-21 use creational language to depict social origins, the "movement from a state of social disorganization, because of unrestrained forces, to structure and security in Yahweh's land. Ancient cosmogonies were primarily interested in the emergence of a particular society. . . . The something new which was not there before is not the mere physical universe but rather the 'world' of human beings."[33]

This broader interest in creation invites a consideration of what traditionally has been called "continuing creation."

2. Continuing Creation. Creation is not simply past; it is not just associated with "the beginning." God does not cease to be the Creator when the work of Genesis 1–2 has been completed nor is God thereafter reduced to the role of creative manager. With reference to Ps 104:30, Anderson rightly claims that the verb used for originating creation in Genesis 1–2 *(bārā')* here refers to continuing creation: "Creation is not just an event that occurred in the beginning, at the foundation of the earth, but is God's continuing activity of sustaining creatures and holding everything in being."[34] While generally helpful, such a statement raises two issues:

(a) To say that God holds "everything in being" claims too much, as does Anderson's assertion that, were it not for the reality that "the Creator sustains the world, it would lapse back into primeval chaos."[35] Rather, several texts witness to God's having established the basic and dynamic *infrastructure* of the world once and for all, guaranteed by a divine promise (Gen 8:22; 9:8-17; see Jer 31:35-37; 32:17-26).[36] God does not, say, make a daily decision to sustain the creation.[37] Because God keeps promises, the future of the creation is assured without particular divine action to that end. God created a reliable and trustworthy world and, while God will be pervasively present (see below), God lets the creation be what it was created to be, without micromanagement, tight control, or interference every time something goes wrong.[38] At the same time, one must not translate a reliable creation into a fixed and static system.[39] Elements of unpredictability and open-endedness, what Eccl 9:11 calls "chance," are an integral dimension of the ways things work in God's creation. Not everything has been predetermined; genuine novelty is possible in God's world, both for God and for God's creatures. And, as Genesis 3 soon informs us, God's creation does not preclude creaturely possibilities that are negative, even anticreational.

(b) As we have noted, continuing creation is often associated only with preserving/sustaining the world. While creation may entail *preservation* in the broadest sense of the term, that word can be misleading, as if it had the sense of preserving creation just as it was "in the beginning" (a "finished product"). Continuing creation cannot be restricted to that understanding; it also refers to the development of the creation through time and space, to the emergence of genuinely new realities in an increasingly complex world. God's continuing creative work is both preserving and innovative.[40] Anderson, too, will make a more inclusive claim: "the Creator not only sustains the order of the cosmos but, more than that, does the 'new thing' that surprises all expectations (see Isa 42:9; 43:18-19)."[41]

This continuing creative activity means that God has an ongoing relationship to the world *as a Creator*, and that relationship, by virtue of who God is, brings into being that which is "new" again and again. God not only continues to care for the creation and provide for its needs, as important as that is, but God also continues to create the genuinely new. God's continuing creative activity enables *the becoming of the creation*. That Isaiah 40–55, for example, can so readily use the language of creation for God's *salvific* action in the return from exile is a specific manifestation of God's continuing creative work between the beginning and the end (e.g., Isa 41:20).[42] The language used for this action of God is "a new thing" (Isa 42:9; 43:19; 48:6; see also Jer 31:22, "the LORD has created a new thing on the earth").[43] The language of divine birthing in Second Isaiah (e.g., Isa 42:14; 49:19-21) is further witness that something genuinely new is brought into being.

As we have noted, creation, while centered in the physical world in many ways, has to do with the continuing activity of God in *all* spheres of life whereby the world, often threatened by the presence of sin and evil, is ordered, maintained, evaluated, and renewed. Generally speaking, those spheres of life include the historical, social, political, and economic—everything that is important for the best life possible for all. "The whole thrust of the Old Testament proclamation guards against any flight into a beyond which is turned away from the world."[44] The broad understanding of creation in ancient Israel was crucial for such a purpose; it helped assure a fundamental earthiness, a down-to-earth understanding of the faith that was related to life as it was actually lived rather than a faith centered in a spiritualistic, futuristic, or sentimental piety.

Moreover, continuing creation is not a neutral reality, as if it were only a matter for God to throw the switches and grease the wheels. God's continuing creation is as "good" as the original creation, pursued and shaped by fundamentally gracious purposes. Continuing creation has to do with the ongoing development of those earthly conditions that are most conducive to the flourishing of life in view of new times and places. Given the realities of sin and evil, such continuing creational activity will not proceed without significant opposition. But God will be creatively at work in the often tragic effects of such overt and covert resistance, unrestingly seeking to bring "good" out of evil, to liberate the captives and to build up communities.

Such understandings of continuing creation also have implications for our view of the human being. The human is not a fixed entity from the beginning but, along with the rest of creation, is in the process of becoming. The human is not somehow exempted from ever new developments taking place in the larger creation. Creation as a whole is open to a future in which the genuinely new can be brought into being, and human beings are among the creatures that are creatively affected. Moreover, human beings are invited to play an important role in the becoming of such a world. Indeed, as we shall see, the texts will speak of God using both human and nonhuman creatures in this ongoing creative activity and such creaturely participation will not be inconsequential. To put that point positively, the creative activity of the human, in particular, has the potential of significantly enhancing the ongoing life of the world and every creature therein, indeed, bringing into being that which is genuinely new.[45]

3. Completing Creation. Creating is also that divine eschatological action whereby God brings a new heaven and earth into being (Isa 65:17-25; Rev 21:1-5). Completing creation assumes that there is an element of incompleteness that is integral to the very structures of created existence, even before sin ("subdue" the earth, Gen 1:28). The character of the eventual completion of this creation is revealing of the direction for all of God's prior work, whether in creation or redemption. The books of Genesis and Revelation provide a creational bracket for the Bible, and texts in between are a continuing witness to the purposive work of God toward this new creation. At the same time, the new creation is not a return to the original beginning—if that were the case, everything that had happened in between would finally be of no consequence. Interwoven by God into this new creation will be continuities with the original creation as well as the new realities that have emerged in and through history (evaluated, of course). But the new creation is not simply a rearrangement of that which has existed; something genuinely new will come to be. We are given a glimpse of this newness in the promises of a new covenant (Jer 31:31-34), wherein disobedience will no longer be possible, as well as a new heaven and a new earth (Isa 65:17; 66:22), and a new heart and a new spirit (Ezek 11:19-20; 35:26-27; cf. 2 Cor 5:17; Col 1:15-20). Such creative acts are characteristic of God's eschatological creative work. The result of such divine work is a new *creation*, of which salvation shall be a key component. At the same time, there will be significant continuities with the original creation; for example, the new creation will be a bodily life and an earthly life.[46]

Creation, Redemption, and Salvation

Several of the words for creation are also used for God's salvific work (e.g., *yāṣar*, "form"; *'āsāh*, "make"; *bārā'*, "create"; *kûn*, "establish"; see Isa 43:1-2; 45:11; 54:5, 14). Such texts (and other factors) raise the issue of the relationship of creation to redemption and salvation. Are acts of creation also acts of salvation or redemption? In turn, are acts of salvation also acts of creation? Is salvation just another word (or "virtually synonymous") for creation? Sometimes? Always? Questions such as these are raised up most directly in discussions of Isaiah 40–55, but they arise in various contexts. My basic reflections on this issue will be developed in the chapters on the creation accounts and the prophets, but some initial comments are pertinent at this point.

First, speaking generally and most basically, creation words and themes are used to place a given subject matter (such as redemption) within the more comprehensive context of God's creational activity.[47] The redemptive work of God takes place within a world, indeed within individual lives that have been brought into being and sustained by God's creative activity. God's redemptive work does not occur in a vacuum but within a context decisively shaped by the life-giving creative work of God both within Israel and without (e.g., in Egypt or exile). God's work as Creator (whether recognized or not) actually and always precedes God's work as Redeemer. Moreover, God's redemptive work does not put an end to God's creative work; God's work as Creator continues through and beyond such historical redemptive actions. The language of "salvation" has reference to both the effects of redemptive actions as well as to the effects of distinguishable acts of continuing creation (e.g., healing; gifts of food and water in the wilderness).[48] Redemption does not do away with the life-giving effects of the Creator but stands in the service of them. The objective of God's work in *redemption* is to free people to be what they were *created* to be, the effect of which is named salvation.

Moreover, by using creation language to speak of God's redemptive work, a point is made that there are matters in these historical events that are analogous to God's creative work. For example, God's actions in both redemption and creation bring life, stability, and well-being for both individuals and communities (that is, salvation). Such a commonality in effects reveals that God's work as Redeemer does not stand at odds with what God is about in creation. At the same time, the use of creation language is not used simply to draw analogies between these activities of God. Creation language is used more basically to give cosmic depth to God's historical activity, as we shall see. This point might be pursued at two levels. On the one hand, with respect to God's activity more generally, "the world of peoples and religions outside Israel and outside the Church is not simply a salvationless void . . . The creation-theological statements of both Testaments name the depth dimension of all of God's activity in the world."[49] On the other hand, more specifically, God's redemptive activity has a special place among God's actions; it not only reclaims Israel as God's own and reconstitutes them as a living, growing people, it also has universal salvific effects, opening the lives of nonchosen peoples to transformation and bringing healing and renewal to the larger nonhuman environment.[50]

Second, our initial questions surface more forcefully with respect to Second Isaiah. Does the prophet use the terms *creator* and *redeemer* (or *savior*) as "virtual synonyms," as some suggest?[51] In view of the discussion to this point, I believe the appropriate answer is: yes and no, depending upon the context. On the one hand, creation in the *originating* sense is not collapsed into salvation/redemption; *no* salvation/redemption language is used in Isaiah 40–55 for God's creative activity such as that depicted in Genesis 1–2. To collapse originating creation and salvation/redemption would be to claim that God's creative activity in the beginning was already compromised by sin and evil and needed salvation; but, at least for Second Isaiah, in the language of 45:18, God "did not create it a chaos."[52] Second Isaiah thus does not use salvation/redemption language for *all* creative activity. On the other hand, some contexts do present God's redemptive activity on behalf of Israel as an experience of God's creational activity (e.g., 41:17-20; 43:1-7, 14-21).[53] This more focused use of creation language probably has to do with the similar effects of divine creative and redemptive activity noted previously: the fundamentally new and life-giving activity of God that has deep and broad effects not only on Israel but on all of creation. Israel's comprehensive belief in God as Creator serves Israel's confession in God as Redeemer and the latter reinforces Israel's confession of God as Creator.

And so Second Isaiah does not equate creation and redemption; rather, the redemptive work of God is a special dimension of God's more comprehensive activity as Creator. To equate the two would collapse all of God's work in the world into redemption and diminish God's more comprehensive work as Creator, including blessing. Generally speaking, God's goal for the creation is not redemption; God's redemption is a means to a new creation, and salvation will be the key characteristic of that new reality. This understanding, in turn, has implications for how one thinks about creation; the creation is not something to be left behind as God works on more important matters, such as redemption. To equate creation and redemption, or to subordinate creation to redemption, is to endanger the status of the world, including human beings, *as creation*. It is also to place in question God's love for the creation in itself, quite apart from redemption, as if God's goal is to get beyond creation to some other reality. Moreover, such an equation endangers the recognition that redemption has to do with much more than spiritual matters; it includes the healing of the body (finally, resurrection), indeed the healing of the environment.

For all the potency of God's redemptive victory, however, this action is not a matter of a divine flick of the wrist, as if everything now is immediately restored to its full creational life. And so, for example, the people of Israel are liberated from Egypt or exile, but they move out into the wilderness, which, however transformed, is still the wilderness. In addition, other oppressive forces can be expected along the way. The redemptive victory of God frees the creation to *become* what God intended. That is, redemption, for all of its decisiveness, does not cancel out the becoming character of creation, a becoming in which God continues to be active as the creator of the world.

God's new *creation*, including every creature therein, is what is at stake in all of this divine activity, even *for God*. The objective of God's redemptive activity is to transform the creation as it moves toward its eschatological goal. God's goal is a new creation, not a new redemption. There must be redemption if creation is to be and become what God intends it to be, but the redemption is not an end in itself; it has finally to do with creation, a new creation.

Can a comparable statement about the relationship of creation and salvation/redemption be made about creation traditions elsewhere in the Old Testament? The answer seems to be usually, if not always. But the possible exceptions seem few and far between. Most now understand that Genesis 1–2 does not depict creation as a victory over the powers of evil, so that creation is salvation, in effect.[54] Yet, certain texts seem to understand creation in these terms (e.g., Ps 74:12-17, which seems to speak of creation as a saving deed). And so Rolf P. Knierim claims that "Creation out of chaos is seen as the first in a chain of salvific actions. Here, world order and Israel's history are united under one purpose, liberation from chaos and oppression. Thus, it can be said that Yahweh is the creator of the world because he is its liberator from chaos, just as he is the creator of Israel because he is its liberator from oppression."[55] Perhaps such an understanding exists, but it is represented only on the edges of the Hebrew Bible, and it is not unimportant that it seems to be present only in poetry.[56] To my mind creation and salvation (or redemption) must not be collapsed into each other in any context.

George M. Landes, in a response to those who emphasize the absence of reference to creation in most of Israel's historical recitals (e.g., Deut 26:5-9; 24:2-13), makes a plausible point that might pertain in several different contexts. Creation was not included in these credos because "the creation of the cosmos by Yahweh was essentially *not* a liberating act . . . not itself reckoned as the initiation of God's redemptive work."[57] Why is this the case? Because there was nothing from which they needed to be liberated! "The primordial waters, which have to be separated before the heavens and earth can be established as such, are not thought of as intrinsically evil or threatening, no more than are the waters from which all of us come from out of our mothers' wombs at birth." While Landes does not pursue this point, his analysis is important because it supports a distinction between a good creation and the origin of sin and evil (often called the fall).[58] If evil is a precreation reality, then (unless one opts for certain forms of dualism) it has its origins in God.[59] I believe that the consistent witness of the Old Testament is that sin and evil do not have their origins in God nor are they written by God into the structures of the universe. Sin and evil have their origins in the human will, not in God or in God's plan. At the same time, when sin and evil do enter into the life of the world, they do *not* become constitutive of what it means to be human (or any other creature). That means that we are not so permeated with sin and evil that we cannot name such forces or work against them. At the same time, it needs to be said that evil is a powerful reality in the world and has become systemic, built up over time into the very infrastructure of creation. A reclamation of creation will be necessary.[60]

A Relational Creator and a Relational World

A basic claim I wish to make about the Old Testament understanding of creation is that it has a fundamental relational character.[61] Here I will lay out the claims for the centrality of relatedness in the Old Testament thought more generally and then summarize some of the ways in which creation fits into that framework.

I begin with a striking quotation from Douglas John Hall in speaking about the Reformers and their grounding in Scripture that captures well the centrality of relationality:

> [The] Holy Writ was relational through and through: this record of a people's history; these complex narratives of the often dramatic relationships between fathers and sons, mothers and children, brothers and brothers, lovers, rivals; these anguished prayers and inspired praises; these dialogues with God and with one another; these stories, steeped in particularity; this tale of wandering, of fiercely remembered promises, of prophetic rage, of apocalyptic spontaneity, of despair and vision. In short, the whole presentation of truth in the one source they took to be absolutely and finally binding *(sola Scriptura)* was relational.[62]

Crucial in thinking through biblical texts regarding creation is the reader's understanding of the God portrayed therein. The imaging of the God of the Bible has tended toward extremes. On the one hand, in a kind of deistic move, God is imaged as a sovereign and aloof landlord, removed from too close a brush with the world; on the other hand, God is imaged as being in absolute control of the world, even to the point of micromanagement. If one or the other image is the primary way in which we portray the biblical God, then we human beings, created in the image of God, are encouraged to be either a passive overseer or a dominating subject in control of the created order. Our most basic images of God will shape our lives, willy-nilly, including how we think about the larger environment in which we live.

In view of such an issue, a key to discussing matters of God and creation is the central place given to *relatedness* in the Old Testament.[63] Relationship talk is nothing new for Old Testament studies. Indeed, seventy years ago, Walther Eichrodt titled the first major chapter of his *Theology of the Old Testament*, "The Covenant Relationship."[64] Or, recently, Walter Brueggemann refers to "a broad theological characterization of covenant as an enduring relationship of fidelity and mutual responsibility,"[65] indeed "everything said about Yahweh is said about Yahweh in relation."[66] But for all the centrality Eichrodt gave to covenant, he understood that "the concept of the covenant never proved adequate to the outpouring of [Israel's] vision of God. In a one-sided portrayal of Yahweh as the founder of the covenant the idea of God could easily become inflexible." The "weakness" inherent in covenant language and which "made it a potential danger to religious life was precisely its legal character."[67] While the word *covenant means* something like commitment, promise, or obligation, it could *refer to* a specific agreement or contract between human parties or even the binding agreement entered into between God and Israel at Sinai.[68]

Covenantal texts reveal that the relationship, indeed an elective relationship, between God and Israel (or an individual) precedes the establishment of any covenant. For example, Israel is specified again and again as God's people before the covenant at Mount Sinai ("Let my people go"). The Sinai covenant has to do not with the establishment of a relationship with Israel but with a formalization of Israel's vocation within an already existing relationship.[69] This understanding is also evident in God's covenants with Noah, Abraham, and David.[70] Each of these covenants is a unilaterally declared divine promise, and each is preceded by divine election, divine deliverance, and the individual's response in faith/worship. These divine promises seem designed to provide a firm grounding within which an already existing relationship can appropriately develop.

The inadequacy of covenant language in specifying the nature and range of the God-human or God-Israel relationship is also evident in the prophets' sharply reduced use of it. The prophets, as Eichrodt himself recognized, make "use of other categories to describe the religious relationship," marital imagery being an example; their "stress is on the personal note in the relationship to Yahweh."[71] From still another angle, through the middle of the last century the strong association in covenant studies with suzerainty treaties tended to associate covenant with monarchial images for God. This perspective often narrowed the understanding of the divine-human relationship. While Ernest W. Nicholson is probably correct in saying that the link to suzerainty treaties has "yielded little that is of permanent value," the monarchial imagery often still fills the room.[72] In any case, the Old Testament clearly understands that the God-human relationship is much more comprehensive in nature and scope than the word *covenant* allows.[73] Generally, of course, all sorts of interhuman relationships are not specified as covenantal.

When monarchial imagery does dominate the discussion, relational language is often used in ways that make the relationship less than fully real; the relationship is formal or "logical," not genuine. What if we took the word *relationship* seriously? What if we spoke of the God-human relationship as real and genuine? What if we understood the relationship with God to be a relationship of integrity, presumably the only kind of relationship God will have? If we did this, what are the implications of such an understanding? I think the biblical material calls us most fundamentally to use relational language for God. But our God-talk may need to be cleaned up so that genuine relatedness is integral to our talk about God and God's interaction with the world.

Now, it is important to say that there will always be some disjunction between God and the language for God, not least the language of relationship. In all such reflection, we should remember that this is a relationship of unequals; it is an asymmetrical relationship. God is God and we're not. But let it also be said that transcendence is not compromised by the language of relationship. Israel's God is transcendent, but transcendent *in relationship* to the world, not in isolation from it. To use Abraham J. Heschel's language, "God remains transcendent in His immanence, and related in His transcendence."[74] We should not think that God is transcendent *and* in relationship, but God is transcendent *in* relationship.[75] God is not less than God in the relationships God establishes. The God who is transcendent remains precisely that in every relationship into which God enters—the Holy One in the midst of Israel (e.g., Isa 12:6; Hos 11:8-9).

The upshot of these introductory comments is that much work is needed in thinking through what the Old Testament has to say about relationship. Covenant language will ultimately be a part of that discussion, but the range of applicable language, texts, and themes means that studies of relationship must be much more comprehensive. Moreover, it seems to me, relationship is so basic a category that it should be placed up front in any overarching consideration of Old Testament theological perspectives.

Three basic categories of relationship seem to be distinguishable in Old Testament literature. In summary: Israel's God is a relational God who has created a world in which interrelatedness is basic to the nature of reality; this God establishes relationships of varying sorts with all creatures, including a special relationship to the people of Israel.

1. *Relationality Is Basic to the Very Nature of God*

"The being of God is a relational being."[76] Such realities as the divine council, the sons of God, and the heavenly messengers witness that

Israel's God is by nature a social being, functioning within a divine community (e.g., Gen 1:26; 6:1-4; Isa 6:8; Jer 23:18-23; Prov 8:22-31). These and other passages witness to the richness and complexity of the divine realm. God is not in heaven alone but is engaged in a relationship of mutuality within that realm and chooses to share, say, the creative process with other divine beings (Gen 1:26). In other words, relationship is integral to the identity of God, prior to and independent of God's relationship to the world. The witness that God is one (Deut 6:4) is not compromised by this recognition of the sociality of God.[77] In addition, the reference to a divine community in association with the creation of the human community is especially to be noted (Gen 1:26; see also 3:22; 11:7). Human beings are created in the image of one who is engaged in a relationship of mutuality and chooses to create in such a way that power is shared with those who are not God (see ch. 2).[78]

2. This Relational God Freely Enters into Relationships with the Creatures

Biblical metaphors for God, with few if any exceptions, have relatedness at their very core (e.g., husband-wife; parent-child; teacher-student).[79] Even nonpersonal metaphors are understood in relational terms (e.g., Deut 32:18; Ps 31:2-3; Exod 19:4, "I bore you on eagles' wings and brought you to myself"). To characterize these metaphors generally, they are usually personal rather than impersonal, ordinary rather than extraordinary, concrete rather than abstract, everyday rather than dramatic, earthly rather than "heavenly," and secular rather than religious. This earthy type of language used for God ties God closely to the creation and its everyday affairs. These kinds of images for God were believed to be most revealing of a God who had entered deeply into the life of the world and was present and active in the common life of individuals and communities. To use Brueggemann's language, "the human person is *a person in relation to Yahweh*, who lives in an intense mutuality with Yahweh."[80]

This divine-human relatedness is also evident in the fact that God gives the divine name(s) to Israel, thereby identifying the divine self as a distinctive member of the community of those who have names. Naming entails a certain kind of relationship. For God to give the name opens up the possibility for a certain intimacy in relationship and admits a desire for hearing the voice of the other (see Isa 65:1-2). A relationship without a name inevitably means some distance. Naming enables truer, deeper encounter and communication; it entails availability and accessibility (in the Old Testament period, the divine name was pronounced). But naming also entails risk, for it opens God up to an experience of the misuse of the name (hence the commandment regarding the divine name; Exod 20:7).

The pervasive use of anthropomorphic/anthropopathic language is also important in this regard. God is one who thinks, wills, and feels. God has a mouth that speaks, eyes that see, and hands that create. This language stands together with the more concrete metaphors in saying something important about God—one who is living and dynamic, whose ways of relating to the world are best conveyed in the language of human personality and activity.[81]

The importance of such relational language is sharply evident in the prohibition of images. The most fundamental concern of this prohibition is to protect God's relatedness. In the words of Ps 115:5-7, the idols

> have mouths, but do not speak;
> eyes, but do not see.
> They have ears, but do not hear;
> and there is no breath in their mouths.

(See also Ps 135:15-18; Jer 10:4-5.) The implication, of course, is that Israel's God is one who speaks and sees and hears and feels. With the idols there is no deed or word, no real presence, no genuine relationship. This understanding is continuous with that point where the Old Testament does speak of a legitimate concrete image, namely, the human being (Gen 1:26). The human being, with all of its capacities for relationships, is believed to be the only appropriate image of God in the life of the world.[82]

It is important to add that this relational God of the Old Testament is not, first and foremost, the God of Israel but of the world. The opening chapters of Genesis, for example, make universal claims for this God. These Genesis chapters portray a God whose universal activity includes creating, grieving, judging, saving, electing, promising, blessing, covenant making, and law giving. And we are not yet to Israel! God was in relationship to the world before there ever was an Israel, and so God's relationship with Israel must be understood as a subset within this more inclusive and comprehensive divine-world relationship. God's acting and speaking are especially focused in Israel, but this divine activity is a strategic, purposive move for the sake of the world (Gen 12:3, "in you all the families [the "families" in Genesis 10] of the earth shall be blessed"). The election of the family of Abraham and Sarah is an initially exclusive move for the sake of a maximally inclusive end.[83]

3. This Relational God Has Created a World in Which All Creatures Are Interrelated

The world of the Hebrew Bible is a spiderweb of a world. Interrelatedness is basic to this community of God's creatures. Each created entity is in symbiotic relationship with every other and in such a way that any act reverberates out and affects the whole, shaking this web with varying degrees of intensity. Being the gifted creatures that they are, human beings have the capacity to affect the web in ways more intense and pervasive than any other creature, positively and negatively, as we know very well in our own time.[84]

This point may be illustrated by the way in which the Old Testament speaks of the effect of the moral order upon the cosmic order. That is, human and nonhuman orders are so deeply interconnected that human sin may have devastating effects on other creatures. The ground puts forth thorns and thistles for Adam (Gen 3:17); the flood is a violent convulsing of the creation that is explicitly linked to cosmic and human violence (Gen 6:11-13); the story of Sodom and Gomorrah tells of an ecological disaster because of human wickedness (see Gen 13:10-13; 19:24-28); the plagues are adverse ecological effects because of the anticreational behavior of Pharaoh and his minions (Exodus 7–11); and the prophets again and again link human sin and adverse cosmic effects (e.g., Jer 4:22-26; Hos 4:1-3).[85]

It is important to recognize that such an understanding of interrelatedness stands over against any notion of a static or mechanistic world, as we will note.[86] Given the genuineness of these relationships, there is a degree of open-endedness in the created order, which makes room for novelty and surprise, irregularities and randomness. To be sure, there are the great rhythms of Gen 8:22 (see Jer 31:35-37): seedtime and harvest, cold and heat, summer and winter, day and night. But, there is no little play in the system; one might speak of a complex, loose causal weave. The God speeches in the book of Job, with their witness to the complexity and ambiguity of the creation, are exemplary illustrations of this kind of world.[87]

That the world is so interrelated makes our attempt to understand how God faithfully relates to its creatures more complex. To speak very generally, God so relates to this interrelated world that every movement in the web affects God as well; God will get caught up in these interconnections and work within them for the sake of the future of all creatures. Or, in other terms, we might say that God honors this interrelatedness and, in acting, takes into account both the order and the play of the creation. God works from *within* a committed relationship with the world and not on the world from without in total freedom. God's faithfulness to promises made always entails the limiting of divine options. Indeed, such is the nature of this divine commitment that the relationship with Israel (and, in a somewhat different way, the world) is now constitutive of the divine identity. The life of God will forever include the life of the people of God as well as the life of the world more generally.[88]

Most basically, the Hebrew Bible urges us to think of God as being in a genuine relationship with every aspect of the creation and intimately involved with every creature. In short, we need an understanding of the God-world relationship in the Hebrew Bible that takes the word *relationship* seriously, which will in turn necessitate some recharacterization of traditional portrayals of the God of the Old Testament.[89]

4. *The Character of the God-Human Relationship (Israel Especially)*

Human beings may "so impact Yahweh in ways that cause Yahweh to be different from the way Yahweh was prior to the contact."[90] Brueggemann goes on to speak of this relationship having "a dimension of mutuality."[91] In seeking to characterize this relationship, Brueggemann proposes this formulation: "*Yahweh is committed to Yahweh's partners in freedom and in passion.*"[92] God truly becomes "involved" with the partner in such compelling ways that the classical attributes usually assigned to God become problematic. Brueggemann speaks of God's "capacity and readiness to suffer with and to suffer for, to stay with a partner in trouble, vexation, and danger."[93] But, for all the strength of such statements, Brueggemann has a "soft" understanding of the idea of "commitment of fidelity." He claims that because God acted freely in establishing the relationship, God can also "cancel the commitment . . . [and] terminate the relationship," indeed, even "to slough off such commitments."[94] If this be the case, then I think we should cease to use the language of commitment or fidelity for Israel's God. The tension provided by the freedom and the passion in the relationship is important, but God's fidelity in the relationship need not be brought into question just because the *human* party to the relationship can decide to be unfaithful, break the relationship, and suffer the consequences. Nor is that faithfulness compromised by divine judgment.[95]

Remembering that the God-human relationship is asymmetrical—that God is God and creatures are not—what might such genuine divine-human relationship entail? I would claim that God's unswerving faithfulness is basic to any understanding of this relationship. Among other divine commitments, the following seem especially pertinent. In thinking through these characteristics, recall what it takes for a genuine inter-human relationship such as a marriage to thrive.[96]

- God so enters into relationships that God is not the only one who has something important to say.[97] The Old Testament will speak of communication between God and both human and nonhuman. Regarding the human, prayer may be said to be God's gift for the sake of a healthy relationship. Exodus 32:7-14, for example, shows that God so values Moses' intercession that God reverses a decision made. Regarding the nonhuman, God calls to the earth (Ps 50:4; Hag 1:11), addresses its creatures (Isa 45:8; Job 37:6), and calls them by name (Isa 40:26; Ps 147:4). They in turn respond to God (Job 38:35; Ps 145:10) and look or cry to God (Ps 104:21; 145:15-16; Job 38:39-41; Joel 1:20).
- God so enters into relationships that God is not the only one who has something important to do and the power with which to do it. Within the very creative process itself, God chooses to share power with the creatures, both nonhuman (e.g., Gen 1:11-13, 20, 22, 24; cf. Ps 65:12-13; Hag 1:10-11) and human (Gen 1:28). Given the divine faithfulness to such a relationship, God will exercise constraint and restraint in the exercise of power in the world. That power-sharing divine move continues into the post-fall world, evident throughout the Old Testament (e.g., Ps 65:12-13; Psalm 8).[98]
- God so enters into relationships that God is genuinely affected by what happens to the relationship. For example, the flood is introduced by a grieving God (Gen 6:6-7) and later, in prophetic texts, God will lament over what has happened to

both people (Jer 9:17-18) and environment (e.g., Jer 9:10; 12:7-13).[99]

- God so enters into relationships that the human will can stand over against the will of God (e.g., Isa 30:1; Ezek 2:5; Zech 1:15).[100] The divine will is resistible; God does not always get God's will done in the world, most especially because of continuing human resistance.
- God so enters into relationships that the future is not all blocked out; for example, Jer 22:1-5 speaks of two possible futures for Israel, depending on how they treat the disadvantaged among them. The people of God, and indeed the larger creation, through the powers they have been given, are capable of shaping the future in various ways, indeed the future of God (note the two possible futures for God in Jer 22:4-5). The future is not simply in God's hands, though that is ultimately the case.

In sum, God has taken the initiative and freely entered into relationships, both in creation and in covenant with Israel. But, having done so, God—who is other than world—has decisively and irrevocably committed the divine self to be in *a faithful relationship*. And because God is faithful to commitments made, God will not suspend these commitments for shorter or longer periods of time.[101]

The Universality of God's Presence in the Created Order

Old Testament scholarship over the last century and more has placed a strong emphasis on divine transcendence, with less concern about divine immanence.[102] Moreover, scholars have commonly insisted that Israel's understanding of God stood sharply over against the religious rituals and formulations of the larger environment.[103]

The perspective of Gerhard von Rad has contributed to such an understanding. He has shown helpfully that the prohibition of images in Israel's life and thought assumes an understanding of God's transcendence relative to the creation. But his formulation is problematic, or at least less than fully clear, when he says that this prohibition entailed a "radical purging of both the divine and the demonic from the material universe;

the world is seen as a single entity, complete and undivided."[104] To speak of a purging of the divine from the material universe suggests that God and creation are like oil and water; room is not left for a perspective that claims that God is deeply immersed in the very stuff of the creation, but not in a pantheistic way.

A viewpoint such as von Rad's has sharply affected the understanding of Israel's perspectives on creation, tending to set Israel's God at a distance from the world of nature, and by extension the creation as a whole. Without sacrificing the truths in this perspective (e.g., God is not to be identified with natural forces), the Old Testament commitment to the presence of God in the life of the world must be more strongly affirmed than it commonly has been. We need to find a clearer way between pantheism and *radical* transcendence. As I have noted, "the immanence/transcendence polarity is not adequate for talk about divine presence. The God who is present is *both* immanent and transcendent; both are appropriate words for a constant divine state of affairs."[105]

From another perspective, claims have been made that Israel's God is so present as to be absolutely controlling of all that happens. To cite von Rad again, he asserts that Israel, refusing to accept any form of metaphysical dualism (which it never entirely avoided), accepted "dualism as a fact within the godhead itself." As an example, he interprets Isa 45:7 in an unqualified way: "Yahweh is the one cause of all things." The world is "always and unceasingly controlled by God."[106] While such a perspective avoids pantheism and deism, it assumes a deterministic perspective. Our work in this volume will carry on an ongoing discussion with such an understanding of the God of the Old Testament. Israel's God is intensely and pervasively present in the created order but in such a way that God allows the creation to be what it was created to be without strict divine control. I begin to spell out that understanding of divine presence in what follows.

God's relationship with the world is comprehensive in scope: God is present and active wherever there is world. God does not create the world and then leave it, but God creates the world and enters into it, lives within it, *as God*. Inasmuch as God fills heaven and earth (Jer 23:24), God is a part of the map of reality and is relational to all that is not God, that is, to every creature. In other terms, God is present on every occasion and active in every event. From the macrocosmic to the microcosmic, there is no getting beyond the presence of God. God cannot be evicted from the world or from any creature's life. At the same time,

God's presence does not mean either divine micromanagement or a divine will that is irresistible, and this is so because of the kind of relationship of which we have spoken. To claim that "the world is full of God" also means that the world, though filled with God, does not cease to be the world—or there would be nothing left for God to fill. The world retains its integrity as creature even while filled with the presence of the Creator. Nor, as noted, does God cease to be transcendent by becoming so involved in the life of the world. God is creator, not creation, but God is deeply caught up in the life of creatures for purposes, finally, of a new creation.

But the Old Testament wants to be even more precise about the nature of the divine presence. In the words of Ps 33:5 (cf. 36:5), "the earth is *full* [filling words again] of the steadfast love of the LORD" (emphasis mine). God is not just here and there, but lovingly present, in every divine act, whether of judgment or salvation. Wherever there is world, God's love is active in relationship to each and every creature. To use the language of Ps 145:9, "the LORD is good to all, / and his compassion is over *all* that he has made" (emphasis mine), and that includes both human and nonhuman creatures. To say that the world is full of the love of God means that God's presence is not static or passive but an active presence in relationship, profoundly grounded in and shaped by steadfast love for the good of all creatures, even in the midst of judgment; as Jer 31:3 puts it on the far side of the destruction of Jerusalem: "I have loved you with an everlasting love."

While God's acting is focused in Israel—and God's speaking is especially articulate there—Genesis 1–11 (and other texts) find this God present and engaged in and with the larger world, and in ways that are remarkably similar to the way God acts with Israel. In that world, God elects, judges, saves, enters into covenant, promises, blesses, and gives the law. God's actions in and for Israel thus occur *within* God's more comprehensive ways of acting in the larger world and are shaped by God's overarching purposes for that world.[107] This understanding means that God was active out and about in the universe before there ever was an Israel (or a church) and, by implication, God has ever since acted often quite independently of the elect people, even in revelatory and salvific ways (see, e.g., Gen 20:3-7; Amos 9:7). God does not cease to act as creator once God acts as redeemer. And, because of the kind of God that Israel's God is, that creative work in the world is effective and good. All creatures, human and nonhuman, the whole world round, daily experience the goodness of God, and God's efficacy in those "unchosen" places will have been rich and pervasive before the people of God show up. Because all of these activities of God in Genesis 1–11 are given a place in the *world's* history, we must be alert to seeing in other biblical texts significant God connections between the chosen people and that larger world, both human and nonhuman.

At the same time, the Old Testament speaks of varying intensifications of the divine presence in the world. In everyday human life, differences in focus, direction, attention, and energy level, as well as the competing presence of others, shape our understanding of the intensity of someone's presence. Something comparable is at work with respect to the divine presence; the texts do not understand that presence in a univocal way. For example, though Jonah flees "from the presence of the LORD" (Jonah 1:3), he still professes belief in a creator God (1:9). The departure of the tabernacling God from the temple (Ezek 10:1-22; 11:22-25) does not mean that God is now absent (see 11:16). The psalmist prays to a God who has forsaken him but is believed to be present enough to hear (Ps 22:1). A continuum moving from general or creational presence to theophanic presence might be suggested, with accompanying and tabernacling presence being intermediate points (actual absence is not a divine possibility in the Old Testament). The language of "glory," often used for an intensified divine presence, is used in connection with both theophanic and tabernacling texts (e.g., 1 Kgs 8:11; Ezek 9:3; Exod 24:15-17).[108] Such texts show that the God of the Old Testament has taken a variety of steps at key times and places to be more intensively present in the life and structures of the world, and Israel in particular. In summary, God is believed to be continuously present, yet God will also be especially present at certain times; God is believed to be everywhere present, yet God will also be intensively present in certain places.

If God fills the world, that would include its structures of space and time. In creating the world, God enters into the space and time of this world and makes them God's own. Regarding time, God's relationship to the world is constituted *from within* its structures of time.[109] At least since the beginning of creation, where it takes God time to create the world, God has freely chosen to enter into the time of the world and truly get caught up in its flow. For example, the common language for divine planning and execution of plans (e.g., Jer 29:11; 51:12) as well as God's being provoked to anger or slow to anger (e.g., Deut 32:21; Exod 34:6) assume that temporal sequence is real for God. At the same time, while God's life is temporally ordered, this claim does not stand over against the eternity of a God who is not subject to the ravages of time. God is the eternal, uncreated member of this world community, but God, too, has a story and will cry out, "How long?" (e.g., Hos 8:5).[110]

The future of the creation has not been totally determined by what God has done in the originating creation. The end of the creation will look different from the beginning, even with all of the continuities. Genesis 1, with its beginning in time (that is, time begins with this beginning) as the movement of seven days suggests, opens up the historical world, and that means change and development. Creation as presented here is not some "myth of the eternal return" or a myth that speaks only of every present moment and has no interest in actual temporal beginnings or the origins of things. God's relationship with the world as depicted in Genesis 1–11 has a fundamentally historical character to it; this is understood to be the beginning of time. And opening up as the creation does into a historical world will mean change, and that also means that creation cannot be understood as a closed system; it must be an open one.[111]

A comparable statement can be made with respect to space. God builds the divine residence into the very structures of the created order (Ps 104:1-3; cf. Isa 40:22; Amos 9:6), so that the heavens (or their semantic equivalent) become a shorthand way of referring to the abode of God *within* the created world. The result, to use the language of Isa 66:1, is that heaven is God's throne and the earth is God's footstool.[112] This could be translated to mean that God has made the creation in its totality God's own home and that heaven is the point of intensified (and uncontested?) divine presence.

God's movement from heaven to earth in many texts is a movement *within* the created order. God—who is other than world—works relationally from within the world, and not on the world from without.[113] The God of the Old Testament is one who is the subject of many verbs that portray movement from the divine life out into the world, an overflowing of the divine love to fill the world. This God is one who comes down to an oppressed people, accompanies the people of God on their journeys, dwells with them, is active on behalf of the world, promises to pour out the Spirit, and rescues and saves those in need. This divine movement from within the world out toward the world in turn shapes the fundamental nature of the human community in the image of God, as a community that moves out from its own sanctuaries and safe places into the life of the world, with all the attendant risks. Being in the image of such an interrelational God always entails for the human being a reaching out toward the other in all of life's circumstances and being graciously there on behalf of that other.

The texts under discussion in this chapter (and throughout the volume) contribute to what might be called *a relational model of creation.* That is, both God and the creatures have an important role in the creative enterprise, and their spheres of activity are interrelated in terms of function and effect. It seems clear that God is not just independent and the creatures just dependent. God has shaped the created order in such a way that there are overlapping spheres of interdependence and creative responsibility shared between Creator and creature.[114] At the same time, God is God and freely brings into being that which is not God. A deep dependence of the creatures upon the Creator for their existence and continuing life is apparent. And creatures can be assured that this God is unalterably committed to their continuing life and will be deeply immersed in that life for the sake of a new creation.

Excursus: Genesis 1–2 and Modern Science

Modern scientific discoveries have created no little dissonance for interpreters of the opening chapters of Genesis. Considerable energies have been expended in seeking to determine how these chapters are to be related to the results of scientific research, especially on the part of those who claim that no conflict exists (or can exist) between biblical and scientific understandings of the created order. The root of the issue is to be found in differing perspectives on biblical authority, or at least the authority of differing *interpretations* of specific texts. I give a high value to biblical authority, but biblical views on "scientific" matters must also be evaluated in relationship to evidence and the arguments pursued by other modes of inquiry.

To claim that God created the world and all that exists is a matter of faith, such a claim is grounded fundamentally in God's self-revelation (see Heb 11:3) and is not the result of scientific investigation. At this level the opening chapters of Genesis are a confession of faith. At the same time, in giving shape to the *content* of the witness to God's creative activity, the biblical writers made use of knowledge of the natural world available to them in their culture.[115] That is, not every concern in these chapters is collapsed into a theological or confessional framework. Israel had no little interest in what we today would call "scientific" issues (see 1 Kgs 4:33). These chapters are prescientific in the sense that they predate modern science but not in the sense of having no interest in these types of questions. "Prescientific" knowledge is evident in these chapters in God's use of the earth and the waters in mediating creation (Gen 1:11-12, 20, 24), the classification of plants into certain kinds (1:11-12), and a comparable interest in animals (1:21-25), as well as the ordering of each day's creation in view of the flow of what is created through the six days. Despite claims to the contrary (often in the interest of combating fundamentalism), these texts indicate that Israel's thinkers carefully pursued questions regarding the *how* of creation, and not just questions of *who* and *why*.[116]

Israel's theologians used this kind of culturally available "scientific" knowledge to speak of creation. In doing so, they recognized that the truth about creation is not generated simply by theological reflection, implicitly discerning that believers in the Creator God must finally draw from various fields of inquiry in order to speak the full truth about the world. The key task, finally, both for that time and for our own, becomes that of integrating materials from various fields into a coherent statement about the created order. In effect, Genesis invites every generation to engage in this same process.

Difficulties arise when it becomes evident that not everything in these chapters can be made congruent with modern knowledge about the world (recognizing that no field of endeavor has arrived at the point of full understanding or is beyond criticism). If our view of the Bible insists that all information in it, of whatever sort, must correspond to scientific reality, then we will have to engage in all sorts of exegetical antics to make it work. But if we understand that those authors did not know everything about the world (e.g., a source for light independent of the luminaries; the age of the world), then we recognize that reality for what it is and move on. We have to take all the additional knowledge we have gained or will gain about the world (e.g., some form of evolution) and integrate it with our confession about God the Creator.

In such an enterprise, we are not called to separate the theological material from the "scientific" material and rewrite the chapter from our own scientific perspectives however much that task must be accomplished for other purposes. The Genesis text remains both an indispensable theological resource and an important paradigm on the way in which to integrate theological and scientific realities in a common search for truth about the world.[117]

CHAPTER TWO

THE CREATION ACCOUNTS IN GENESIS

Genesis is a book about beginnings.[1] It moves from the morning of the world and all its creatures to the ordering of families and nations. Only then does the book witness to the birthing of the fathers and mothers of Israel (11:27-30). Genesis 1–11 gives to God's election and redemption of Israel *a universal frame of reference*. Israel is chosen to serve creation, the entire creation. God's initially exclusive move stands in the interests of a maximally inclusive end: a new creation in which the wolves will play with the lambs and a little child shall lead them (Isa 11:6-9). Genesis 1–11 also testifies to the beginnings of God's activity in the world. Creation is a new day for God, too, and given the divine commitment to the creation, God will never be the same again.[2]

The creation accounts in Genesis 1–2 are among the most studied texts in the Bible.[3] These chapters have generated reflection from every conceivable viewpoint and controversies regarding their interpretation continue apace. Among the many questions these chapters raise for the modern reader, perhaps none are more pertinent than this: *Is Genesis 1–2 an adequate statement for our reflections about creation?* In many ways these chapters will continue to provide readers with an indispensable foundation for these reflections, including the images of God and the human, the relationship between God and the world, and the nature of human and nonhuman interrelationships. In addition, these chapters provide a paradigm that we can use to integrate our theological reflection with truths about the world gathered from other spheres of inquiry and our own experience.[4]

At the same time, Genesis 1–2 is not a fully adequate statement for contemporary readers regarding creation. We have learned truths about the origins, development, and nature of the world from modern science of which the biblical authors never dreamed. We are confronted with issues that they never faced regarding, say, the environment and the role of women. In some ways these chapters have created more problems than solutions for any adequate consideration of such matters. While interpreters of these texts have often exacerbated the problems, we must not discount the long history of the negative effects of the texts themselves; these texts have in fact contributed to the environmental crisis and to a second-class citizenship for women in church and society. It will take generations for newer readings to overcome these effects and, even then, the biblical material will not finally stand beyond critique.[5] In seeking finally to address contemporary issues in a responsible manner, we must go beyond the text and draw on insights from other biblical texts and from postbiblical learning and experiences in and through which God has been at work.

Basic Characteristics of Genesis 1–2

The book of Genesis is usually seen as a composite work, drawn from various sources and edited over the course of many centuries. The classical consensus spoke primarily of three interwoven sources (Yahwist [J], Elohist [E], Priestly [P]). These sources were gradually woven together by editors over five hundred years or more, from the United Monarchy (tenth century B.C.) to the postexilic era. This long-prevailing consensus regarding source divisions has come under sharp challenge from several perspectives over the last generation in particular. From within the source-critical perspective, the nature, scope, and dating of the sources have been regular subjects of debate. Few scholars doubt that Genesis consists of traditions from various historical periods, but little consensus exists regarding the way in which they were brought together in their present form. Moreover, newer literary approaches have called into question many of the assumptions and conclusions of the source-critical consensus. These strategies focus on issues of literary criticism rather than literary history, on the texts as they stand rather than their history prior to their present shape. These newer approaches have contributed significantly to our understanding of these texts.[6]

Did Israel understand these texts (and Genesis 3–11) to be telling a story of an actual time in the past? It is likely that the answer to this question is both yes and no. While these stories often mirror human life in every age, the past and the present are not simply collapsed into each other.[7] Taken as a whole, these texts do purport to tell a story of the past, yet they are not historical in any modern sense ("history-like" is a term sometimes used). A concern for the beginnings of things is evident in several ways, including the atypical aspects of some texts (e.g., the long-lived patriarchs belong to an irretrievable past, as does the reality of one language, 11:1) and the interest in genealogy and chronology (e.g., 8:13-14).[8] On the other hand, that which is typical in human life may be reflected in matters such as the use of the word *'adam*, which refers to generic humankind (1:26-27), the first man (2:7), or Adam (4:25).[9]

This interweaving of the typical and the atypical provides a richness and depth in the story and carries important *theological* implications. For example, Genesis 3 speaks both of a past, *subsequent* to the creation when sin and its evil effects emerged into the life of the world, *and* of a typical encounter with the reality of temptation. The tendency in recent scholarship has been to emphasize the latter.[10] But, if the reader does not attend to the presentation of these materials as *past* and views them only as ever-present and typical, then any distinction between God's creation and the entrance of sin into the world is collapsed and God is made directly responsible for sin, while human responsibility is significantly diminished. From such an angle, sin would be viewed not as a disruption of God's good creation but as integral to God's intentions for the world. Sin would then be more a divine problem than a human one.

For all the importance of historical and literary work on Genesis 1–2, interpreters should not forget that these texts are most basically the product of a community of faith engaged in theological reflection on creation: God is the primary subject in these accounts. This is true of both creation accounts in their own way, as we shall see.

Given the rhythmic cadences of Gen 1:1–2:3, this material has a doxological character and may have been honed in and through liturgical usage and the regular round of the community's praise of God the Creator (see Job 38:7).[11] Worship interests also clearly appear in the links between these accounts and other texts associated with tabernacle, temple, sabbath, and religious festivals (developed in later chapters).[12] In its present form, however, Gen 1:1–2:4*a* may be identified as a didactic account, shaped by liturgical interests. This liturgical character should be related to a probable textual interest in proclamation, even though the form of the text is not homiletical. Walter Brueggemann states that "Israel has no interest in bearing testimony to Yahweh as the one who creates, except as Yahweh can be linked to the practicalities of living faithfully in the world."[13] As long as one understands that "living faithfully" includes theological reflection, this can be an important way of thinking through the text. Whether or not one can speak precisely of a "practical" context in Israel's history is unlikely, but Brueggemann shows how the text might have functioned for anxious and dispirited people of God in exile: "the intent and the effect of this liturgical narrative is to enact by its very utterance a well-ordered, fully reliable, generative world for Israelites who are exiles in Babylon."[14] More generally, the narrator writes in view of the world within which he lives, understanding it in contrast with the original world as given by God, though not without significant continuities. Creation is seen as a gift by a God who knows what is good for God's own creatures and who grants these necessities for lives lived in flourishing ways.[15]

Genesis 2:4*b*-25, on the other hand, takes the form of an often told story and is much more focused on the human situation. Yet, its witness to God the Creator is just as profound in its own way. In the language of Odil Hannes Steck regarding this text, the world is depicted not as "a certain state of affairs, not a static object. . . . For [the Yahwist] the world is an event, a process."[16] This understanding will be developed later in this chapter.

That creation is presented in two such different types of literature is theologically important. On the one hand, the first account, with its highly structured presentation, speaks of creation in terms of order and stability, of separations and boundaries. On the other hand, the second account in story form bespeaks creation in more open terms, with the story form qualifying the first account. Yet, not everything in the first account is as structured and static as might initially appear to be the case;[17] readers may note the account's asymmetry or variability and conclude that, amid the structured presentation, God's creation does have a dynamic, open character. Moreover, the second account, for all the ambiguities the story presents, also speaks of boundaries (the law) and separations. Hence, the two accounts in their own way witness to the "ordered freedom" of the creation. Traditional understandings have tended to favor the lofty formulations and familiar cadences of the first chapter, emphasizing the sovereignty, unilateral action, and even remoteness of God, at the expense of the more "naive" story in 2:4*b*-25.[18] In parallel fashion, the role of the creatures has been portrayed largely in passive and dependent terms. To the extent that interpretations have been attentive to the creaturely role, they have focused on the human being as created in the image of God, with the accompanying command to have dominion (Gen 1:26-28). These verses, however, have seldom been related theologically to other texts in these chapters that speak more fully of the status and responsibility of the creatures.[19]

Traditional theological interpretations of the creation accounts have commonly been reinforced by critical decisions. During the heyday of source criticism, Gen 1:1–2:4*a* was usually thought to be a Priestly (P) product worked out in independence from the earlier Yahwistic (J) version in Gen 2:4*b*-25. P and J were believed to have distinctive perspectives on creation. This separation of sources has often been accompanied by a subtle or not-so-subtle conviction that Genesis 1 is a more mature theological statement about the Creator and the creation and Genesis 2 a more primitive account. This critical perspective has often buttressed the traditional image of God as a radically transcendent Creator, operating in total independence, unilaterally speaking the world into being.[20]

In more recent studies, however, P is often understood to be the redactor of Genesis 1–2, drawing upon J and other materials and putting them together essentially as we now have them.[21] This would mean that, while chapter 1 is P's special contribution, it was shaped with a view to what is now present in 2:4*b*-25 and was never intended to stand by itself. From this perspective, the P understanding of creation is to be found *only* in Genesis 1–2 as a single whole.[22] The often noted differences between Genesis 1 and 2 may then be understood as internal qualifications. A theologically coherent perspective on creation, which the P writer presumably had, is to be found in these two chapters *in interaction with each other*. In effect, these chapters together become the *canonical* perspective on originating creation; indeed, given the speculative nature of efforts to discern the original scope and context of the J material, Genesis 1–2 together constitute the only perspective on creation of which we can be certain. The differing theological voices of the tradition, woven together, have become a more sophisticated theological perspective on creation and more closely approximate the understanding that Israel, finally, discerned regarding Creator and creature and their interrelationship.

In view of such an understanding, several theological emphases emerge that are different from those traditionally emphasized. The praiseworthy language about a transcendent Creator certainly continues to be affirmed, but it is now placed in a more comprehensive theological context in which other images for God and the God/creature relationship come more clearly into view. The purpose of my work in this chapter, finally, is threefold: (a) to draw out images for God in both chapters that are deeply relational and qualify the nature of divine sovereignty that is commonly claimed, especially for Genesis 1; (b) to show that creation is not presented as a finished product; (c) to place the creative role of the creature (both human and nonhuman) alongside the initiatory and decisive role of God and draw out the implications that these complementary roles have for an understanding of creation.[23]

Modes of Creation

Initially, I focus on various *modes of creation*. While the character of the Creator is constant, much inner-biblical variety exists regarding the mode of creation. We focus on Genesis 1–2, which speaks of creation from several (overlapping) perspectives. I draw in other biblical texts to illustrate and expand this list. Amplification of these modes of creation will occur as the discussion moves along.[24]

1. God creates by means of the word (e.g., 1:9; see Pss 33:9; 148:5).
2. God creates by means of the word, followed by deeds of separation or other creative actions (e.g., 1:6-7; cf. Pss 33:6, 9; 147:15-18; 148:3-5; Isa 48:13; 55:10-11).
3. God speaks with others (divine beings and other creatures) and invites their participation in the creative process (e.g., 1:11, 26).
4. God uses that which has already been created as "raw material" to bring still other creatures into being (e.g., 2:7-8, 19; cf. Pss 8:3; 95:5). Various images depict this mode, e.g., God is builder (2:22) and potter (Job 10:8-9; Pss 33:15; 94:9; 103:14, dust; Isa 27:11; 29:16; 43:7; 44:2, 21, 24; 45:9, 11; 64:8; Jer 10:16; Zech 12:1).
5. God creates by bringing order to that which already exists (e.g., the earth in 1:2, 9).
6. God creates some creatures out of nothing (e.g., 1:14-16).
7. God and human beings name creatures, thereby bringing further order to the creation (e.g., 1:5-10; 2:20).

8. God evaluates what has been created, the results of which entail further creative work on the part of both God and creature (e.g., 2:18-23).
9. God creates by means of the spirit/breath (1:2; 2:7; see Job 33:4-6; Pss 18:15; 104:30; Isa 42:5), commonly synonyms (Job 27:3; see Job 4:9).
10. God creates by wisdom (Prov 3:19; 8:22-31; Jer 10:12; 51:15; Pss 104:24; 136:5).
11. Some would claim that God creates through combat with chaotic forces and victory over them (see below).

Several remarks on the opening verses of Genesis 1 are important for discerning the context within which the seven-day structure of the chapter unfolds.[25] Genesis 1:1-3 refers to the beginning of God's creating, but the translation and interpretation of these verses remains uncertain. Three differing translations (and four interpretations) of these verses seem possible:[26]

1. A temporal clause, subordinate to the main clause in verse 3 (God said, "let there be light"), with verse 2 a parenthesis regarding prior conditions (see JPS). Though this translation may be favorably compared to 2:4-7 and the Babylonian *Enuma Elish* (see Excursus at the end of this chapter), the parallels are inexact; moreover, such a long opening sentence is uncharacteristic of the style of this chapter and other genealogies.

2. Verse 1 is a temporal clause, subordinate to the main clause in verse 2 (see NRSV, NAB, NEB). This rendering is less problematic, but a better case can be made for the next option.

3. Verse 1 is an independent sentence (see NIV, RSV, JB, NJB, REB). As such, the sentence could be interpreted to refer to the first act of creation, with the following verses portraying new phases; yet, this interpretation breaks up the seven-day pattern.

4. Alternatively, the independent sentence could be interpreted as a summary of the chapter, with verse 2 describing prior conditions and verse 3 narrating the first creative act.[27] The latter interpretation is most convincing because other genealogies (note "generations" as descriptive of what *precedes*, 2:4*a*) begin with an independent sentence that provides a summary of what follows (see 5:1; 6:9; 10:1; 11:10).[28]

The word *beginning* probably refers not to the absolute beginning of all things but to the beginning of the ordered creation, including the temporal order (see below on 2:1-3). The author does not deny that God created all things,[29] and God is assumed to exist prior to "the beginning" (note that God is not introduced to readers), but God's creative work in this chapter begins with "raw material" that already exists (described in v. 2)—the origins of which are of no apparent interest or are simply assumed to have had their origins in prior divine activity. The interest of the author focuses on the organized "heaven and earth" (see Ps 89:11), the totality of the ordered world.[30] It is significant that the heavens are a part of the world *as created*; hence, they would have reference to God's abode *within the world* (as in Ps 104:1-3; Isa 40:22; Amos 9:6).[31] At the same time, certain creatures are not developed from the raw material in verse 2 and, hence, could be said to be created out of nothing (light, firmament, luminaries).

The spirit/wind of God "hovers, moves" over the face of the waters in 1:2; this image suggests that which has an ever-changing velocity and direction (cf. the use of this language for a drunken walk in Jer 23:9; on wind and spirit, cf. John 3:8). But to what end? Since the spirit/wind is related to God, the activity is in some sense creative (see Job 33:4; Ps 104:30 for a creative use of "spirit"). The image of the spirit/wind of God (the sole entity of v. 2 not mentioned in the balance of the chapter) brings God and raw material together and gives a dynamic rather than a static sense to the creative process. Moreover, verse 2 exhibits a mediated understanding of creation as the spirit of God works in and through already existing material to bring about an ordered creation.[32] This sense is in keeping with the dynamic understanding of creation in the balance of the chapter.

Images of God the Creator

Some twenty images of God the creator can be discerned in Genesis 1–2; they are correlated in various ways with the modes of creation noted above. When considered in interaction with one another, these images provide a more relational model of creation than has been traditionally presented. In what follows, I consider several of these images for God as they provide support for this more comprehensive understanding of creation.

God as Creator/Maker

Genesis 1:1–2:4*a* uses two major verbs for God's creative work (*bārā'*, 7 times; *'āsāh*, 11 times; commonly translated "create" and "make").

Notably, these verbs are used interchangeably; for example, in Gen 1:26-27, "let us make" is followed by "so God created."[33] The verb *bārā'*, the most common verb for creating in the Old Testament, is used both in the sense of originating and continuing creation.[34] The verb sometimes has reference to re-creation or a transformation of existing realities (e.g., Pss 51:10; 102:18; Isa 41:20; 65:18). Scholars commonly emphasize that the verb is used in the Old Testament with only God as subject and without an object of material or means. This usage has sometimes been thought to be evidence for a "creation out of nothing" perspective in this chapter, but such an idea can only be affirmed for the creation of firmament, luminaries, and possibly light.[35] But such an understanding fails to take into account the even more frequently used verb *'āsāh*, an everyday verb that is commonly used for human activity.[36] The use of this verb elsewhere for God as Maker of heaven and earth (Isa 37:16), Pleiades and Orion (Amos 5:8), and human beings (Isa 17:7; 27:11; 57:16) clearly implies that God's creative activity is not thought to be without analogy in the human sphere (see above on the modes of creation). This usage thus parallels the creative images of God in Genesis 2, such as potter (*yṣr*; 2:7-8, 19; cf. Isa 64:8) and builder (*bnh*, 2:22), which speak of God creating humankind out of already existing material. At the same time, the use of the verb *bārā'* may witness to an understanding that no analogy drawn from the human sphere can *exhaust* the meaning of God's creative activity.[37] What is accomplished here is, finally, only possible because of God's initiative and decisive activity.

God as Speaker

Creation by means of the divine word is not an idea unique to Israel, as Egyptian texts in particular demonstrate (see Excursus at the end of this chapter).[38] Creation by word means that creation is not an accident but a deliberate act of the divine will. The word expresses what God intends, and this, in turn, personalizes what God does; God is not removed from or indifferent to the creation. The word also bespeaks divine transcendence, expressing the separateness of God from that which is created; what is created is not a divine emanation or birthing (though birthing imagery is used in some texts).[39]

At the same time, this creative activity does not simply entail God's unilateral speaking the world into being; these texts witness in several ways to a much more complex understanding. For one thing, God's speaking is usually accompanied by God's making (e.g., 1:6-7, 14-16); even the creation of light is not complete until it is separated from the darkness (1:4; God's separating actions do not occur with living creatures, though 2:22 could be so understood). God does not create so much by "word events" as by "word-deed events." The varied placement of the phrase, "and it was so," makes it likely that the divine speaking usually announces the divine *intention* to create, and the creative act is not completed until the making language has so informed the reader.[40]

Moreover, and especially important, the divine creating often entails a speaking *with* that which is *already* created: let the earth bring forth (1:11, 24); let the waters bring forth (1:20).[41] Genesis 1:12 differs from 1:20, 24 in that it specifically states that "the earth brought forth." That such a statement is not present in 1:20, 24, however, should not be interpreted to mean that the earth and waters were not actual participants in these cases; rather, God's creative act is mediated in and through these creatures, and God as sole stated subject is a variation of 1:11-13, where the earth is stated as the only subject. Grammatically, the use of the jussive "let" means that God's speaking does not function as an imperative; it leaves room for creaturely response, not unlike the cohortative "let us make" (1:26) leaves room for consultation and the "[let them] have dominion" (1:28) entails a sharing of power. The "let" associated with the luminaries (1:14-15) entails the giving over to them the governance of the temporal realities of days, seasons, and years; God's governance is not unilateral but mediated. Hence, the divine speaking in this chapter is of such a nature that the receptor of the word is important in the shaping of the created order. What happens in these cases is best characterized as mediate rather than immediate creative activity; creation takes place not from outside the created order but from within.

Such a perspective indicates that creation in Genesis 1 is seen in terms of process and not simply as punctiliar event, for temporal space is given for response. The use of a seven-day sequence rather than a single creative moment for all things also suggests this understanding (see below). Both human and nonhuman creatures are called to participate in the creative activity initiated by God. This perspective is sharply reinforced by the creational images of Genesis 2, as we have seen. This divine way of creating, in choosing not to act alone, is also revealing of a divine vulnerability, for in so involving those who are not God, room is given for the activity of finite creatures, with all of the attendant risks in allowing creatures to be themselves.

God as Molder of Existing Matter

A point of significant interest in Genesis 2 is that God actually comes into contact with that which is material and earthy. Genesis 2 understands that God has assumed human form and come incredibly close in the creative process; God forms, breathes, plants, and constructs a woman out of flesh and bone. God is imaged as a potter who molds a human being (and animals, 2:19) out of the dust of the earth (2:7-8; see also Job 33:6; Isa 45:9; 64:8; cf. Jer 18:1-6; Pss 103:14; 139:15) and breathes into this new creature the breath of life.[42] God is imaged as a surgeon who removes a part of the man's body and closes up the incision. God is imaged as architect and builder who designs and "constructs" a woman out of human flesh and bone (2:21-22).[43] This understanding continues in Genesis 3–4, where God walks in the garden in the cool of the day (3:8), designs and makes clothing out of animal skins (3:21), and engages Cain in conversation (4:1-16), a kind of "unmediated" human relationship with God.[44] In these texts God comes into the closest possible contact with material reality, with the stuff of earthly life. The common notion that the Creator is completely external to the creation, perhaps in the interests of avoiding pantheism, amounts to a concealed deism. It should be stressed that these ways of imaging God are not naive or primitive. The imaging of God in the form of a human being links this text with later theophanic passages (e.g., Gen 18:1-2) and other texts where human beings are ushered into the divine presence (e.g., Exod 24:9-11).[45] The testimony of Genesis 1 to the *goodness* of all forms of material reality undergirds God's *tangible and tactile* engagement with the creatures in Genesis 2.[46] Not only are finite, material realities capable of being "handled" by God (see Ps 95:5, "and the dry land, which his hands have formed") without compromising God's Godness, they are capable of actually bearing God bodily in the life of the world. And, in some sense, the reverse is also true; as God breathes God's own breath of life into the nostrils of a human being (2:7), something of the divine self comes to reside in the human—*and in an ongoing way*.[47]

Efforts to spiritualize, allegorize, or otherwise discount these images in the text have been common through the centuries,[48] usually in the interests of a narrowly spiritual and/or radically transcendent understanding of God. But readers should let the witness stand: God is tangibly involved with this earth and its creatures. More generally, God, by creating in such a way, has made room in the divine life for the very earthy creatures that

God has brought into being; indeed, as noted above, Genesis 3–4 witnesses to comparable levels of divine-human bodily engagement in post-creation times. This testimony regarding God, standing at the head of the canon, should inform our understanding of God in the rest of the Scriptures.

God as Evaluator

After each creative act (except day two) God responds to that which has been created: "And God saw that it was good." That is, God discerns a decisive continuity between God's purposeful intention and the result. And, notably, the creatures are declared good in themselves, quite apart from any usefulness for the human (a point also made by Job 38–41). And because it is God who declares that each creature is good, that conveys a sense of worth and value to each and every creature that cannot be matched by any human evaluation. Valuation of the creature is God-given, not something generated by how human beings think or feel. Francis Watson draws out the environmental implications well: "Human acts which treat the non-human creation simply as the sphere of use-value or market-value, refusing the acknowledgement of its autonomous goodness, are acts of terrorism in direct opposition to the intention of the creator."[49] He goes on to speak of the divine declaration of goodness as a reference to every creature not only being itself good but also being good for others (e.g., vegetation for the good of other creatures, 1:29-30).

Notably, God does not remain removed or uninvolved with the creation once the creature comes into being. God does more than speak and act. In evaluating, God sees, indeed *experiences*, that which has been created and is *affected* by what is seen, thereby revealing an *ongoing* relationship of consequence with that which has been created.[50] Readers may well wonder why God would evaluate God's own work; wouldn't it be good just by being a creature of God's own making? A clue to this evaluative process may be found in 2:18, where God observes what has been created and declares that "it is *not* good." That is, the creation of human beings to this point does not fulfill the purpose God intends for them; further creative work is needed. This negative *divine* evaluation of God's own work suggests that creation is conceived not in static terms but in terms of a process wherein the divine response to what has been created leads to further development of the creation and of intracreaturely relationships. That God pauses after each day of creation means that God takes time to evaluate what has been created before moving on to the next day. This is testimony to creative process rather than punctiliar event or series of events between which nothing of importance occurs. The time between days and acts of creation is taken up by the divine consideration of what has been done and an evaluation thereof.

Moreover, in 2:18-23, God engages the human in the task of evaluation. If God not only evaluates the world as good but reevaluates an aspect of the world as "not good" (2:18) and if the only creatures capable of evaluating are human beings made in the image of God, then God here sets a key human task within ongoing creation. Human beings are called to be ongoing evaluators and reevaluators, and, given this role of God within creation, that *human* task is integral to the ongoing creative task (the initial evaluation of the man is of the woman, 2:23).

"Good" does not mean perfect, despite the claims of some scholars that "perfection" is an attribute of the "good" creation: "God pronounced his workmanship good and blessed it. The creation rested in its perfection; no further work was needed."[51] Such an assessment is not appropriate, however, not least given the ongoing evaluative process noted. Moreover, the idea of perfection does not take sufficiently into account God's call to the human to "subdue" the earth, explored further below. Still further, if the creation was "perfect," how could anything ever go wrong?[52]

God responds to what has been created in other ways as well; God names (1:5-10) and God blesses (1:22, 28; 2:3). By naming the creatures, God responds in still another way to what has been created (human naming in 2:18-23 does not overlap God's naming). Naming, which involves knowledge of and relationship to the creature, *continues the creative process* (understood in terms of ordering) by a discernment of the place of the creature in relationship to other creatures. As with evaluating, so in the divine naming, God's creating involves a process of both action and interaction with what has already been created, leading to further creaturely developments. That God is so engaged in creative activity over time suggests that God's creating work is not fixed in the beginning but is ongoing, in constant interaction with creatures that already exist.

God's response of blessing is specifically related to land animals (1:22), human beings (1:28), and the seventh day (2:3). To bless others is an act of giving power and potentiality to them; it is another dimension of the divine power-sharing activity we have discerned in these chapters in other ways (see below on 1:28); this action is revealing of the kind of relationship God establishes with the creatures. God gives over to the creatures what is God's to use as they will. With respect to animals and human beings, the gift of blessing relates particularly to the propagation of their own kind; with respect to the Sabbath, a particular temporal order is given such a creational status that its honor (or neglect) can deeply affect creation. Blessing is understood to be integral to the creative process itself; it enables creatures to participate in the ongoingness of creation. That blessing also continues to play a role throughout the biblical materials makes it clear that creation has to do, not just with the beginnings of things, but with a continuing process of becoming.[53]

God as Consultant of Others

The "let us" of Gen 1:26 (and the following "our") images God as inviting that which is not God to participate in the creation of human beings;[54] the "us" (also in Gen 3:22; 11:7; Isa 6:8) is commonly understood to be a reference to divine or semidivine beings of the heavenly realm or divine council/assembly (see 1 Kgs 22:19; Job 38:7; Ps 8:5-6; Isa 6:1-8; Jer 23:18-23).[55] The creation of humanity is thereby shown to be the result of a dialogical act—an inner-divine consultation—rather than a monological one. Such an understanding has immense significance for how one views the stature of the human being.

It is important to say that such mutuality within heavenly precincts does not entail an equality of God and the divine beings; God is God, and they are not. At the same time, the texts do not suggest that God's role in their relationship is that of a king relating to his subjects (though monarchial imagery likely lies in the background). The relationship between God and the divine council is of such a nature that genuine interaction and mutual interdependence are characteristic (cf., e.g., Job 1–2). God certainly takes the initiative and extends the invitation to the divine council, but their participation is not understood to be perfunctory or minimalist; they have a genuine role to play, so much so that the product of their creative work is understood to be in the image of all involved.

This perspective has at least two related levels of importance: (a) God chooses not to create (human beings) unilaterally or in isolation but shares the creative process with others. (b) Human beings, created in the image of God, are specifically (and uniquely) said to be the result of this inner-divine consultation. This relationship of mutuality within the divine realm is thus implicitly extended to those who are created in the divine image. We are thereby led to expect that God may involve human beings in the creative process in some way. This engagement of the human now follows in both 1:28 and 2:18-25; each text will call for more detailed consideration below. The latter text continues the theme of divine consultation, this time with the human being, created in the image of the kind of God revealed here.

God as Victor?

Some scholars interpret Gen 1:2 in terms of creation as the result of God's conflict with and victory over the forces of "chaos" *(Chaoskampf)*, a threatening or evil force, evident in the word *tehôm* ("deep") and its putative link with Babylonian Tiamat.[56] This conclusion regarding Gen 1:2 is also drawn with an eye to other texts that seem to portray creation in these terms (Pss 74:12-17; 77:12-21; 89:10-15) and especially to ancient Near Eastern parallels regarding creation through conflict and victory (see Excursus at the end of this chapter). In response to this perspective, we first consider Gen 1:2 and then move to other biblical texts that suggest this *Chaoskampf* interpretation.

Many scholars disagree with the *Chaoskampf* interpretation of Gen 1:2.[57] David Toshio Tsumura's interpretation is representative: "This Hebrew term *tehôm* is simply a reflection of the Common Semitic term **tihām-* 'ocean' and there is no relation between the Genesis account and the so-called *Chaoskampf* mythology."[58] Tsumura also shows that the phrase *tōhû wābōhû* ("formless void") "has nothing to do with 'chaos' and simply means 'emptiness' and refers to the earth which is an empty place, i.e. 'an unproductive and uninhabited place.'"[59] William P. Brown similarly concludes: the verse "designates nothing more than formlessness, a static, amorphous state, tantamount to nothingness . . . jumbled, undifferentiated mass."[60]

This point of view denies that verse 2 depicts evil as being a constitutive dimension of the created order, even in limited sense. God may be said to say no to what is present in verse 2, for that state of affairs is not what God intends for the creation. But God does not engage in conflict with it; rather, God uses it as "raw material" or a starting point for further creations (e.g., the earth of v. 2 is made to "appear" in v. 9). The situation laid out in verse 2 is not described as "evil" (or other such language).[61]

Jon D. Levenson puts forth a kind of middle ground regarding this issue but in a way not entirely satisfactory. He speaks of Gen 1:1–2:3 (and

Psalm 104) as a depiction of "creation without opposition" and hence not a portrayal of creation as combat.[62] At the same time, he identifies the "primordial chaos" of 1:2 as "a malign power," "evil," and "dark, ungodly forces."[63] Even so, for Levenson, Genesis 1 does not speak of God's "banishment of evil, but about its control." Yet, a few sentences later he claims that these primordial forces are "effortlessly *overcome* by placement in a structure in which they are bounded by new realities created by divine speech alone."[64] In such a formulation, "control" entails an action to "overcome"; with this kind of language, some kind of victory must be in view, however effortless it is. Can one speak of overcoming evil and not introduce a combat element into Genesis 1 in some sense?[65] Levenson's perspective on verse 2 will not do, not least because he nowhere makes the case that this verse is descriptive of *evil*.[66]

In this formulation "chaos" is interpreted as an evil force persisting beyond God's ordering activity and constituting an ever-present, potential threat to God's creation. The question becomes whether one can speak of the reality of Gen 1:2 as a continuing ontological reality and what its character might be. I claim that to designate this reality as "evil" is not supported by the text; yet, in some sense "chaos" persists. A key to considering this issue is the divine command to "subdue the earth" (1:28).[67] If this command has the sense of bringing order out of continuing disorder, as seems likely, then some dimensions of the realities of 1:2 do continue. For some disorder to persist beyond God's originating creative activity is necessary for the proper development of the creation; such elements of disorder are "good." W. Sibley Towner is right to say (also calling attention to Job 38–41): "If there were no freedom in this creation, no touches of disorder, no open ends, then moral choice, creativity, and excellence could not arise. The world would be a monotonous cycle of inevitability, a dull-as-dishwater world of puppets and automatons."[68] This direction of reflection regarding "chaos" could profitably relate Gen 1:2 to recent developments in physics, namely, "chaos theory."[69] While Genesis 1 obviously does not reflect a modern physicist's knowledge of the world, at the least it can be said that the literary variation in the chapter, the good-but-not-perfect character of God's evaluation, the need for the creation to be subdued, and the interconnectedness of all creatures make for some rough edges in the creation and constitute an openness to change and ever new developments.

A key human responsibility set out in the command of Gen 1:28 is *to work creatively with that disorder*. Human beings could, however, be so irresponsible with respect to this task that the disorder would move beyond "good" and life would revert more and more toward the situation of Gen 1:2. What is important to stress here is that such consequences are the effect of *creaturely* irresponsibility and God's judgmental response and not that of some evil forces. We will see in the next chapter that this is one way to understand Gen 6:11-13; the earth had "gone to ruin" because of creaturely violence.[70] While the flood is an initial effect of such irresponsibility (Gen 6:11-13), post-flood divine promises (8:21-22; 9:8-17) limit future threats; this limitation would mean that any intensification of disorder constitutes a threat only to one or more discrete entities within the creation (e.g., Sodom and Gomorrah) and not to the created order as such. In other terms, given the deep interconnectedness of all creatures, moral order has the potential of adversely affecting cosmic order (as we know so well in our own time). Notably, if the cosmic order could be so affected by moral order, this constitutes another argument that the ecosystem is understood in dynamic terms and not as a fixed entity that functions in a mechanistic way.

This perspective is consonant with the use of "chaos" imagery in later texts (e.g., Pss 74:12-17; 77:12-21; 89:10-15). Chaos in these texts does not have reference to a resurgent evil force but is used in connection with human sin and its effects and the associated "wrath of God," as Jer 4:23-26 shows so clearly.[71] It is important that these references are allusive in character and are present only in poetic literature. To assume that Israel understood such poetic imagery in a literal way may be as profound a mistake as to think these Genesis chapters are journalistic prose.

But, how this imagery is interpreted is important. Some scholars set the poetic imagery over against literal description.[72] For Dennis J. McCarthy, for example, whatever associations this language might have had with ancient Near Eastern traditions, "Early in its history Israel is so free from seeing any reality in the *Chaoskampf* theme that it has become a mere source for figures of speech."[73] And so, in Exod 15:1-18, for example, terms from the *Chaoskampf* are a source for imagery, but the waters have become the weapon of God rather than the enemy. Because these themes had lost their literal meaning, they could be applied figuratively to various historical nations and figures.[74]

Yet, McCarthy and others go too far to the other side of the issue in speaking *simply* of imagery, with these themes totally demythologized. That is, in such a formulation, the creation themes have become so devoid of creational import that they have become, in McCarthy's language, simply "images of salvation." Others take a mediating position, namely, the *Chaoskampf* language is neither demythologized nor historicized but is used to give cosmic depth to historical events. God's founding of Israel has universal impact and implications. Exodus 15 may not be "a story of creation in any meaningful sense," except as Israel applies creation words to God's formation of a people,[75] but the creational themes carry a deeper level of cosmic significance.[76]

God as King?

It has been suggested that God the Creator is imaged as a king in Genesis 1.[77] Moreover, while interpreters might not use the king metaphor for God, the language of divine "rule" or "sovereignty" is common. This understanding is grounded in several observations:

1. The portrayal of the Creator God using monarchial imagery in several Old Testament texts (Pss 8:5-6; 24:1-2, 7-10; 93:1-2; 95:3-5; 96:5, 10; 149:2; Isa 43:15; Jer 10:10-12).[78] Even more, it is sometimes suggested that, given a (problematic) decision that kingship is a central or root metaphor for God, other metaphors need to be drawn into that orbit of understanding (for example, building).[79]

2. Royal parallels in ancient Near Eastern texts in Egypt and Mesopotamia, including those that associate "image of God" with the king[80] and divine rest with enthronement (which, in turn, may be linked with royal texts such as Ps 132:13-14).[81] These links suggest that the God of the creation account is portrayed as a king and that ancient Near Eastern understandings are directly transferable to Israel's perspective.

3. Ezekiel 28:11-19 portrays a "royal first man" that is sometimes thought to have connections with the Eden story in Genesis 2.[82] In Ezekiel this text is part of the oracles against the nations and constitutes a "lamentation" over the fall of Tyre. Portrayed as a royal figure, he was originally at home in Eden (situated on "the holy mountain of God") and was endowed with wisdom and bedecked with precious stones. Though originally blameless, his pride corrupted his wisdom and made violent his ways, and God, through a guardian cherub, cast him off the mountain to earth and utterly destroyed him. The human could be depicted as having assumed royal prerogatives that were exclusively those of God. Whether and how this text is related to Genesis 2–3 is much debated, but it seems that the text is too vague to support a link between creation and divine kingship.[83]

A note on the Garden of Eden: Contrary to some reflections, Eden is not considered a garden of God in Genesis 2–3.[84] While there are ancient Near Eastern parallels to garden settings for the gods and while it is true that Eden is a place where God is present and comfortably strolls in it, earth is not turned into heaven.[85] Eden is a genuinely earthly place within which God has chosen to dwell.[86] But the presence of God in the garden is not unmediated; God appears in human form—certainly a mediated divine presence! Moreover, while Eden is a garden for human beings, it is not simply so; other creatures also have a home there. God placed the human in the garden to care for what was already there (2:15) and, while the presence of the human was crucial for its life and health (2:5), the garden is also a home for other creatures as creations of God. Unlike the view of other ancient Near Eastern creation texts, human beings were placed in Eden not to serve the gods but to serve the creation.

In response to arguments for God as king, it should be stressed that no *specific* monarchial language for God is used in Genesis 1–2 or associated with the image/likeness language of 1:26-27. Moreover "image of God" is never used of a king in the Old Testament (so the only evidence comes from "outside the text"),[87] and *creation* in the image of God is not found in the texts with royal connections.[88] Moreover, the rest/enthronement language is used in texts that follow upon the conquest of an enemy, an understanding that is not present in the creation accounts (see above section). But, an even more decisive argument against such an understanding is the democratization that is inherent in the claim that *every* human being is created in the image of God.[89] If the royal language has been democratized, then royal links that may be present have been subverted and nonhierarchical perspectives prevail. Moreover, the only "rule" language in Genesis 1–2 is used for the luminaries (1:16-18) and for *all* human beings, without regard to station in life (1:28; see discussion below). As such, this text is at least an amonarchial text, probably even an antimonarchial text.[90] This kind of interpretation may be overly subtle to fit such a polemical purpose, but that may have been necessary in a setting where monarchs were prominent figures. Monarchs would not have appreciated the social "leveling" in this text! This direction of thought fits well with the other images of God in Genesis 1–2 of which we have spoken.[91]

It may be that the use of monarchial language for God the creator on the part of some scholars has contributed to an emphasis, perhaps subtly so, on divine power and control in the interpretation of Genesis 1, which in turn could negatively shape what it means to be in the image of God.[92] In thinking through issues related to the power and control of God the Creator, John Macquarrie's reflections are worth pondering: for God, it is

> not so much an exercise of power as rather an exercise of love and generosity, an act of self-limitation and even of self-humiliation on the part of God. His love and generosity lead him to share existence with his creatures. He puts himself into the creation. He commits himself to it and takes responsibility for it, though at the same time he commits a share of the responsibility to the creatures.[93]

And to the latter issue we now turn.

The Creature and the Creative Process

The creation accounts demonstrate that God chooses not to act alone in bringing the creation into being. While God is certainly the initiator and primary actor in creation, God certainly involves both the human and the nonhuman in the continuing process of creation; it is important to stress that human beings are *not unique* in having the powers of creative activity. In what follows, I lift up key texts that speak of nondivine involvement in the creative process.

Genesis 1:26-28

The phrase "image of God" has been the subject of much discussion over the centuries.[94] An unfortunate aspect of this discussion has been an almost exclusive focus on the meaning of the words *image* and *likeness*; less attention has been given to the import of the word *God* in view of the portrayal of God in the larger context (perhaps in part due to the lack of epithets used for God). The content of the word *God* at this point in the text has fundamentally to do with God's *creative* activity; so the human vocation to be in God's image, at least as specified in this chapter (especially 1:28), is to be modeled on the creative words and actions of God.[95]

So, it has been a crucial interpretive task for us to gather images for God in these accounts and seek to discern the kind of God portrayed there, for it will decisively shape what it means for human beings to be the image of God in the world. For example, if the God who is portrayed in Genesis 1 is understood only or fundamentally in terms of overwhelming power, absolute control, and independent, unilateral activity, then those who are created in God's image could *properly* understand their creaturely role in comparable terms. In such an understanding, the relationship of God's image to the rest of creation is to be one of power over, absolute control, and independence. By definition, the natural world becomes available for human manipulation and exploitation. Readers might ask: has not the human tendency over the years to dominate the nonhuman creation been an effort, recognized or not, to act in the image of the dominating God often thought to be portrayed in Genesis 1?[96] If all the creatures of Genesis 1 are understood to be but passive putty in the hands of God, then does not that invite a comparable treatment of them by those created in the image of such a God?

On the other hand, if the God of the creation accounts is imaged more as one who, in creating, chooses to share power in relationship, then the way in which the human as image of God exercises dominion is to be shaped by that model. If, as I have sought to show, the images of God as Creator do not include those that are military or monarchial (or only vestiges thereof), it seems out of place to focus on divine sovereignty in a traditional way. I now look more closely at God's relationship with the human, with its implications for developing what it means to be created in the image of this kind of God.

The very first words that God speaks to the newly created human beings assume the gift of power and its (potential) exercise: be fruitful, multiply, fill the earth, have dominion, subdue the earth (1:28). Given the imaging of God we have discerned up to this point, these words of commission should be interpreted fundamentally in terms of *creative word and deed* and not domination or violence. God's relationship with the world is such that God, from the beginning, chooses not to be the only one who has creative power and the capacity, indeed the obligation, to exercise it. God certainly takes the initiative in distributing this power to the creatures and God is the one who invites their participation in the use of power. But, having done so, God is committed to this way of relating to them in such a way that forfeiting or suspending this role is not a divine option. God is a power-sharing God, and God will be faithful to that way of relating to those created in the divine image.

Human beings are not only created *in* the image of God (this is who they are); they are also created *to be* the image of God (this is their role in the world). The latter means that God really does give over the care of the world to the one created in the divine image, come what may; God will not intervene to fix things every time the creature does not get it right (concern about the effects of human action would then be sharply diminished). Image language entails that the roles given by God are "a matter of vocation" for the human; this human vocation "is necessary for the successful continuance of the created world." Moreover, inasmuch as this divinely given vocation is included in the evaluation, "very good," having dominion and subduing are understood *originally* as completely positive for the life of the other creatures.[97]

The commission to "be fruitful and multiply, and fill the earth" (1:22, 28) is possible to fulfill because God blesses these creatures.[98] Note that blessing is an act subsequent to their creation.[99] Blessing is a word of empowerment, of divine power-sharing with the creature, which is then capable of fulfilling the named responsibilities.[100] It has been common to link the image of God with the task of dominion; it is less common to link it with the call to procreate or "male and female."[101] God intended that the world be a settled place, and that means that procreation is crucial to what God intends for the creation (see Isa 45:18). If creative power is an essential element in the imaging of God in the creation account, then human likeness to God in one respect consists in our procreative capacity.[102] Indeed, procreation is stated as an obligation of the community of human beings for the sake of continuity in creation. To that end, God builds into the very structure of these creatures the capacity to generate new life.[103] God (unlike the gods of Canaan) does not assume responsibility for these generative activities. By being what they were created to be and without the need for divine intervention, they can "naturally" be productive of new life and perpetuate their own kind.[104] God remains involved in the process (see Ps 139:13) but not in a micromanaging way so that human decisions and actions do not count or potentially random events cannot wreak havoc (e.g., the randomness of the gene pool). Humans will do the procreating, not God! Reproduction is a responsibility that human beings have in order to be the image of God they were created to be.[105]

The genealogies, so prominent in Genesis 1–11, witness to the fulfillment of this human responsibility; the genealogies may be said to speak of the spread of the image of God throughout the world. Most basically, the genealogies tell us that human beings are reproducing themselves and life goes on. Human *stories* may receive less attention in Genesis 1–11 because of the importance of getting human beings into existence and perpetuating the image of God. Notably, the genealogy in 5:1-3 speaks of human genealogy in the specific terms of image of God and procreation (see below).

The concerns of 9:4-6 link image of God with the sanctity of human life, and these verses are bracketed in part by a repetition of the command to be fruitful and multiply (9:1, 7). Murder means that human beings, who carry the divine image, would be in danger of no longer perpetuating themselves, the divine image, into the future. That the Cain and Abel story is the first story is not fortuitous (followed shortly by 5:1-3); it says something crucial about the perpetuation of the human species. "Taking the life of an individual entails the nonlife of all his potential descendants, the destruction of life to an almost infinite degree (in Abel's case, exactly half of all potential human beings)."[106] That is one of the primary forms of evil manifest in the world: the killing of human beings, which is the killing of an image of God. One might also note that abusive procreational practices are a key factor leading to the flood (6:1-4).

The discussion of law in the creation account will be picked up in chapter 5, but the implication of these commands for "natural law" might be anticipated here. Given the understanding of creation as becoming will mean that new occasions teach new duties. And so it should not simply be assumed that these commands are as applicable today as in Israel's world. Given, say, the patterns of population growth in the modern world, perhaps the word from God today is: Don't multiply so fast! The earth is already full. Another dimension of this issue relates to whether being in the image of God *necessarily* entails procreation for every human being. This matter must not be so construed that childless couples (for whatever reason) or singles (whether by choice or not) are somehow understood to be less than fully human.

The next divine word to the human beings is to have dominion (*rādāh*), centered on the animals.[107] This verb apparently belonged to the sphere of ideal conceptions of royal responsibility (see Ps 72:8-14; see especially Ezek 34:1-4, where "force" and "harshness" are needed to qualify the verb; so also Lev 25:43, 46). At the same time, given the antimonarchial understanding of image we have suggested and the fact that every human being is in view, the focus of the royal imagery should be placed on what the king *does*, not who the king *is*. The verb *rādāh* should thus be understood in terms of caregiving, even nurturing, not exploitation (so also 2:5, 15); the killing of animals is a post-sin reality (9:2-3), shown not least in Gen 1:29-30, where only plants (not living creatures in that world's understanding) are given for food.[108] This creaturely activity is directed toward the world of creatures not the world of the gods (or God), but God does not remain unaffected by how creatures proceed with their responsibilities.

Noah is the first person who sees to this care of the animal world; he is repeatedly obedient to God's command to bring the animals onto the ark in the face of a destructive storm (Gen 6:19-20).[109] In the words of Dietrich Bonhoeffer,

> this freedom to rule includes being bound to the creatures who are ruled. . . . [they] constitute the world in which I live, without which I cease to be. . . . I am not free from [them] in any sense of my essential being, my spirit, having no need of nature, as though nature were something alien to the spirit. On the contrary, in my whole being, in my creatureliness, I belong wholly to this world; it bears me, nurtures me, holds me.[110]

The verb *kābaš*, "subdue," may have primary reference to the cultivation of the earth, a difficult task in those days.[111] While the verb may involve coercive activities in *interhuman* relationships (see Num 32:22, 29), no enemies are in view here, as we have noted. That this text is the only instance where the verb is used with reference to the nonhuman creatures means that one cannot simply transfer to this text understandings from its usage for human activity. Given the lack of specificity in "subdue," and the images of God present in the context, the verb may be best understood as a more general reference to creational development, to the becoming of the world (often experienced as a harsh reality in that time). God's creative activity relative to the earth (e.g., 1:2 with 1:9-10) entails an ordering of the not yet ordered; human continuity with this divine activity suggests a meaning of "subdue" along the lines of "to bring order out of disorder."[112]

As we have noted, the word *subdue* makes clear that the divine evaluation "good" does not mean that the creation is "perfect" in the sense of needing no further development or attention or, for that matter, being unable to fail. Declaring the creation as "very good" does not mean that its goodness was a means to another end but that each creature is good for being what it was created to be. At the same time, because God creates for a purpose, the creation is not static but dynamic and going somewhere; the potential of becoming is built into the very structure of things. To be called "good" means that nothing God has created, most of which was sheer matter, is evil. In some sense, creation is a "project" of God, begun "in the beginning" and developing through the millennia in and through the agency of creatures (especially human beings). In time it will need salvific work in view of sin and evil, which will move the creation toward a goal: a new heaven and new earth.[113]

Genesis 2:5-17

The point made about the role of the human in 1:26-28 is essentially the same as that stated in 2:5. The absence of a human being to "till" (*'ābad*, "serve") the ground is considered crucial for the becoming of the creation that God intended. The earth was in this precreation state not only because God had still further creating to do but also because no human being was yet active. Responsible human beings are said to be as important to the development of the creation as is rain! The divine purpose for the human being that is specified in 2:15, to "serve" *('ābad)* and to "protect" *(šāmar)* the earth (more natural translations of these verbs), specifically connects back to 2:5. The tasks outlined in these two texts give to the human a responsibility not only for the maintenance and preservation of the creation but also for intracreational development. This human activity stands in the *service* of the nonhuman world, moving it toward its fullest possible potential; at the same time, no precise future is suggested; the future is open-ended to some degree.[114]

Ellen F. Davis notes that the words in 2:15 describing the human work in the garden are not most fundamentally words drawn from the fields of horticulture and agriculture; in fact only rarely are they used for cultivating the land. Even more, they are words that are primarily related to human activity in relationship to God: to serve or work on behalf of or worship (e.g., Exod 9:1, 13).[115] To serve the land would thus imply "that we are to see ourselves in a relation of *subordination* to the land on which we live . . . deferring to the soil. The needs of the land take clear precedence over our own immediate preferences."[116] And this is shown to be the case not least because, as Gen 1:29-30 indicates, human beings are heavily *dependent* upon the land for their very life.

The verb *šāmar* ("keep, observe") has a primary reference to keeping Torah (e.g., Exod 13:10; 20:6). What it means to "keep" the soil is akin to what it means to keep the commandments. To keep the commandments has both positive and negative dimensions, namely, to promote the well-being of others and to restrain violence and the misuse of others. And so to "keep" the land is to promote its well-being and keep it from being violated through human misuse. Davis also points out that the verb *keep* is related to the care of the less fortunate and the vulnerable in the sense of "watch over" (see Pss 16:1; 17:8; 86:2). And so, the charge in 2:15 "can be heard as an extension of that prophetic concern for the vulnerable, expanding the sphere of covenant obligation to include the soil itself."[117]

Even in the wake of human sin, God still entrusts the human with power and responsibility; the use of the language of 2:5, 2:15 in the post-fall context of 3:23 indicates that there is a basic continuity in human responsibility for the care of the earth.[118] God may well be imaged as a parent at this point, still entrusting the human creatures with important creational responsibilities even though they have failed. The narratives that follow also continue to speak of the human being as created in the image of God (5:1-3; 9:6; the use of comparable language in the postfall Psalm 8 should also be noted).

Notably, rain is considered as important for the development of the creation as is the human (2:5), as is water more generally (2:6). The crucial role given to water is further developed in 2:10-14, as rivers flow out of Eden to water the larger garden and the earth beyond (probably all of the regions of the then known world).[119] Even life outside the garden is "good" (v. 12) so that when Adam and Eve move out into that world, they will not move from a world of blessing to one devoid of blessing. God's good creation will be there to continue to support life, so crucially dependent upon water.

Even more, the ground (*'ădāmāh*, a play on *'ādām*) proves to be a crucial ingredient for the creation of the human. Human beings are not created "out of nothing," but out of an already existent nonhuman creature, a creature that has creative capacities (1:11-13, 24). The ground proves to be an indispensable medium for the creative work of God the potter (of nonhumans as well as humans, 2:19). With the trees (2:9, 16) the ground remains basic for continuing human life (1:29; 2:5), even when it suffers because of human sin (3:17-19). In other words, human beings are keenly dependent upon the ground not only for their sustenance and livelihood but also for their very being. Without the ground they would neither exist nor survive. At the same time, as we have noted, the ground depends on the human for its proper development. Issues of dependence and interdependence in a highly interrelated world are here brought to the forefront.

With these considerations in place, we return briefly to the understanding of *image* and *likeness*. The word *likeness* makes it clear that *image* is not to be construed in the sense of identity. At the same time, the word *image* suggests that "the pattern on which [human beings are] fashioned is to be sought outside of the sphere of the created."[120] The image refers to the entire human being, not to some part, such as the reason or the will; it is important to say that it includes the body, for Israel certainly understood that human beings are "material, bodily beings, and are so essentially."[121] In the language of Bonhoeffer, "Humankind is derived from a piece of earth. Its bond with the earth belongs to its essential being. . . . The body belongs to a person's essence . . . a human being is a human body."[122] This claim links up with one of the foremost characteristics of God in the opening chapters of Genesis; God assumes bodily form, performs certain actions that entail a bodily form (e.g., shaping, breathing), and personally interacts with Adam, Eve, and Cain as if God were another human being. The bodily appearances of the "messenger of God" elsewhere in Genesis are also important in this connection (e.g., Gen 16:7).[123]

In addition, the text speaks of human beings created in the image of God neither as isolated individuals nor as a generalized humanity, but as *social, relational beings*—male and female—and thereby correspondent to the sociality of God ("let us"; see Gen 1:26; 3:22; 11:7; cf. 9:6).[124] The significance of human bodily existence returns at this point; human beings are related to each other and to other creatures as bodies; bodily existence is an essential element of this relationality. This relational understanding of image is affirmed by God's own declaration that the isolated or totally independent *'ādām* is "not good" (Gen 2:18).[125] Generally speaking, human beings are given such gifts that they have a *communicating relationship* with one another and with God (recall that they are the product of inner-divine communication, 1:26) and can take up the God-given responsibilities specified in 1:28.[126] As the image of God, they are to mirror God to the world, to be as God would be to the nonhuman, to be an extension of God's own creative activity in the continuing development of the world.

To return to our earlier discussion, the image of God, whatever its royal roots, has been universalized, indeed democratized so that all humanity—male and female[127] and with no regard for race or class—belongs to this sphere; all interhuman hierarchical understandings are set aside. This democratization has the effect of leveling any monarchial images that may lie behind the text, indeed making the text subtly antimonarchial.[128] This consideration relates back to the basic imaging of God of these chapters in the nonmonarchial terms of which we have spoken.

In so understanding the human in God's image, we see again that God intends from the beginning that the created order not remain just as it is initially created. And this is the case not just because God does not exhaust the divine creativity in the first week of the world (!), but because of the creative capacities that have been given to the creatures. God creates a paradise, but this is not a static state of affairs. The creation is not presented as "a finished product,"[129] all wrapped up with the big red bow and handed over to the creatures to keep exactly as it was originally created. God creates a dynamic world in which the future is open to a number of possibilities and in which creaturely activity is crucial for proper creational developments.

Genesis 2:18-25

These themes are developed in a striking way in 2:18-25. This segment is probably intended to retell the events of (primarily) the sixth day of creation in story form, though certainly not in any precise or linear way. In this text God evaluates the creational situation and declares that something God has created is not (yet?) good: "It is not good that the *['ādām]* should be alone" (2:18). To whom is God speaking here? It is likely that the reader is once again permitted to overhear the inner-divine reflective process, providing a connection back to the "let us" of 1:26; the *'ādām's* not being alone is correlated with God's not being alone. Here God identifies a problem within the divine creative work up to this point and moves to find a solution, to make those changes that would enable a different evaluation: it is now good.[130] Notably, relationship with at least one other human being is considered essential for human beings to be evaluated as "good." Some representative interpretations of these verses will help us focus on one major issue; each of them lifts up a key dimension of the text.

1. This text speaks of divine experimentation, a trial and error method of creation. After a "false start," God finally creates what the *'ādām* needs.[131] Unfortunately, this view has often been adjudged naive or primitive, and hence to be left behind theologically. From my perspective, this is an experimental divine move within the very process of creation that has deep theological implications. Both God and the *'ādām learn* from the experience.[132] The *'ādām* learns that the animals, linked though they are by virtue of their common origins in the *'ădāmāh* (2:19), will not do as partner or helper (reinforcing the human role of dominion of 1:28). God learns from what the human being actually does with the task that has been divinely assigned. At the same time, think of the high value

given the animals in that God considered them as a potential resource for resolving the issue of human aloneness (witness the role that some animals do in fact play in this regard even today in, say, nursing homes).

2. From another perspective, God here "engages in a sharp secularization of the human creature."[133] God does not intend to be the helper of the *'ādām*, at least in this sense; God's presence is not the solution to the problem of human aloneness. The help that the *'ādām* needs regarding this matter is to be found among the creatures, not among the gods. The net effect of this angle of interpretation lifts up the divine honoring of the human decision-making process.[134]

3. On the naming of the animals, for Westermann, it is the *'ādām* who "decides what sort of helper corresponds to him." The naming indicates that the *'ādām* "is autonomous within a certain limited area," whereby he "puts [the animals] into a place in his world."[135] Von Rad speaks of the naming as an act of ordering but also in terms of the use of language "as an intellectual capacity by means of which [the *'ādām*] brings conceptual order to his sphere of life."[136] It is important to stress in this connection that language shapes reality and hence has a creative function. These suggestions of Westermann and von Rad move in the right direction but need to be filled out in terms of a more comprehensive understanding of the role of the human in creative activity.

How God responds to the evaluation of "not good" is impressive. Twice, God "brings" some other creature—first the animals, then the woman—before the human being. Twice, God lets the *human being* determine whether the animals or the woman is adequate to move the evaluation of the creation from "not good" to "good." The human being, not God, deems what is "fit for him." The future of the human race in some basic respect lies in human hands.[137]

This portrayal of God, the creator of heaven and earth, leading all the animals one by one, and then the woman, to a face-to-face meeting with the *'ādām* is truly remarkable. This activity suggests the image of God as a servant: God the Creator places the divine self at the service of the "good" of the human being, indeed at the service of creaturely creativity. God's role is the placing of various creative possibilities before the human being, but it is the creature that is given the freedom to decide. God so values human freedom that God will take into account the free human response from within the creative process in shaping the future.[138]

That the human being does not simply acquiesce to what God presents is remarkable. After all, this is God, the creator of heaven and earth! But, what God initially provides, the human being in freedom does not accept! God, in turn, accepts the human decision and goes back to the drawing boards. God takes the ongoing creational process into account in shaping new directions for the creation. Divine decisions interact with human decisions in the creation of the world. Creation is process as well as punctiliar act; it is creaturely as well as divine.

The future is genuinely open here. It depends on what the human being does with what God presents. Will the human being decide for the animals? The question of not only how but, indeed, whether humanity will continue beyond this first generation is left open-ended, suspended in the midair of this creative moment. How the *human beings* in their God-given freedom decide will determine whether there will be a next human generation. The human being at least in part determines how God will be able to move into the future. The human judgment will shape the nature of the divine decision, indeed shape the future of the world. Phyllis Trible has put this point in a most helpful way. She notes that God, who has so dominated the narrative to this point (though not as much as she implies), now recedes into the background. God is now present, "not as the authoritarian controller of events but as the generous delegator of power who even forfeits the right to reverse human decisions."[139] Without any qualification in the text, *whatever* the human being called each animal, that was its name (2:19). Whatever!

The human being's naming of each creature is meant to be parallel to the divine naming in 1:5-10. This act is not a perfunctory utilitarian move, a labeling of the cages of the world zoo. Naming is a part of the creative process itself, discerning the very nature of intracreaturely relationships. Human decisions are shown to be important in the ongoing development of the created order. It is not that human beings have the capacity to stymie God's movement into the future in any *final* way, but God has established a relationship with human beings such that their decisions about the creation truly count.[140]

The *'ādām* finally recognizes that the woman, created by God in an act of separation from the *'ādām*, will address the stated need (cf. God's acts of separation in ch. 1, never of living creatures). The woman, who is, finally, created from the same creaturely stuff as is the *'ādām*, is recognized as a genuine counterpart. God recognizes the creational import of the human decision, for no additional divine word or act is forthcoming. God lets the man's exultation over the woman fill the scene (2:23); in lieu of a statement from God, the *human word* (the first uttered in

Genesis) counts for the evaluation that the creation is now "good." The translation of Everett Fox puts it well, "The human said: This-time, she-is-it!"[141] It is left to the narrator to note the rightness of this creative move by drawing the reader into the closeness of the male-female bond, citing the implication of the human decision for the future of the creation. At the same time, this bond is not reduced to matters of procreation; indeed, the narrative stresses other matters: companionship, intimate and otherwise. Even more, Adam's exultant cry does not make the point that the woman is sexually different; he lifts up her common humanity not her sexuality.

It is noteworthy that the prohibition regarding the tree occurs just prior to this narrative unit, concerning which no debate is invited (2:16-17). This command (and note the presence of law before sin, a matter to be taken up in ch. 5) indicates that, for all the creative power God entrusts to human beings, the human relationship to God provides an indispensable matrix for the proper exercise of that power. To obey the command regarding the tree is to recognize that human creativity is derivative, that human beings are not freed from all limitations in its exercise or from God's good intentions for creaturely life. The tree is a concrete metaphor for the limits of creatureliness. But, within these limits, 2:18-23 depicts some remarkable divine moves relative to the role of the human in the ongoing development of the created order.[142]

Before concluding this segment, it is important to speak about recent exegetical work relative to an androcentric perspective often thought to be present in these verses. Standing at the forefront of any such discussion should be the claims made in 1:26-27. With no signs of hierarchical arrangements, both male and female are created in the image of God. This claim must shape the interpretation of the texts that follow. A comparable claim is made by the *'ādām* in exulting over the woman (2:23); no subordination of the woman is in view, for the same descriptive language is used for both male and female (bone, flesh).[143] When Gen 3:16 states that the man will rule over the woman, this development recognizes patriarchy as a consequence of human sin and contrary to God's intentions for the creation.[144]

A brief discussion of a few problematic texts may be helpful at this point. (a) For the woman to be called "helper" *('ēzer)* carries no implications regarding the *status* of the one who helps; indeed, *God* is more often called the helper of human beings (e.g., Psalm 121). The suggestion that Eve's helping has to do with motherhood is insufficient,[145] not least because the immediate outcome specified in 2:24-25 does not lift up this concern; in fact, children are not explicitly in view in this story. (b) For the woman to be created from the rib (or, more likely, side) of the *'ādām* entails no subordination any more than the *'ādām's* being created from the ground implies his subordination to it. Indeed, the *'ādām* and the animals are created from the same material (2:19). (c) For the woman to be named by the *'ādām* (2:23; 3:20) does not entail the authority of man over woman any more than does Hagar's naming of God (Gen 16:13).[146] Naming has to do with an act of discernment regarding the nature of relationships, as in the naming of the animals by *'ādām*. Moreover, if the *'ādām* is already ruler over the woman in chapter 2, then the sentence of 3:16 is no judgment.[147] (d) Being created last has nothing to do with being subordinate; one could claim that the creation of woman is the climactic moment in the story (as the creation of humans in Genesis 1 has often been so interpreted).[148]

Genesis 4:1; 5:1-3

The notice regarding the birth of Cain (4:1) and the opening segment of the genealogy of Seth (5:1-3) continue the theme of the human as creator that we have observed in the creation accounts. In 4:1, though the translation is somewhat uncertain, we are likely told of Eve's participation with God in the creation of a new human being. The verb (*qānāh*, a play on the word Cain) can refer to God's creative activity (Gen 14:19, 22) and the preposition can have the sense of "together with" (Exod 18:22; Num 11:17). It may be said that Eve lives up to her name (Gen 3:20), that God's blessing has been active (Gen 1:28), and that the man has played an appropriate role (4:1). But it is Eve who gives a *theological* interpretation of what has occurred: She has created a child with the help of the Lord. Eve is the decisive agent here, the subject of the verb of creation; she is the *creator* of this new man-child. Only God had been involved in the creation of human beings up to this point (though without the agency of a mother). Eve recognizes that in giving birth she has been caught up by God in a continuation of that creative work. Her unusual reference to having created a "man" (*'îš*) rather than a child expresses her creative continuity with Adam's interpretation of God's action in 2:23, namely, that woman was taken out of "man" (*'îš*).[149]

In 5:1-3, we are provided a unique introduction to a genealogy. God's creating of humankind in 1:26-27 is specifically recalled and related to the human genealogy that now follows. As God created humankind in the divine image and likeness, so Adam "creates" (literally, "became the father of") Seth in his "likeness" and "image."[150] This link suggests that human procreation is understood to be a genuinely creative act and finds its true parallel in God's own creative activity. In the words of the text, human beings have now taken over from God the role of creating the image of God or, more precisely, still further images of God, each of whom would carry on God's own breath of life into successive generations (2:9, cf. 9:6). In other words, the story of human generation that now follows stands in the tradition of that divine creative activity. It may indeed be that from "the standpoint of genealogical structure, to place God at the beginning of the genealogy, as the text has done, is to place him in the position of 'father' to Adam."[151] God's creative role may be distinguished from Adam's in several ways, not least by the absence of begetting language, the initiative taken in creation, the creativity evident in the "product" that emerges from the divine hand. Yet, this creative act on the part of the human is no minor role but is vital to the future of the creation as framed by God's initial creative work. Continuity in naming is also stressed in this text; God named the male and female "Humankind" and Adam named his son Seth.[152] We have noted above that naming is a genuinely creative activity (seen especially in 2:19-20), and that is recognized in specifying this divine-human parallel.

Creation and Sabbath, God and Time

"Creation reaches its highest level not in fireworks—in some impressive-looking action—but in rest" (2:1-3).[153] At the same time, the creation is not "finished" *until* the seventh day! That is to say, the seventh day as a day of rest is built by God into the created order of things. The very temporal framework of six days plus one, a work/rest rhythm, is understood to be an integral part of what God has created. Creation thus has to do not simply with spatial order but with temporal order as well. Steck puts it well: "the world was created, not only *in* time, in the six days of creation, but also *with* time as one of its constituents."[154] Wherever there is world, there is time; it is an ongoing, constitutive dimension of life in God's good creation. To honor the day of rest is to be in tune with a God-intended temporal framework of creation; because God's hallowing of the day of rest is creational, it has a status quite independent of Israel.[155]

The word *day* signals the creation of time, distinguishing it from its predecessor (i.e., eternity). The commands regarding Sabbath in Exod 21:11 and 31:17 seem to understand the six days of creation as "actual days and a unique, unrepeatable lapse of time in this world."[156] Other possibilities for understanding *day* (symbolic; sequential but not consecutive; liturgical) are less likely. Efforts to understand *day* in terms of, say, evolutionary periods, betray too much of an interest in harmonization.[157]

The Sabbath is also a break from creating or, more accurately, a divine move to a different sort of creating (God "finished" on that day). Resting on God's part means giving time and space over to the creatures to be what they were created to be; God will be present and active but not be invested in the control of their lives. God will rest and let them be. God will "sit back" as it were and let the creatures function with all the capacities they have been given. God rests so that the creatures can thrive. While the creatures will finally not be able to manage on their own and God's presence will undergird their lives, God's resting shows that they are creatures with a will and a power of their own. God doesn't create with strings attached; God doesn't keep the creatures on a leash; God lets them be creatures that are genuinely other than God. Jürgen Moltmann says it well: "God does not create merely by calling something into existence, or by setting something afoot. In a more profound sense he 'creates' by letting-be, by making room, and by withdrawing himself."[158]

The narrative of creation along a time line also establishes links with Israel's worship life, especially the seven-day sequence, the Sabbath, and the times and seasons of the "rule" of the luminaries. Israel through its faithful worship becomes attuned to a temporal order built into the very structure of creation. So the creational temporal order is linked to the religio-cultural order and its special times. The sabbath as a sanctified time does not, however, set aside that day as more divine than the other days. The divine rest is not an atemporal dimension of Genesis 1; it is as temporal as the other six days. The sabbath is revealing of a God who takes time seriously and takes "time out" to let the creatures have their own freedom to be what they were created to be.

When Sabbath is commanded for Israel in Exod 20:11 and 31:17, the texts link that prescription to the working/resting pattern of the creation account (Sabbath is first commanded in Exod 16:23, *before* the Sinai legislation). Because of this creational orientation, Sabbath-keeping is not conceived simply in terms of human rest. The Sinai commandment makes clear that the Sabbath is as much for (domestic) animals as it is for humans (Exod 20:8-11; Deut 5:12-15). The laws regarding sabbatical and Jubilee years show that the land, too, must have its Sabbaths (see Lev 25:1-24), the neglect of which would have an adverse effect on the land (Lev 26:27-45). Moreover, Israel is to model that weekly pattern for others. These texts recognize that only by keeping the Sabbath would creatures be attuned to the creation that God intended. Sabbath-keeping is an act of creation-keeping with cosmic implications; if Sabbath is not kept, that neglect can have adverse effects upon the entire creation. Positively, Levenson speaks of the sabbath as "a *weekly* celebration of the creation of the world."[159]

But, even more, Sabbath-keeping is important for what it has to say about God. By resting on the seventh day, God is thereby shown to have entered into the time of the created order.[160] Though God's direct involvement in the temporal order is implicit in the evening/morning references (Gen 1:5-31), it is now repeatedly stated that God did something on a particular day (Gen 2:2-3). God is here attending to, indeed entering into the temporal order of the world. Henceforth Bible readers are invited to think of the temporality of God. God's relationship with the world is not to be understood in terms of divine timelessness; rather, God has freely chosen to include the community of creatures that have a past, a present, and a future within the divine life.[161] God takes the time to contemplate, to take in the reality of what has been created. And God, by so immersing the divine self in time, *sanctifies or hallows* that very temporal reality (Gen 2:3).

The creation of the universe takes time—even for God.[162] There have been efforts over the centuries to claim that God created the universe instantaneously (e.g., Augustine). Certainly the all-powerful God would not need to take any time to bring the world into being! But these are actual days to which God attends here, moving from evening to morning for six days. God's varied modes of creating take time if the creation is to develop in a dynamic way. As Michael Welker makes clear, the interest of this chapter is not simply to claim a divine "production of anything and everything."[163] To speak of creation over time, coming into being along a time line, lifts up the theme of creation as dynamic process and not simply product (and never finished product). Creation takes time, and God, who involves the creatures themselves in further creational developments (e.g., Gen 1:11-13, 20, 24), takes the time necessary for creation to come to be what it is. However literally one interprets the seven days, they are emblematic of any period of time that it takes for the creation to come into being and develop. Extension along a time line is believed necessary to develop clear distinctions among the creatures and to assure that their domains and interrelationships are carefully established (not least for the sake of human knowledge of the creation).[164]

Moltmann helps capture another dimension of Sabbath-keeping for God:

> By "resting" from his creative and formative activity, he allows the beings he has created, each in its own way, to act on him [see above on God as Evaluator]. . . . By standing aside from his creative influence, he makes himself wholly receptive for the happiness, the suffering and the praise of his creatures. . . . The God who rests in the face of his creation does not dominate the world on this day: he "feels" the world; he allows himself to be affected, to be touched by each of his creatures. He adopts the community of creation as his own milieu.[165]

Israel, in mirroring God's way of being on this day, sets aside one day when they attend not to their own responsibilities and freedoms, as important as they are, but to God's ordering of life, including its time. They, too, must take time to "feel" the world and be touched by all God's creatures (see Job 38–41). This act honors God's larger creative purposes, worshipfully acknowledging that God is the Creator.

It has been noted, at least since Augustine, that the absence of a "seventh day" formula in 2:1-3 leaves the future open-ended for further creative activity.[166] The creation is "finished," but that does not mean that God's work has come to an end, as if God's creativity had now been exhausted; it has simply been "rounded off." Creative activity will be taken up once again, both by God (e.g., Ps 104:30) and by human beings and other creatures (see 2:18-25).[167] Such ongoing creative work, however, must attend to the Sabbath rest if it would be properly attuned to God's intentions for the creation.

Excursus: Creation Stories in the Ancient Near East

Creation literature is not unique to Israel. Sumerian, Mesopotamian, Egyptian, and Canaanite creation accounts (or remnants thereof) have been unearthed in the nineteenth and twentieth centuries.[168] As a result of comparing these extrabiblical texts with the biblical literature, it is apparent that Israel participated in a culture with a lively interest in questions regarding creation. While some scholars have claimed that Israel depended directly on one or more of these accounts, it is now more common to speak of a widespread fund of images and ideas upon which Israel drew that helped shape its own creation accounts. Included among these parallels are the primordial waters, divine rest,[169] creation as separation, images of the creator as potter, farmer, and speaker of the word, and the textual sequence in Genesis 1–9.[170]

Scholarly efforts initially focused on the Babylonian *Enuma Elish* in the century following its appearance in 1876. Its opening lines are:

> When on high [= Enuma Elish] the heaven had not been named,
> Firm ground below had not been called by name,
> Naught but primordial Apsu [male waters], their begetter,
> (And) Mummu-Tiamat [female waters], she who bore them all,
> Their waters commingling as a single body;
> No reed hut had been matted, no marsh land had appeared,
> When no gods whatever had been brought into being,
> Uncalled by name, their destinies undetermined—
> Then it was that the gods were formed within them.[171]

The syntactical construction "When . . . Then" resembles the opening lines of Gen 2:5-6 (and, some think, 1:1-2), as do the primordial waters and the absence of human beings. The birthing of the gods is obviously not paralleled in Genesis. Marduk, one of the gods birthed, leads the assembly of the gods against Tiamat; from her slain body, he creates the universe and becomes king over gods and human beings, which are created to serve the gods. This creation account was recited at the Babylonian New Year festival and was believed to "trigger" the renewal of the earth, beginning the agricultural year.

More recent work has concentrated on the Babylonian *Epic of Atrahasis* (about 1600 B.C.E.), published in 1969.[172] Its significance is evident primarily in its sequence of creation-disruption-flood-repopulation, corresponding to the ordering of the biblical account. Only Atrahasis is saved from the divinely ordained plagues and flood. The gods permit a limited (but unsuccessfully calculated) repopulation of the earth because of the capacity of human beings to serve the gods.

Special attention has also been given to Egyptian parallels.[173] No Egyptian creation accounts as such have been discovered; understandings of creation in Egypt have had to be pieced together from a variety of sources. Several parallels with biblical texts are evident, the most notable of which are those between the great hymn to the sun god Aten and Psalm 104.[174] Another important link can be seen in the understanding of creation by means of the word of a god named Ptah: "for every word of the god came about through what the heart devised and the tongue commanded."[175] In Simkins's words, "In this myth Ptah is identified with the creative principle which is actualized through his thoughts and speech."[176] In addition, the image of God the potter in Genesis 2, who breathes the breath of life into human nostrils, has its parallels in activities of the god Khnum:

> You are the all-powerful one,
> And you have made humans on the wheel.
> . . . .
> you have formed everything on your wheel each day
> In your name of Khnum the potter.

Again, "The sweet breath of wind goes out from him for the nostrils of gods and humans."[177]

Regarding Canaanite (Ugaritic) writings from Ras Shamra, no cosmogony such as those found in Mesopotamia has been discovered, and the presence of a creation myth is disputed by scholars. Yet, the Baal Cycle, wherein Baal defeats Sea and Death (symbols of chaotic forces) and brings renewed fertility to the earth, contains words and themes present also in several Old Testament texts relating to creation (e.g., Pss 74:12-17; 77:12-21).[178]

It is important to examine closely all such accounts and seek to determine their relationship, if any, to the biblical texts. The delineation of similarities has long belonged to such work, some of which have been noted here. But, dissimilarities from the biblical account have more often been the scholarly focus.[179] They include: the basic purpose (e.g., the absence of explicit Israelite political interests), emphasis upon history rather than nature, the lack of a theogony and a conflict among the gods, the absence of interest in primeval chaos (see above), the prevailing monotheism, and the high value given human beings. These often noted dissimilarities have differing values. For example, the sharp contrast often drawn between nature and history has been overblown. The ancient Near Eastern gods were also gods of history,[180] and Israel had a lively interest in matters of nature and the created order.[181]

At the same time, to conceive of the biblical account's relationship to these other stories fundamentally in disjunctive or polemical terms can miss their genuine contribution to Israel's own reflection about creation.[182]

Israel certainly believed that God had been active through the years in the life and thought of other cultures, including their thinking about creational issues (as well as other matters, such as law), and they were not fearful of drawing on such reflection. Such an understanding would be witness to the activity of God the Creator, not only before Israel existed but also during the history of the chosen people.[183]

CHAPTER THREE

CREATION AT RISK: DISRUPTED, ENDANGERED, RESTORED (GENESIS 3–11)

The kind of relationship God established with the created order necessarily entailed risk; genuine relationships always entail risks (at least pre-eschaton). What creatures do with their God-given freedom makes a difference regarding the course creation will take. As we have shown, God's creating work did not result in a finished product, nor was the future of the world divinely mapped out from the beginning. If God works with a blueprint of the course of the created order, it is in a constant state of revision in view of what creatures say and do. Moreover, God has freely chosen to share the continuing process of creation with the creatures, especially human beings. God's creatures, because they are finite, can fail in the fulfillment of their tasks and responsibilities, of course, and that can have negative effects on the entire created order. But sin can have even deeper and more destructive effects.

And sin they do. And the effects of their actions on the creation are massive and nearly fatal. Genesis 3–6 testifies that human beings used their freedom to violate their relationship with God, leading to an inevitable and pervasive wickedness. In the climactic words of Gen 6:5, "The LORD saw that the wickedness of humankind was great in the earth, and that every inclination of the thoughts of their hearts was only evil continually." Or, according to Gen 6:11-12, "the earth was filled with violence . . . all flesh had corrupted its ways upon the earth" (see also 6:13). Human corruption *(hišḥît)* led to destruction *(šḥt)*. The same Hebrew word refers to both cause and effect; in everyday parlance, what goes around comes around. To be sure, God mediates these effects, but the impetus and direction had already been decisively set by human behaviors. Moral evil had cosmic effects, as we know all too well in our own time; that is the way God created the world to work. For God to have forced compliance to the divine will and not allowed creatures the freedom to fail would have been to deny any genuine relationship. We now need to sketch the thrust of the narratives that led to this catastrophic point, the divine action that follows, and the implications these texts have for Israel's understanding of creation.

Genesis 3:1-24—The Originating Sin

Genesis 3 has had a high level of value in the history of biblical interpretation, though apparently not within the Old Testament itself (Ezek 28:11-19 has some uncertain connections).[1] This text did not gain such a status until post–Old Testament times (e.g., Sir 25:24; Wis 2:24) and early Christian use (e.g., Rom 5:12-21; 1 Cor 15:21-22, 45-49). At the same time, care must be used not to overdraw this point. The placement of this text at the head of the canon gave it a certain theological stature. It is not my purpose to engage in a full-scale analysis of this passage; that work is available elsewhere.[2] My concern is to lift up those dimensions of this text that bear particularly on the study of creation.

Genesis 3 does not stand isolated, of course, and its larger context should play a more important role than it commonly has. While the literary and thematic links with chapter 2 are often noted, less attention has been given to connections with the chapters that follow. Similarities in the thought progression of 3:1-24 and of 4:7-16 have been noted, keeping these texts closely interrelated.[3] But this link should be extended through 6:1-5, where the cosmic effects of sin are mythically conveyed with 6:5 summarizing the situation at that juncture, namely, the universality and inevitability of human sinfulness. No such claim is made at the end of chapter 3, though that has been a common interpretation through the centuries. Rather, chapter 3 describes the "originating sin," and the chapters that follow speak of a *process* by which sin became "original," that is, universal and inescapable (no genetic understandings are conveyed). When this processive understanding of sin's emergence is combined with the text's primary imagery of separation, estrangement, alienation, progressively greater distances from Eden, and the decreasing ages of human beings, "fall" language, at least in the traditional sense, is reductionistic and not entirely appropriate for Genesis 3 alone.

In view of such observations, a number of scholars have claimed that "fall" language does not do justice to this text. James Barr claims, "Old Testament scholars have long known that the reading of the story as the 'Fall of Man' in the traditional sense . . . cannot stand up to examination through a close reading of the Genesis text."[4] Rather, in the words of Claus Westermann, these chapters depict the human's "state as a creature" at every time and place.[5] But, as we have sought to show, this perspective discounts the role of the narrative as a "story of the past," temporally removed from the story of creation in Genesis 1–2. Unless this is recognized, creation and fall are collapsed and God becomes essentially responsible for these adverse developments rather than the human being. It seems that "fall" language of some sort is truer to the text.

Some interpreters (both traditional and revisionist) have suggested a "fall upward" approach to this text, which the "becoming like God" theme might suggest. Most of these scholars have interpreted this understanding of fall negatively: human beings transgress the limits of creatureliness and assume godlike powers for themselves. Yet, this understanding of fall and sin is insufficiently primal, for it assumes a more basic problem, namely, mistrust.[6] Other interpreters have taken the "fall upward" theme in a positive direction (at least since Irenaeus in the second century). In this view, human beings move out from under the parental hand of God, a necessary move for a child on its way to true maturity. Yet, in such an interpretation, God becomes the problem in the text, setting arbitrary limits in the first place, opposing maturity, and overreacting when humans transgress them. The text gives few suggestions that the human lot actually improves, from either the divine or human perspective, as relationships at every level fall apart. If the sin of the humans is minimized, then so are the effects of the sin specified in 3:14-19, including the patriarchy that now ensues. At the same time, to speak of a fall in the sense of falling "out" or "apart" would resonate well with this basic imagery that is used throughout these chapters.[7]

Although no ancient Near Eastern fall story has been uncovered, understandings of sin in the broader culture no doubt influenced Israel's reflections regarding these matters. A universal and pervasive understanding of sin can be discerned in several of these Near Eastern texts.[8] A Sumerian penitential prayer reads:

> Who is there who has not sinned against his god,
> who has constantly obeyed the commandments?
> Every man who lives is sinful.

Or, consider a Sumerian wisdom saying: "A sinless child was never born of its mother." Or, this penitential lament:

> Though my transgressions are many—free me of my guilt!
> Though my misdeeds [be innumerable]—let your heart be still!
> Though my sins be countless—show mercy and heal (me)!

Or, ponder this remarkable invocation to the goddess Ishtar:

> Forgive my sin, my iniquity, my wickedness and my offence
> . . . .
> Loose my fetters, secure my deliverance
> . . . .
> Let my prayers and my supplications come to you
> (and) may all your grace be with me.
> Those who see me in the street will glorify your name.

Or, this song of thanksgiving to the Egyptian god Amun-Re:

> If it is the nature of the servant to commit sin,
> it is the nature of the Lord to be gracious.

It is clear that these profound understandings of sin are nothing peculiarly biblical, let alone Christian. In other words, God's work *as creator* among "nonchosen" peoples resulted in a sophisticated understanding of sin, upon which Israel drew for its own theological reflections. We are the inheritors of a rich theology of sin from the prebiblical world of God's good creation, though it is seldom acknowledged.

No word for "sin" occurs in chapter 3; good storytellers don't have to name the game. The word *sin* first appears in 4:7, where it is given an enticing, possessive character. This absence of specific sin language has made it difficult to agree on the nature of the primal sin; what do the human beings do that is wrong? And what are the effects of what they do? A closer look at some details of the story will assist readers with such questions. It will be important to see that this text does not simply speak of the effects of sin in terms of a breakdown of the God-human relationship; all creatures are caught up in the snowballing effects of human sinfulness, becoming creation-wide in its scope.

The chapter begins with an introduction of the "serpent" (the everyday Hebrew word for "snake") as a creature of God's own making (3:1). The language for the snake is identical (in Hebrew) to that used for the animals that God had made and the *'ādām* had named (!) in 2:19-20 ("animal of the field").[9] Moreover, after its encounter with the human beings, God identifies the snake as an animal in 3:14. No language is used in 3:1 to suggest that the snake is malevolent or demonic (though that claim has been made since intertestamental times, Wis 2:24; cf. Rev 12:9; 20:2).[10] Moreover, the humans seem to understand the snake in quite innocent terms; they express no fear or wonderment, perhaps because animals in the garden were thought to have capacities of thought and speech (cf. Job 12:7-9).

The snake is an ambivalent symbol in Israel's world, associated with both life and death (see Num 21:4-9) and also with craftiness (cf. "sly fox"), perhaps because of its ability to sneak up silently on others. The verbal link (in Hebrew) between the "naked" humans and the "crafty" snake suggests that human beings may be *exposed* at times to shrewd elements in God's world—language appropriate for temptation. So, at one level, the snake is a metaphor, representing anything in God's *good creation* (N.B.!) that could present options to human beings, the choice of which could lead them away from a true relationship with God. The snake facilitates the options the tree presents. And note: God does not accept Eve's excuse that the snake had tricked her (3:13). Human beings cannot escape responsibility for what happens by a claim such as "the devil made me do it."

At the same time, though the snake does not set out to seduce the humans away from their relationship with God, the snake does not emerge from this encounter as completely innocent in that regard. The divine word to the snake in 3:14-15 implies that the snake also bears responsibility in view of what happens ("because you have done this"). True to life in an interrelated world, the ophidian facilitator participates in the consequences of the choice that humans make. As such, the snake is established as a metaphor of temptation for all future generations (3:14-15; already in 4:7 the temptation to sin is described in snakelike terms: "lurking at the door," ready to strike). This point regarding the snake may be linked to our considerations in the preceding chapter regarding creaturely participation in the creative process and the possibility of failure. Though it strikes against the grain of modern sensibilities, in some sense a nonhuman creature is here understood to fail, though it is not finally responsible for human sin, and its failure can only be named as such in view of the way in which human beings respond (see below on the significance of "all flesh" in the violence of Gen 6:12-13).

Chapter 3 brings readers into the middle of a conversation between a snake and two human beings; 3:6 makes clear that the man is present the whole time (though the woman has borne the brunt of the blame in the history of interpretation). Such an interaction between human beings and a nonhuman creature is important not least because it demonstrates the close linkage, indeed communicating capacities of human with nonhuman in a pre-sin creation. The reader overhears the conversation at the point it evolves into a question about God and the prohibition (3:1). The snake asks questions that carry the conversation along and responds in ways that are truthful, or at least potentially so: their eyes are opened (3:7), they do become like God,[11] knowing good and evil (3:22), and they do not die, at least physically; in fact, they could eat of the tree of life and continue to live (3:22).

The snake may not tell the whole truth but neither does God; that now becomes a key issue. The phrase "God knows" (3:5) is apparently decisive in leading to the eating. This claim highlights the fact that God has not told the humans the full truth. And the question is thereby raised as to whether God, having kept something from them, indeed something that seems beneficial, could be fully trusted with their best interests. The issue of knowledge at its deepest level is an issue of *trust*. Can the humans trust God while pursuing the truth about God? Can they trust that God has their best interests at heart even if they do not know everything? Can they trust that not all knowledge (or its apparent "benefits") is for their good? The primal sin may thus best be defined as mistrust of God and God's word, which then manifests itself in disobedience and other negative behaviors (e.g., blaming). Faced with the choices the tree presents, the human beings mistrust God and violate the divine prohibition (2:16-17). Sometimes (dis)obedience is considered to be the central issue,[12] but disobedience of the law, certainly present in this text, is always symptomatic of a more basic issue, namely, human mistrust of God.

The snake has presented possibilities through words (only), and the humans draw their own conclusion. Rather than speak to God about the issue, they silently consider the tree and the wisdom it offers (without specifically recalling the prohibition). The issue is not the gaining of wisdom in and of itself, however, but the way it is gained ("the fear of the LORD is the beginning of [wisdom/] knowledge," Prov 1:7). The issue is not the use of the mind or the gathering of experience, but the mistrust of God that the human move assumes. When mistrust of God is combined with possible new levels of knowledge, certain negative effects are forthcoming. The humans do not have the perspective or the wherewithal to handle their new knowledge very well (a recurrent problem); only God can view the creation as a whole and make appropriate decisions in view of that perspective.

In some sense, the story creates a symbol out of the serpent; it will remind all who encounter it of the subtleties of such conversations about the truth, especially theological truth, and the humiliating and conflictual consequences of mistrust in God and in what God is about in creation. But the serpent is not out to seduce human beings or challenge God; it is more of a neutral figure, a third party, mediating possibilities within God's good creation that can provoke reflection on the truth about God.[13]

The woman takes of the fruit and—with no tempting words—gives it to her silently observing partner (3:6). Even now, he raises no questions and considers no religious issues; he simply and silently takes his turn. The man and the woman are in this together. Their eyes are opened, that is, they see each other and the world differently—entirely through their own eyes; left to their own resources they are indeed naked, both literally and metaphorically. Their human resources—loincloths—prove inadequate, as they hide from God (3:10). Their clothing reveals more than it conceals (as does God's clothing the already clothed in v. 21). In 3:8-13, the man is the primary subject, balancing the female subject of 3:1-7. The Creator of the universe—no aloof God this—does not leave the humans alone or walk elsewhere. God seeks a response from the fearful and ashamed human beings, but they move to the "blame game" rather than confession. The sin has led to dissonance in every relationship, between humans, humans and God, humans and animals, humans and the earth, and within the self (shame).

Most would say that 3:14-19 is descriptive (of what happens in the wake of sin) rather than prescriptive (divinely established orders for the future).[14] At the same time, the language of divine judgment is appropriate if understood as God's *announcement* of what the sinful deeds (including those in vv. 8-13) have wrought. They reap the consequences of their own deeds in terms of their primary roles in that culture; God sees to the connection between deed and effect. Every aspect of creaturely life is touched: marriage and sexuality; work and food; birth and death. It is especially remarkable that the "rule" of the man over the woman is seen as a consequence of sin; hence it stands over against God's creational intention. More generally, humans wanted control over their own lives; they now have control in grievously distorted and unevenly distributed forms. They wanted to transcend creaturely limits; they have found newly intensified forms of limitation. They now have the knowledge they desired, but not the perspective to handle it well.

But this state of affairs has not been put in place for all time to come; no new orders of creation are established. Indeed, as with any consequences of sin, or divine judgments (witness the rebuilding of Jerusalem), every effort should be made to relieve the toil, pain, patriarchy, and negative effects on nature ("thorns and thistles"). Such endeavors (from anesthesia in childbirth to labor-saving devices in farming to efforts to overcome patriarchy) harmonize with God's intentions in creation, though continuing sinfulness impedes the effort.

Even in the wake of these effects, God remains in relationship with the creatures and hopeful signs for the future emerge, though expulsion from the garden becomes necessary. The naming of Eve anticipates that life will go on; God acts to cover their shame with more substantial clothing (3:21); even exclusion from the possibility of never ending life could be interpreted as gracious, given what they had become. The humans leave the garden with integrity and are not described in degrading terms; they are still charged with caring for the earth (3:23). While being "like God" severely complicates life, it also bears some potential for good and advancement.[15]

Is death one of the effects of the sin of Adam and Eve? The traditional interpretation closely links sin and death, commonly formulating an ontological change: humans who are not immortal become mortal. Most scholars now conclude that the text makes no such claim; I would agree, given certain clues. In 3:14-19, there is no referral back to the prohibition and no forthright statement that death shall now be their lot, no sense of death as enemy or threat—only a proverbial saying in verse 19 that the man (not the woman) shall have difficulty farming until he returns to the dust out of which he was created. This saying is followed by exclusion from the tree of life (3:22), implying that even though they had sinned they could still live forever by eating of the tree.

I would speak of death in two ways, as the experience of death within life and as realized mortality.[16] If human beings were created immortal, the tree of life would have been irrelevant. *Death per se was a natural part of God's created world.*[17] Yet, the tree of life was a potential vehicle for receiving some form of ongoing life. Now, even in sin, this remains a possibility (3:22). So God makes a further move beyond death within life, namely, exclusion from the tree, so that their mortality is realized. The upshot of this interpretation is that Paul's understanding of sin and death in Rom 5:12-21, while developing these themes beyond the scope of the story, is right to read the story in terms of an etiology of *the full reality of death*, if not mortality per se.

Genesis 4:1–6:5—The Snowballing Effects of Sin

The effects of these garden events on family and community life now follow, initially expressed in the story of Cain and Abel (4:1-16). Life now takes place outside of the garden (the garden continues to exist), though God seems to be as available to Cain as to Adam and Eve in the garden and still appears in human form. But life outside the garden is life away from the home God had intended. The story of the world's first children in Genesis 4 presupposes a more densely populated world (Cain's wife, building of a city, and concern for his life). The text may belong with others that collapse the distance between the "then" of the story and the "now" of the reader (e.g., 2:24). This story of violence portrays how the effects of sin cross generations, afflict even families (a basic order of creation), and lead to intensified levels of violence (4:23-24; 6:11-13).

This story is important for the theme of creation not least because it reflects God's involvement with a family apart from the ministrations of the community of faith. From Eve's confession of God's help in the birth of Cain (4:1),[18] to the calling on the name of the Lord (4:26), God is present and active in this postgarden community. The story also sets in place key themes for the rest of Genesis: family conflict, sibling rivalry, God's freedom to elect one brother rather than another (and not choosing the elder), and divine promises given to the nonchosen (e.g., Ishmael).

The story of Cain and Abel begins positively with responses to God's commands in 1:28: to be fruitful and multiply (Eve), to have dominion over the animals (Abel), and to subdue the earth (Cain). The initial focus on worship is remarkable in that it represents it as integral to God's good *creation* quite apart from specific divine revelation. The brothers bring appropriate offerings; God, however, rejects Cain's offering—an election for reasons known only to God.[19] Cain's dejected response to God's choice is not the problem as much as his failure to respond positively to God's interaction with him about it. God makes clear that Cain is able to master his anger (4:7), but Cain kills his brother anyway. God, having been called by the blood of one unable to seek justice (4:10), calls Cain to account for the murder. The murder is wrong, though no law against it exists, assuming some notion of natural law available to all human beings apart from specific divine revelation.[20] When Cain deflects the question, God more intensively applies to him the earlier curse on the ground (3:17), the banishment, and the distancing from God's presence. When Cain objects to what amounts to a death sentence, God mercifully ameliorates the sentence by promising (!) to be Abel's brother's keeper and sealing the promise with a mark (its nature is uncertain). Ironically, the restless wanderer proceeds to build a city. Such an image again mirrors the experience of dispersed peoples, including Israelite exiles, who settle in a place that is less than truly home.

The following genealogies portray two different family lines (Cain, 4:17-24; Seth, 4:25–5:32) that flow from this conflicted family. Both positive and negative developments *within the created order* are portrayed. Positively, a powerful rhythm within life that works for good in God's creation persists: intimacy that brings new life into being, creative advances in the arts of civilization (4:20-22), diversification in the work that human beings are called to do. Progress in human development continues apace.[21] In addition, the text witnesses to the worshipful invoking of the name of Yahweh (4:26), remarkably, by those who are not Israelites! And people walk with God, such as Enoch (5:24) and Noah, in and through whom God works on behalf of the created order (5:29). These texts witness to a *continuing goodness in God's creation*. Human sin has not changed God's good creation into an evil creation; God continues to be effectively at work for good across the created order and people are responsive to that divine activity among them. Such understandings are revealing of Israel's strong sense of God's continuing creative work *apart from the chosen community*.

At the same time, negative effects abound. Human violence becomes more intense (Lamech; 4:23-24), and the diminishing age spans probably depict the debilitating effects of sin over time (see also the ages in 11:10-

27). Long lives are characteristic of other ancient Near Eastern lists of kings and patriarchs, but even though the ages in Genesis 5 are much more modest, the context suggests that they carry a point regarding the effects of sin. Progress in civilization is always accompanied by progress in sin and its effects, so that "progress" becomes an ambiguous reality within God's world. But, for all the ambiguity, God's creative work continues apace, and that activity is efficacious, bringing goodness into the far-flung corners of that world.

The effects of sin and its aftermath are now extended to the cosmic sphere, first in 6:1-4 and then in the flood itself. The first text has never been satisfactorily explained by interpreters. Its depiction of the crossing of boundaries between the heavenly and earthly realms may portray the cosmic effects of sin, with new possibilities for violence. This would, then, be a natural lead into the flood story, in which the entire cosmos is caught up in the effects of sin's violence and is threatened with extinction.

In sum, Genesis 3 witnesses to an originating sin that begins a process, an intensification of alienation, extending over chapters 3–6, by which sin becomes "original" in the sense of pervasive and inevitable, with effects that are cosmic in scope. However generalizable the story in Genesis 3, it alone cannot carry the weight and freight of the traditional view; the fall is finally not understood to be the product of a single act. But that act is a beginning of no little consequence, and Genesis 3–6 witnesses to a reality that subsequent generations can with good reason call a fall.

Genesis 6:5–8:22—The Flood: The Great Divide

This text is usually recognized as an interweaving of J and P stories of the flood. That Israel would have preserved more than one version of the flood is not surprising since flood stories circulated widely in that world, of which the one in *The Gilgamesh Epic* is the most well known. The basis for these stories is probably a severe flood in the Tigris-Euphrates Valley (one occurred ca. 3000 B.C.E.), which in time was interpreted by Israel's theologians as a flood that covered the then known world as a judgment of God on human sin.[22]

The focus of the present text is signaled by the repeated conviction about human sinfulness that brackets the account (6:5; 8:21) and the associated disclosures regarding divine sorrow, regret, disappointment, mercy, and promise. God appears not as an angry judge but as a grieving and pained parent, distressed at developments (6:6-7); yet, the judgment as initially announced is thorough and uncompromising ("I will blot out" in 6:7 allows for no exceptions). This inner-divine tension is resolved on the side of mercy when God freely chooses Noah (6:8). Noah, whose faithful walk with God is exemplified by his obedience (6:9, 22; 7:5, 9, 16; 8:18), including his stewarding of the animals (see 1:28), becomes a vehicle for God's new possibilities for the creation (anticipated in the announcement of 5:29).

The flow of the story leads up to and falls away from God's remembrance of Noah and the wild and domestic animals in 8:1. In the midst of cosmic catastrophe, the divine memory of the creatures enables a new creation. The story itself gives repeated attention to the boarding of the ark, to lists of people and animals/birds that are saved, to what God does to bring salvation rather than judgment, and to the chronology of the event. Remarkably little notice is given to the disaster itself, to the plight of its victims, and to the feelings of the participants; no dialogue is reported, and Noah does not speak. The flood is described in natural terms as the effects of sins (of violence in particular) with no divine act of intervention; only with the subsiding of the waters is God's activity stated explicitly.

The environmental themes in the story are significant. Humans have had a deeply adverse impact on the creation; thorns and thistles (3:18) grow to cosmic proportions and the world's future is endangered. Yet, God's announcement of a future covenant (6:18) and provision for temporal limits to the flood (7:4) assures that the orders of creation will not break down completely. Moreover, God's remembrance of the animals, creeping things, and birds, indeed "every living thing" (6:19; 8:1), belongs to the same divine initiative as God's remembering Noah.

Does the flood story also witness to the failure of creatures that are not human (as noted above regarding the snake, 3:14-15)? This understanding may be reflected in Gen 6:12-13, where it is said that "all flesh" (both human and nonhuman creatures) had "corrupted its ways upon the earth" (cf. Isa 24:20, the "transgressions" of the earth, for a comparable notion). This interpretation of "all flesh" is supported by 6:17, 19 (and throughout this section), where the phrase clearly includes animals. Hence, the judgment must come upon "all flesh." With such an interpretation, this text correlates more closely with Gen 9:1-17. In 9:5, animals are held accountable by God for taking the life of another.[23] Moreover, God's promise extends to the nonhuman world (Gen 9:8-17), where the repeated reference to "all flesh" makes clear that God here makes commitments to both human and nonhuman creatures. What does it mean for our environmental considerations that God has made *promises* to nonhumans?

Scholars have proposed overlapping purposes for the flood: Clearly one such purpose is the direct parallel that can be observed in 1:31 and 6:12: "And God saw." By such a juxtaposition of seeing verbs one can observe what the world has come to.

1. God intended to *purge* the world of its corruption. Water would thus be understood as a cleansing agent. The language of blotting out (6:7) suggests a wiping clean of the slate of the world and beginning anew. Yet, 8:21 makes clear that human beings are just as sinful after the flood as before. If the purpose was to cleanse, it was in some basic sense a failure. Perhaps the purging of the negative *effects* of human sin on the created order is what is in mind.[24]

2. God intended to *undo* the creation and begin again.[25] Water would thus be understood as an instrument of destruction. The references to a return of the watery chaos (7:11; cf. 1:2), the use of *rûah* in 8:1-2 issuing in the return of the dry land (8:13-14), and the blessings of 8:17 and 9:1, 7 suggest this interpretation. Löning and Zenger even refer to 5:1–9:29 as "the second act of the creation of the world."[26] Yet, this understanding does not take into sufficient account the fact that the "old" creation was not destroyed and major continuities with the original creation remain (vegetation; light; firmament; luminaries; ark occupants). There is a beginning again, but the essential preflood creation remains intact, including a sinful humanity; the only thing that is genuinely new is a divine promise never to do that again.

3. The flood story represents a *typical threat to life*. The flood waters symbolize a threat to ordered life, always lurking at the edges of existence.[27] Water is thus used as in, say, the lament psalms (Ps 69:1-2) as an image of difficulty, suffering, and catastrophe. Yet, while flood *imagery* may be used to depict such moments, God's promise at the end of the flood story indicates that the flood was an event that would not be repeated.[28] Hence, the flood should *never* be used as a type or illustration of divine judgment. Rather, the story functions to declare the certainty of God's promise that there will never be such an event again (as in Isa 54:9-10).[29] Notably, the "chaos" that erupts in this story is not said to be due to resurgent forces of evil (sometimes related to Gen 1:2) but to *God's* activity in mediating the effects of human sin (cf. the reversal of

creation themes in Jer 4:23-26, said to be due to human sin and divine wrath).[30]

4. The flood story represents a *polemic against other religious understandings*. Hence, efforts have been made to show the "obvious" superiority of the biblical flood story over against the polytheistic stories current elsewhere in that world. But, though the differences from other stories are significant, this agenda is often overplayed. Israel learned much from the peoples round about regarding God's world, and the purpose of the flood story was certainly intended to make more than a negative point.

5. This narrative testifies that *not all post-sin behaviors are a betrayal of trust*. Noah is named a righteous and blameless man (Gen 6:9), whose care for the animals, in exemplary obedience to God, enables their continuing life beyond the flood. This is certainly an important theme for all that follows; God will continue to place confidence in human beings for the carrying out of their responsibility for the creation (9:1, 7). A basic creaturely goodness continues to characterize God's creation, and that witness must not be downplayed.

6. The flood story focuses on *God and God's commitment to the world*. This God: expresses sorrow and regret; judges but does not want to; goes beyond justice and decides to save some, including animals; commits to the future of a less than perfect world; is open to change in view of experience with the world and doing things in new ways; and promises never to do this again. What God does here "*recharacterizes*" the divine relation to the world. God ameliorates the workings of divine judgment and promises an orderly cosmos for the continuation of life. God will never do this again! God is the one who has changed between the beginning and end of the flood, not human beings (though there are fewer of them around!).[31]

God's regretful response assumes that humans have successfully resisted God's will for the creation. For God to continue to interact with this creation in the wake of such defiance involves God's decision to continue to live with such resisting creatures (not the response of your typical CEO). In addition, God's regret assumes that God did not know for sure that this would happen (as elsewhere, see Gen 22:12; Deut 8:2).[32] Moreover, the text provides no support for a position that claims God planned for the creation to take this course. What has happened to the creation is due to human activity, not divine. At the same time, God bears some responsibility for setting up the creation in such a way that it could go wrong and have such devastating effects.

While this story does recharacterize the divine relationship to the world, it also makes clear that God is not simply resigned to evil. God must find a new way of dealing with the problem of evil. Two complementary directions are taken:

(a) For God to promise not to do something again entails an eternal self-limitation regarding the exercise of divine freedom and power. God thereby limits the divine options in dealing with evil in the life of the world. And, given the fact that God will keep promises, divine self-limitation yields real limitation. The route of world annihilation has been set aside as a divine possibility. Divine judgment there will be, but it will be limited in scope. And hence no simple retributive system is put into place; sin and evil will be allowed to have their day, and God will work from within such a world to redeem it, not overpower the world from without. This divine direction with the world is developed further in 9:8-17.

(b) Genesis 6:5-7 makes the bold claim that this kind of divine response means that God will take the route of suffering.[33] For God to decide to endure a wicked world, while continuing to open up the divine heart to that world, means that God's grief is ongoing. God thus determines to take suffering into God's own self and bear it there for the sake of the future of the world. It is precisely this *kind* of God with whom ancient readers are involved, and it is primarily the divine commitment to promises made that they need most to hear.

Genesis 9:1–11:26—A New World Order

The postflood account of the Priestly writer (9:1-17) picks up the theme struck by the narrator in 8:21-22. There God "said in his heart," but now, using first-person discourse, God speaks directly to the flood's survivors regarding both continuities and changes in the divine relation to a still sinful world. This world is no new Eden, but every creature—human and nonhuman—is assured that the basic divine relationship to the world established in the initial creation still holds, with its blessings and (adjusted) commands. At the same time, God introduces changes in the divine relationship to that sinful world that will have significant effects. From the perspective of Löning and Zenger, the section 9:1-29, following the flood story, becomes "the *culminating theological statement* about the world as God's creation."[34]

I find an admixture of realism and promise in this text. On the one hand, human beings remain sinful creatures through and through (6:5; 8:21). The flood cuts them off from life in paradise; access to that world cannot be bridged by gradual improvement or sudden insight. The basic creational order still remains, but the dominion charge is complicated by sin and its effects. The animals will be filled with "fear and dread" because of human violence. While the human diet can be supplemented with meat as a concession in a famine-ridden world (a theme in chs. 12–50), the proscription regarding the eating of blood (= life; see Lev 17:11) stands as a sharp reminder that killing animals must not be taken lightly, for God is the source of their life. Violence remains a part of the earth's fabric, and this command suggests an effort to control the problem of 6:11-13. The only creaturely violence of explicit concern, however, whether on the part of animal or human, has to do with the endangerment of human life, whether on the part of animal or human (cf. 4:13-14). And hence this divine command is put in place: the lifeblood of human beings is not to be shed. At the same time, human life is not absolutely inviolable; humans can forfeit their right to life if they take another's life. Indeed, murderers are directly accountable to God for their actions, though human agents are no doubt in mind (but no court system is mentioned). This provision provides a continuing way of dealing with the ongoing violence evident in 6:11-13, but the effects will never again assume floodlike proportions.

On the other hand, God herein directly addresses human beings, giving them responsibilities within the created order that are not unlike those received in Gen 1:28. The commands to "have dominion" and "subdue the earth" are not repeated with the other commands in 9:1, 7. Yet, because both animals and vegetation (9:3, 4) are given over to the human for their limited use means that these commands, while qualified, are not set aside. Human beings remain in the image of God and have a fundamental dignity as human beings that is not to be ignored, trammeled upon, or snuffed out (9:6), and they retain fundamental responsibility for the larger created order (9:1-7). Psalm 8 hymns this status of human beings in a postfall world. Whatever else one might say about the effect of sin upon human beings, it does not mean that God has ceased to trust them or refuses to work in and through them.[35] The existence of these so-called Noachic laws in a time and place before Israel comes into existence is significant (continuing the creational laws of 1:28 and 2:16-17).[36]

But sinful human beings do not possess sufficient resources for the responsibilities they have been given; only God can assure the creation's future. Hence, God determines to ameliorate the workings of divine judgment and promises an orderly cosmos for the continuation of human and nonhuman life. To this end, God makes a covenant with those who have endured the flood (9:8-17). Covenant in this text is an unconditional promise, publicly stating the divine commitment of 8:21-22. The repetition of words and phrases in this text emphasizes its promissory character—never again!—and the inclusiveness of its recipients, both human and nonhuman, through all generations. This covenant promise makes all subsequent covenants possible.[37]

This unilateral and unconditional covenant is an obligation that God alone assumes regarding the future of the created order; remembering this covenant is exclusively a divine responsibility and it will never need to be renewed. The point may be stated in these terms: "the creator God has a relationship of love and faithfulness toward the earth and says a fundamental and irrevocable 'yes' to *this* earth and *these* human beings."[38] This covenant will stand forever and be as good as God is, and so human beings can rest back in its promises. This covenant will remain in force regardless of how human beings respond to it. Even more, God will uphold this covenant independent of the community of faith, quite apart from Israel's life and mission; all human beings, whether persons of faith or not, experience the effects of this divine promise. Efforts to qualify this promise by claiming that it includes only destruction by water fail to appreciate the general references to destruction (8:21). Humans may, by virtue of their own behaviors, put themselves out of business, but not because God has so determined it or because the created order has failed. Or, less comprehensively, human sinfulness may adversely affect that created order so that it does not function in the way that God intended in its creation. But God's promise will remain intact through thick and thin.

In this text, covenant stands in the service of the creation, indeed all of its creatures.[39] The covenant in itself does not "restore" creation, but comes as a new divine initiative on the far side of restoration.[40] The future of the creation is at stake and God is concerned to provide for its sure and certain future for the sake of "all flesh," indeed the entire earth. It is *creation* that is most basic in this text, not covenant;[41] covenant is a divinely chosen *means* whereby creation can continue to thrive, even in the face of the worst human evil and violence.[42] If the preflood creational "system" were simply continued beyond the flood, such human evil would threaten the created order again and again. Hence, the covenant promise is in the interests of removing such a threat. This does not mean that evil consists of an eternal chaos that stands ready to intrude upon creational life and threaten its future; the issue is human sin and its potentially destructive effects.[43] It may be helpful to recall here that creation is not a finished product (ch. 2); in making such a promise, God is engaged in moving in new directions with that unfinished creation. The covenantal promises of God are related, however, not to creational details but to its basic infrastructure, clearly stated in 8:22.

God's good creation, necessary for the very life of "all flesh," will continue to thrive come what may in the way of sin and evil. It is helpful to say that "It is only by God's covenant with Noah, God's self-obligation to keep the creation going despite the evil in it, that one can trust the creation and its orders."[44] But it is important to note that God's decision lies in the distant past (not as a specific point in history but as a divine commitment that lies in the past) and that the creation and its orders are in fact trustworthy in perpetuity, for God will not suspend this ancient divine commitment to the world for shorter or longer periods of time. It is just such a trustworthy world that is the fundamental concern for every generation that endures any experience of evil and violence. Covenant is a means to that divine end for creation.

In view of that point and in the light of other Old Testament texts, this covenant also serves as proclamation, filled as it is with verbs that have only God as the subject. That is, God is faced with a specific need on the part of the survivors of the flood: will they have to continue to worry about and/or prepare for another such future, especially in view of the fact that evil will continue to pervade the life of the world? The gracious, promissory word of God for the survivors of the flood is clear: Never Again! God's establishment of a covenant becomes the word that survivors of any era need to hear if any hope for the future is to develop among them.

It is striking that this understanding of the relationship between creation and covenant is picked up again in an exilic context.[45] In Isa 54:6-10, the promise of Genesis 9 is used to assure exiles that destruction, exile, and divine abandonment as the judgment of God will not be repeated; God will establish a "covenant of peace" with them that is as sure as the promise to Noah and all flesh.[46] Ezekiel 34:25-31 and 37:26 also speak of a "covenant of peace," and the entire natural order is made the recipient of the promise. This reference is similar to the covenant of

Genesis 9, with its "all flesh" orientation and God's broad reference to a "covenant between me and the earth" (Gen 9:13); moreover, some of the specifics in Gen 8:22 are picked up with the reference to the seasons and sustenance. In addition, Ezek 37:26 explicitly links this promise with Gen 9:1, 7, where the command "to be fruitful and multiply" becomes a promise: *God will* multiply them! Antipathy between human beings and at least the wild animals is still present in Ezekiel 34, however; only in texts such as Hos 2:18 is a genuine covenant of peace with the wild animal world envisaged (cf. also Isa 11:6-9; 65:25). Jeremiah 31:35-36 and 33:14-26 are also pertinent, especially with the contextual reference to a new covenant (31:31; 32:40).[47] God's covenant with day and night (33:20, 25) is essentially synonymous with God's commitment to the "fixed order" of creation (31:35-36); God's absolute commitment to the creation is used to ground God's commitment to Israel. Israel can be as sure of its covenant with God as it can with God's covenant with the creation. The sign of the rainbow serves *God's* remembering (see, comparably, Exod 12:13), that is, divine action with respect to a prior commitment (see Exod 2:24; 6:5; Lev 26:42); but it also becomes a secondary sign for people in which they can take comfort and hope.

This divine restraint in dealing with evil sets the direction for a different approach to dealing with sin and evil and to the redemption of the world. The covenant with Noah and all flesh provides the context within which other covenants become possible; its universal character provides the umbrella under which all other covenants find their place. This covenant makes possible, indeed provides the grounding for, the promises to Abraham and Israel (close links with the covenant with Abraham in Gen 17:1-8 exist). This text shows that promises are one of God's most basic ways of relating to the world, and that universal promissory reality generates more particular promises to serve the divine strategy, which now will focus on the redemption of the world.

The remaining segments in Genesis 1–11 (9:18–11:27) serve several purposes in thinking through an understanding of creation. They do help prepare the creational ground for God's choice of Abraham, but they also have importance independent of that election. Two basic points may be made.

1. These texts bring the reader into a world of extended families, whose peoples and places reflect known historical realities (e.g., Babel), though not all of the names can be identified. Nations as well as families are *orders of God's good creation* (though, given the reality of evil, not every particular nation or family). All of these peoples, as descendants of "Noah and his sons" (9:1, 8, 19), bask in the brightness of God's covenant with "all flesh"; Israel has no special place at the table when it comes to this universal covenant. All peoples will be drawn into the call of Abraham (12:3), but here, in the wake of God's covenant with all flesh, they are given an integral place in God's creation and are made the recipient of God's promise. At the same time, a kind of secularity is present in 9:18–10:32, for God does not speak or act. Yet, the text provides some clues to show that God is understood to be present and active among these peoples (9:26-27; 10:9; 11:1-9).

2. Problems and possibilities of various sorts—both good and evil—take on a communal aspect. The new Adam (Noah) and his sons, who represent all existing peoples, get caught up in the spiraling effects of sin and evil (9:18-27). This theme of the dysfunctional family sets the stage for the rest of Genesis. The community that would build a tower is also caught up in these effects (11:1-9). Yet, goodness persists alongside human failure. The blessings of God's creation continue to abound in the proliferation of families (evident in the genealogies), the development of cities and nations, including the appearance of the family of Shem. Abraham emerges from within this family and this kind of world, and it is for their sake that he and his family are called, so that "all the families of the earth shall be blessed" (12:3).

The first text in this section (9:18-29) contains difficulties that cannot be pursued here. One key to interpretation is that Noah's sons are presented both as individuals and as ethnic units (e.g., the Canaanites), as in chapter 10. God's postflood blessing begins to take effect amid the world of the curse (see 5:29), ameliorating its effects. The vineyard and its wine, for example, symbolize God's blessings of life and fertility (see Ps 80:8-16). At the same time, human sin (drunkenness and parental disrespect of some sort, perhaps the public disgrace of the father) and intrafamilial conflict abound, leading to communal difficulties—including slavery—among the descendants (9:25-27). The move from individual behaviors to systemic forms of evil is remarkably in tune with reality and will perdure as an ongoing pattern adversely affecting God's good creation. God will work against such human developments, but not in a way that will destroy the creation or compromise the divine promise.

The second text (10:1-32), the table of nations, delineates all the known peoples of the world eponymously, that is, in terms of their descent from Noah's three sons. Such multiplying and ordering of the peoples into an international community is witness to God's continuing creational work. Problems of identifying the nations in the genealogy remain, but basically the horizon of the list extends from Crete and Libya in the west to Iran in the east, from Arabia and Ethiopia in the south to Asia Minor and Armenia in the north (the world then known). The recurrent use of the word *families* (10:5, 20, 31-32) testifies to God's ongoing creative work on behalf of the life and well-being of all families and is linked to Abraham's calling to bring God's blessing into their lives.

The third text (11:1-9), centered on the city/tower of Babel, seems out of place after the table of nations, where people are already scattered (10:18) and Babel is named (10:10). But the two sections are not in chronological order; 11:1-9 reaches back and complements chapter 10 from a negative perspective. Links with later Israel in Babylonian exile may be seen in the scattering of the people from the city—note the "whole earth" reference (11:1), which suggests that this text is both a story of the past and a typical story of humankind.

The basic human failure in this text is not easy to discern, but it seems focused in the motivation, "otherwise we shall be scattered abroad upon the face of the whole earth" (11:4). Largely because of this, building a tower and making a name become problematic, namely, as an attempt to secure their future isolated from the rest of creation. These activities constitute a challenge to the divine command to fill the earth (1:28; 9:1) and have dominion; human concern for self-preservation places the rest of the creation at risk. God counters these efforts by acting in such a way—confusing languages—that they have no choice but to scatter and establish separate linguistic communities. God thereby promotes diversity at the expense of any kind of unity that seeks to preserve itself in isolation from the rest of the creation and thereby places that creation at risk. This story combines with the "environmental" concerns of Genesis 1 in bracketing Genesis 1–11.

From one of these scattered and multilingual families Abraham is raised up for God's mission with respect to all such families, indeed all creation.

CHAPTER FOUR

CREATION AND THE FOUNDATION NARRATIVES OF ISRAEL

Creation in Genesis 12–50

Genesis 12–50 is not about creation in the sense that Genesis 1–2 is, but these chapters are decisively creational in setting, character, and theological focus. A preliminary listing would include: famine and other natural catastrophes that threaten life and resources, agricultural dimensions of everyday living, sickness and health, and difficulties in conceiving and birthing children. From another angle, the complexities of social life within families and other forms of community reveal a creational concern; for example, the economic and political activities of Joseph as vizier of Egypt have to do with the preservation of human life more generally, indeed the life of "all the world" (Gen 41:57). Moreover, the contexts within which God chooses to be at work, from blessing to various forms of interaction with characters outside of the family of promise (e.g., Gen 14:18-20; 16:7-14; 20:3-7; 21:8-21), evidence a concern for the creational dimensions of individual and communal life. In fact, so dominant is the creational theme in these chapters that James K. Bruckner's language is apt: "the particular and dominating cosmo-logic of the narrative is rooted in creational relationships."[1]

It has long been a practice to drive a sharp wedge between Genesis 1–11 and the beginnings of Israel's ancestral story. More recently, under the impact of literary-critical readings, there has been a renewed interest in the integrity of Genesis as a whole.[2] In some ways the traditional division is appropriate; Genesis 12 does mark a new stage in God's relationship with the world. But even those who sharpen this break often note that Gen 12:1-3 is a fulcrum text, linking Abraham with a key theme of the immediately prior chapters, "all the families of the earth" (see "families" in Gen 10:5, 20, 31-32). And so it has been common to claim that God's election of Abraham had a universal purpose: to extend God's special blessing through this family to the entire world. Yet, with the longstanding emphasis on "salvation history," the creational perspectives of the ancestral story have been neglected.

The universal theme introduced by Gen 12:1-3 has often been tracked through chapters 12–50, with particular attention not only to its verbal repetition (18:18; 22:18; 26:4; 28:14) but also to the numerous contacts made by Israel's ancestors with the "nonchosen" peoples. Even a cursory reading shows that remarkably little polemic is directed against these "outsiders" in the Genesis text (Sodom/Gomorrah is the exception).[3] In fact, as will become evident, these "unchosen" folk will often play a positive role in Israel's life and God's economy. The way in which Israel's ancestors interact with these individuals and groups, whether negatively or positively, carries an important word about God's creational designs.

Genesis 17:4-5 will express this theme in somewhat different, genealogical terms: Abraham is the "father of a multitude of nations." Sarah, too, will give rise to "nations" (17:15-16), with her descendants giving birth to peoples that extend well beyond Israel (e.g., Edomites). In these terms, the posterity of Abraham and Sarah will have a creational impact by expanding the world of nations.[4] Strikingly, the genealogies in this section of Genesis are focused on these "outsiders" (Ishmael, 25:12-18; Esau, 36:1-43), even though their inclusion is not necessary for Israel's story line. The genealogies in Genesis "constitute a unified system affirming the common humanity of all nations." As in the Bible generally, the foreigner "is not the opposite of the Israelite, not a quintessential Other, but a person with a full range of human possibilities."[5] The genealogies and stories of these outsiders demonstrate the extent to which God's life-giving and life-preserving work in creation extends well beyond the borders of the chosen family.

Human Beings in Community: Family, Nation, and Land

Genesis 1–11 presents human beings as individuals and as communities in ways that are carried through the rest of Genesis. As such, all Genesis texts are a witness to creational concerns and to God's creative work in the world.

To begin the discussion, it is important to say that Genesis 1–11 has presented human beings as good and responsible creatures. Created in the image of God, as well as from the dust of the ground, human beings are given work to do in God's world. Mindful of their created status, they are still called to be cocreators with God, in and through whom God will work. Divine activity does not entail human passivity in working toward God's goals for creation. Human beings become sinful and this development darkens everything they say and do, but they remain God's good creation, in the divine image, with the same call to responsibility (3:22-24; 5:1-3; 9:1-7). Indeed, faithfulness to God remains a human calling, and an obedient Enoch and Noah show the way (5:24; 6:8–7:5).

As we have already noted, texts in the rest of Genesis are concerned with a vision of what human beings are to be about in the world. God engages them in an enterprise on behalf of the creation, and God will relate to them with integrity, though it is not uncommon for interpreters to denigrate the importance of human activity.[6] The call to faithfulness will animate these texts, especially the story of Abraham (Gen 15:6; 22:1-19). The faithfulness of Joseph shows itself in still another way. Joseph is no passive member of the community but becomes deeply engaged on behalf of the public good. He rejects violence and revenge and brings closure to the snowballing effects of familial dysfunctionality and its deleterious effects upon the social order. His careful attention to environmental issues, including the anticipation of times when the land will not produce because of famine, provide an exemplary way in which individual leadership can be harnessed on behalf of the best life for all in God's often precarious creation. When Israel as a people comes into view, they are called to be holy, merciful, and just, as God is (Lev 19:1; Deut 10:12-22). Again and again, the text will press its concerns for human engagement on behalf of life, health, justice, and community well-being (Deut 30:19).

Make no mistake, sin has the effect of breaking down harmonious relationships at multiple levels; it creates divisions between human beings and God, among human beings (men and women, siblings, parents and children), between human beings and the land ("thorns and thistles"), and within the self (shame). Sin adversely affects the spheres of family and work, of culture and community (4:17-24), of national life (chs. 10–11), indeed the larger creational order (the flood). In fact, sin is so deep-seated that "every inclination of the thoughts of their hearts was only evil continually" (6:5); even the flood does not change that (8:21). Yet, human beings can act against such inclinations (4:7; cf. Deut 30:11-14) and decide for that which is life-giving rather than death-dealing. This tension regarding human beings who are both good and sinful, including both chosen and nonchosen, will pervade the texts in Genesis 12–50.

Human Beings in Community

Human beings are never presented as isolated individuals; they are always members of communities. Genesis 1–11 has introduced readers to families and nations, fundamental *orders of God's creation* that are essential to human life and well-being (see especially the genealogies). Genesis 12–50 continues this strong and pervasive interest, especially the creational order of the family; indeed, these chapters are often referred to as "family narratives."[7]

To be concerned about the development and continuing dynamic of *the family* is a creational matter. One contemporary way of looking at these chapters is through the lens of family systems theory, observing especially the signs of a dysfunctional family. Examples include the wife/sister issues for both Abraham/Sarah and Isaac/Rebekah (12:10-20; 20; 26); the strife between Abraham and Lot over land (13); and the triangulated relationship among Sarah, Hagar, and Abraham as well as Jacob, Leah, and Rachel. The vital and usually positive role that women—Rebekah, Leah, Rachel, and Dinah—play in these conflicts has received increased attention.[8] These conflicts should not be reduced to issues of sociology or psychology. A key to understanding the family stories is that God's choosing, speaking, and acting generate much of the conflict. At the same time, God does not leave the principals to stew in their own often ill-conceived interactions. God remains at work in and through an amazing range of family problems and possibilities, finally for purposes of reconciliation (Gen 50:20).

Further dimensions of family life belong within the sphere of God's concern, and these go well beyond religious and spiritual matters. The narrative gives much attention to such everyday community concerns as birth (especially complications; e.g., 25:21-26; 29:31–30:24), love (24:67) and marriage (e.g., issues of endogamy/exogamy, 24:1-67), parenthood (e.g., identity and age, 17:15-19), and family death and burial (23:1-20), even the concern about who attends the funerals of Abraham (25:9) and Jacob (50:7-14). While the chosen family remains the center of concern throughout, other families are drawn into the orbit of consideration.

One of the more obvious effects of sin has to do with familial issues. Within Genesis 1–11, this is evident in the emergence of tensions and inequalities between husband and wife (3:12, 16), the envy and violence between brothers (4:1-16), and the disrespect shown to parents by children (9:20-27). The narratives that follow in Genesis 12–50 pick up on these themes; conflicts mirror a wide range of family life, among both the chosen and the nonchosen. Consider these conflicts: Abraham/Sarah/Hagar; Jacob/Esau; Jacob/Leah/Rachel; Jacob/Laban; Joseph and his brothers. Again and again family life is disrupted because sinfulness is rooted so deep in the human heart. The same could be said for national life, and that will become evident in Genesis 37–50.

In addition, concern for the life of *the nation* is evident, beginning with the Table of Nations in Genesis 10. This creational concern is carried through into Israel's foundational narratives. The promises of God to the chosen family consist of a strong emphasis on "the nation" (Gen 12:3), indeed, Abraham and Sarah will give birth to a "multitude of nations" (17:4-5, 16). In the narratives that follow, the birth of Israel as a nation is given shape. But, a concern for national life more generally is also evident. For example, in the Joseph story especially (Genesis 37–50) attention is given to issues of economics, agriculture, and the dynamics of political and governmental life more generally. This story draws important links between family life and national life and, and in the person of Joseph, demonstrates the importance of good national leadership for the proper development of social life, indeed God's entire *creation* (Gen 41:53-57). National life is often compromised by the sinfulness of individual leaders and systemic forms of evil (including Joseph), but the nation remains a key structure of creation in and through which God is at work for life and blessing (cf. 47:13-26).

Another way in which creational themes are developed in Genesis 12–50 is through the interrelationships established by the family of Abraham and Sarah with other families and nations. This family regularly encounters outsiders: Egyptians (Pharaoh, Gen 12:10-20; Hagar,

16:1; 21:9); other nations, including pre-Israelite rulers of Jerusalem (14); Sodom and Gomorrah (18–19); Canaanites (20; 21:22-34); Hittites (23); and Aramaeans (24). In addition, the narrative is interested in the progenitors of the Moabites and Ammonites (19:37-38) as well as the Ishmaelites and other Arabian tribes (25:1-18). This narrative interest is certainly related to the call to Abraham to be a blessing to such families (12:2-3). How well this call is fulfilled may be discerned in the various ways the chosen family relates to these various peoples. The narrative develops models that are both positive (Abraham interceding for Sodom and Gomorrah, 18:23-33) and negative (Abraham endangers Abimelech and his family, 20:1-18).

This call to be a blessing is repeated with Jacob, especially as it is anticipated that his descendants will be dispersed throughout that world (28:14). Jacob's contacts with outsiders are more limited than Abraham's (cf. relationships with Canaanites in chs. 26, 34), not least because the story is preoccupied with Jacob's relationship to Esau, the progenitor of Israel's Edomite neighbors. Their conflict has been generated by God's word and shaped by parental preferences (25:21-28) and their continuing relationship has an ambiguous character (e.g., 33:14-17). Each can be faulted for behaviors toward the other as they compete for the blessing. In the end, they both receive ample blessings, evident for Esau in his genealogy (36) and specific references to wealth (33:9; 36:7). The other outsiders in the story of Jacob are the Aramaeans, his kinfolk in Haran. Despite the conflict, both sides recognize that Jacob's presence among them has indeed mediated blessing (30:27-30). God even appears to Laban and speaks to him (31:24, 29). Jacob and Laban somewhat warily conclude a covenant of peace (31:51-52), but such an ambiguous development is perceived positively in view of the potential for ongoing conflict.

In the story of Joseph, the Egyptians are the chief outsiders. The contributions of Joseph to their well-being are considerable. Blessings come to these people through his political acumen and economic savvy (39:5; 41:46-49); indeed, the entire world comes into view, as all peoples receive benefits from his God-given wisdom (41:53-57). At the same time, the Egyptians treat the chosen family in such a way that their lives are preserved and they are able to develop as a community in an alien land (47:27); their grieving of Jacob's death (50:7-14) witnesses to possible relationships that can be developed between the chosen family and outsiders. Given this basically positive portrayal of the Egyptians, readers will have difficulty demonizing them when they come to the book of Exodus.

These texts clearly witness that God has been at work among the Egyptians for good. Such is the activity of the Creator God.

Another creational interest in these narratives focuses on *the land.*[9] The foundation narratives of Israel are regularly punctuated with interest in and concern for the "natural" world. The land is a key theme in Genesis 12–50. The promises of God include land (12:7), which is fought over within the family (13) and without (14; 21:22-34). God, however, seals this promise in a covenant (15:7-21), and it is reinforced by Abraham's purchase of a burial site in chapter 23.

At the same time, this promised blessing has a precarious character. For example, this gift of God is often subject to famines (12:10; 26:1; 42:5; 47:13); in other terms, the land can become something other than what it was created to be and not consistently sustain its inhabitants. The texts do not always lay the responsibility for such negative developments for the land at the feet of human sin; the land is apparently understood to be subject to such realities as drought just by virtue of its createdness. But human sin plays an all too common role in negative developments for the land. Sodom and Gomorrah is an example. The land that Lot chooses, where Sodom and Gomorrah are located, is described in paradisiacal terms. But the reader is alerted that it will experience an ecological disaster (13:10), which is realized in 19:24-29 (cf. its ecological makeup, 14:10). This move from Eden to environmental nightmare is grounded in human behaviors (13:13; 18:20-21). In other words, cosmic order is linked to moral order, a reality that moderns can understand. The same claim is not made for the several famines that are reported, but Israel does make such a link in other texts (Deut 11:13-17; 28:22-24). How God is related to these natural disasters is difficult to discern.[10] One approach speaks of judgment as other than an explicit divine decision. God's judgment does not introduce something new into the situation; rather, God facilitates the moral order, that is, tends to the orders of creation. These orders do not function in a precise way, but commonly function in such a way that the consequence corresponds to the deed. And so, anticreational deeds will often have negative creational effects.[11]

"Implied Law" in Genesis 12–50

Throughout Genesis 12–50 the law is given an important place. Indeed, law is central to the life of the ancestral family, so much so that

Abraham's obedience of the law is prominently noted: "Abraham obeyed my voice and kept my charge, my commandments, my statutes, and my laws" (Gen 26:5). It has commonly been stated that law in these chapters is anachronistic, written with Sinai law in view; what is important for our purposes is that it is *represented* as happening prior to the giving of the law on Mount Sinai, and that has theological implications. This text testifies that law for Israel is not simply to be associated with Sinai. Laws were certainly formulated in the pre-Mosaic world, and Abraham was obedient to the laws that were available to him.

James K. Bruckner's work on "implied law" (points at which an "ought" or an "ought not" is assumed) is important in thinking through this matter.[12] He is concerned with implied law in the Abrahamic narrative, especially Genesis 18–20; we use his work as one way of illustrating the point about the pervasive creational character of Genesis 12–50.[13] Bruckner argues that the implied, creational law that undergirds these narratives "discloses a dynamic cosmological connection between the physical creation and the human moral order under judgment by God."[14] Focusing on Genesis 18–20, the questions of both Abraham (18:23-25) and Abimelech (in 20:4) assume a cosmological relationship between the physical and the moral order, that is, that "communities are at physical risk, regardless of individual innocence, because of a violation of the moral order."[15] The sins of Sodom threaten the bountiful ecosphere of the entire region (described in Gen 13:10), and that is what in fact happens—the destruction of not only people and cities, but even what "grew on the ground" (19:25). Or, the barrenness and sickness that follows in the wake of Abraham's sin against Abimelech and Abimelech's (unknowing[16]) taking of Sarah (20:17-18) shows the cosmological connection between the moral and natural orders. Anticreational and immoral acts adversely affect not only human health and welfare but also the well-being of the larger environment, sometimes catastrophically so. Characters in biblical narrative are often caught in "a web of cosmological consequence,"[17] whether they are guilty or just happen to live in the vicinity of the consequence.

This connection between moral order and cosmic order does not function in some deistic way; these linked orders have been created by Israel's God in the first place, and they are maintained and facilitated by God over the course of human life in a creational community. At the same time, these orders are not micromanaged by God. As such, these orders do not function in a mechanistic or predictable way; the looseness of the causal weave is such that randomness and irregularities occur. God honors these orders as creatures, letting them be what they were created to be. The effect of this divine way of working within such a created order is that while evil does not go unchecked in the life of the world, the innocent may not be exempted (e.g., women and children in both Genesis 19 and 20) and what goes around may not come around. Witness the apparent lack of negative effects of Abram's actions on himself in Gen 12:10-20.[18]

This functioning of law is also evident in the treatment of other characters and their activities throughout Genesis 12–50; no forensic or juridical categories are in view, no court ever goes into session. Rather, "the oughts are presented as an organic [or creational] ethic by means of creational motifs that are embedded in the narrative. . . . Because . . . oughts and ought nots are woven into the foundations of human experience."[19] Importantly, "outsiders" are made accountable to law in these texts (e.g., Egyptians, Canaanites, Aramaeans). Law is an integral part of their life and functions independently of any specific covenant relationship. Moreover, such implied law has the same purpose as does God's giving of the law to Israel, "that you may live, and that it may go well with you" (see Deut 5:33). These texts are a profound witness to the work of the Creator God, who builds such a moral order into the creation. It is assumed that, because of the presence and activity of the Creator God in the lives of all peoples, they would be able to recognize the law quite apart from specific divine revelation.

The law implicit in the ancestral narratives is nowhere made explicit in prior texts. Laws had indeed been laid out in Genesis 1–11, both before sin entered the world and after (2:16-17; 9:1-7), but these particular laws are only evident on the edges of these ancestral stories.[20] At the same time, natural law is assumed throughout Genesis 1–11; for example, it is assumed that Cain's killing of Abel violates the social order and is revealing of implicit creational commands. By building the law into the created order, the point is made that every human being, not simply the chosen people, is to attend to the law *for the sake of the creation and all its creatures*. We know from ancient Near Eastern literature that laws had long been in place before Israel came into being. The sheer existence of such bodies of law testifies to the work of God the Creator in and through such lawgivers who, quite apart from their knowledge of God, mediate the will of God, however dimly perceived, for their societies.

As another example of the work of law in Genesis 12–50, we observe the lively interest in matters of governance in the Joseph story (Genesis 37–50), which integrates family matters with national and political history. The primary concerns throughout this story are creational, from issues of family order to natural disaster (especially famine), from socioeconomic crisis and its management to national structures. Matters of public policy are very much in play in this story (e.g., Gen 41:37-57; 47:13-26). The witness of the text is that God is very much present and involved—usually behind the scenes—in the administrative directions that Joseph takes in social and economic matters, particularly in times of national crisis among a nonchosen people. To speak of God as involved with such chosen and nonchosen leaders in far-flung places, working out the detail of public life, is to speak of the work of the Creator God. God's purposes throughout this story are to preserve life and well-being for all persons involved, chosen or not, including blessings of the land, wise leadership, and family growth. The creational words of Gen 1:28 are fulfilled for Israel (47:27), which are in turn extended to Pharaoh (47:7-10), the Egyptians (47:13-26), and "all the world" (41:53-57).

Rightness or wrongness in Genesis 12–50, then, is not determined by reference to a law code or by ordinances that have been specifically revealed by God, but by the dynamics of long-standing experience in everyday relationships. In other words, *human* wisdom, *human* discernment, and *human* perception have been integral to the shaping of what is right and what is wrong. Certainly Israel would want to claim that God the Creator has been at work in the lives of those who were engaged in the development of societal principles and practices related to the good ordering of life in community. But God has chosen not to engage in the development of these dimensions of creational life in either a direct or unilateral way. As with the relational model of creation with which we have been working, we have here *a relational model of the development of law*.

When Israel is given the law at Sinai (and subsequently), it is thereby given responsibilities in the tradition of both Genesis 1–11 and Genesis 12–50.[21]

Images of God

The focus of the discussion of Israel's foundation narratives has traditionally been so sharply placed on "salvation history" that creational themes have been neglected. One direction for restoring balance in the treatment of these narratives is to discern the extent to which key creational themes in Genesis 1–11 are continuous with those in Israel's ancestral story. We have noted in chapter 1 that Genesis 1–11 is not laid out simply to give the reader some basic information about the world or the beginnings of things. Rather, the strategy is to catch the reader up into *a universal frame of reference*. Readers are invited to view a screen that is cosmic in scope and to engage in an act of the imagination that carries them beyond—way beyond—their little corner of the world. In the service of this strategy, Genesis 1–11 presents a rhythmic interweaving of story and genealogy that focuses the mind on certain recurring images, especially those of God and the entire creation. These creation-wide images set the tone and direction for *reading all that follows*, including the ancestral narratives. That is, the images of God and world introduced in Genesis 1–11, before there ever was an Israel, are ones that readers will regularly encounter as they move through Israel's foundational narratives. And so we explore, in turn, images of God in the interests of lifting up this universal reference.

Most fundamentally, the images of God in Genesis 1–11 witness to a God who is present and active in the world more generally, not just in Israel. The way God is imaged in *pre-Israel* narratives prompts readers to be on alert for how this God continues to be present and active in the vicissitudes of daily life and, more particularly, among peoples other than Israel. The foundation narratives of Israel in Genesis 12–50 are such a witness to the worldwide range of activity on the part of the *Creator* God.

Having set the "agenda" for Abraham to be a blessing to all "families," God remains engaged in the lives of these "outsiders," often in ways independent of their relationship to the chosen ones. Moving through the narrative: God is engaged in Egypt and within its royal house (12:10-20), which anticipates God's later involvement with the house of Pharaoh; in conflicts with ancient empires (14:20); in the ministrations of the king-priest Melchizedek (14:18-20); in the life of the Egyptian slave, Hagar, and her son Ishmael (16; 21:8-21); in the judgment on Sodom and Gomorrah (18:16-19:29); and in the life and dreams of the Canaanite Abimelech (20) and Egyptian leaders (40–41).

God is less frequently the subject of verbs relating to outsiders in the Jacob story. But God remains related to Esau, the progenitor of Israel's Edomite neighbors (see 33:9; 36:7). And, while Esau never mentions God and God does not act or speak relative to him after 25:23, Jacob does see the "face of God" in Esau's reception of him (33:10). Moreover, Abimelech will once again interpret God's activity (26:28-29; see 21:22-23), and the relatives in Haran (Aramaeans) continue a God-fearing stance. Laban, trickster though he is, so gives witness (31:49-50, 53) and God speaks to him (31:29; cf. 30:27).

The God Who Speaks/Reveals

On the first page of Genesis we are introduced to a speaking God. This Creator God is evident in the texts that follow, as God speaks to several pre-Israelite individuals (Adam, Eve, Cain, and Noah). Genesis 12–50 is introduced with reference to this speaking God (12:1-3), and so begins a journey of communicative interaction between God and the chosen family. But it is very important to observe that God's speaking is not confined to interactions with this family. The God who speaks to the nonchosen in Genesis 1–11 provides a pattern for God's continuing speaking ways with outsiders in Genesis 12–50. Initially, readers might note the assumption of Gen 14:18-20 that God has been revealing of self to Melchizedek. But especially noteworthy are the stories of God's speaking relationship with outsiders such as Hagar (Genesis 16; 21), Laban (Gen 30:27; 31:24, 29), Abimelech (Genesis 20), and the dreams of Egyptians (Genesis 40–41).[22] God is not revealed as one who is aloof, distant from the life of the world, but is on speaking terms with even outsiders. God takes the initiative in these interactions and speaks first, but God is also revealed as responsive to what the human party has to say in response to the divine initiative.

The God Who Elects

In Genesis 1–11, God's electing is set as a basic way in which God chooses to work in the *world*. For example, God chooses Abel's offering rather than Cain's (4:4-5); this divine choice of the younger over the older brother relates to issues of primogeniture in the chapters that follow (e.g., Isaac rather than Ishmael; Jacob rather than Esau; cf. also 38:27-30; 48:13-14). Moreover, God chooses Noah (6:8-9) as the one to be saved from the flood. With him, God begins again with the human family and, at the end of the flood, enters into covenant with "all flesh." In other words, this divine electing activity is not an end in itself; God elects for the purpose of preserving the creation alive in a reasonably stable world environment.

Such purposes of life and well-being for the entire creation are continued and brought into sharper focus in God's election of Abraham/Israel. The purpose of God's loving choice of Israel in keeping the oath to its ancestors (Deut 7:6-8), as well as in giving the law, has a creational focus: so that "you may live, and that it may go well with you, and that you may live long in the land you are to possess" (Deut 5:33; cf. 6:24). In other words, God's objectives in choosing Israel are fundamentally creational in their focus and most basic concerns: creational stability and communal stability are linked in this divine work. As we have seen, this divine purpose for Israel is not simply for the sake of the chosen; God has God's world in focus. God's exclusive move in choosing Abraham/Israel is not an end in itself, but a divine strategy for the sake of a maximally inclusive end. The blessing of Israel's ancestors for the sake of all the families of the earth (including the nonhuman family, given 9:8-17) is in tune with the universal divine purposes of life and well-being. These divine objectives are intended, finally, for all of God's creatures. Divine election does not entail having a corner on participation in the goodness of God's creation.[23]

The God Who Saves

A related theme from Genesis 1–11 is the image of God as Savior, seen especially in God's deliverance of both human beings and animals from the flood (e.g., 8:1). Given human sinfulness and the dire effects let loose in God's creation, God chooses to be savior. This divine move demonstrates that God is active in saving activity out and about in the creation independent of Israel and the mediation of the community of faith (see Amos 9:7 for a prophetic witness).

This God, shown to be savior of *the world*, becomes the savior of the progenitors of Israel (e.g., Gen 14:20), and that activity will come to a climax in God's delivering Israel from slavery in Egypt (Exod 3:8; 6:6; 14:30; 18:11) and beyond. More important, these saving activities of God are not narrowly spiritual in character; as is evident in Exod 15:2 ("the LORD . . . has become my salvation"); salvation language will be used with respect to matters that are social and political as God enables deliverance from the world's oppressors.[24] This divine concern is so wide-ranging that God will bind the divine self to the Torah in acting in saving ways, on behalf of those who have been abused, whether Israelite or "resident alien," even if Israel itself proves to be the perpetrator (Exod 22:21-27). The concern for the stranger and alien is particularly evident in the laws (e.g., Deut 24:19-22), and Israel is commanded to follow God in extending justice and love to them (Deut 10:19); the people of God are to "love the alien as yourself" (Lev 19:34), which includes extending the effects of God's saving deed on behalf of Israel to all others.

In Genesis 12–50, God the Creator *continues* to engage in specific saving actions with respect to outsiders in the service of God's more universal purposes on behalf of the creation. For example, God is present with Hagar and Ishmael and delivers them from certain death in the wilderness (16:7-14; 21:15-21), and God is explicitly said to be "with the boy" after Ishmael has left the home of the chosen (21:20). God here acts in both word and deed *outside* the boundaries of what we normally call the community of faith. God's acts of deliverance occur out and about in the seemingly godforsaken corners of the world, even among those who have been explicitly excluded from the "people of God." Here, the delivering God is at work among the outcasts of the world, an experience that parallels that of later Israel (in exile) in basic respects. Moreover, God delivers Abimelech and his family from the effects of the sins of the righteous (20:17-18), and God is open to deliverance of the cities of the plain upon Abraham's intercession (18:16–19:29). In the story of Joseph, God acts behind the scenes, weaving the threads of goodness and mercy into the texture of ordinary life, both private and public, for both insider and outsider. The narrator has both Egyptians and Joseph witness to God's presence, God's spirit, and God's preservation of life (39:1-23; 41:38; 45:4-9; 50:20). God's saving activity includes the Egyptian people, indeed "all the world" (41:57).

The God Who Makes (Covenant) Promises

The God of the covenant promise, integral to the rhythm of Genesis 1–11, constitutes a basic image for all that follows. After the flood, God makes a covenant with Noah and all flesh (9:8-17; cf. 8:21-22). In this unilateral, unconditional covenant with the entire creation God binds self—thereby limiting the divine options—with respect to the future: God will never destroy the earth again. God decides to go with the world, come what may in the wake of continuing sin and evil. Notably, God makes this promise precisely *because* humankind is sinful through and through (8:21). Sinfulness so defines humanity that, if human beings are to live, they must be undergirded by the divine promise. Only God can assure the future of creation.

Covenant is thus introduced into the biblical narrative as a word with universal associations. Apart from Israel, God has established a promissory relationship with creation, revealing God's most basic way of relating to the world: in commitment, patience and mercy, not in anger or capriciousness. The covenants that God now makes with Abraham/Israel are grounded in this prior promise and can be confidently assumed to be as good as it is; the God with whom Israel has to do is as trustworthy as the God here is revealed to be (see the arguments of Jer 31:35-37; 33:14-26; Isa 54:9-10).

The covenant with Noah and all flesh is also revealing of the basic *structure* within which subsequent covenants are framed, which, in turn, has theological implications. God elects (6:8); God saves (6:18; 8:1); human beings respond in worship and faith (8:20), and only then does God establish covenant. This fourfold structure is characteristic of God's covenants with Abraham (12:1-3; 12:10-20 and 14:20; 15:6; 15:18 and 17:1-8), with Israel (the covenant is not made until Exodus 24), and even with David (2 Samuel 7). We have explored some of the implications of this structure in our opening chapter on relationship as basic to Israel's understanding of God.

While God does not explicitly "make a covenant" with any nonchosen people in the ancestral narratives,[25] God does make *repeated* promises to Hagar and Ishmael (Gen 16:10-11; 21:18) and to Abraham regarding Ishmael (17:20; 21:13) in language remarkably similar to the covenants with Abraham, Sarah, and family (cf. 12:2; 17:15). These stories carry an image of God as *Creator* who makes promises to those who do not belong to the "people of God."[26] The chosen people are thereby reminded that they cannot confine God's promising activity to their own precincts. As Walter Brueggemann puts it, "God has not exclusively committed himself to Abraham-Sarah."[27]

Interhuman covenants between insiders and outsiders are also made in the Genesis narrative (e.g., 21:22-34; 31:44). Such human commitments may be said to stand in the tradition of a God who makes promises; human faithfulness to promises made is a possibility for those who stand outside of the explicit covenant promise. Such promising is again a witness to the work of God the Creator. Promise is to give basic shape to the life of all human beings, chosen or not.

The God Who Blesses

Blessing is a gift of God, usually mediated through human or nonhuman agents, that empowers recipients to experience and bring forth life, goodness, and well-being, including spiritual and more tangible expressions. God's blessing is given creation-wide scope from the beginning (Gen 1:22, 28), and continues in the post-sin, pre-Abrahamic world (9:1).[28] Through acts of blessing, God provides a life-giving, life-enhancing context for all creatures within *every* sphere of their existence. As such, blessing belongs primarily (but not exclusively) to the sphere of creation, both originating and continuing creation. Initially, God blesses both animals and human beings in order that they might be fruitful and multiply (1:22, 28); God even blesses the temporal structures of the created order (2:3). In the wake of sin, the curse—natural effects of sin that God mediates—begins to have a devastating effect upon the creation (3:14, 17; 5:29). Yet, even in this post-sin, pre-Abrahamic world, God's blessing abounds (Gen 9:1, 7, 26) and ameliorates the effects of the curse (8:21-22). The genealogies throughout Genesis continue the testimony to this reality.

Inasmuch as blessing belongs primarily to the sphere of creation, the non-elect peoples are *not* dependent upon the elect for many forms of blessing; it rains on the just and the unjust, and families who have never heard of Abraham continue to thrive. The ancestral narratives assume that God is active for good in every human life, not just among the Israelite ancestors. The genealogies of the nonelect, two of which bracket the story of Jacob, demonstrate this point (Ishmael and Abraham's other sons, 25:1-18; Esau, 36:1-42); witness also Esau's prosperity (Gen 33:9; 36:6-8).

This understanding of blessing in universal terms stands in some tension with the focus on blessing in Gen 12:1-3 and its mediation, by God and members of the ancestral family, throughout chapters 12–50. The phrase, "in you all the families of the earth shall be blessed," repeated throughout Genesis, seems to suggest that blessing must be mediated by the Abrahamic family (see 30:27, where Laban is blessed because of Jacob; 39:5, where Pharaoh's house is blessed because of Joseph; so also 47:7, 10). Yet, it is to be emphasized that Gen 12:3 ("I will bless those who bless you" [see 27:29]) immediately recognizes that blessing is not simply something that the elect are able to extend to others; the nonchosen can also mediate blessing to the elect. This point is illustrated several times in the larger narrative (12:16; 20:14; 26:12-14). Melchizedek bears witness to the activity of God in Abraham's exploits and blesses him (14:18-20). Later, the foreign seer Balaam will be used by God to bless the people of Israel (Numbers 22–24).

This reality raises a question: If God as Creator already blesses the world after Abraham but independent of the chosen family and if the nonelect can mediate blessing to the ancestral family, of what purpose is Abraham's election? Though the narrative is remarkably reticent about this question, it is helpful to see that blessing in Genesis encompasses two different though not unrelated realities:

1. The general, creational realities such as fertility, prosperity, and success in the sociopolitical sphere, which all of God's creatures can mediate and experience independent of their knowledge of God. The texts noted above illustrate this type of blessing, as do those cases where Joseph becomes a vehicle of blessing on Egyptian and other nonchosen communities. Even within the ancestral family, the blessing Isaac extends to Jacob in 27:27-29 may be so described.[29]

2. God's specific, *constitutive* promises to the elect family, initially through Abraham (son, land, many descendants, nationhood; 12:1-3, 7; 13:14-18; 15:4-5, 18-21), and never mediated by the nonelect. I call them "constitutive" because they are community-creating, without which Israel would not have come to be. These promises are called "the blessing of Abraham" in 28:4, are repeated to Isaac (26:3-4, 24), and commended by Isaac to God on behalf of Jacob (28:3-4), who extends them to Jacob (28:13-15; 35:10-12).[30]

The creational blessings are life-enabling and life-enhancing, but they are finally not sufficient for the fullest possible life. The constitutive blessings mediated through the elect are essential if the best life possible is to be experienced for everyone. They bring focus and intensity to the blessings of creation, make them more extensive and abundant, and decisively give new shape to both the human self and the larger community. Through relationships with the chosen family, life for individuals and communities has the potential of becoming even more correspondent to God's will for goodness and well-being in creation. As an example one might cite the resolution of the barrenness of Abimelech's wife and slaves in and through Abraham's prayer (20:17-18) or Laban's experience of blessing because of Jacob (30:27-30). The larger issue at stake in the divine choice of this family is a universal one: the reclamation of the entire creation in view of sin and its deleterious effects upon life.[31]

As for the chosen family, it is not as if, given God's blessing to Abraham initially, they stand in no further need of divine creational blessings along the way. The ongoing blessing work of God can be seen in the theme of barrenness and birth. This issue is introduced early in the narrative with the barrenness of Sarah (11:30, not necessarily a physical problem), and it remains a key theme in the story of Abraham, resolved only with the birth of Isaac (21:1-7). God becomes similarly involved with Rebekah, Leah, and Rachel (25:21; 29:31; 30:22). With respect to the people of Israel, God's blessing is to be spoken over them regularly (see Num 6:22-27). Blessing is not a onetime gift; the chosen and redeemed people of Israel are in need of continuing blessing all along their journey for the sake of continuing life, health, and well-being.

God as Judge

The image of God as judge is sharply evident in Genesis 1–11. The sin of Adam and Eve (and their descendants) is not treated lightly by God, as if it were a minor matter. The judgment of God, which may be defined as the mediation of the moral order (seeing that sins do have consequences), plays a key role so that sin and its effects do not have the last word. In other words, this divine move is made not simply because God is offended but because social and cosmic stability is at stake.

To that end, God announces and mediates the effects of sin on the primary spheres of human life and vocation (3:14-19) and declares a catastrophic end of all life (6:5-6). Only Noah's finding favor with God ameliorates the range of the catastrophe. At the end of the flood story, God promises never to destroy the earth again; this promise builds into the very structures of the world a limitation with respect to the range of God's judgment. God's judgment will never again be universal in its scope. The divine promise regarding judgment in Genesis 8–9 does not mean, however, that God will never enter into judgment in less thoroughgoing ways. The theme of divine judgment will play a significant role in Genesis 12–50, with respect to both chosen and nonchosen individuals and peoples. Such divine judgments against the nonchosen are especially evident in the story of Sodom and Gomorrah (Genesis 18–19).[32]

God as Relational

Through the lens provided by these various images, the God of the opening chapters of Genesis is seen to be a highly relational God. Most basically, God is present and active in the world, enters into a relationship of integrity with the world, and both world and God are affected by that interaction. In this relationship, God has chosen not to stay aloof but to get caught up with the creatures in moving toward the divine purposes for creation, and in such a way that God is deeply affected by such engagement. For example: God involves the human in creational tasks; God walks in the garden and engages the human; God ameliorates judgment (4:15); God suffers a broken heart (6:6); God limits the divine options in relating to sin and evil (8:21-22). And readers are not yet to Abraham!

The rest of Genesis, indeed the Pentateuch, witnesses to this kind of God. For example, God responds to human prayer, from petition (24:42-51), to lament (25:22-23), to intercession, and that on behalf of the unchosen (18:22-33; cf. Exod 32:7-14; Num 14:19-20). Moreover, God genuinely interacts with these "outsiders," including Hagar (16:7-13), Abimelech (20:3-7), and Pharaoh (41:15-36). This divine-human relationship is thereby revealed as having a genuine dialogical character.

To conclude this point: the opening chapters of Genesis reveal a complex rhetorical strategy with respect to the implied audience to which they are directed. These chapters provide a universal frame of reference and reveal a God who is present and active in the larger world beyond Israel and in such a way that the readers—wherever they may be located—can count on such a God for their future. These chapters also set forth an understanding of humanity that lifts up goodness and responsibility—for the entire creation—in the midst of continuing sinfulness in a way that need not lead either to hubris or despair. No matter the past, God remains committed to the future of the creation. These images set the tone and direction for reading all that follows regarding the more particular story of Israel. At every turn, the reader is asked to keep the larger nonchosen world in mind. God's purposes are of such a universal scope, encompassing all peoples, that the nonchosen provide an essential dimension for all the more particular divine activities within the community of the chosen.

Creation in Exodus

Until quite recently, the interpretation of the book of Exodus has been almost exclusively concerned with the theme of redemption, so much so that standard introductions to the Old Testament often start at this point.[33] The theme of creation is often ignored or noticed only with respect to selective texts (e.g., the tabernacle). It is my conviction that the book of Exodus is shaped in a decisive way by a creation theology. This can be recognized in the book's verbal, thematic, and structural concerns.[34]

The present form of Exodus is not socially disinterested; it was written with the problems and possibilities of a particular audience in view. An exilic provenance is likely. Israel in exile finds itself in straits similar to its forebears in Exodus in two major respects: captive to outside forces (chs. 1–15) and suffering under just judgment because of disloyalty to God (chs. 32–34); it stands in need of both deliverance and forgiveness. Issues related to law and obedience, divine presence and absence, and appropriate worship places and practices are also central for both Exodus and exilic Israel.[35] At the same time, the material in Exodus is presented in such a way as to resonate with other comparable situations.

Generally speaking, God's work in *creation provides the basic categories and interpretive clues* for what happens in redemption and related divine activity.[36] God's work in creation is lifted up initially in the book and shown to be life-giving, life-preserving, and life-blessing (Exod 1:7, 12, 20). What God does in redemption is in the service of these endangered divine goals in and *for the creation*. For example, the hymnic celebration of that redemptive act in Exodus 15, as we shall see, is permeated with creation talk, evident in its vocabulary, structure, and theme. And so, on the one hand, an *experience* of God's work as creator is necessary for participation in the exodus—otherwise there would be no people to redeem. On the other hand, an *understanding* of God's work as creator is indispensable for the proper interpretation of what happens—there would be no exodus *as we know it* without its having been informed by that understanding. It is the Creator God who redeems Israel from Egypt.

A creation theology provides the *cosmic purpose* behind God's redemptive activity on Israel's behalf. While the liberation of Israel is the focus of God's activity in Exodus, it is not the ultimate purpose. The deliverance of Israel is ultimately for the sake of all creation (see 9:16). The issue for God is, finally, not that God's name be known in Israel but that it be declared to the entire earth. God's purpose in these events is creation-wide. What is at stake is God's mission for the world, for as 9:29 and 19:5 put it, "all the earth is God's" (cf. 8:22; 9:14). God's redemptive activity on behalf of Israel is not an end in itself; it stands in the service of the entire creation. The divine calling to be a kingdom of priests and a holy nation appears within the context of that phrase, "the whole earth is [God's]" in 19:5; Israel is called to a commission on behalf of God's earth.[37] Hence the *public character* of these events is an important theme throughout the story.

God's redemptive activity is set in terms of *a creational need.* The fulfillment of God's creational purposes in the growth of Israel is endangered by Pharaoh's attempted subversion thereof. If Pharaoh succeeds in his antilife purposes at that point at which God has begun to actualize the promise of creation (1:7-14), then God's purposes in creation are subverted and God's creational mission will not be able to be realized. God's work in redemption, climaxing in Israel's crossing of the sea on "dry land," constitutes God's efforts at re-creation, returning creation to a point where God's mission can once again be taken up.

God's redemptive activity is *cosmic in its effects.* Generally, the Lord of heaven and earth is active throughout Exodus, from acts of blessing to the use of the nonhuman creation in the plagues, the sea crossing, the wilderness wanderings, and the Sinai theophany. More specifically, Exodus 15 confesses that God's victory at the sea is not simply a local or historical phenomenon but a cosmic one. God's defeat of the powers of historical chaos not only results in Israel's liberation but also brings about the reign of God over the entire cosmos (15:18).

God's calling of Israel is given *creation-wide scope.* The theme "all the earth is God's" is picked up again in 19:4-6, a divine invitation to Israel to be a kingdom of priests and a holy nation. Israel is called out from among other nations and commissioned to a task on behalf of God's earth. The combination of religious and political language in these designations of the chosen people suggests that Israel is to function among the nations as a priest functions in a religious community. Israel's witness to God's redemptive activity (see 18:8-12) and its obedience of the law are finally for the sake of a universal mission. The redemptive deeds of God are not an end in themselves. The experience of those events propels the people out into various creational spheres of life. Redemption is for the purpose of creation, a new life within the larger creation, and, finally, a new heaven and a new earth.

A creation theology is built into the very structure of the book of Exodus. This reality can be seen not least in the parallels between Exodus and Genesis 1–9: (a) a creational setting (cf. Exod 1:7 with Gen 1:28); (b) anticreational activity (cf. Exodus 1–2, 5 with Genesis 3–6); (c) Noah and Moses (Exod 2:1; 25:1; 33:12); (d) the flood and the plagues as ecological disasters (Exod 7:8); (e) death and deliverance in and through water, with cosmic implications (Exod 15:1); (f) covenant with Noah/ Abraham and at Sinai, with commitment and signs (Exod 24:1; cf. 31:17); and (g) the restatement of the covenant (Exod 34:10). Moreover, Exodus 25–40 may be viewed in terms of a creation, fall, re-creation structure.

Within the book of Exodus, several text segments are deserving of further attention in view of these creational themes. They include the opening chapters, the plagues (Exodus 7–11), the Sea Crossing (14–15), the wilderness wanderings (15:22–18:27), and the tabernacle (25–31; 35–40).

Creational Growth and Threat in Egypt

Exodus 1:7 states a key theme for the book: "the Israelites were fruitful and prolific; they multiplied and grew exceedingly strong, so that the land was filled with them." The parallels between 1:7 (and 1:9, 10, 12, 20) and Gen 1:28 indicate that the growth of the people of God in Egypt is a key fulfillment of a divine *creational* purpose, not simply a divine historical promise (Gen 17:2-6; 48:4).[38] This text specifies a microcosmic fulfillment of God's macrocosmic design for a creation filled with life. Israel is here seen as God's starting point for realizing the divine intention for all creation. Moreover, the growth passages in Exodus 1 are a witness to God's ongoing work of creation and blessing, that flowing, rhythmic, nondramatic divine activity. The reticence to speak of God at this point (God is not mentioned until 1:17) is testimony to a behind-the-scenes kind of divine activity in which God works in and through creatures to accomplish the divine purposes. The Egyptians, who have experienced (if not yet known) God's work as creator, are included among these creatures, for it is in their land and through their hospitality that this growth occurs (recognized also in Deut 26:5; Ps 105:24; Acts 7:17-22). The God who will redeem is seen here to be at work in life-giving ways (cf. Gen 45:5-7; 50:20). This divine creative activity is an indispensable foundation for the later work of redemption, without which there would be no people to redeem. God's redemptive work does not occur in a vacuum: God's work in creation provides the basis for God's work in redemption; God's work in redemption fulfills God's work in creation.

But this creational development is threatened by historical forces embodied in an oppressive pharaonic regime. Pharaoh, a historical symbol for the anticreational forces of death, seeks to subvert God's life-giving work with death-dealing efforts, to close down God's work of multiplication and fruitfulness. Such efforts are a threat to undo God's creative work, with negative macrocosmic ramifications. God's activities on behalf of Israel are directed toward overcoming this creational threat and, given the nature of the threat, will have to be comparably cosmic in their scope. The future of the creation is at stake. When liberation does come, the entire creation will be affected.

In seeking to overcome this threat to creation, God initially works primarily through women. The narrator presents these activities in a deeply ironic way; those without power in that culture prove to be powerful indeed.[39] The midwives' vulnerable but creative resistance to a powerful pharaoh parallels God's creative activity (1:15-22). The clever maneuvering on the part of Moses' mother and sister enables God's chosen leader to live on for a new day. Pharaoh's daughter exhibits the kind of care and concern, developed outside of the community of faith (the work of the Creator God), that not only saves Moses' life but enables his growth and education for future responsibilities (see Acts 7:22). Her activity directly parallels God's later work (see 2:23-25; 3:7-8): she "comes down," "sees" the child, "hears" its cry, takes pity on him, draws him out of the water, and provides for his daily needs. The activities of these women make a difference, not only to Israel but also to God. God is able to work in and through these trusting women, and that creates possibilities for God's way into the future that might not have been there otherwise. Indeed, the activities of these women and their effects, fundamentally creational in origin and orientation, not only make possible Israel's experience of redemption but also constitute a paradigm for that experience.

The Plagues as Ecological Signs of Historical Disaster

Some brief comments on introductory matters.[40] Source analysis has discerned three interwoven strata in Exodus 7–11. The J account is usually considered the most extensive, with seven plagues and the basics of the present structure of the text. The degree to which these prior forms of the plague tradition have been preserved in the present text remains uncertain, however, and hence interpretations of their import will always be problematic. The use of the plague tradition in Psalms 78 and 105, with seven plagues presented in ways different from each other and from Exodus, makes the traditional-historical analysis even more complex.[41] Without discounting the importance of this enterprise, I will work with the final form of the text, the most basic shape of which is probably to be identified with the P redaction.

In terms of rhetoric, repetition is noteworthy in these texts. For example, the word *kōl* ("all") is pervasive, used over fifty times; it may provide an interpretive clue to the narrative. While used in every plague, there is an explosion in its use (as well as *'ereṣ*, "earth"—to which we return) as one moves into the seventh plague. This is an extravagance of language, perhaps even a failure of language, in an effort to speak of the increasing intensity in the final plagues: every tree, all the fruit, no one can see, not a single locust, the whole land. Everything is affected or nothing. A hyperbolic way of speaking has taken control of the narrative. These outer limits of language match and convey the content of a creative order breaking out of its normal boundaries. As such, this language serves both a literary and a theological purpose.

This language participates in a dramatic form that has no real biblical parallel.[42] There are significant continuities with certain prophetic traditions, especially Ezekiel. Also to be noted are texts such as Deuteronomy 28 and Leviticus 26, which view Israel itself as the potential object of the plagues (cf. Exod 15:26 with Deut 7:15; 28:27, 60). Regarding social setting, there are links between 10:2 and the retelling notices associated with ritual in 12:26; 13:8; and 13:14. The highly stylized form may reflect the dramatization of some experience that was less comprehensive and intense; a dramatized presentation in a cultic setting is a possibility.

Common parlance refers to these events as plagues (i.e., a blow/stroke), but the text itself primarily uses the language of "sign" (*'ôt*, 4:17; 7:3; 8:23; 10:1-2) and "portent" (*môpet*, 4:21; 7:3, 9; 11:9-10). The sign character of these materials must be taken more seriously than has been the case heretofore. I work with this definition of sign:[43] a specific word or event that prefigures the future by the affinity of its nature (cf. 1 Sam 2:34; Jer 44:29; 1 Kgs 13:2; 2 Kgs 19:29; 20:9). As signs/portents, the intent of the plagues is not finally to leave observers with mouths open in amazement. Rather, having gotten the readers' attention, they point beyond themselves toward a disastrous future, while carrying a certain force in their own terms. They are both acts of judgment in themselves and point toward a future judgment, either Passover or sea crossing or both, and each plague must be examined in these terms.[44] Generally, it may be said that the plagues are ecological signs of historical disaster. They function in a way not unlike certain ecological events in contemporary society, portents of unmitigated historical disaster.

The most basic perspective within which the plagues are to be understood is a theology of creation. They are most fundamentally related to the natural order of things, God's nonhuman creation. The collective image presented is that the entire created order is caught up in this struggle against Pharaoh's anticreational designs, either as cause or victim. Pharaoh's activity has cosmic effects and the only appropriate and effective way of dealing with these issues is through comparably cosmic activity.

H. H. Schmid and others have shown that in Israel and the ancient Near East, the just ordering of society—reflected in its laws—was brought into close relationship with the sphere of creation.[45] A breach of those laws was considered a breach of the order of creation with dire consequences on all aspects of the world order, not least the sphere of nature. One must speak of a symbiotic relationship of ethical order and cosmic order. This understanding of the created order undergirds the plague cycle in Exodus.[46]

In sum, Pharaoh's oppressive measures against Israel are antilife and anticreation. They strike right at the point where the creational promise of fruitfulness is being fulfilled in Israel. Egypt, Pharaoh in particular, is an embodiment of evil forces that threaten the future of the creation.[47] The plagues are the disastrous effects of Pharaoh's anticreational sins, the functioning of which may be described as divine judgment. *That* there are consequences to sins is named as the judgment of God. At the same time, the plagues are signs pointing beyond themselves to unmitigated historical disaster. The following paragraphs work this out in greater detail.

A. The Plagues as Portents of Disaster

The correspondences between the plagues and the Passover/sea crossing are both verbal and imagistic. Each of the plagues is examined in turn.[48]

1. *Exodus* 7:8-13. The swallowing of the magicians' staffs by Aaron's does not represent Aaron's (or God's) superior power to do magical tricks! It is a sign of the fate of the Egyptians at the sea.[49] The only other use of the verb, *bāla'*, "swallow," occurs in 15:12, where it refers to the swallowing of the Egyptians in the depths of the earth beneath the sea. This effect is a result of God's "stretching out his right hand," a reference to God's working through Moses' staff (cf. 7:15; 14:16). Moreover, this serpent, *tannîn* (different from the word used in 4:3), is a more terrifying creature than a snake. Elsewhere, this word refers to the enemies God defeated in the exodus (Ps 74:13; Isa 51:9) and is a symbol for the Egyptian pharaoh (Ezek 29:3-5; 32:2; cf. Jer 51:34). The symbolism shows this to be an ironic reversal. The staffs of the magicians become *tannîn* and Aaron's *tannîn* swallows theirs. Here God turns the tables, using a dragon to swallow up the dragon, as God will use the waters in chapter 15. This action is a sign of Pharaoh's fate.

2. *Exodus 7:12-24.* The phrase "there was blood *[dām]* throughout the whole land of Egypt" (vv. 19, 21) suggests the sign value. The comprehensiveness of the blood in the land is more than hyperbole. While *dām* is not used in chapters 14–15, the *image* is one of the sea becoming red with Egyptian blood. The oracle against Egypt in Ezek 32:6 links blood in land and water (cf. Ezek 29:4-5; 5:17; 14:19; 38:22; Isa 34:7). These references show that this sign is more than just a bloody mess, a lot of dead fish, and a headache for waterworks personnel. Blood, which will be a sign of deliverance for Israel (12:13), here becomes a sign of disaster for Egypt (cf. the nationwide "cry" in 11:6).[50]

3. *Exodus 7:25–8:15.* The sign value of this wonder for Pharaoh is focused at three points. The verb *nāgap*, "smite" (8:2), is not used again until 12:23, 27, where it refers to the smiting of the firstborn (cf. 12:13; 9:14; Josh 24:5). This strong word often means a fatal blow and is used in contexts of divine judgment (Isa 19:22; Ps 89:23). It is anomalous that the narrator, out of all the plagues, should raise the specter of fatal blows in connection with frogs! The plague functions as a sign of something more deadly on the horizon. The reference to the stinking land (8:14) is also an image of destruction. The death of so many children and animals in the final plague (12:30) would have created a comparable problem for Egypt, and the image of Egyptians piled dead on the seashore (14:30) creates a similar picture. Pharaoh's own nose should have told him that something is amiss here! The phrase "covered *[kāsāh]* the land of Egypt" (8:6) may also portend an ominous future: the sea waters "cover" the Egyptians (14:28; 15:5, 10; cf. Ezek 30:18).

4. *Exodus 8:16-19.* This sign functions in terms of images, as the "dust of the earth" is turned into gnats. Dust is that from which human beings have come and to which they return upon death (cf. Gen 3:19; Eccl 3:20; Job 4:19; 10:9; Ps 104:29) and can refer to the grave or the netherworld (Job 17:16; Ps 22:29; Isa 26:19). The image suggests the end of the Egyptians and the humiliation of those who oppose Israel's God, including the kings of the earth (Isa 26:5; 41:2; 49:23; Mic 7:17; Job 40:13; Ps 72:9). The use of dust as an image of mortality and humiliation is a sign that Pharaoh ignores at his peril.

5. *Exodus 8:20-32.* The sole use of sign language within a plague narrative (8:23) highlights the division between Egypt and Israel. To have flies stopped at the Goshen border, as if by an invisible wall, should have been a sign of some magnitude to Pharaoh (cf. his concern in 9:7). This distinction between Egyptians and Israelites will be disastrously realized in 11:7. Its sign value is enhanced by the reference to "all" the land being "ruined" (*šāhat*, 8:24; note the repetition of "land"). Such language seems too strong for a fly infestation! This root plays a key role in the Passover story (12:13, 23; cf. its use in Gen 6:11-12 for the preflood state of affairs; Ezek 5:16). The flies are a sign of the destroyer that will pass through the land of Egypt on that fateful night. Moreover, the flies were removed so that "not one remained" (8:31; cf. 10:19), a phrase repeated in 14:28, where not one Egyptian remained. God's re-creative act is also a sign, a sign of judgment on the oppressors. As it was with the flies, so it will be with the Egyptians. They did comparable damage to the land; they will share a common end. The sign is thus found in both the plague and in its removal.

6. *Exodus* 9:1-7. This sign takes a significant step beyond nuisance and discomfort. Its sign value lies at two points. The use of *deber* for the plague is an ominous word (note the play on *dābār*, "thing," in vv. 5-6); it is used exclusively in divine judgment contexts, whether in Israel (Deut 28:21; Ezek 5:12) or among Israel's enemies (and with cosmic effects, Ezek 38:22; Hab 3:5). Moreover, the distinction between Israel's and Egypt's animals (see Ezek 32:13) is again portentous, a distinction also present in the final plague (11:5; 12:29). The use of the word *kōl* for the death of livestock also enhances its sign value.

7. *Exodus* 9:8-12. This sign is prefigured in the sign in 4:6-7; there Moses' hand became leprous and was returned to normalcy. Leprosy is mentioned elsewhere in the Old Testament with the verb *pārāh* ("break out") and is specifically linked with boils (Lev 13:18-23). This is an ominous sign of a disease that will be even more devastating for the Egyptians; while the plague that finally falls on them is not identified, it is likely a more intensified form of that which is experienced here.[51] The disease, an obvious sign of mortality and judgment, would serve as an image of more severe possibilities. The power of this plague's significatory value is seen in the later recollection of the "boils of Egypt" as a possible judgment on Israel (Deut 28:27, cf. v. 60; 7:15).[52]

8. *Exodus* 9:13-15. This plague's intensity enables it to function as a sign of the incomparability of the plague of death (11:6). Comparative language now begins to be used (see 9:18, 24; cf. 10:6, 14). The extensive use of *kōl* and *'ereṣ* vivify this frightful experience of the weather.

Weather-related phenomena often function as images in theophanic contexts (Pss 18:12-13; 77:16-20) and is a powerful image of divine judgment contexts (Isa 28:2, 17; 30:30-31; Ezek 13:11-13; 38:22-23; Hag 2:17). Experienced in such an intense form, it should function as a sign for any who would listen.

9. *Exodus* 10:1-20. The extensive use of *kōl*, "all" (eleven times), and *'ereṣ*, "earth," again, intensifies the gravity of the locust devastation. Moreover, the sign values of the plague become more numerous. That locusts are often a symbol of divine judgment (Deut 28:38, 42; 2 Chr 7:13; Jer 51:27; Amos 4:9; 7:1; Joel 1–2) certainly makes this a portentous sign. As with the frogs (8:6), they "cover the land" (10:5, 15), a portent of the water covering the Egyptians (14:28; 15:5, 15). A sign may also be present in the phrase "no one will be able to see the land" (10:5); when the destroyer moves through Egypt (12:13, 23), not seeing the blood on the doorposts means tragedy. Once again, the twice-noted incomparability language (10:6, 14) anticipates 11:6. Moreover, the east wind is drawn into the fray (10:13) as it will be at the sea (14:21). Finally, the phrase "not a single locust was left" (10:19; 8:31), having been driven into the Red Sea, again prefigures the sea crossing (14:28). As it was with locusts and flies so will it be with the Egyptians. They will meet a common end. The significatory value of this plague is rich and varied.

10. *Exodus* 10:21-29. The darkness language, anticipated in 10:5, 15, has a high sign value. "Heavy darkness" *('ăpēlāh)* is a symbol of divine judgment (Isa 13:10; Joel 2:10), including Ezekiel's oracle against Egypt (Ezek 32:7-8). The infrequent language of "feeling, groping" *(māšaš)* is also present in such contexts (Deut 28:29; Job 5:14; 12:25). The narratives that follow are filled with darkness language, both with respect to the tenth plague (11:4; 12:12, 29-31, 42) and the sea crossing (cf. *hōsek* in 14:20-21). The darkness is a reversion to a precreation state of affairs (see Gen 1:2);[53] that is why it is the most serious plague, except for the last. The sign is beginning to participate in the reality of destruction for Pharaoh. There will be no stopping the disaster at this point.

Such an extensive correspondence of vocabulary and images between the plagues and the Passover/sea crossing is hardly fortuitous.[54] The balance of this segment will seek to draw out the implications.

B. The Plagues and the Created Order

The plague narrative has an overarching creational theme. The pervasive usage of the word *'ereṣ*, "earth, land," in every plague story—over fifty times, and intensely from the seventh plague—also provides a clue to this focus: What is happening to God's earth/land? While the center of attention is on the land of Egypt, the word sometimes has a more comprehensive sense. It is commonly recognized that the "knowing" texts are among the most important, theologically, in the cycle; three of these are concerned with earth/land: God is Lord in the midst of the earth (Exod 8:22); there is no God like Yahweh in all the earth (9:14); the earth is the Lord's (9:29; cf. 19:5; Ps 24:1-2). It also appears in the central verse, 9:16: "so that my name may be declared throughout all the earth." For the sake of the mission of God—the creation-wide proclamation of the divine name—there is a concern for the earth.[55]

Generally for Exodus, God's liberation of Israel is the primary but not the ultimate focus of the divine activity. The deliverance of Israel is ultimately for the sake of the entire creation. The issue for God finally is not that God's name be made known in Israel; the scope of the divine purpose is creation-wide, for all the earth is God's. God's purpose is to so lift up the divine name that it will come to the attention of all the peoples of the earth. Hence, the public character of these events is very important. To put this in different words: in order to accomplish God's mission in the world, God must have a world teeming with life. If Pharaoh persists in his antilife policies at precisely that point at which God has begun to actualize the promise of creation (clearly laid out in 1:7), then God's very purposes in creation are being subverted and God's mission is threatened. God's work in and through Moses, climaxing in Israel's crossing of the sea on "dry land," constitutes God's efforts of re-creation; the goal is to return creation to a point where God's mission can once again be taken up.

The plagues are fundamentally concerned with the natural order; each plague has to do with various nonhuman phenomena. The collective image presented is that the entire created order is caught up in this struggle, either as cause or victim. Pharaoh's antilife measures against God's creation have unleashed chaotic effects that threaten the very creation that God intended.

First, a word about those elements of the nonhuman order that are on the *victimizing* side; they are all out of kilter with their created way of being. Move down the list: water, frogs, dust and gnats, flies, cattle epidemic, ashes and boils, weather phenomena, locusts, and darkness. None of them appear as they were created by God to be. They all appear in distorted form. Water is no longer simply water; light and darkness are no longer separated; diseases of people and animals run amok; insects and amphibians swarm out of control. What must the numbers have been when every speck of dust in the land became a gnat (8:17)? What size must the hail have been to "shatter every tree" (9:25)? And the plagues come to a climax in the darkness, which in effect returns the creation to the first day of Genesis 1, a precreation state of affairs. While everything is unnatural in the sense of being beyond the bounds of the order created by God, the word "hypernatural" (nature in excess) may better capture that sense of the natural breaking through its created limits, not functioning as God intended. The plagues are hypernatural at various levels: timing, scope, and intensity. Some sense for this is also seen in recurrent phrases to the effect that such "had never been seen before, nor ever shall be again" (10:14; cf. 10:6; 9:18, 24; 11:6).

Second, regarding the *victims* of the plagues, scholarly attention has tended to focus on their effects on Pharaoh and other human beings (a typical anthropocentrism). But in every plague there are devastating effects on the environment—water, the land, various plants and animals, even the air—every sphere of the created order is adversely affected. The stress on the word "all" *(kōl)* serves to show that nothing in the entire nonhuman order escapes from these ill effects. Even more, the effects (like the causes) are hypernatural. The hail strikes down every plant and shatters every tree. There are boils on every beast and every human being. The locust devastation is such that "nothing green was left" (10:15) and not a soul can see the land—except, of course, in Goshen, where the hypernatural extends in the other direction, with not a single cow dying from plague, not a single swarm of flies, not a single hailstone falling, and the pitch-black darkness stops dead in the air precisely at the border. The exemption for Israel is but another form of participation in the uncharacteristic, hypernatural behaviors of the natural order.

This means that attempts to see these signs as simply natural occurrences are far removed from the point of the text. There is sufficient continuity with the natural to show that it is in fact creation that is adversely affected. Their sequencing does have a certain naturalness to it: frogs leaving bloody water, flies drawn to piles of dead frogs, and so on. But these continuities really serve this purpose: to show that the elements of the natural order are not what they were created to be and do. Their "behaviors" break the bounds of their createdness. It is a picture of creation gone berserk. The world is reverting to its precreation state. It is a kind of flood story in one corner of the world—that corner where God's creational purposes were beginning to be realized.

C. The Plagues and the Moral Order

The theological grounding for the plagues is an understanding of the moral order, created by God for the sake of justice and well-being in the world. Pharaoh's moral order is bankrupt, severely disrupting this divine intent, and hence he becomes the object of the judgment inherent in God's order. A key word is *šepet*, "judgment" (6:6; 7:4; 12:12; cf. Gen 15:14; note its predominant use in Ezekiel, including references to Egypt, 30:14, 19). God sees to the moral order of things, enabling the working out of the effects of Pharaoh's sinfulness. Such judgments are not imposed on the situation from without but grow out of and have an intrinsic relationship to the sinful (or good) deed.[56]

Correlation between deed and consequence is prominent in these texts. It is sharply evident in 4:23: the death of the Egyptians' (including Pharaoh's) firstborn correlates with that experienced by Israel at his hands. Other verbal and thematic correspondences are: (1) The unjust oppression of the Israelites over an extended period of time and a prolonged oppression of the Egyptians by the plagues. (2) The losses experienced by the Israelites—general well-being, property, land, life—and those experienced by the Egyptians. (3) The bondage of Israel and its ill effects on their personhood and the hardening of the Egyptians' hearts (14:17), an experience of enslavement. The "broken spirit" (6:9) of the Israelites that prevents them from hearing the good news finds a correspondence in the hardening of Pharaoh's heart that inhibits his hearing the word of the Lord. (4) The indiscriminate death experienced by Israelite babies at the hands of a pharaoh bent on genocide and the death of Egyptian firstborn at all levels of society (11:5; 12:29). (5) The "cry" *(sĕʿāqāh)* of the Israelites in bondage (3:7, 9) and the "cry" of the Egyptians on that fateful night (11:6; 12:30). (6) The cosmic sphere in which the plagues function correlates directly with the creational sins of Pharaoh so central in the narrative. Pharaoh has been subverting God's creational work, so the consequences are oppressive, pervasive, public, prolonged, depersonalizing, heartrending, and cosmic because such has been the effect of Egypt's sins upon Israel—indeed, upon the earth—as the pervasive "land" language suggests.

In those instances where God removes the plague, the appropriate language is that of re-creation. God overcomes the chaotic situation and returns those elements of the natural order to a closer semblance of their created scope and intensity. In some cases the sign of judgment is retained, as we have seen with the phrase "not one remained" (8:31;

10:19; 14:28). Here, re-creation entails ridding the world of the perpetrators of evil. These reversals of the plagues are anticipatory of God's re-creational activity in the narratives that follow. The song at the sea is filled with creational language, and the divine victory over this embodied chaos assumes cosmic proportions. Moreover, these re-creational themes are played out in the gifts of water and food in the wilderness (see below).

God is certainly portrayed in these texts as active in the interplay of Pharaoh's sin and its consequences (though not without mediation), but in effect God gives Pharaoh up to reap the "natural" consequences of his anticreational behaviors (hardening of the heart—making the heart something other than it was created to be—is another such instance). God's seeing to this order is not a passive "letting it be," but, given the divine faithfulness, God does function within the limits provided by that order. The plagues are thus not an arbitrarily chosen divine response to Pharaoh's sins, as if the vehicle could just as well have been foreign armies or an internal revolution. The consequences are cosmic because the sins are creational. God thereby acts to reestablish the rightness of the created order (ironically confessed by Pharaoh himself in 9:27: "The LORD is in the right" *[saddîq]*). The divine power over all forms of pharaonic power is demonstrated through the moral order for the purpose of re-creating justice and righteousness in the world order.[57]

The sin-consequence schema is not understood in mechanical terms, however, as if all of these results were inevitable and programmed to occur within a certain temporal and causal frame; there is a "loose causal weave" in the moral order. Pharaoh was given opportunity to break into the schema, to turn the situation around. Note also the warning in 9:19-21, where the fear of the word of Yahweh provides relief from judgment, mitigating the effects and the sense of inevitability (cf. 10:7). God personally enters into the prolongation of the consequences (see 9:16) for the public purpose of mission. But, finally, in the face of continuing and resolute refusal, the only way into the future was for God to drive the consequences to their deepest level.

More generally, such a correspondence at the cosmic level is reflective of the symbiosis between the human and the nonhuman natural orders commonly observed in the Old Testament, from Gen 3:17-18 on (e.g., Hos 4:1-3; Jer 9:10-16, 20-22).[58] The combination of plagues and judgment is also a feature of many prophetic passages, as we have seen. The fall of Jerusalem is, in effect, a time when Israel also becomes the recipient of plagues (see Deut 28:27-29; Lev 26:14-39; Exod 15:26; Jer 4:23-28).[59]

The complexities of the divine, human, and cosmic interaction in the narrative cannot all be factored out, but the divine purpose for Israel in and through this entire experience is clear: to get Israel through the waters of chaos and enable them to walk on the "dry ground" of creation. Hence, the creation themes will become prominent once again in Exodus as God works a re-creative deed (15:1-21).

In this environmentally sensitive age we have often seen the adverse natural effects of human sin. Examples of hypernaturalness can be cited, such as deformed frogs and violent weather patterns. The whole creation groaning in travail waiting for the redemption of people needs little commentary today (Rom 8:22).

Cosmic Salvation at the Sea

It has long been recognized that Exod 15:1-18 employs the language, style, and literary structure of the creation myths of the ancient Near East.[60] What is not agreed on, however, is the extent to which this pattern has influenced the theology of this chapter. For example, Bernhard W. Anderson claims that, whatever may have been the case in other Old Testament literature, in Exodus 15, "there is no suggestion here of creation in a cosmic sense"; rather, the language is entirely in the service of historical concerns, namely, the coming to be of a people.[61]

This formulation is problematic for several reasons. (1) It suggests that the admittedly mythological material can somehow remain selectively relevant, carrying only a historical point. (2) It seems to set myth and history against each other, as if the text could affirm only one or the other. (3) It fails to account for the profound role of the cosmic in the text, on both sides of the conflict. (4) Issues of intertextuality seem not to be taken with sufficient seriousness, that is, that other Old Testament texts do indeed interpret the exodus in both historical *and* cosmic terms (e.g., Ps 74:12-14; Isa 51:9-10).

It must be said that the mythological themes evident in the text have not been stripped of their cosmological significance and reduced to a historical claim. To cite Ronald A. Simkins: "Cosmic metaphors are applied to a historical account in order to attribute cosmic meaning to the historical events."[62]

From a theological perspective, Passover and sea crossing keep redemption and creation firmly together, but without collapsing them (Exod 12:1–15:21).[63] The sea crossing lifts up the cosmic side of the divine activity, bringing God's creational goals to a climax. It is only at the sea that the evil embodied in Pharaoh and his minions is decisively overcome and the created order is established on firmer moorings.[64] God's victory at the sea is not simply an event of local significance, vanquishing a historical enemy, however important. It is a cosmic victory.[65] Without that cosmic element, Israel's liberation from anticreation forces would be only as far-reaching as the next trouble it encounters on its journey.

At this point I recall the extent to which cosmic issues play a role in the conflict between God and Pharaoh. Pharaoh seeks to subvert the divine creational work among the Israelites (1:7) and the cosmic effects of this conflict are especially evident in the plague cycle (see above). A number of Old Testament texts identify evil forces with Pharaoh/Egypt (see Ezek 29:3-5; 32:2-8; Ps 87:4; Isa 30:7; Jer 46:7-8); this identification may be recognized in Exodus at those points where the conflict at one level is within the realm of the divine (e.g., 12:12; 15:11; 18:11). Egypt is considered a historical embodiment of cosmic forces of evil, threatening to undo God's creation.

Given the anticreational forces incarnate in Egypt and the pharaoh, no simple local or historical victory will do; God's victory must be and is cosmic in scope. God, therefore, fights with "weapons" appropriate to the enemy; it is God's activity in *creation*—primarily, the use of nonhuman rather than human forces—that conquers these cosmic forces.[66] God's redemption is an overcoming of anticreational forces at every level, including the cosmic. It is precisely because what happens here is cosmic that it has universal effects. In the words of George M. Landes, "it is because the Creator-God is the Liberator-God that liberation has universal dimensions."[67] Hence, all of Israel's future enemies between the sea and the promised land tremble and "melt away" (15:13-16). After the divine victory such conflicts are already settled, and the enthronement of God in the promised land is a reality *already at the sea* (15:17-18). A kind of "realized eschatology" is in place here.

When God delivers Israel from bondage under Pharaoh to service under Yahweh, the people of Israel are reclaimed for the human situation intended in God's creation. In redemption, God achieves those fundamental purposes for life and well-being inherent in the creation of the world. When the anticreational forces embodied in Pharaoh have been destroyed, life begins to grow and develop once again in tune with God's creational designs. It is important to note that this is not a "back to Eden" scenario, as if the effect of God's redemptive work were a repristination of the original creation. The image to be considered here is spiral, not cyclical. This consideration has to do with two major factors: the character of the original creation and the effects of redemption.

1. To recall our earlier observations regarding Genesis 1–2, the command to subdue the earth (Gen 1:28) indicates that the meaning of *good* does not mean that the earth is static or perfect. What is envisaged is a world that changes in such a way as to make the creation look quite different than it did on the seventh day. God's creation is a living, moving, dynamic reality. For the creation to stay exactly as God originally created it would be a failure of the divine design. Continuities with the original creation certainly exist (see Gen 8:22), but development and change are central to what God intends in creation.[68] Exodus 1:7 already witnesses to a new creational reality, far beyond Eden. The rest of Exodus testifies to God's continuing work in creation, bringing into being that which is genuinely new. There is no aspect of daily life that does not testify to this ongoing creative work of God (e.g., Pss 104:27-30; 139:13; Job 10:8-12; 12:10; 34:14-15). God did not exhaust the divine creativity in the first week of the world!

2. God's redemption, being the historical act it is, enters into a point in history where some of that becoming of the world has already begun to take place. Because God's continuing creative work is not neutral or negative, redemption does not do away with these proper creational developments. God's redemptive acts reclaim all that makes for life, including that which is truly human. *Redemption is in the service of creation*, a creation that God purposes for all. Because God is a God of life and blessing, God will do redemptive work, should those gifts be endangered. *The objective of God's work in redemption is to free people to be what they were created to be.* This redemptive act is being delivered, not from the world but to true life in the world. Negatively, this redemptive act entails freeing Israel from all that oppresses or enslaves or victimizes, from inner spirit (see Exod 6:9) to sociopolitical sphere to cosmic realm. Positively, God's redemptive act reclaims Israel as God's own and reconstitutes them as a living, growing people. Even more, this act restores the life-giving potential of all aspects of the created order, to which the wilderness texts testify (see below).

What happens in redemption, then, is not something extrahuman or extracreational, something fundamentally different from what God gives in creation. Redemption makes ordinary human life possible once again. Yet creation and redemption, though integrally related, are not to be equated with each other. Redemption as well as distinguishable continuing creative acts (e.g., in the wilderness) are the *means*; creation or new creation is the *end*.[69] *Redemption is in the service of a creational end*, ultimately a new heaven and a new earth (Isa 65:17; cf. 2 Cor 5:17), preliminarily realized in the wilderness and in the rest in the promised land (see Exod 3:8). The effect that God intends in the act of redemption is a new creation—in the dynamic sense.

For all the potency of God's redemptive victory, however, this reclamation of the creation is not a matter of a divine flick of the wrist, as if everything now is immediately restored to its full creational life. The people of Israel are indeed liberated, entirely by God's doing, but they move from the Red Sea into a godforsaken wilderness, where the effects of redemption only begin to be realized in the gifts of food and water and in the overcoming of still existing oppressive forces such as the Amalekites (Exod 15:22–18:27). The redemptive victory of God frees the creation *to become* what God intended. Redemption, for all its decisiveness, does not cancel out the becoming character of creation, a becoming in which God continues to be active as the creator of the world. The gifts of God in the wilderness, by which God enables new life and growth for Israel *and* the nonhuman order, are the initial stages of the history of God's *continuing creative giving* to the community on its way.

I return to the salvation wrought by God at Passover and the sea crossing. When the Israelites sing the song of Exodus 15, "the LORD has become my salvation," it is important to note what *salvation* means in this context. *Salvation* means that the Israelites are delivered from the effects not of their own sin but of the sins of other people (the Egyptians). When God delivers Israel from this abusive situation, the people are reclaimed for the life and well-being that God intended for the creation. As such, God's salvation stands, finally, in the service of creation, freeing people to be what they were created to be and having a re-creative effect on the nonhuman world as well, as life in the desert begins to flourish once again.

Wilderness Wanderings

In the crossing of the sea, the divine victory over the forces of evil has assumed cosmic proportions. But that is not the end of the story, for God's salvific activity has to do not only with human beings, but also with the nonhuman world. Those elements of the created order that were adversely affected in the plague cycle need to be dealt with, and so God acts to bring healing to that creation. These re-creational themes are played out in stories of the gifts of water and food in the wilderness (15:22–18:27). Several parallels between the plagues and the wilderness stories are evident:

Exodus 15:22-27. The result of the first plague was that "they could not drink the water" (7:24). When, in 15:23, "they could not drink the water," the bitter water is made sweet and potable. In fact, the wilderness is filled with springs of water (15:27; cf. 17:6). This re-creation will also be the cosmic effect of a later divine victory, when "waters shall break forth in the wilderness, / and streams in the desert" (Isa 35:6).[70] At the same time, these signs of the new creation are related to the shape that Israel's life is to take (15:25*b*-26). The symbiotic relationship between moral order and cosmic order is universal, a matter to which Israel must attend as much as Egypt. The "diseases [= plagues] of Egypt" also stand as a possibility for Israel (15:26; see Deut 28:27, 60).

Exodus 16:1-36. Whereas in the seventh plague God had "rained" *(mṭr)* hail upon Egypt, destroying the food sources (see 9:18, 23), in 16:4 God "rains" bread from the heavens. In the eighth plague, locusts "came up" *('lh)* and "covered" *(ksh)* the land (10:14-15), destroying the food. In 16:13, the quails "came up" and "covered" the camp, providing food. In the Numbers parallel to this story (11:31), the wind brings quail rather than locusts (Exod 10:13).

Exodus 17:1-7. In the first plague, Moses used his staff to strike the water and the water became unfit to drink (7:20-24). Now, in 17:5, "the staff with which [Moses] struck the Nile" brings water that is fit to drink.

These divine actions are providential, certainly, but they are more than that. The interpreter's focus should not be simply on the provision of the daily needs of the people; in addition, the wilderness itself is genuinely renewed. Elements of the nonhuman order are deeply and positively affected by God's saving deed and the relationship with the human community becomes more what God intended it to be. Salvation is experienced by both human and nonhuman.

How one assesses the "miraculous" character of these wilderness provisions is important in thinking through the nature of divine providence. Some would understand God's actions as contrary to what is natural for nature; so, for example, William H. C. Propp speaks of God actually producing "food and drink from thin air and thick stone,"[71] and describes these events as "supernatural."[72] But the texts themselves speak of these events in terms that are usually much more natural. And so, water is sweetened by the use of a piece of wood with certain properties (15:22-27), water courses through rock formations, the striking of which could expose the water (17:1-7), and manna and quail are natural entities in that part of the world (16:1-36).[73] To speak of such events as natural does not necessarily remove them from God's involvement; rather, God, who always works through means, works in and through the natural (and the human) to work out the divine purposes. Consideration of divine providence should not be divorced from a clear recognition of nature's God-given potentialities and the gifts of the human in surfacing those potentialities.[74] God's providence is often shown in leading Moses (and others) to *help that is already available in the world of creation*. Notably, one element of the creation is used to put right another element from that order (cf. the modern use of natural elements to develop medicines).

Tabernacle

Verbal and thematic links between the accounts of creation and tabernacle (Exodus 25–31; 35–40) have long been noted.[75] Jon D. Levenson puts it well: "the function of these correspondences is to underscore the depiction of the sanctuary as a world, that is, an ordered, supportive, and obedient environment, and the depiction of the world as a sanctuary, that is, a place in which the reign of God is visible and unchallenged, and his holiness is palpable, unthreatened, and pervasive."[76] In other terms, the tabernacle is a microcosm of creation (cf. Pss 11:4; 78:69; Isa 66:1-2); it is the world order as God intended, writ small in Israel. While not fully re-creative of the world, it was a crucial beginning in God's mission to bring creation to the point where its life is perfectly reflective of the divine will, where "the earth will be full of the knowledge of the LORD / as the waters cover the sea" (Isa 11:9).

In this understanding, the worship of God at the tabernacle is a world-creating activity, a God-given way for the community of faith to participate in God's *ongoing* re-creation of a new world in the present, for Israel and for all.[77] God's continuing work in and through the worship of Israel is creative of a new world for Israel; it is a means whereby the community itself can take on the characteristics of the new creation in every aspect of its life. Inasmuch as sin had sharply disrupted that created order (witness Exodus 32–34, which stands between the two tabernacle accounts), God provided Israel's worship with rituals with which to restore that broken world. And so, for example, the sacrificial system immediately follows the completion of the tabernacle (Leviticus 1–7). In and through sacrificial actions and worship activities of various sorts, God worked salvation in and through human beings in moving toward the restoration of the created order. Though these laws were intended specifically for Israel, the concerns and the effects of such *local* ritual activity were *cosmic* in scope.

More particular themes common to Genesis 1–11 and the tabernacle texts illustrate the importance of this matter for Israel.[78]

The Ark of Noah

Both ark and tabernacle are portable, viewed as means by which the people of God can move in a secure and ordered way beyond apostasy and through a world of disorder on their way to a new creation. Even more, they provide a vehicle for the moving presence of God with this people.[79] This community on its way can be assured of the continued divine presence, which is not finally to be confined to Israel but is to stream out from there into the larger world. Parallels between Noah and Moses are also present; they find favor in God's sight and are perfectly obedient to God's commands in their respective building projects.

The Spirit of God

The moving of the spirit of God in Gen 1:2 is paralleled by the spirit-filled Bezalel and other craftsmen who build the tabernacle (31:1-11). The same living, breathing spirit that grounds the creation of the world is engaged in the completion of this worship world for Israel. Their intricate craftsmanship mirrors God's own work (and the work of participating creatures).[80] The precious metals with which they work take up the very products of God's beautiful creation and give new shape to that beauty within the creation. Just as God created such a world in which God himself would dwell (not explicit in Genesis, but see Ps 104:1-4; Isa 40:22), so now these craftsmen re-create a world wherein God may dwell once again in a world suitable for the divine presence.

New Year's Day

The dedication of the tabernacle occurs on new year's day (40:2, 17), which corresponds *in liturgical celebration* to the first day of creation. If, as seems likely, Genesis 1 is a hymnic piece celebrating the Creator, the tabernacle becomes the liturgical context for that hymnic activity, which shows forth before the world the effects of God's re-creating deed.

Seven Divine Speeches

The seven divine speeches in Exodus 25–31, followed by seven acts of Moses (Exod 40:17-33), correspond to the seven days of creation. Some of the speeches have parallels with creation days, and both accounts conclude with a concern for keeping the Sabbath (Gen 2:1-3; Exod 31:17); the reference to Genesis in Exod 31:17 makes the creation connection explicit. Just as the first tabernacle account ends with a Sabbath notice, the next account begins with it (35:2-3). The enclosure of chapters 32–34 with these tabernacle references suggests that God's decision to renew the covenant with Israel makes for the possibility of picking up the narrative at the point where it was interrupted by Israel's apostasy. God's gracious response to Israel means that work on the tabernacle can proceed forthwith; in spite of deep sinfulness, God's promise to dwell among the people still stands (29:45). The keeping of a *time* that is in tune with the created order is once more a reality in Israel, and this prepares the way for the hallowing of a particular *space* for God's dwelling in Israel. Exodus 31 ends on a note of harmony, rest, and preparedness. It is a paradise scene, Genesis 2 revisited, but decisively marked by the temporal order. This opens the way to think of the golden calf (Exodus 32) as Israel's particular experience of the fall. So the ordering of these materials may be described in terms of creation (25–31), fall (32–34), re-creation (35–40).

Shape, Order, Design, Intricacy

Readers are invited to "see" the embroidery (36:37; 38:18), including color (36:8, 35; 38:18-23), in both structure and furnishings. This may be said to correspond with the orderly, colorful, artful, and intricate creation of Genesis 1. It is especially to be recalled in this connection that God's creative activity is sometimes mediate, working in and through that which is already created (Gen 1:11-12, 20, 24, 26). The end product of the "construction" in both instances is a material reality that is precisely designed, externally beautiful, and functionally "literate." There is careful attention to the relationship between form and function. God is present and active in both creation and tabernacle, not simply in the verbal but also in and through that which is tangible. In both instances the creative work of God ranges widely across the physical order of things, integrating the world of nature and that which is built with human hands. The prominent use of the general word for "making" *('āsāh)* in Genesis 1 shows that God's creative work is not without analogy in the human sphere. The tabernacle is one such instance. Israel's use of these interrelated spheres in its imaging of God (e.g., God is rock; God is shield) demonstrates the theological import of this confluence of the various physical orders of the world. Both heavens and earth (Ps 19:1) and tabernacle show forth the glory of God.

It Is Good

God looks at the finished world and sees that it is very good (Gen 1:31); this corresponds to Moses "seeing" and evaluating the finished product to be exactly as God had commanded (eighteen references in Exodus 39–40). An act of blessing also occurs in both (Exod 39:43; Gen 2:3). The end result in the "building" of both creation and tabernacle is that they are essentially the products of the divine command. Just as the creation through the word of God meant that the creation was completed precisely according to the will of God, so also the completion of the tabernacle according to a heavenly "pattern" (25:9, 40) meant that it corresponded exactly to the divine will. This is one spot in the midst of a world of disorder where God's creative, ordering work is completed according to the divine intention just as it was in the beginning.

At this small, lonely place in the midst of the chaos of the wilderness, a new creation comes into being. In the midst of disorder, there is order. The tabernacle is the world order as God intended writ small in Israel. The priests of the sanctuary going about their appointed courses is like everything in creation performing its liturgical service—the sun, the trees, human beings. The people of Israel carefully encamped around the tabernacle in their midst constitutes the beginnings of God's bringing creation back to what it was originally intended to be. The tabernacle is a realization of God's created order in history; both reflect the glory of God in their midst.

Moreover, this microcosm of creation is the beginning of a macrocosmic effort on God's part. In and through this people, God is on the move to a new creation for all. God's presence in the tabernacle is a statement about God's intended presence in the entire world. The glory manifest there is to stream out into the larger world. The shining of Moses' face in the wake of the experience of the divine glory (Exod 34:29-35) is to become characteristic of Israel as a whole, a radiating out into the larger world of those glorious effects of God's dwelling among Israel. As a kingdom of priests (19:5-6), they have a role of mediating this vision and purpose of God to the entire cosmos.

CHAPTER FIVE

CREATION AND LAW

We have seen that the giving of the law is integral to the creation accounts.[1] By building the law into the created order, the point is made that every human being, not simply the chosen people, is to attend to the law *for the sake of the creation and all its creatures*. We know from ancient Near Eastern literature that laws had long been in place before Israel came into being. The sheer existence of such bodies of law testifies to the work of God the Creator in and through such lawgivers, who quite apart from their knowledge of God, mediate the will of God, however dimly perceived, or imperfectly expressed, for their societies.

We now take a closer look at the relationship between creation and law and seek to relate that discussion to other aspects of Israel's law.

Bible readers commonly do not know what to do with the law texts in the Pentateuch; as a result they are often neglected. Among the reasons given: their ancient cultural context, their claimed obsolescence, their hard-nosed (albeit selective) use by some believers, confusion over the polysemic word *law*, and their remarkable capacity to make readers feel uncomfortable (e.g., Exod 22:21-28; Deut 15:7-11). A less visible but perhaps more basic reason for this neglect is the sense that Old Testament laws are to be understood in static terms, given by God and never to be changed; hence, readers will either agree or disagree and treat them accordingly. I will argue that the texts themselves understand the law in dynamic terms and as most fundamentally related to creation.

At stake in these reflections is not only an understanding regarding whether and how individual laws pertain to religious faith and life but also a continuing positive view of the basic concerns that undergird and inform these laws. Specifically, many laws articulate Israel's deep concern for justice for the less advantaged; by neglecting these law texts we lose so much grist for consideration of these issues. More generally, these laws, both individually and in their entirety, are a gracious gift of God for the sake of the life, health, and well-being of individuals in community. This is made especially clear in the book of Deuteronomy.[2] As Deut 5:33 puts it: these laws are given to God's people "that you may live, and that it may go well with you, and that you may live long on the land that you are to possess." God gives the law in the service of life. For that, if for no other reason, they deserve close attention.

Scholars have long been at work tracking the development of Israel's legal tradition. While the canonical presentation of the emergence of Israelite law covers a span of some forty years (from Mount Sinai to the plains of Moab), interpreters usually understand that these laws developed over many centuries, from premonarchial times to the postexilic period. Various repetitions and inconsistencies in the laws have been especially important in drawing this conclusion. Broadly speaking, it is now commonplace to distinguish the book of the covenant (Exod 20:22–23:33), Deuteronomy 12–26, and the Priestly tradition (Leviticus); and that is the usual chronological ordering. At the same time, these complexes of law are themselves composite, and it is usually thought that they underwent a complex development over many centuries in view of ongoing changes in community life before being drawn into their present canonical orbit.[3]

Yet, while there has been a long-standing awareness that Israel's laws developed over time and were not understood in a static sense, this has been more a historical judgment than a canonical one.[4] Is the *canonical* presentation of law, set as it is in the wilderness period, revealing of a comparable perspective regarding law? I will argue that, despite the ascription of all law to the Mosaic era, there are several different signs that the law as canonically presented is not understood to be timeless and immutable.

I make several claims as a way of beginning. The laws that God gives Israel are understood basically in terms of creation and vocation. For example, for the Pentateuch to speak so basically and persistently of the law as being in the service of life and well-being means that its understanding of law is dynamic and is fundamentally creational in its orientation. To speak so of the Pentateuch also carries the claim that its understanding of law is seen basically in vocational terms. God gives the law not only for the sake of the life of those who receive it but also for the sake of the life of the neighbor, indeed all of creation, whom they are called to serve.

Creation and Law

Links between the law and the creation story in Genesis have often been noted,[5] but here I speak of the relationship between law and creation in the Pentateuch more generally. The sequence of redemption followed by law in the book of Exodus can be misleading; it may prompt a view that the laws were promulgated in view of God's act of salvation.[6] But such an understanding cannot be maintained. Rather, Israel's laws are grounded in God's work in creation. As B. D. Napier stated long ago, "Hebrew Law, in its present total impression, has its clearest roots in [Israel's] creation-faith."[7] Generally speaking, that many pentateuchal laws have their predecessors and parallels in other ancient Near Eastern law codes (e.g., the Code of Hammurabi) demonstrates their roots in creation rather than redemption (which Israel recognized, see below on Deut 4:6-8). More specifically, in his study of creation in Israel and the ancient Near East, H. H. Schmid claims unambiguously, "legal order belongs to the order of creation." In his view there is a symbiotic relationship between cosmic and social orders. Negatively, "an offense in the legal realm obviously has effects in the realm of nature (drought, famine) or in the political sphere (threat of the enemy)."[8] Positively, the law is a means by which the divine ordering of chaos at the cosmic level is actualized in the social sphere, which is thereby brought into closer conformity with the creation that God intended. The law is given because God is concerned about the *best possible life* for *all* of God's creatures.

The book of Genesis supports this understanding of creational law. Law is integral to God's creative work and is formulated both as prohibition (Gen 2:15-17) and as positive command (Gen 1:26-28). Law is thereby recognized as a pre-sin reality, part and parcel of God's good creation, given for the sake of a good life for all its creatures. This creational law is reiterated and extended after sin enters the life of the world in view of new times and places (Gen 9:1-7), and these early narratives are revealing of creational law (e.g., the story of Cain and Abel assumes that Cain should have known that murder is wrong, Gen 4:10-13).

The ancestral narratives also witness to pre-Sinai law.[9] Especially to be noted is Gen 26:5 (cf. 18:19, 25): "Abraham obeyed my voice and kept my charge, my commandments, my statutes, and my laws." This text is no simple anachronistic reference to the law given at Sinai; it witnesses to the narrator's understanding of the place of law in the pre-Sinai period.[10] This text stands in basic continuity with earlier articulations of God's will in the creation. Abraham's conforming to the will of God shows that his life is in tune with God's creational purposes and also models for later Israel the right response to law. These ancestral texts also demonstrate that law cannot be collapsed into the law given at Sinai. At the same time, they show that Sinai law basically conforms to already existing law; that is, the law given at Sinai stands in fundamental continuity with the law obeyed by Abraham. Other Genesis texts could be drawn on to illustrate this point.[11]

The place of law in Exodus 15–18 makes the same point (e.g., 15:25*b*-26; 16:4, 26; 18:13-27). Exodus 18:13-27 may carry a special force, situated as it is just before the revelation at Sinai (and somewhat disjunctively so).[12] On the one hand, Moses states that in adjudicating cases among the people, he is making "known to them the statutes and instructions of God" (Exod 18:16), though, of course, there has not yet been any Sinai revelation. Moses makes use of already existing law, not specifically identified in the narrative as having been revealed by God, and interprets it as the law of God. On the other hand, Jethro, in his giving counsel to Moses, identifies his wisdom regarding the right ordering of the community with what God has *commanded* (18:26), even though he had not received a revelation from God. So, both Moses and Jethro speak of laws of God that have not been specifically revealed to them as such. The understanding of law that undergirds this narrative is important for at least two reasons.

One, it makes possible a more open understanding of the ascription of the Sinai laws to God's specific revelation. If Moses and Jethro can attach a "God commands you" to their own discernment, then readers are put on the alert that the phrase "the Lord spoke to Moses" (or the like) does not necessarily exclude human insight and reflection in the development of these laws (though no explicit credit is given in the Sinai texts). This understanding may be parallel to the description of mediated divine *action* in Exod 3:7-10 where both God and Moses are agents of the exodus, though God is often the only subject of the verbs (e.g., Exod 14:13, 31). This point may be supported by the textual recognition of the distinction between God speaking the Decalogue directly (see Deut 5:22-27; Exod 20:18-21) but mediating other laws through Moses. Even more, the additional distinction between law spoken by God to Moses (Sinai) and law spoken by Moses (Deuteronomy) makes the latter one step further removed from the mouth of God. In the latter, God's laws pass through a human mind (narratively) and that inevitably involves interpretation and reflection (not unlike Acts 15:28, also in a law-giving context). God's revelation is the decisive but not the only factor in the giving of the law.

Two, "The *specific revelation of God at Sinai*, now to be presented, is thus seen to stand in *fundamental continuity* with the discernment of the will of God in and through *common human experience*."[13] The "law given at Sinai, then, is not a new reality. . . . Sinai is a drawing together of previously known law, and some natural extensions thereof; it intensifies their import for this newly shaped community. In most respects, Sinai is simply a re-giving of the law implicitly or explicitly commanded in creation."[14] To cast this point in general terms, human constructs for the ordering of community may be revealing of the divine intention quite apart from the reception of a specific divine directive to that effect. This observation, in turn, links back to the development of law in ancient Near Eastern societies and, I might add, in every society since that time.

This understanding may be supported further by Deut 4:6-8. We know that many of Israel's laws find their parallel in ancient Near Eastern law codes. That Israel also knew this to be the case is clear from this text. Other peoples do have "statutes and ordinances," but they are not as "just" as Israel's (4:8); theologically, this recognizes the work of God *the Creator* among such peoples in the development of law. Note also that the difference in the "just" character of the laws involved pertains to the "entire law"; this may recognize that the *individual ordinances* of other peoples could not always be described as less just. Even more, the knowledge of the law by other peoples entails a quality of discernment on their part; they recognize the wisdom of Israel's laws (4:6; cf. their discernment in Deut 29:24-28; Jer 22:8-9). To be able to do this means to apply some standard that can successfully determine whether they are good laws. That those who are not people of God can make such a determination successfully means that the laws are understood to conform to a standard other than "God said so." In other words, the laws are binding not just because of the God who gave them; somehow God's giving of the law is thought to conform to the existing moral order, which could be discerned by those who were not people of God.[15]

These texts understand that however much the textual claim is made that these laws have their origins in God, ultimately there were *human agents*—both within and without Israel—involved in the ongoing evaluation and development of Israel's laws. To use terms that we have used heretofore regarding creation, one must speak of *a relational model of law*. That is, the origin and development of law in Israel is understood to be an ongoing task in which God works in and through human agents.

The law is given in creation for three fundamental reasons, all of which are basically concerned about life:

(a) Most basically, law helps order human life so that it is in tune with the creational order intended by God. Given the interconnectedness of moral order and cosmic order, such obedience will have a salutary effect on the nonhuman world.[16] And so the law is given in creation so as to keep cosmic order and social order integrated in a harmonious way.

(b) Because life in creation is not free from all threats, law is given for the sake of both the preservation of God's creative work and the provision of the most welcoming context possible for ever new creational developments. For example, creation will not remain "good" and engendering of life regardless of what human beings do with the gifts they have been given. The created order is not so fixed that it is immune to (significant) damage; human sin can negatively affect the created order so that it ceases to serve life in the way that God intended (see Deut 11:13-17; Hos 4:1-3). This creational context for law also means human beings are not free of creational demands just because they do not belong to the chosen people. It is just such an understanding that informs many biblical texts relating to non-Israelites (e.g., Deut 4:6-8; the oracles against the nations, e.g., Amos 1–2).[17] Nations are held accountable to creational law quite apart from their knowledge of the God who gave it.

In this context, we briefly consider several specific laws that pertain to care for the nonhuman creatures. Their life in God's good creation is not free from threat, not least because of the behaviors of human beings. The liveliness of God's relationship with nonhuman creatures is such that laws for their protection are built into the heart of the Torah. Two perspectives may be noted. One, more indirectly: given the interrelatedness of social order and cosmic order, sinful human behaviors of any sort can adversely affect the nonhuman world (e.g., Deut 11:13-17; Jer 4:23-26; Hos 4:1-3).[18] Hence, all laws regarding human behavior have a dimension that includes the care and protection of the nonhuman. Two, more directly: human beings may savage the land and the creatures that live on it. Hence, laws are formulated for the well-being of domestic and wild animals (Exod 23:4, 11-12; Lev 25:7; Deut 22:1-4; 25:4; cf. Prov 12:10) because God is concerned about their welfare (Ps 104:21, 27-28; 145:15-16). Indeed, the Sabbath law was instituted in part out of concern for the animals (Exod 20:10; 23:12; Deut 5:14). Still other laws evidence a divine concern for the trees (Lev 19:23-25; Deut 20:19-20) and the birds (22:6-7). As John Barton indicates, "these laws seem to presuppose some idea that human beings have obligations to the animal and vegetable world, that certain ways of acting towards them are 'unfair' or exploitative."[19] Even the food laws "take seriously the ecology of human beings in the natural world in a way which deserves our admiration."[20] Certain boundaries are set for human beings as they relate to the land and its creatures; they are not given the freedom to do with them as they please. This is testimony to a unified creation, wherein humans and nonhumans are interrelated in intricate ways and called to live together in ways that honor and support the other.

A divine concern for the land itself is also evident in the law, calling for a basic human respect for the earth. This is to be done, because "the earth is the LORD's" (Ps 24:1) and the animals and land belong to God (Ps 50:10-11; Lev 25:23). Given this close relationship between God and land, the land is an issue of divine right, not human rights, and human beings are to treat it accordingly, as gift not possession. For example, every seventh year the land was to lie fallow and vineyards were to remain unpruned. The land was thereby given a rest, a sabbatical year, not unlike human beings and the domestic animals were given a sabbath rest (see Exod 23:10-11). The fallow year for the ground is "consistently interpreted as something the land has a *right* to."[21] The failure to observe this practice is understood to have deeply negative effects; in Lev 26:34-35, for example, the removal of people from the land (the exile is in mind) is stated sharply: so that "the land shall enjoy its sabbath years." This effect is not understood "in an agricultural but in a moral sense; the people's sins had put an intolerable strain on the land, from which it needed a fallow period to recover. The sabbatical years, like the weekly sabbath, represent a restoration of the land to an actually or symbolically unworked condition, in which it could be itself without human interference."[22] The honoring of the jubilee year (every fiftieth year) had the same basic concerns as the sabbatical years, though it was extended to include other provisions (Lev 25:1-55).

(c) Law is given to serve the proper development of God's good but not perfect creation. As we have seen in chapter 2, the command to "subdue the earth" (1:28) indicates that the creation was not fully developed at the beginning. God does not establish the created order as a fixed, polished entity; it was not intended to remain forever just as it existed at the end of the first week of its life (and the history of nature so demonstrates). This openness to the future exists not only because God did not exhaust the divine creativity in the first week of the world (see Ps 104:30) but also because of the creative capacities built into the order of things and the charges given its creatures (see Gen 1:11-12, 20, 24, 28; 2:18-23).[23] To be sure, there are the great rhythmic givens of creation that perdure: seedtime and harvest, cold and heat, summer and winter, day and night (Gen 8:22; Jer 31:35-36); but God's creation is also understood to be a work in progress. God creates a paradise, but the effect is not a static state of affairs; the creation is a highly dynamic reality in which its future is open to a number of possible developments.

If the law was given in creation in the service of developing God's creation toward its fullest possible life-giving potential, then for the creation to stay just as God originally created it would be a failure of the divine design. Development and change are what God intends for the creation, and human beings are charged with responsibilities for intracreational development. A fundamental implication of this kind of reflection is that "natural law" is not understood to be a fixed reality; it, too, is open to development in view of a changing world. In other words, a proper creational understanding of law entails something other than the maintenance of the status quo; existing understandings of "natural law" are in need of ongoing scrutiny in view of what creation is becoming (and this is borne out by experience). For example, the command to "multiply, and fill the earth" (Gen 1:28), understandable in view of its ancient setting, may need to be reexamined in view of changing population patterns. New situations will teach new duties in view of the developing created order, including natural law, such as: don't multiply so fast!

As with the relational model of creation with which we have worked, we have here *a relational model of the development of law.*

Divine Commandment and Natural Law

The above considerations regarding law and creation need to be expanded beyond the Pentateuch.[24] A key question has to do with a possible distinction that texts make regarding the basis for moral obligation.

One basis consists of those laws that are directly commanded by God, especially in the Pentateuch; God has thereby explicitly declared what is right and what is wrong. A second basis for discerning moral obligation is natural law, a basic moral sense that God has built into the very structures of the created order.[25] Natural law is able to be discerned from observations of the world and how it best works, from what most people think is right and just (e.g., incest is wrong in most cultures), quite apart from a person's relationship to God or a particular faith tradition. In view of this common moral sense, individuals and nations are held accountable to natural law and for overstepping generally accepted boundaries, apart from any knowledge they might have regarding what is explicitly given by God.[26] We have seen above how this understanding is present in pre-Sinai narratives (e.g., Gen 20:9; 26:5; 34:7; Exod 18:13-27).[27] Generally speaking, as Barton puts it, "the biblical writers often argue not from what God has declared or revealed, but from what is apparent on the basis of the nature of human life in society."[28] They appeal to self-evident standards of morality, a shared perception of that which is right, a basic sense for the created order of things.

James Barr picks up the argument that the distinction between natural law and Israel's explicitly revealed laws is not as sharp as surface indicators may suggest. The issue at stake in this distinction is not divine revelation as such, but the *kind* of revelation being referenced.[29] Formally, the Torah texts claim that the laws are directly given by God, but certainly in terms of substance there are significant points of indebtedness to ancient Near Eastern law or just to the dictates of common sense: "the actual content makes very good sense if we think of it as derived from the social experience of the community."[30] The source of Israel's explicit laws is at least in part due to "human beings pondering the legal problems of the society, noting difficulties and unclarities in existing law, offering suggestions and reforms . . . on the basis of thoughts and experiences."[31] And so, as a comparison of Israel's laws and other ancient Near Eastern law codes indicates, Israel's explicit laws were often likely developed from the natural law embodied in such law codes. In other words, the revelation of the law given by God at Sinai builds upon human insights regarding morality that were available over a wide spectrum of ancient Near Eastern society.

At the same time, to emphasize the theological point, these general cultural understandings and laws were understood to be the product of *God the Creator's work* among the various peoples (see Deut 4:6-8, discussed above). From this theological perspective, one might claim that no inherent contradiction between revealed law and natural law exists; the "natural" is divine in origin as well.[32] But, whatever the nature of God's work as Creator, human moral discernment, shaped as it is by finitude and sinfulness, is a complex reality when it comes to working out what the *specifics* of "natural law" might be, what implications they may have for daily life, and how important they are relative to those laws that the texts represent as specifically revealed. These cultures did not, of course, always get things right in their moral reflections! Whether Israel always correctly understood what the texts represent as God's explicit commands is a question that will also need careful consideration.

John Barton has also raised these issues in his work on the oracles against the nations in Amos 1:3–2:3.[33] In these texts, "moral obligation seems to be regarded as a matter of human moral consensus," but then, more problematically, "not necessarily resting on a theological basis at all."[34] And so Amos denounces several of the nations surrounding Israel for atrocities committed by individuals or armies against the humanity of others (e.g., treatment of pregnant women, Amos 1:13; see 1:9, breaking a "covenant of kinship"). In effect, the prophet argues that they should have known better! Not because of any law code that they failed to obey, or at least not one that is cited explicitly, but because of their common humanity and moral sensitivities. At the same time, it is important to say that non-Israelite nations did have law codes and rules of conduct in war that should have prompted different behaviors from those that Amos denounces. The likely assumption is that Amos understood that God the *Creator* had been at work in their cultures over the centuries—and hence a "theological basis" was at least implicitly present. The theological point was that the Creator was working behind the scenes to generate customs and laws that would be in the best interests of the life and health of all communities and to which these peoples were held accountable quite apart from their knowledge of the source of these expectations and laws. Amos assumed that his Israelite audience would have been familiar with these understandings of God's work as Creator and hence could understand his point. Such an understanding would also be assumed in speaking of Israel's God as the subject of the judgment on these nations for their behaviors (the same language is used for Judah/Israel as for the other nations).[35]

Barton understands that Isaiah moves toward a more explicit natural law understanding of things. Like Amos, Isaiah understands that non-

Israelite peoples are being held accountable, less with respect to behaviors they should have known were wrong than for their pride (Assyria in Isa 10:12-15; Babylon in 13:11-13; Dan 4:28-32). Such arrogance and pride are behaviors not generally drawn up in law codes, but it is assumed that they reflect certain moral orders that people should have known from observation and life experience and for which they would be held accountable. Israel, too, should have known better, apart from the law:

> The ox knows its owner,
>   and the donkey its master's crib;
> but Israel does not know,
>   my people do not understand. (Isa 1:3)

(See also 5:20-21; Jer 8:7; Amos 6:12.) Even issues of idolatry—for example, thinking of human beings more highly than God—may also be available in the general culture (see Isa 31:1-3).[36]

These understandings of natural law are also evident throughout the Wisdom literature. Close study of the complexities of human experience over time is revealing of basic human standards of morality (Job 20:4-5; Proverbs; Sir 39:1-11; Wis 7:15-22), as is an analysis of the natural order (Job 12:7-12).[37]

A brief discussion of Psalm 19 is in order at this point, given its close linking of creation and law; other close associations of creation and law in the Psalms can be seen in Pss 93:1-5; 119:89-96; 147:12-20 (cf. Ps 97:6).[38] A key issue in the interpretation of Psalm 19 is the nature of the relationship between the two major parts of the psalm and whether the psalm should be interpreted as a unity.[39] Psalm 19:1-6 focuses on God's revelation in creation, 19:7-13 on the law.[40] Among the interpretive options, the most persuasive to me focuses on creation and law as two different, yet closely related ways in which God reveals the divine self to human beings. Löning and Zenger say it well: this psalm is a "bold attempt to think the voice of creation and the voice of the Torah together in such a way that the voice of creation on the one hand becomes Torah and so that, on the other hand, the Torah is declared to be a concentration of the voice of creation."[41]

In the first section of Psalm 19, just as the heat of the sun (one example among the heavenly bodies) is regularly and universally experienced by all creatures (19:4*b*-6), so the word of God and knowledge about God is made available to "all the earth," though not in the usual articulate human speech (19:1-4*a*).[42] These verses are not to be aligned with the theme of nature's praise to God (see ch. 8), but nature's word to human beings—from heaven to earth. It is perhaps a measure of our verbal culture that the conveyance of knowledge in nonverbal ways tends to be diminished in importance and effect. In the second section of Psalm 19, the law is described in comparable terms; the law is as reliable, clear, life-giving, spirit-reviving, enlightening, joy-giving, supportive, guiding, piercing, and sure as are day and night and the workings of the heavenly bodies. The "biblical law [is] of the same order as the laws of nature, the inner mechanism of creation."[43]

Notably, no reference is made to the law of Moses or to the giving of the law on Mount Sinai in verses 7-13; this could suggest that law has reference to instruction that is available both in the Torah and in the natural order.[44] The means in and through which the divine will has been made known to human beings cannot be narrowly constricted to the limits of Israel's life and thought, however central that might be viewed. God has ways of getting through to individuals and communities—including the extraordinary works of the Creator God—that move beyond the often narrowly guarded boundaries of the chosen people (cf. Rom 1:20). Levenson's comments regarding Psalms 19 and 119 are helpful in concluding this point: "the commandments that the psalmist practices, even those which may be Pentateuchal, constitute a kind of revealed natural law. They enable him to bring his own life into harmony with the rhythm of the cosmos and to have access to the creative and life-giving energy that drives the world."[45]

Creation and Worship

Those commands that may be said to be peculiar to Israel's life with God do not stand over against this understanding of law and creation.[46] To the extent that there are laws intended specifically for the redeemed community (e.g., pertaining to worship), they are *both* grounded in, and in the service of, divine creational purposes. At one level, commands regarding worship as a creational reality are implicit in the story of Cain and Abel and the appropriateness of their offerings; other such texts include those regarding the Sabbath (Gen 2:1-3), calling on the name of the Lord (Gen 4:26), and Noah's postflood sacrifice (Gen 8:20-21). Of course, Israel's sacrificial system (see Leviticus 1–7) has deep roots in ancient Near Eastern worship practice, as do other levitical laws.

At another level, Israelite worship is a means by which the world is created and re-created in every new ritual activity. A study by Frank H. Gorman Jr., building on the anthropological work of Mary Douglas and others, demonstrates this integration of worship and the creation: "The Priestly ritual system is best understood as the meaningful enactment of world in the context of Priestly creation theology."[47] This is defined as "the bringing into being and the continuation of the order of creation . . . that reflects the original good order of God." Certain rituals are necessary for the continuation of the world order; others are needed to effect a restoration upon disruption. In view of Genesis 1, "human beings are called to become participants in the continual renewal and maintenance of the created order." The ritual legislation becomes one means by which human beings act out this role in creation. Thus, even though these laws are intended specifically for Israel, the concerns and the effects of such *local* ritual activity are *cosmic*. Obedience is not simply conceived in individual or even social terms but as actions that affect and encompass the entire created order.[48]

I emphasize several matters from the preceding discussion. The parallels to many Israelite laws in the cultures surrounding Israel must be placed within a theological context centered in creation. Few of the social laws are in fact uniquely Israelite and there are many parallels to various ritual activities (e.g., sacrifices); what is unique is the particular configuration of material collected here and its being related in specific ways to Israel's life under Yahweh. But the existence of much of this legal material in the surrounding cultures is testimony to God's work as Creator among these peoples. One result of this divine activity was the development of law for the ordering and preservation of human life, and this divine creative activity occurred prior to and independent of God's redemptive work. God uses such laws for the benefit of life, quite apart from redemptive activity as well as from the nations' "knowledge" of the origins of their laws. This point is further evidence for the fact that the law does not grow out of redemption but is brought more clearly into the light of day for Israel as the law of God for the sake of creation. It is now made clear to the redeemed people what their responsibilities in God's reclaimed world are. The law is given to be of service in the ongoing divine task of the reclamation of creation. In the obedience of the law, Israel in effect becomes a "created co-reclaimer" of God's intentions for the creation.

Law and Vocation

The covenant at Sinai with its accompanying laws is concerned most fundamentally with Israel's vocation in the world in the service of life. The Sinai covenant does not establish God's relationship with Israel; the Israelites are "my people" early in the book of Exodus (e.g., 3:7-10). These people are the inheritors of the promises given to their ancestors (Exod 3:15-17; 6:4, 8), a covenant that God remembers (2:24; 6:4-5) as given to the ancestors and to their "descendants" (Gen 17:7). It is this ancestral covenant that grounds Moses' appeal to God when the people break the Sinaitic covenant (Exod 32:13), indicating that the Abrahamic covenant is more foundational for the God-Israel relationship. The Sinai covenant is a matter of Israel's vocation, not its status. It is a formalization of Israel's role in the world—to be a holy nation and a kingdom of priests (Exod 19:5-6). The giving of the law to an already redeemed people is in the service of this vocation, to which the people agree to be obedient (Exod 19:8; 24:3, 7).

In being given the law at Sinai, Israel, like the first human beings, is caught up by God in a vocation that involves the becoming of the creation. Sinai law is not a new reality but a fuller particularization of how the community can take on its God-given *creational* responsibilities for the sake of life in view of new times and places. Sinai draws together previously known law and develops new law for this redeemed and called community. In most respects, Sinai is simply a regiving of the law implicitly or explicitly commanded in creation or made evident in common life experience (within Israel and without).[49] The exodus gives Israel some new motivations for keeping the law, indeed empowers Israel to that end, but the law is grounded in Israel's creation-faith not God's redemptive activity. To obey the law is to live in harmony with God's intentions for the creation. As Deuteronomy especially never tires of telling readers, the law is given for the sake of the best life possible; the law stands in the service of a stable, flourishing, and life-enhancing *community* (the community language is important). Sinai law sketches a vocation to which Israel is called for the sake of the neighbor and the creation. Because of the way in which Deuteronomy often identifies the neighbor in relationship to specific life situations (e.g., 24:10-22), it is revealing of a dynamic sense of law.

The central concern of the law for the poor and disadvantaged is for the sake of life or, in other terms, to make sure that God's *salvation* extends deeply into the life of the community. God's work of salvation has the effect of reclaiming and enabling not only true human life and freedom but also *responsibility* for the sake of life for all. As a newly redeemed community Israel stands before God and is, in effect, addressed as human beings were on the sixth day of creation and called to take up this vocation.

A Dynamic Understanding of Law

I now consider various matters that more fully indicate that the law is understood to be a dynamic rather than a static or fixed reality.

Law and Context

It is of no little import that the wilderness is the context for all pentateuchal law. This is true of the major blocks of law given at Sinai and Moab, but especially to be noted are the wilderness narratives (Exod 15:22–18:27; Num 10:11–36:13), where laws emerge periodically as new situations develop for the journeying community (e.g., Exod 15:25*b*-26; Numbers 15; 18–19; 27–36). The book of Deuteronomy, whether viewed canonically (forty years after Sinai) or historically (the seventh century B.C.E.), is a major exemplar of law emerging in view of changing circumstances. The forty years between Sinai and Deuteronomy should not be downplayed, especially in view of its recollection of Israel's most recent history and its anticipation of a new context in the promised land. This span of time is sufficient to demonstrate that the text recognizes that Israel's life situation has now changed and new formulations of law are needed. Deuteronomy would have to be interpreted quite differently if its laws had been given at Sinai.

In tracking the way in which the law is literarily presented in Exodus through Deuteronomy it is immediately apparent that law and narrative are interwoven.[50] In other words, the law is not presented as a code but is integrated with the ongoing story of the people of God, unlike the law codes of the ancient Near East (or in contemporary societies). Law for Israel is always intersecting with life as it is lived—filled with contingency and change, complexity and ambiguity.

That Israel's laws emerge in connection with the wilderness experience is significant; in other words, the wilderness is an image for the basic character of law. On the one hand, the law provides something of a compass for wandering in the wilderness. On the other hand, the contingencies of wilderness wandering keep the law from becoming absolutized in a once-and-for-all form and content. Law in and of itself tends to promote a myth of certainty regarding the shape of life; actual life, however, especially when seen from the perspective of the wilderness narratives, is filled with contingencies, in which nothing on the ship of life seems to be tied down. This means that new laws will be needed and older laws will need to be revised or perhaps put on a back burner. So, for example, in Deuteronomy there are laws regarding kingship and prophecy in anticipation of the coming settlement in the land (17:14-20; 18:9-22).[51]

The image of wilderness lifts up that which is basic to the development of law (and all relationships for that matter): constancy and change. Law takes ongoing experience into account while remaining constant in its objective: the best life for as many as possible. Both constancy and change are basic to law because they are basic to life, indeed the life that God intends for all creatures. They are also basic for God, a matter to which I now turn.

Law and God

That all pentateuchal law is attributed to God has created something of a problem in thinking about the God of these texts, especially in view of their inconsistencies. Is God inconsistent or represented as inconsistent, or is some other explanation possible? Various harmonistic efforts, both rabbinic and Christian, have been attempted to make sure that a consistent God emerges, but at the expense of a straightforward reading of the text. At the same time, critical scholars sometimes make claims about God that may intensify the God issue unnecessarily. Below are some implications of the interweaving of law and narrative that we have noted.

One, the law is a gracious gift of God. The law is more clearly seen to be a gracious gift because it is episodically integrated with the story of God's other gracious activities. God's actions in the narrative show that the law is not arbitrarily laid upon the people but is given "for our lasting good, so as to keep us alive" (Deut 6:24). The gracious purposes of God for Israel evident in the narrative demonstrate that the law is fundamentally gift not burden.

Two, the law given by God has a fundamentally personal and interrelational character. God introduces the law with highly personal statements regarding what God has done on behalf of the people (Exod 19:4;

20:2). Obedience to law is thus seen to be a response within a relationship, not a response to the law as law. Moreover, in the narrative readers are confronted with a God who personally interacts with Israel through every stage of their journey. God's giving of the law does not stand at odds with this kind of interactive God-human relationship. And so God does not give the law in a once-and-for-all form but takes the ongoing relationship into account in giving shape to the law.

Three, God's gracious gift of law meets a creational *need*. God's ongoing work of providence and salvation in pentateuchal narrative is always related to the needs of the people, for example, delivering them from Egyptian abuse and providing food and drink in the wilderness. That God's narrative actions are so correlated with the people's needs argues for a comparable understanding of law. God's law takes into account what the people need for the best possible life. This means that the laws are not arbitrary; they are given in view of specific human needs—and this at several levels. For example, God gives the sacrificial laws in Leviticus 5 because of the people's need for atonement. At the same time, it is made clear that the wealth of the worshiper is taken into account in determining the type of offering (Lev 5:7, 11). Individual situations of need affect how the law is to be applied.

Four, the basic shape for a life lived in obedience to law is drawn most basically from Israel's narrative experience with God, rather than from abstract ethical argument or even divine imperative. God "loves the strangers, providing them food and clothing. You shall also love the stranger, for you were strangers in the land of Egypt" (Deut 10:18-19). "Be merciful, just as your Father is merciful" (Luke 6:36). God's will for Israel does not function at the level of general principle; it moves into life in all of its particulars, for that is where the law makes the most difference for people's well-being (e.g., Deut 24:19-22).

That the law is developed as an exegesis of divine action means that believers are always being called to go beyond the law. The range of God's actions is not *legally* circumscribed (e.g., Jer 3:1-5). God is always doing new things, and so this will mean imagining ever new ways in which the law and the consequent shape of people's everyday lives can reflect God's actions in the world. This understanding also prevents the believer from equating obedience to the law and doing what is right. Law may not have caught up with the community's confession regarding God or its understanding of life and well-being (and so it may be that the legal act is not necessarily a moral act).[52]

Five, God does not simply give the law to the people by divine fiat; God accompanies the law with motivations to obey the law.[53] These motivations are revealing of the kind of God that stands behind the law; God does not just lay down the law, but gives Israel good reasons to obey. For Deuteronomy (e.g., 5:33; 22:6-7), it is in Israel's self-interest and in the best interests of the human and nonhuman community, especially the vulnerable and marginalized, to obey—that it may go well with you and that you may live long. This, of course, is not reward talk; rather, such benefits are intrinsically related to the deed; they grow out of the deed itself. To obey is a reasonable thing to do (Deut 4:6); right obedience is always an intelligent obedience.[54] The concern of the law is not to bind Israel to some arbitrary set of laws but to enable them to experience the fullness of life in relationship.

The most basic motivation given Israel for obeying the law is drawn from its narrative experience with God as deliverer. "Remember that you were a slave in Egypt" (Deut 24:18, 22). Therefore, you shall, for example, shape your lives toward the disadvantaged in ways both compassionate and just. God's saving deeds call forth response from Israel. For what is Israel to be grateful? Most basically, it is the gift of life, and obedience to law extends that gift out into all the highways and byways of the community and the larger creation.

Six, God's giving of the law, understood in vocational terms, means that God has chosen to use human agents in carrying out the divine purposes in the world. God moves over, as it were, and gives to the human an important role to play in taking initiative and assuming responsibility for the world of which it is a part, including furthering the cause of justice and good order in Israel and the larger creation. God is the kind of God who has chosen not to do everything "all by himself."

Seven, given these comments about the law, let me interact briefly with statements about God made by two scholars who have been very helpful in developing our thinking about the law.

James Watts in his excellent book makes certain claims regarding the God of the law that are sometimes problematic.[55] He states: "Because YHWH rules in Israel, fidelity and obedience is demanded and enforced."[56] But this kind of formulation implies an unacceptable purpose for God's giving laws to Israel. It is as if God reasoned, "I'm king and you're my subjects, and hence you are obligated to obey me." God's purpose in giving the law looks quite different if understood in more creational and relational terms. That is, God gives the law and commands obedience for the sake of the life and well-being of the creatures not out of a virtually self-serving notion that the people must obey, because God is, after all, their ruler.[57]

In a recent article, Bernard M. Levinson asks some rhetorical questions about the God of the law that are also problematic: "Once a law is attributed to God, how can it be superseded, which is to say, annulled, without the prestige or authority of the divine law being thereby impaired? . . . Could one imagine, for that matter, that the divine himself should suddenly deem inadequate one of his own rules?"[58]

These questions assume that the will of God (and God?) is immutable, at least as revealed in the law. But on what grounds is such a claim made? Why would a divine change in God's own law be considered problematic for either the law or God?[59] Would it not be much more problematic for both God and the law if God were not able to revise God's own law or to choose to set one or more laws aside in view of new needs in the people's lives? God's (and the law's) "prestige" and "authority" are more tied up with the divine ability to know what is best for people's lives not the ability to put laws in place that never need changing. It might be noted that the *historical* recognition on the part of most scholars that the canon reveals an ongoing revision of God's own law has probably enhanced the divine reputation not damaged it.

Law and Spirit

One of the more striking characteristics of the law, especially in the book of Deuteronomy, is the passion and energy with which the law is set forth. The parenetic form of presentation ("preached law") addresses the reader directly. This spirit in which the law is presented is revealing of a dynamic understanding of law that often entails a degree of openendedness. For example, Deut 15:7-11 speaks of the treatment of the poor in the language of spirit rather than letter: "do not be hard-hearted and tight-fisted toward your needy neighbor. You should rather open your hand, willingly lending enough to meet the need"; "give liberally and be ungrudging when you do so"; "open your hand to the poor and needy neighbor in your land."

This hortatory language is not related in a literal way to the actual law regarding remission of debts (15:1-3). Rather, the language urges readers to *interpret* the law and even go *beyond the law* (e.g., "give liberally"; "enough to meet the need"). Once this rhetoric is introduced into the text, then what it takes for individuals (or the community) to obey the law becomes a somewhat open-ended matter, subject to interpretation (for example, "liberally" is not defined and discerning what is "enough" to meet the need is left open). The laws regarding the less advantaged are often generally stated (e.g., Exod 22:21-24); what it means to care for them entails the use of the imagination (Exod 22:25-28 may provide an illustration of the general principle articulated in the prior verses).

Revision of Law within the Pentateuch

The literary history of pentateuchal law is ostensibly denied by the attribution of all law to God in the wilderness setting. Levinson in his penetrating study of Deuteronomy seeks to uncover the human voice that lies beneath the surface of the text. While some aspects of Levinson's proposal are problematic, his work opens up new avenues for conversation.[60] He speaks of a "rhetoric of concealment" in Deuteronomy whereby, through various literary devices, changes in the law are deliberately camouflaged through a variety of literary means, not least casting the whole in terms of its ancient Mosaic setting. They employed "the garb of dependence [on the Covenant Code] to purchase profound hermeneutical independence."[61] While the text of Deuteronomy presents the law in terms of the divine voice, Levinson's proposal reveals the concealed human voice in the material. His proposal joins other analyses of the text that give evidence for ongoing human involvement in the development of law.

I would like to pick up on a somewhat isolated statement by Levinson regarding the juncture between his historical work and the canonical shape of the law; he calls the inclusion of both the Covenant Code and Deuteronomy within the Pentateuch "a major irony of literary history."[62] In other words, the canonical process has given a status to the book of the covenant that the Deuteronomic authors would not have shared. Whatever one may think of Levinson's historical proposal, Deuteronomy has been placed on a canonical continuum that includes older law; in that very fact Deuteronomic law is considered a revision of prior law and has in turn been opened up for further revision.

Notably, the inconsistencies in the laws are not ironed out in the canonical form. What if one worked with the assumption that these inconsistencies are a plus and are revealing of a complex understanding of the development of law *within* the canonical shape of things? This dynamic understanding of the law may be demonstrated by a comparison of law texts to one another. A long-recognized example is the changes that Deuteronomy makes with respect to the laws in the book of the covenant in view of new times and places (changes in Leviticus and Numbers could also be noted).[63] These changes are not explicitly acknowledged in Deuteronomy (hence Levinson's proposal), but readers of the final form of the Pentateuch would recognize them as such.

To illustrate, two texts may be cited. The Ten Commandments, redactionally placed at a crucial position in both Exodus and Deuteronomy, introduce the two major bodies of law in the Pentateuch. Given their standing, it is striking that the Deuteronomic version varies from that in Exodus; the changes are minor, but that they exist at all is important. The coveting commandment(s) are notable, with the interchange of "house" and "wife" (Exod 20:17; Deut 5:21); this change may reflect a change in the status of women in Israelite society (and any modern revision would make sure that the "neighbor" is no longer only the male). This change may be related to a more significant revision in the slavery laws, where, for example, Deuteronomy does not distinguish between treatment of male and female slaves in their manumission whereas Exodus does (cf. Deut 15:1-18, esp. v. 17, with Exod 21:2-11, esp. vv. 2, 9).[64]

This recognition of inner-biblical development in the law is of considerable import, not only for understanding biblical law but also for postbiblical developments. The tensions and inconsistencies in the law texts are testimony to the ongoing, unresting divine effort to link the law to life in ever new times and places. Watts says it well: "Contradiction in Pentateuchal law . . . authorizes legal change as a natural part of Torah."[65] Because God is the author of all these laws, Israel's legal traditions "cast God as the principal instigator of change within law."[66] If these law texts were (are) all smoothed over, then they would be testimony to an immutable law for which new times and places would be irrelevant. The very roughness of the material is an ongoing witness to the changing character of life and the changing character of the will of God as it relates to that life. And so *development in the law* is just as canonical as individual laws or the various collections of law. God's will for Israel is understood to be a living will. God moves with this people on their life's journey, and God's will for them changes because they are changing. For God's will to be linked to life in such a central way makes the law an even more gracious gift than it would be if understood as immutable.

Even more, the Pentateuch's *preservation of older law alongside newer law* is an important matter to consider. Letting the book of the covenant stand in the canon in its given form along with Deuteronomy is not considered a threat to the law's integrity; rather, old law and new law remain side by side as a canonical witness to the process of unfolding law. At the same time, all laws remain the laws of God—older laws from God and newer laws from God—and hence cannot be declared devoid of value. As such, the book of the covenant maintains its value for ongoing legal reflection and innovation. This means that in moving toward any new formulation of law, every word from God was thought to need careful consideration. In revising the law it was deemed necessary to go back over all the laws from God; it was precisely in the imaginative interaction of older laws and current laws that new laws were generated for changing times and places. As such, pentateuchal law unfolds in a way comparable to the ways in which new law is developed in our own time, where older laws that are no longer "on the books" continue to be a resource for legal reflection.

And so, instead of an immutable, timeless law in the Pentateuch, we have preserved for us a developing process in which experience in every sphere of life over time is drawn into the orbit of the law and preserved for the consideration of successive generations—for the sake of the best life possible!

The New Testament Pattern

The New Testament picks up on this Old Testament witness to a dynamic, unfolding law. The New Testament community doesn't simply accept every Old Testament law as binding law; it works through the laws in a variety of ways in view of the new situations in which it finds itself (e.g., Acts 15:1-35; note especially vv. 28-29, "it has seemed good to the Holy Spirit and to us"). As such, it follows a trajectory already set by the Old Testament community.[67] The New Testament thereby provides a broad pattern for interpretation and sets an agenda for both church and society in its ongoing consideration of Old Testament laws.[68]

For example, the laws regarding clean and unclean food are rethought (e.g., Mark 7:1-23; Acts 10:1-16) and the result is that older laws regarding these matters now have a different standing in the canon for Christians. At the same time, the food laws have not been cut out of the canon or declared of no value. They remain the laws of God for an ancient time and place, but they have an ongoing import precisely because of that. They served life at one time and it remains to be asked: how might the most basic concerns that inform the food laws continue to be of value for contemporary life? That is to say, readers need to make a distinction between (1) the law as law and (2) the concerns that generated the law in the first place. And so, while the texts themselves witness at times to laws *as laws* no longer being applicable, it always needs to be asked whether the concerns that generated those laws may continue to be important for the community and its ongoing formulation of new law. And so, while the food laws as laws may no longer be applicable for some religious communities, food laws will still be needed for the sake of the health and well-being of the community. One may well look to modern food laws designed to preserve life and health as descendants of that ancient biblical concern (e.g., the Food and Drug Administration). I would argue that every law of God continues to have value for present-day communities *at some level*, especially at the level of the concern that generated the law in the first place.

A Point of Contemporary Significance

Over the course of the last two centuries much blood has been spilled over the question of the continuing applicability of particular Old Testament laws. In the nineteenth century, disagreement over texts regarding slavery spawned conflict and split communities, churches, and families. In more recent times, disagreement over law texts regarding homosexual behavior threatens to do the same. In my estimation, these conflicts have not been accompanied by much sophistication in understanding how to work with these and other laws. However well intentioned the discussion is, such argumentation regarding the place of law is all too often a cut-and-paste enterprise.

The postbiblical formulation of new laws by human beings should be seen as being in tune with the divine intention regarding creational life and well-being evident in biblical law. Because these ever-emerging laws, however, are usually associated with legislatures, courts, and church assemblies and developed by human beings, we tend not to think of them as God's laws; but, of course, they are. It may well be that some of these newer laws will stand over against their biblical predecessors, but this would be not unlike their biblical predecessors in, say, Deuteronomy.

The above discussion of inner-biblical development in the law—as much a canonical reality as the laws themselves—may provide a canonical warrant for thinking through postbiblical developments in the law in a new way. Interpreters should not make a blanket statement about all biblical laws, as if they were all equally applicable or obsolete; we are called to study each and every law seeking to discern whether it continues to serve the life and health of the community, indeed the larger created order, and see what might come of that conversation. While the New Testament has done some of that work for us, we are called to do a careful and thorough consideration of the old, to think through God's purpose in giving the law, and to read back through all prior laws for insights they may continue to provide in moving toward new formulations. It is precisely in the interaction of older word from God and newer word from God—words that may stand in tension with one another—that revisions or abrogations of law are determined and new laws are developed.

If it is established that the biblical law texts witness to a dynamic process of revising law in view of new times and places, then that testimony provides an important canonical basis for considering every biblical law as open to revision but without treating any one of them with disdain. This way of thinking about biblical law may change attitudes toward the law and, I might add, toward the God who has so graciously given us such a dynamic law for the sake of the creation and its life.

CHAPTER SIX

CREATION, JUDGMENT, AND SALVATION IN THE PROPHETS

Creation is a much more common theme in the prophets than is commonly recognized.[1] Within the prophetic corpus, creation has been especially associated with Isaiah 40–55, and for good reason, given the frequency of reference to creation. In this chapter, I consider several dimensions of this major topic: creation and judgment and creation in Amos, Jeremiah, and Second Isaiah; other prophetic texts will be drawn into the discussion along the way.

Creation and Judgment

How shall we speak of divine judgment in today's world? Some interpreters of the current world scene are not hesitant in responding. They point to the depletion of the ozone layer and global warming, "unnatural" developments in the animal world (e.g., deformed frogs), the spread of deadly diseases, and weather patterns that seem uncommonly violent. Aside from the heightened rhetoric and undisciplined certainty that often accompany such claims, is there not a kernel of truth in the linkage of such phenomena with the judgmental activity of God?

Even those who do not draw such conclusions and who recognize our inadequate knowledge of the history of nature, the difficulties of comparative measures, and the "wildness" and randomness that are integral to God's good creation have often been given to a nagging bewilderment.

What is the import of these developments for the future of the earth and its inhabitants? Many would claim that such "unnatural" events are at least in part due to human activities that have disrupted the delicate balance of the earth's ecosystem. The truth of such a claim is commonly accepted, both within and without the church. But is such an "explanation" sufficient?

For believers in a living and active God, further questions must be asked: how might *God* be involved in these developments and to what end? Even for those who are properly reserved in making theological claims about environmental events, these questions are important because they are raised by many biblical texts that link divine judgment with natural catastrophe. One thinks of the flood narrative (Genesis 6–8), the story of Sodom and Gomorrah (Genesis 18–19), or the plagues in Egypt (Exodus 7–12). While each of these texts indicts sinful human behavior for what happens to the ecosystem, God is certainly portrayed as deeply involved. Indeed, doesn't God make matters worse for the environment? If readers were to move beyond these stories to prophetic texts, this impression would often be reinforced. Jeremiah 4:22-26, for example, is certainly one of the most vivid biblical portrayals of environmental catastrophe (see also Jer 9:10-11; 12:4, 7-13). Again, while human behaviors are cited (v. 22), the climactic point in the text links these natural disasters to the "fierce anger" of God (v. 26). For all the talk about God being committed to the stewardship of the earth, in these texts we find God contributing to the degradation of the environment!

What might the interpreter concerned about the environment have to say about such texts? While certainly human sinfulness and divine judgment are key dimensions of the topic, undergirding such texts is an understanding of the created order as a highly interrelated reality. To begin, I consider the prophetic understanding of judgment.

Perspectives on Judgment

Generally speaking, judgment has reference to ruling in an equitable way (Ps 72:2). As such, judgment may mean good news or bad news. Divine action against the wicked (Ps 94:2; cf. Rom 2:2-3) can mean deliverance of the poor and needy from oppression (Pss 76:9; 82:8) or vindication for those who have been wronged (Ps 26:1). Most commonly, God's judgment is related to the effects of sin; this is especially evident in the formal link ("therefore") between the prophetic indictment for sin and the announcement of judgment (e.g., Jer 5:12-17; 6:13-15). Most basically, judgment is thereby shown to be not a capricious divine act but a response to human sinfulness.

Many shortsighted views on divine judgment exist. They may include a stress on individual, eschatological, religious, or spiritual perspectives on judgment as well as neglecting communal, historical, socioeconomic/political, and psychical/bodily perspectives.[2] Generally speaking, the more narrowly we speak of judgment, the more restricted our understanding of salvation will be. If, for example, judgment is only or primarily a spiritual matter, then the healing of the body or the environment will tend not to be comprehended within the understanding of *salvation*. The wide range of biblical thinking about divine judgment merits more attention than it has been given.[3]

The metaphor of God as judge is often a decisive factor in thinking through divine judgment, and for good reason. At the same time, the metaphor prompts one to think of judgment solely or primarily in forensic terms, as if each judgment were the result of a specific divine decision. Though the language of "judgment" is associated with the court of law, juridical categories do not fully or sufficiently comprehend the workings of divine judgment. This is true from several perspectives. For one, God's judgment is never simply justice. In terms of straightforward legal thinking, God is much too lenient. God is patient, forbearing, and "slow to anger" (e.g., Jonah 4:2), and open to changing the divine mind—both before and *after* (!) the judgment has been exercised (e.g., Jonah 3:8-10).[4]

For another, judgment is understood fundamentally in relational terms; a relationship is at stake, not an agreement or a contract or a set of rules. God does not bring judgment in terms of a legal statute with sanctions. As we will see, God does not impose anything new on the judgmental situation but mediates the consequences of sin.

From still another perspective, Erich Zenger is helpful in showing that, in thinking about God as judge, "the public system of justice remains only an analogue for what is at stake in talk about God." God is not at all "a neutral representative of an independent court of justice."[5] Human judges, when they are doing their job well, dispense sentences with dispassionate objectivity. (What would courtrooms be like if judges were constantly displaying their personal anger and anguish?) God, on the other hand, is not cool and detached. God has a binding relationship with those at whom the divine anger is directed, is openly anguished over present and future possibilities (e.g., Hos 6:4), and is personally caught up in the situation. Such features of the prophetic portrayal of God constitute a no in the use of the metaphor of God as judge that must stand alongside any yes. In other words, the personal dimension of wrath qualifies any legal or juridical understandings. At the same time, the juridical/political sense qualifies the personal. The personal and political senses of divine wrath must remain linked, but not collapsed, and each must qualify the other. When thinking of God as judge, remember that the judge behind the bench is the spouse of the accused one in the dock.

Divine judgment is properly understood as the effects of human sin. But the issue is made more complex by still another reality. One characteristic of communal and historical judgment is that no clean distinction is made between the righteous and the wicked (e.g., all suffer in the fall of Jerusalem). Because life is so interconnected, the righteous and the innocent (e.g., children) are often caught up in the judgmental effects of sins that are not their own. In other words, they will undergo the *experience* of judgment in ways that are often devastating to their life and health.[6] This is the issue raised with God by Abraham in connection with the judgment on Sodom and Gomorrah.[7] More generally, judgment can be a reality for the elect:

> You only have I known
>   of all the families of the earth;
> therefore I will punish you
>   for all your iniquities.
>   (literally, "I will visit all your iniquities
> upon you") (Amos 3:2)

The prophets, who may be considered proponents of a "religion against itself," brought the elect themselves within the operative sphere of judgment. No individual or community was immune from historical judgment.[8]

To extend the point, divine judgment may also adversely and "unfairly" affect nonhuman realities, including animals and the land, indeed the entire ecosystem. The world of nature is also caught up in divine judgment due to no fault of its own. This reality is further testimony to the interconnectedness of life. God has created the world in such a way that the moral order affects the cosmic order. Human sin and its judgmental effects ripple out and adversely affect the entire created order.[9] We will return to this issue below in our discussion of creation in Jeremiah.

God Judges through Means

In judgment, God works in the world through means, including human beings (within and without the community of faith) and, potentially, all nonhuman creatures.[10] This divine way with the world is true for both judgment (Nebuchadnezzar) and deliverance (Cyrus). Such agents are no less "real" than Yahweh. Interpreters must not diminish the distinction between God and God's agents or discount the stature and the very real power of a human army. Just how God is involved in this activity cannot be factored out with precision, though Jer 51:11 (and 50:9; 51:1) may contain a clue with the reference to God as having "stirred up *['ûr]* the spirit of the kings of the Medes" (cf. Isa 13:17; 41:25; 45:13; Ezek 23:22; Joel 3:7).

Nonhuman Agents

The Red Sea crossing is an example of how God uses nonhuman creatures as agents for similar purposes—the wind, waves, water, clouds, and darkness (Exodus 14–15). Nonhumans are the judge and the savior of the human! God's use of nonhuman agents is common throughout the Old Testament (e.g., Ps 104:4; Isa 30:30; Jer 12:9; 21:14; Joel 1; Amos 4:6-11), including sickness and famine (e.g., Num 11:33; Deut 28:20-24, 58-61; 2 Sam 24:15-18; Pss 88:16; 90:5-8). Servant language is even used for the birds and animals of the land in Jeremiah; they will "serve" the king of Babylon in his judgmental work (Jer 27:6; see 7:33; 12:9; 16:4; 19:7; 28:14; they are parallel with "the sword" in 15:3). While animals may be used as metaphors for the Babylonians (e.g., 4:7; see Isa 56:9), these texts speak of the agency of the animals themselves. Note also God's command to cut down the trees to make siege works (Jer 6:6) or the use of the hot wind (4:11; 22:22) and fire (5:14). Indeed, desolation of the land as an effect of human iniquity is used by God as instrument of judgment (3:2-3; 5:24-25; 14:2-12). "Victim" language for the land and its animals insufficiently recognizes this "vocation" to which God calls them in service of the divine purposes, a vocation that may entail suffering.[11]

Foreign Army Agents

Perhaps the most common of the divine agents are foreign empires such as Assyria and Babylonia ("the weapons of his wrath," Jer 50:25; cf.

Isa 10:5; 13:5). These empires execute the wrath of God. Jeremiah's language regarding God the Creator's use of nonchosen peoples is especially striking. For the purpose of judging Israel, God calls King Nebuchadnezzar "my servant" (Jer 25:9; 27:6; 43:10)! God's use of such agents is testimony to a sophisticated creation theology; God is active out and about in the world, working in and through peoples outside of the chosen community. God as creator makes choices among human beings and sociopolitical realities to carry out God's work in the world (Jer 27:5-6; see 50:44).

This divine choice does not mean "the power and significance of Babylon are completely nullified,"[12] not least because Babylon uses its power in inappropriate ways (see Isaiah 47; Jer 27:7; 25:12-14; 50-51).[13] God makes free choices, but they are constrained by relationships established and are related to the powers that are available in and through which God can work.[14] To all external observation, God is not involved in these military and political activities, but the claim of these texts is that God is at work in and through them on behalf of God's global purposes. Observers cannot factor out just how God is so involved, but the text *confesses* that God's will is somehow at work. Notably, such texts witness that *God's actions in history are grounded in an understanding of God as Creator*. God's purposes span the globe, and God's actions with Israel are interconnected with these creation-wide designs. This formulation is an Old Testament perspective often neglected in the long-standing rush to connect God's activity in the world with historical realities in particular, resulting in a neglect of the work of God as Creator, with no little negative impact on the larger environment.[15]

A stunning juxtaposition of God and the means God uses for purposes of judgment is evident in Jer 13:14 and 21:7; both God and Nebuchadnezzar "will not pity or spare or have compassion" in the destruction of Jerusalem (see 27:8, "I *[God]* have completed its destruction by *his* hand," emphasis mine). Throughout Jeremiah, language used for Nebuchadnezzar and the Babylonians is also used for God. Among other things, both God and Babylon break, destroy, scatter, drive away, fight, strike down, and pursue Israel and then send them into exile. In a somewhat disturbing way, these characterizations of God in judgment are often conformed to the means that God uses.[16]

What conclusions might one draw from this common fund of language? Such harsh words appear to be used for God because they are used for the actions of those in and through whom God mediates judgment. These parallels suggest that *the portrayal of God's wrath and violent action in Jeremiah are conformed to the means that God uses*. God is portrayed in terms of the means available. Both God and human agents have a crucial role to play, and their spheres of activity are interrelated in terms of function and effect. God is not only independent and the humans involved only dependent. God has so shaped the created order that there are overlapping spheres of interdependence, and responsibility is shared by God with human beings. In some sense God has chosen to be *dependent* on Nebuchadnezzar in carrying out that judgment.[17] This decision to work through less than perfect means is a risky move for God because God thereby becomes associated with the agent's (often violent) activity.[18] God thereby accepts any fallout that may accrue to the divine reputation (guilt by association).

This perspective is testimony to a fundamentally *relational* understanding of the way in which God acts in the world.[19] There is an ordered freedom in the creation, a degree of openness and unpredictability, wherein God leaves room for genuine human decisions as they exercise their God-given power. Even more, God gives them powers and responsibilities in such a way that *commits* God to a certain kind of relationship with them. This entails a divine constraint and restraint in the exercise of power in relation to these agents. They overdid it!

Divine Judgment and the Created Moral Order

The most common agent of divine judgment is the created moral order. That is, God has created the world in such a way that deeds (whether good or evil) will have consequences. Generally speaking, the relationship between deed and consequence is conceived in intrinsic rather than extrinsic terms. That is to say, the consequences grow out of the deed itself; they are not a penalty (or reward) introduced by God into the situation. *That* good deeds have consequences may be called blessing; *that* sins have consequences may be called judgment. We focus on the latter in this context.

Several matters of translation and interpretation come together in thinking through this issue.[20] Initially, I focus on the common use of moral order language in Jeremiah.[21] Sometimes this word refers to the wickedness of the people, sometimes to the effects of their wickedness, commonly translated "disaster" (the word *'āwôn*, "iniquity," is also used in both senses in the Old Testament; see Gen 19:15).[22] In other words, the same Hebrew word is used to speak of both the wickedness of the people and of its consequences ("disaster"). This verbal linkage makes it clear that the judgment experienced by the Israelites flows out of their own wickedness (*rā'āh* leads to *rā'āh*).

This understanding of *rā'āh* issuing in *rā'āh* may be observed in several formulations. God brings disaster *(rā'āh)*, which is "the fruit of *their* schemes" (Jer 6:19, emphasis mine; see Hos 8:7; 10:13). Or, "I will pour out *their* wickedness upon them" (Jer 14:16, emphasis mine). Or, God gives to all "according to their ways, / according to the fruit of their doings" (Jer 17:10; see 32:19). Ezekiel 7:27 puts the matter in these terms: "according to their own judgments I will judge them." Like fruit, the consequence grows out of (or is intrinsic to) the deed itself. This leads to a certain amount of correspondence thinking in the prophets, that is, like produces like (e.g., Jer 50:29); the people will stew in the juices they themselves have prepared. This type of thinking may have its roots in a fundamental concern for fairness, namely, in terms of any human canons of accountability, the judgment fits the crime.[23]

How is God involved in the move from sin to consequence? Several images have been suggested: God mediates, midwifes, facilitates, sees to, carries the mail, greases the skids for, puts in force, or completes the connection *(šālēm)* between sin and consequence. God's personal anger may be said to be a "seeing to" this movement from deed to consequence that is the moral order. In some texts God takes a more active role, at other times a more passive, withdrawing role (e.g., delivering them into the hands of their enemies, Isa 64:6-7; Ps 81:11-12).[24] A related image is God's giving people up, reflected in many Old Testament texts (e.g., Ps 81:11-16; see also Isa 34:2; 43:28; 47:6; 64:7; Jer 29:21; Rom 1:24-28). This "giving up" is not an arbitrary divine act, but a giving the people up to the consequences of their own choices. Ezekiel 22:31 is a striking text in this respect. God declares: "I have consumed them with the fire of my wrath." What that entails is immediately stated: "I have returned *[nātan]* their conduct upon their heads."[25] Again, such language is witness to an intrinsic relationship between sinful deed and consequence.

This dynamic understanding of sin and its effects can also be observed in the use of the verb *pāqad*, "visit." Its translation as "punish" in NRSV is often problematic, as in Jer 21:14: "I will punish you according to the fruit of your doings." A more literal translation is clearer: "I will visit upon you the fruit of your doings" (see 5:9; 14:10).[26] It needs to be considered whether the word *punish* is ever an appropriate translation of the verb *pāqad* (see also the related noun *peqûdāh*, often translated "punishment," e.g., Jer 46:21).[27]

While the understanding of sin-consequence in these texts could be expressed in language such as "your sin will find you out," or "you reap whatever you sow" (Num 32:23; Gal 6:7), God is not removed from the connection between sin and consequence; Israel's understanding of God is not deistic. But, generally speaking, judgment is not something that God introduces into the sinful situation, such as imposing a penalty specified in the law; rather, God mediates the consequences that are intrinsic to the wickedness itself.[28] God thereby sees to the moral order—a reality that God has built into the very structures of creation. In other words, given the interrelatedness of all creatures, Israel's sin generates certain snowballing effects or negative "fallout." At the same time, God is active in the interplay of human sinful actions and their effects, and "third parties" may be used by God as agents for that judgment (e.g., the Assyrians). Both divine and creaturely factors are interwoven to produce the judgmental result. In more modern terms, our own sin and the sins of our forebears press in upon us, but no less the hand of God. For history is our judgment and God enables history—carrying the world along, with a personal attentiveness in view of a relationship of consequence. God's salvific will remains intact in everything, and God's gracious concern is always for the best; but in a given situation the best that God may be able to offer is burning the chaff to fertilize the field for a new crop.[29]

This moral order does not function in any mechanistic, precise, or inevitable way; it is not a tight causal weave. And so it may be that the wicked will prosper (Jer 12:1), at least for a time, and the innocent will suffer for unknown reasons (Job) or get caught up in the effects of the sins of others, as we have noted. Ecclesiastes 9:11 even introduces an element of chance or randomness in relating human deeds to their effects: "time and chance happen to them all." God is to some degree subject to this just order (see Abraham's question in Gen 18:25), though this cannot be factored out except to say that the looseness of the causal weave allows God to be at work in the "system" without violating or (temporarily) suspending it and, in these terms, God is certainly an agent.

This point leads back to Israel's understanding that roots its own law in a creation theology.[30] And so Israel's violation of matters relating to social justice, and God's wrath related thereto, cannot finally be reduced to matters of covenant. *God's creation is at stake in Israel's behaviors, not simply their more specific relationship with God.*

The Oracles against the Nations

Divine judgment is also directed against foreign nations.[31] Prophetic oracles against the nations (OAN)[32] are remarkably common (e.g., Isaiah 13–23; Jeremiah 46–51; Ezekiel 25–32; Amos 1–2; Nahum; Obadiah). A motivation for the announced judgments often focuses on issues of human justice, especially in the conduct of war, including wars against Israel (Isa 10:12, 25; Jer 10:25; 50:25; 51:45, 49; Ezek 25:14, 17; 36:1-7; Amos 1–2; Nahum; Obadiah; Zech 1:14-15; 8:2; see also Pss 2:5, 12; 56:7; 79:5-7; 110:5).[33] Such a perspective roots these texts not in any covenantal understanding (no covenants between God and these nations are in view) but in a creation theology. Knowledge regarding matters such as social justice is believed to be available to those outside Israel, in terms of which they can be held accountable. In the pattern established throughout the prophets, human evil *(rā'āh)* issues in divinely mediated disaster *(rā'āh)*, not simply for Israel but for all nations.[34] One after another, these nations are held responsible for who they are and what they have done, and they will suffer the consequences. No matter the justifications or defenses or excuses they might bring to the case, they will not be able to escape from the effects of their own behaviors. No matter how great their empires, how sophisticated their policies, how brilliant their officials, God will hold them accountable.[35] The OAN demonstrate that God's purposes at work in and through these nations are universal in scope. God's work has the world in view. Again and again, the parallels between Israel and the nations are drawn out; all nations, chosen or nonchosen, are subject to the created moral order.

That the predominant theme of the OAN as well as the oracles against Israel is one of judgment bespeaks a word to Israel: God is consistent in the way in which God acts in the world. God's word of judgment against Israel is not rooted in caprice but is part and parcel of God's ways with the nations more generally. Hence, Israel would not be able to claim that God was being unfair, as if they had been divinely singled out for judgment and held to a higher standard of behavior than other nations. On the other hand, the nations could not claim unfairness either, as if God played favorites and never visited the chosen people with judgment. All nations are accountable to God and God works consistently among them in terms of sin and its consequences (e.g., Egypt for its pride and militarism, Jer 46:8).

That God, however, is not the only effective agency in these disastrous events is made clear by the divine judgment on *Babylon* (Jer 25:12-14; 50–51; see Isa 47:6-7; Zech 1:15). In effect, Babylon exceeded its mandate, going beyond its proper activities as a divine agent for judgment, and committed iniquity itself in making the land an "everlasting waste." The exercise of wrath against Babylonian excessiveness shows that God did not micromanage their actions; they retained the power to make decisions and execute policies that flew in the face of the will of God. The will and purpose of God active in these events (cf. Jer 49:20, 30) is not "irresistible."[36] In some sense God risks what the Babylonians will do with the mandate they have been given. One element of that risk is that God's name will become associated with the violence, indeed the excessive violence, of the Babylonians.[37]

It is not uncommon that communities of faith reduce God to the God of their particular domain. For example, it may be claimed that God's only or primary business is to look after Christian folk. God's presence and activity elsewhere in the world, while probably professed in a general way (e.g., God is omnipresent), is seldom fully acknowledged or seriously woven into reflections regarding God and the larger world of peoples and nations. But these OAN testify that God is not simply present to all peoples, God is actively at work among them in the pursuance of God's purposes for the world. Some such creational claim is probably the most fundamental theological grounding for these oracles. To put it succinctly: God is present on every occasion and active in every event. All people have experienced God's presence and activity in their lives. They may not realize it, of course, but God's activity has indeed been effective among them.

This universal reach of the divine purpose means that the issue addressed by these OAN is not to claim that God rules over the nations (see Jer 46:18; 51:57) but that God is about the restoration of the entire creation. Jeremiah's call, for example, specifies that he is appointed "over nations and over kingdoms" as a "prophet to the nations," not simply for the purpose of judgment but also "to build and to plant" (1:5, 10). In several subsequent Jeremiah texts, God is portrayed as being at work among the nations for purposes of restoration and salvation (e.g., 3:17; 12:14-16; 16:19-21; cf. 18:7-10, "a nation or a kingdom"). Amos 9:7 fits this understanding, as God is imaged as acting in a salvific way on behalf of nonchosen folk such as the Philistines and Aramaeans (see Zech 8:22-23; Isa 45:14, 22-23; 56:3-8; 66:18-19, 23).[38] The God of the prophets is no local deity, concerned simply about the people of Israel. God is the Creator God, the "God of all flesh" (Jer 32:27; see 25:31; 45:5), who works out the divine purposes for the entire creation in and through the movements of nations and peoples. God is interested in these nations for who they are in themselves, not simply in their relationship to Israel. At the same time, *the particularity of God's work in and through Israel remains intact amid the universality of God's work among the nations*.

The OAN in Jeremiah are remarkable in their repeated reference to the nations as God's "daughter" (Jer 46:11, 19, 24; 48:18; 49:4; 50:42; cf. Isa 23:12; 47:1). Israel is referred to in such terms, of course (Jer 6:23; 18:13; 31:4, 21), but it is theologically significant that Israelites are not the only people who are considered to be the children of God. These references are testimony to God as Creator of all people; as such, God as parent is concerned about the welfare of all of God's children, not just God's elect. And that divine concern will be manifested not only in terms of judgment but in terms of salvation (in the broadest sense of the term). God will even so act on behalf of the Egyptians, who are, ironically, called "my people" (Isa 19:20-25; cf. Jer 46:26; Ezek 29:13-14); other nations come into the view of such a promise as well (Jer 48:47; 49:6, 39). All peoples are God's children and God's choice of Israel is ultimately for the sake of every one of these children.

Amos's Creation Doxologies

The eighth-century prophet Amos, the first of the writing prophets, speaks often of creational matters. The book as a whole is bracketed by the theme of creation, moving as it does from the withering of vegetation before the judgment of God (1:2) to the thriving of the vineyards in the wake of the new creative action of God (9:11-15). Moreover, the universal reach of God's judgmental activity against the nations at the beginning of the book (1:3–2:3) is matched by the universal presence and activity of God among the nations in the concluding chapter (9:1-8). Along the way, Amos's sharp words to an unfaithful people link creation and judgment in a startling way.

In several texts the creation theme is presented in hymnic fashion in the context of strong oracles of indictment and judgment (4:13; 5:8-9; 9:5-6; cf. 8:7-10).[39] These hymnic segments interweave themes of originating creation (5:8*a*; perhaps also 4:13*a*; 9:6*a*, though see NRSV) and continuing creation, demonstrating that God's creative work is ongoing and exhibits continuity across the ages (cf. the use of creation themes in the Psalms and Second Isaiah). They have been called "doxologies of judgment,"[40] each of which uses the phrase, "the Lord (the God of hosts) is his name." Their purpose has been variously described, including "to motivate repentance and covenant renewal,"[41] to emphasize "the power and might of the omnipotent God of creation whom Israel is about to confront in final judgment,"[42] and to "acknowledge . . . God's just judgment" and the divine "responsibility both for the enduring, predictable side of this world . . . as well as for its changing, unexpected occurrences."[43] I suggest here a somewhat different way of articulating the purpose of these doxologies.

We have seen above that the moral order is fundamentally a matter of creation, built into the very infrastructure of God's cosmic design. That sins will have adverse consequences is fundamentally a matter of the way in which the world works; ill effects are intrinsically related to the deed. And so, it is a natural theological move for the prophet to follow the strong indictment and oracles of judgments (experienced and anticipated) with a word about creation.

God is certainly involved in these ongoing workings of the created order, mediating the movement from sins to their effects; indeed, the texts often use the first person to speak of such divine involvement. And so Amos 4:4-12, climaxing with a claim about God the Creator (4:13), contains a string of verbs with God as subject: I gave, withheld, struck, laid waste, sent, killed, carried away, and overthrew. Most, if not all, of these actions relate to the natural order (famine; drought; blight and mildew; locusts; pestilence/plagues; the destruction of Sodom and Gomorrah) as effects of human sinfulness.[44] Those who live in these environmentally troubled times should have no difficulty in discerning the link between such natural catastrophes and human sinfulness (see the opening paragraphs of this chapter). God has mediated these adverse effects on the natural order before (cf. Hos 4:1-3) and is about to do so again (v. 12). The concluding statement about creation (v. 13) makes clear that the reader is to think of the foregoing divine involvement as a matter of God personally tending to the created moral order, not arbitrarily imposing a series of sanctions (cf. Hos 4:1-3).

The doxology in 5:8-9 seems interruptive in its context, but that is less the case if creational themes are seen as integral to talk about judgment.[45] The doxology is preceded by a lament for the death of the nation (5:1-2) and a call to "seek the LORD and live" or suffer the consequences of God "breaking out" and "devouring" (5:3-7); the doxology is followed by more indictments, oracles of judgment, and exhortations (5:10-17). God the Creator, who acts in creation to turn "deep darkness into the morning, / and darkens the day into night," has created the world in such a way as to make "destruction flash out against the strong, / so that destruction comes upon the fortress" (5:8-9). As certainly as Pleiades and Orion (probably related to weather patterns),[46] darkness and light, day and night work according to their created ordering, so also will God mediate adverse effects upon those who "trample on the poor / and take from them levies of grain" (5:11; cf. Job 5:8-16; 9:5-10). The larger context picks up the theme of justice especially (5:7, 10-15; 5:21–6:14). This theme is fundamentally creational in orientation; the absence of justice in Israel disrupts not only the social order but also the cosmic order. The people have polluted the land through their lack of care and concern for the needy and disadvantaged (cf. Jer 3:1-5, which links human wickedness with adverse cosmic effects; Joel 2:10).

Amos 8:7-10 may be of some help in working this issue through.[47] Because of human wickedness, the earth will be affected (8:7-8). The relationship between verses 8 and 9 is striking. Events in the celestial sphere, probably a solar eclipse (v. 9), are made parallel to the adverse effects of sin on the human community (v. 10).[48] As such events occur in the natural order so will human sinfulness have such negative effects on Israel. These realities are all of one piece: the divinely mediated working out of the created order of things. It is noteworthy that the theme of justice returns in this context (8:4-6) and those verses introduce the creational themes.

The context of Amos 9:5-6 again helps the reader to see the function of the doxologies. A key point of 9:1-4 is that the judgment will be universally effective; there can be no escape from the judgment to be visited upon the people. God then grounds that word in a claim about the Creator God, who has a universal reach, whose touch extends across the entire face of the cosmos (9:5-6). Amos 9:7 is an extension of the same point, namely, that God is the God of all peoples, acting in the stories of nonchosen nations. Nothing escapes "the eyes of the Lord" (vv. 4, 8; cf. Prov 5:21; 15:3), a theme that brackets the doxology. This point has been sharply introduced in the opening chapters of the book, namely, that judgment is experienced by all peoples, not just Israel (1:3–2:16). Again, the sheer worldwide range of divine activity is related to claims made about the Creator God.

All of these texts about the created order fit well with the description of the new creation at the end of Amos (9:11-15). This text is bracketed by the ill effects of human sinfulness on the environment in Amos 1:2. One of the characteristics of this new world is that *the natural order* will be rid of the adverse effects of human sinfulness. Even more, the creation will function in ways that outstrip God's original creational intentions. The vineyards will be so productive that human efforts will not be able to keep up with the abundance. There is no return to Eden here, no myth of the eternal return. The prophets move beyond Eden in their vision of the future.[49]

Amos's recurrent use of references to the natural order and the linkage he draws to human words and deeds cannot be reduced to poetic imagery. This language is "not just hyperbole. Rather, the prophets employ numerous cosmic metaphors to underscore the significance of the historical events that occasion their oracles."[50] The word *metaphor* is appropriate here, providing one does not deny continuity between language and reality, recognizing the yes as well as the no in all metaphoric language.[51] The natural order is *actually* affected by human behaviors; social order and cosmic order are in fact deeply interrelated. Even more, we see again that to so depict the human predicament in cosmic terms lends a depth to the human situation that catches up the entire environment. Those of us who live in this environmentally troubled time should have no difficulty seeing the truth of this remarkably rich interrelatedness of social and cosmic orders.

Creation and Judgment in Jeremiah

The book of Jeremiah voices a concern for creational issues more commonly than is generally recognized.[52] In this segment I review the more basic perspectives on creation in Jeremiah and then use a close study of Jeremiah 12 as a way of illustrating the special interest in the land on the part of the prophet.

The following theological claims regarding creation are basic to Jeremiah.[53]

1. ***God "made the earth"*** (Jer 33:2; cf. 10:12-13= 51:15-16; 27:5; 32:17) and continues to uphold the "fixed orders" of creation (31:35-36; 33:20, 25). Such "fixed orders" refer to the great rhythms of creation (the sea, sun, moon, stars, day, night; see Gen 8:22). But, notably, this

language does not bespeak a mechanistic world or a divinely determined one, for the land can become desolate and mourn, the animals and birds can be swept away (12:4), and human behaviors can wreak havoc in God's good creation, and with impunity (12:1). God does not "control" or micromanage the world, however much God's actions are deemed to be effective.

This perspective regarding the world entails an openness in the "system" that allows for genuine creaturely decision making and (lack of) responsiveness. Again and again in Jeremiah, the people are given choices that will shape their future, which in turn will shape the future of all other creatures as well as the future of God (God will do different things depending on what creatures do). The various "if, if not" constructions in Jeremiah (12:14-17; 17:24-27; 21:8-10; 22:1-5; 38:17-18; 42:9-17) demonstrate such an openness to the future. God "plants" the people, but it is they who take root, grow, and bring forth fruit (12:2). What creatures "grow up into" and the fruit they bear make a difference both for themselves and for their world, for good or for ill. People can make God's "pleasant portion / a desolate wilderness" (12:10); the God who is "near" and "far" (23:23) can be "far from their hearts" (12:2); and Babylonian armies can exceed their divine mandate with devastating effects upon land and people (12:14; see 8:16; 25:11-14; 51:24). From another perspective, there is room for an incalculable and frustrating randomness in God's created order (e.g., Jer 12:1, the "way of the guilty" can prosper) so that no theory of retribution (or any other) can "explain" the way the world works.

2. ***God "fills heaven and earth"*** (Jer 23:23-24). At the least, this means that God is present and relational to all that is not God, whether "near by" or "far off" (in creaturely terms). Inasmuch as God "fills heaven and earth," the latter exist as realities to be filled; hence, all creatures are a genuine "other" to God. Given the comprehensive character of "heaven and earth," the divine relationship with the other is not limited to the human sphere. God as the "God of all flesh" is one formulation in Jeremiah that moves this relationship beyond the human (32:27). Moreover, that the desolate land mourns *to* God (12:11; see 4:28; 23:10; Joel 1:10, 20) demonstrates that it has a relationship with God that is independent of God's relationship to the human (see Job 38–41; Pss 104:21, 27; 145:15-16; 147–48). That God in turn addresses the land (16:19; see 22:29) also evidences such an independent relationship. Such language regarding the nonhuman cannot be reduced to figurative

speech, poetic license, or worshipful exuberance. Rather, this language of interresponsiveness shows that God's presence to and relationship with the earth and its creatures is more than external; there is an inwardness or interiority characteristic of the earth and its creatures such that a genuine relationship with God exists. To speak in this way does not necessarily lead to a panpsychism or vitalism, only that some kind of *internal* relationship with God is claimed.[54]

3. ***This relational God has created a relational world.*** An interrelatedness exists among all creatures for Jeremiah (and for Israel). The world could be imaged as a giant spiderweb. Every creature is in relationship with every other, such that any act reverberates out and affects the whole, shaking the entire web in varying degrees of intensity. This may be illustrated by the virtual drumbeat of Jeremiah that moral order affects creational order, though not mechanistically or inevitably. Again and again, we read how human sin has an adverse effect upon the earth, indeed upon the entire cosmos. Because of human wickedness it does not rain (2:12; 3:3; 5:24-25; 14:4), the land is made desolate (12:10-11; see 23:10), the animals and birds are swept away (12:4; see 4:25; 9:10; 14:5-7; Hos 4:3; Zeph 1:3), and the land is polluted (3:2, 9; 16:18; see 2:7; Isa 24:5) and mourns (12:4; see 4:28; 23:10; Isa 24:4-7; 33:9; Hos 4:3; Joel 1:10-20) to God (12:11). Indeed, the entire earth and heavens seem to be reduced to a precreation state of being (4:23-26), though that very context (v. 27) insists that no "full end" of the earth is in view.[55] Modern understandings of the interrelatedness of the ecosystem connect well with these biblical insights.

4. ***The God of Jeremiah is no aloof God,*** somehow present and related but detached. God is a God of great passions (pathos); deep and genuine divine feelings and emotions are manifest again and again. Sorrow, lament, weeping, wailing, grief, pain, anguish, heartache, regret, and anger all are ascribed to God in Jeremiah.[56] While these divine passions are focused on an unfaithful people, the earth and its creatures also get caught up into God's vulnerable heart. To God, Israel and its land are "my house . . . my heritage . . . the beloved of my heart . . . my vineyard . . . my portion . . . my pleasant portion" (12:7-10; see Ps 50:10-11). This recurrent "my" shows that the relationship God has with people and land is not perfunctory in character; God is deeply involved in their lives and is profoundly affected by that engagement.

At the same time, this display of divine emotion is no sentimental or romantic matter. God manifests not only sorrow (12:7; see 3:19-20; 9:10,

17-18[E]; 13:17) but also sword-wielding anger (12:12-13; see 4:26; 7:20). Indeed, into the midst of this language of closeness and possession comes the strong expression of hate (12:8; see 44:4; Amos 5:21; Hos 9:15). As we know from close interhuman relationships, the sharp juxtaposition of love and hate indicates something of the trauma of this broken relationship for God. These are emotions of great intensity, evidencing the depth to which God's own "heart and soul" are affected (see 32:41) by what has happened to the people and to the land.

This considerable detail regarding the importance of creation in Jeremiah provides the theological grounding for the understanding of Jeremiah as "a prophet to the nations" (1:5, 10) as well as the variety of ways in which the nations become the subject of various oracles (especially chs. 25, 46–51). Because God is the God of all creation, God is the God of all peoples and nations. God is present and active among them, even though they may not recognize this to be the case. Moreover, God's purposes for all creation include these various peoples (cf. 12:14-17; 18:7-10), whether as agents for judgment (see above), as objects of judgment (cf. 10; 25; 50–51), or as objects of divine deliverance (see 3:17; 4:2; 16:19-21; 46:26; 48:47; 49:8, 39).

A Close Study of Jeremiah 12

Jeremiah 12 provides a concentrated look at the importance of creational issues for the prophet.[57] Jeremiah 12:1-4 has long been considered a confession/lament of the prophet.[58] The charge that Jeremiah puts before God (12:1) is focused on the injustice of the prosperity of the wicked; he urges God to give them their just due (12:3). But the rationale for his argument is not fully apparent until 12:4. The lament climactically moves to an appeal to God on behalf of the land and its nonhuman inhabitants ("How long?"). God's response (12:5-17), while initially addressing Jeremiah's personal concerns (12:5-6), moves in 12:7-17 to focus on Jeremiah's concern about the land.

This perspective may be supported by Jeremiah's use of imagery regarding the land in verse 2. The land on which God planted these people (Israel) is a bountiful land (see 2:7, 21; 11:17). This land has had a life-giving capacity to enable them—even the wicked!—to take root and thrive (v. 2; "it rains on the just and the unjust"). But the "hearts" of the guilty and treacherous, unlike Jeremiah's "heart" (v. 3*a*), are bearing the fruits of wickedness (see above discussion; 6:19; 17:10; 21:14). One such fruit is devastation for the land (v. 4), a virtual refrain in Jeremiah (e.g., 2:8; 3:2-3; 4:26; 9:12[E]; see Hos 4:1-3). The land is not the problem; the issue is the people who live on it. In the wake of their wickedness, the land, which could take the occasional drought in stride (see 17:7-8), has become a veritable dust bowl (see 14:2-6). What kind of divine justice is it that the wicked can have such effects on the land and apparently get away with it? In this reading, Jeremiah's personal situation is seen as part and parcel of the situation faced also by the land. Both mourn because of the fruits of the wicked.[59]

And so Jeremiah, whose wrath conforms to the wrath of God (6:11; 15:17), urges God to pull the wicked out of circulation from among God's sheep—violently (v. 3). May they be led to the slaughter as they have led him (11:19)! Remove them from the land—not only for his sake but also for the sake of the land. How long must the land mourn? Only by removing this people from the land can the land be saved. Because of them the land mourns. The grass of *every* field withers. The animals and the birds are swept away. And the people deny any connection between this situation and their sin (v. 4*c*; see 5:12). God does take some responsibility for this situation for the land (v. 7), as we will see, but this is because of the prior reality—"the wickedness of those who live" on the land (v. 4*b*).

The translations of verse 4*a* vary in view of the fact that the same verbal root may mean both "mourn" and "dry up" (see Isa 24:4). But "mourn" is the usual focus of the verbal root and it clearly has that meaning with land as subject in 4:28, where it is parallel with the verb "grow black" (see Joel 1:9-10). Probably both meanings are in view. The verb may pertain concretely to drought and desertification (see the parallel with "wither," also in 23:10). Yet, such a reference does not sufficiently attend to the land as a genuine subject in a larger lament-filled context. The land mourns not only because it is drying up but also because it has been polluted by Israel's infidelities, devastated by foreign invasions, and forsaken by God. The land joins with Jeremiah and God in lamenting what has happened to the land. Even the people, stretched to the limit, can join in (14:2).

God's response first focuses on Jeremiah's personal situation (vv. 5-6; cf. 15:19) and then centers more comprehensively on the land and God's response to the wicked about whom Jeremiah has complained (vv. 7-13). The initial reply contains an enigmatic reference to the land as a "safe land" (v. 5*b*; or "land of peace"); it may be a proverbial reference to the land. In verse 12 the land is not at peace ("safe") anymore. The point is that the land is a land of peace compared to what it will become; if Jeremiah has difficulty now, how will he fare when things really get rough (= "thickets of the Jordan")? If Jeremiah thinks that family/friends (= "foot-runners") have been difficult (see 11:18-23), and God admits they have been (v. 6; cf. v. 2*b*), what will he do when all the wicked in Israel (= riders on horses) descend on him?

Verses 7-13 continue God's response to Jeremiah, whose concern for the land (v. 4) now becomes the focus of divine consideration; appropriately, the wicked are also in view. As noted, these verses are a *divine lament*, not an announcement of judgment—which seems to be already in progress.[60] God's lament over the land matches Jeremiah's lament in verse 4; indeed, the land itself laments and that lamenting has reached the heart of God (v. 11). People have not laid to heart the suffering of the land (v. 11), but God's heart (v. 7) has been deeply touched by it. At the same time, God's forsaking action is also complicit in these developments for the land (see Ps 107:33-34).

This focus on the land is especially evident in the use of the word *heritage (nahălāh)*, God's own possession, used five times in this chapter.[61] The word usually refers to Canaan in Jeremiah, as God's gift to Israel or God's own possession (2:7; 3:19; 16:18; 17:4; 50:11). The word may also refer to the people as God's possession (v. 8; 10:16; see Deut 9:29; 32:9). Norman C. Habel understands the word in terms of a God-people-land "symbiosis." In Jeremiah 12, *heritage* usually refers to the land (vv. 7, 9, 14-15); in verse 8 it refers to the people—whom God hates because they lift up their voice "against me." *Heritage* is best focused on the land in this text but extended to incorporate the people of the land; both are God's own possession. God's "house" may refer to temple, land, or people and all may be in view in this text.[62] God's forsaking is comprehensive in scope; God has left temple, land, and people. Readers would recall that temple and land are interrelated. From this sanctuary, God's special dwelling place in the land, blessings flow out into all the land (e.g., Psalm 132). But if God forsakes the temple (see Ezek 8:6), then it no longer has the capacity for blessing.

Jeremiah 12:10 uses "my" language again—"my vineyard" (2:21; 5:10; 6:9; see Isa 5:1-7) and "my (pleasant) portion," a variant formulation of *nahălāh* that reiterates that the land is God's land. It is striking that, with all these "my" references affirming divine ownership of the land, God cannot take care of the land any better than this. But, as noted above,

God's way of possessing does not entail "control." God delegates responsibility for the land to others, with all the attendant risks, and will not micromanage their handling of their duties, intervening to make sure every little thing is done correctly. This way of relating to people and world reveals a divine vulnerability, for God opens the divine self up to hurt should things go wrong—and we hear that hurt expressed here in anguished tones.

God's lament begins with a virtual refrain regarding what God has done with respect to the land and people. God has forsaken (9:2[E]; 25:38), but this is not a divine initiative; God has forsaken because the people have forsaken God (2:13, 17, 19; 5:7, 19). God has abandoned (7:29; 23:33, 39), but (again) because the people have abandoned God (15:6). God has given them over to their enemies (as in 21:7) because of their wickedness. Notice the passive language in verse 7; God gives them over to the effects of their sins (see Isa 54:7-8; 64:7). It is important, however, not to claim too much for the divine abandonment. It is not that "God's withdrawal has caused fertility to end and exposes the land . . . to chaos,"[63] but that the already devastating effects of the people's wickedness are thereby brought to completion in the moral order, which God mediates. Also, to assert that "Yahweh has withdrawn fidelity" suggests that God is not faithful in judgment; judgment may in fact be the only way in which God can be faithful in this particular situation.[64]

Jeremiah 12:8 specifies the key factor in this divine move; Israel has become like a lion to God. Heretofore, the lion metaphor has usually been used for the foe from the north that will devour Israel (e.g., 2:15; 4:7; 5:6; see 5:17). But in this text, as in Israel's persecution of the prophets (2:30), Israel has turned on God like a roaring lion, making God its prey. This self-identification of God as prey is remarkable! But God is not a victim, for God is not without significant resources. In response God "hates," that is, God treats Israel as enemy and sends in the lions and other wild animals.

Inasmuch as these are animals of the land, to label the land a "victim" is not adequate; the animals bring resources to fight for the land (see above on animals as servants). Heretofore, other preying animals have been used to speak, literally and metaphorically, of God's instruments of judgment (wolf, leopard, snakes, 5:6; 8:17). That list is expanded with the use of hyenas and birds of prey, indeed God calls "all" the wild animals to be instruments of judgment (v. 9). The hyena image in verse 9*a* (the translation is uncertain) probably implies that the land has been so polluted by its inhabitants (see 2:7; 3:2) that it has become food only for such scavengers. The hyena greedily moves in on its prey while the vultures circle above, and God commands other animals to join in the devouring of Israel (15:3; see 5:17).

A what-goes-around-comes-around understanding informs this text (see above discussion). The people have become lions to God, and hence the lions will attack them. They have made God their prey and hence they will become prey. At the same time, the land gets caught in the middle; it too becomes prey. In God's repetitive, personal, and emotion-laden words (vv. 10-11): the land has become desolate, desolate, desolate, desolate! The land gets hit from several sides. One, it suffers from drought, so that farmers reap only weeds and thorns (vv. 4, 13; 3:3; 5:23-25; 14:2-6; see Gen 3:18). Two, Israel's wickedness and neglect adversely affect the land (vv. 8, 11; see 2:7; 3:2-3). Three, invading armies (v. 10)[65] trample on the land and its vineyards, destroying crops and making the land a wilderness (vv. 10-11; see 2:15; 4:7, 26-27; 9:10-12[E]; 10:22). They have entered into the land across every caravan route (or every hill, v. 12) and plundered it. Four, God is active in and through all these desolating events for the land (vv. 7, 9, 12-13). "No one shall be safe" (v. 12), perhaps especially the land!

Readers, who are apt to focus on the effects of these judgments on people, should ponder the sheer force of all of these agents arrayed against the land. The land doesn't stand a chance and becomes prey. In this respect, the land is like the people but is more like God. Like God! Land and God are both undeserving of what has happened to them. The land shares with God the status of "prey." Land and God are also alike in that both mourn. But, while there is this mutuality in mourning over what has happened, there is a deep inequality as well: the land mourns to God (v. 11), but God is able to marshal resources for this moment that the land cannot.

But Jeremiah's (and the readers!) questions in verse 4 now return, only in a higher decibel. What kinds of resources does God bring? Why is God lamenting? Is not God also to blame? Doesn't God make things even worse for the land? After all, God has forsaken and abandoned; God has hated; God has commanded the "animals" to gather over the corpse that is Israel. And now (v. 12), it is *God's* sword that devours the people from one end of the land to the other and no one is safe. As verse 13 puts it, the "fierce anger of the LORD" has been a key factor in what has occurred. Given *God's* actions, the land is mourning even more now. God's sword-wielding anger across the length and breadth of the land has resulted in a land that is more devastated and desolate (v. 12). How long will the land mourn? Jeremiah had asked God to pull the people out of the land for the sake of the land (vv. 3-4). God's response in vv. 7-13 is that the resolution of Jeremiah's lament is more complicated than Jeremiah (and often readers) thinks.

Yes, Jeremiah is right, the people must be uprooted from the land for the sake of the land, but that end cannot be accomplished with a divine flick of the wrist. The enemies of God and land cannot be dealt with in a moment, with no collateral damage. God's sword does not cut clean, for God has chosen to relate to the world through means that are available—and only violent means may be available—rather than do things "all by himself" (see above on agency). And God does not perfect people before working through them, including armies led by "my servant" Nebuchadnezzar (25:9; 27:6). And so, God responds to the mourning of Jeremiah and the land, but it will take a complex series of often violent events to bring about a "land of peace" once again.

This divine move may sound suspect, but we are helped in thinking about it by the other dimension of God's response to the situation, namely, grief. The personal, emotional, and repetitious language shows how much this is a genuine loss for God. Given the divine commitment to people and land and the centuries-long relationship with them, God cannot (!) respond indifferently. God is truly caught up in what has happened here and mourns the loss. Abraham J. Heschel captures this thought well: "With Israel's distress came the affliction of God, His displacement, His homelessness in the land, in the world. . . . Should Israel cease to be home, then God, we might say, would be without a home in the world."[66] Yes, God forsakes and abandons and gives over the land with its people, but at tremendous loss for God. Yet, divine suffering is necessary for the sake of a future for the land (see 31:20; Isa 54:7-8), and verses 14-17 begin to address that issue.

Verses 14-17 speak to a question that exilic readers may have asked: will the invaders who plundered people and land get away with it? As noted, these verses could also be understood as a response to Jeremiah's lament: How long will the land mourn? In an exilic context, Jeremiah's question about the wicked (v. 1) would be expanded to include the overreaching, proud Babylonians and their allies and their mistreatment of the land (see v. 14; 25:11-14; 50:29; 51:24). These marauders have not spoken the last word about the land. God has a future for the land beyond all of this desolation, and these verses begin to address that. Jeremiah's book of consolation will continue this theme, for example, 30:16:

> all who devour you shall be devoured,
> . . . .
> those who plunder you shall be plundered,
> and all who prey on you I will make a prey.

(More positively, see 31:5, 12, 14; 32:41-44; 33:10-13; 50:19.) The land *will* become a "land of peace" once again.

Continuing the use of the personal "my" (12:14), God announces judgment on "my evil neighbors." These nations surrounding Israel, especially Babylon, had "plundered" the heritage (so NAB; the NRSV translation "touch" seems weak). Notably, God refers to them as "my" evil neighbors; God includes himself in the Israelite community and a resident of its land! The enemies of Israel and its land are God's enemies. The nations that God used to "pluck up" Israel will now themselves be plucked up (see 1:10; 18:7-10). This verb also refers to the people of Israel (= the house of Judah) whom God will "pluck up" (in a positive sense) from the nations where they have been dispersed. The third usage of this verb (v. 15) seems to refer to all ("everyone") whom God has uprooted in the past, whether the nations or the house of Judah. God will have compassion on them, and return them again to their heritage/land. Hence, the focus on land is finally not simply on the land of promise but on the heritage/land of all peoples. God's concern about land has universal dimensions (see the positive words in the OAN, 46:26; 48:47; 49:6, 39). Jeremiah is truly a prophet to the nations (1:5, 10).

Then, 12:16-17 seem to refer solely to the "evil neighbors" upon whom God has had compassion and has returned to their homelands. They are to learn the ways of Yahweh as assiduously as they had earlier taught the people of Israel to worship Baal and swear by that god. If they do this, they shall be built up in the midst of God's people (again, see 1:10). If they will not listen, then God will uproot that people from their land and destroy them. This conditional future offered to the other nations is at least in part for the sake of the future of God's own people and God's own land. The implication to be drawn with respect to Israel and the land seems to be this: Never again!

God's purposes in the world must be conceived in relation to the story of all of God's creatures, including the land. Using Isaiah's language (65:17-25; see 11:6-9), God is creating a new earth and it will be populated by animals, vegetation, and people (see Hos 2:18-23). Comparably, the salvation oracles of Jeremiah are remarkably inclusive in their orientation, including non-Israelites (e.g., 3:17; 12:14-17; cf. 29:7) and the land itself (31:5, 12, 14, 27; 32:42-44; 33:10-13; 50:19). When the trumpet sounds and God rides the cloud chariots into a new heaven and a new earth, the children will come singing, leading wolves and leopards, and playing among the snakes. And they will not hurt or destroy, for God will, finally, "give rest to the earth" (50:34; see Isa 14:7; 51:3) and all creatures will "shout for joy" (Jer 51:48).[67]

Creation and Salvation in the Prophets

I focus in this segment on Isaiah 40–55, while drawing in other prophetic texts along the way. Creation is a theme more frequent in the oracles of Isaiah 40–55 than in any other prophet.[68] This frequency is likely the case because of the historical situation into which the oracles were addressed—deep into the Babylonian exile (ca. 550–540 B.C.E.). These oracles are a proclamation to a dispirited people of Israel, still reeling from the devastations wrought by Babylon's armies, deeply wondering, even despairing whether they had any future (Isa 49:14; 40:27). What word from God would be most fitting for a people in such a situation? From the perspective of Isaiah 40–55, a word regarding creation is crucial if the situation is to be appropriately addressed.

Creation verbs are common in Isaiah 40–55 compared to Isaiah 1–39 or Isaiah 56–66.[69] At the same time, creation themes in Isaiah 1–39 canonically ground the emphasis in Isaiah 40–55 (e.g., Isa 2:1-4; 11:6-9; 24–27), and Isaiah 56–66 will extend them to include foreigners (56:1-8; 60:10-16; cf. 66:18-20) and a vision of the creation of "new heavens and a new earth" (Isa 65:17; 66:22). The book of Isaiah is bracketed by visions of a new creation (Isaiah 2; 11; 65–66).

The role that creation language plays in Isaiah 40–55 is multifaceted. A key question will help us explore this role: how is the word regarding creation related to Israel's desperate historical situation? A common response takes its cue from the opening verses, echoed throughout: "Comfort, O comfort my people, / says your God" (Isa 40:1-2; see 49:13; 51:3, 12, 19; 52:9; 54:11; cf. 57:18; 61:2; 66:13). This direct word from God is a word designed to comfort the "afflicted, storm-tossed" exiles (Isa 54:11). But, how is a word about creation a comforting word? We here examine the ways in which that claim works itself out with respect to various issues and concerns.

Creation and Israel's Self-Identity

The most urgent aspect of the exile's situation to be addressed was their very identity as human beings in the world and in the sight of God. Their deep failure issuing in destruction and exile led them into the depths of divinely recognized self-deprecation (see 41:14; 42:18-19; 43:8—worms, insects, blind, deaf). Fearful of their own future (41:10, 13-14; 43:1, 5; 44:2, 8; 54:4), they are weighed down by faintheartedness, weariness, and exhaustion (40:29-31; 54:6). Thomas W. Mann puts the question well: "How do you convince people who think of themselves as worms that they are, instead, still the beloved people of God? . . . how do you persuade people who think of themselves as 'nobodies' that they are 'somebodies.'"[70] From Israel's perspective, given its own apostasy, God could set this people aside and move on to others. From the perspective of Isaiah 40–55, a key word to bring to such a dispirited and uncertain people is a word from God regarding who and whose they are: "You are precious in my sight, / and honored, and I love you" (43:4; cf. also 43:1; 44:1-2; 46:3-4; 51:16; 54:8, 11). Such a powerful direct word from God to a people that had deeply failed their God is no objective statement about Israel's identity; it is straightforward proclamation: in spite of all that has happened, you are mine and I love you.

One basic function of Isaiah's use of creation language is to undergird and reinforce this point: God has created you, that is, God has chosen you to be a special people, unlike any other (creation language is not used for any other specific people in Isaiah 40–55). The point is made clear again and again, using several creation verbs: Israel is a people "created for my glory, / whom I formed and made" (43:7; see 43:1, 15, 21; 44:21; 45:9, 11; 51:13). God long ago elected Israel and made promises to this people, and God will be faithful to God's long-standing commitments. Consistent with this creation language is the use of birthing (and rearing) imagery; Israel has been formed in the divine womb (42:14; cf. 46:3-4; 49:19-21; 66:6-13) and "carried from the womb, even to your old age";[71] the God who has made them will continue to bear them and save them throughout their days (46:3-4). From God's own perspective, Israel "will not be forgotten" (44:21); even if, unthinkably, human mothers may forget their children, "I will not forget you" (49:14-15); hence Israel can "forget" the shame of its youth and "remember no more" the disgrace of its youth (54:4). In this connection God links creation language with marriage imagery to designate this relationship, "Your Maker is your husband" (54:5; cf. 62:3-5), assuring Israel that no bill of divorce has been served (50:1-3).

Creation language, related as it is to every stage in Israel's life—from birth to death—is used to speak rich words of comfort and assurance. At a time when Israel has been cut off from its particular history, given to wonder about the value of its *historical* heritage, *creation* language could reach deeply into the substratum of life and thought, into the heart of their very identity as human beings. When the matters to be confronted include the exiles' loss of a sense of worth and place, then a word about creation is of central importance, for only such a word can get at the heart of the issue of human worthwhileness. To hear directly from God that "you are precious in my sight, / and honored" (43:4; cf. 49:5) is to hear God's personal declaration about their value *as human beings*. They are human beings first of all; only then can they properly begin to think about their special place in God's designs for the world. Only from such a creational base can their place as God's people be properly appreciated and discerned. Only from assurances that they are God-formed human beings of value can they begin to speak of hope for the future. Only creation language can fully convey the "conviction that Israel owes the totality of her existence to Yahweh," and not just its redemption.[72]

Even more, the prophet recognizes the *human* dimensions of the exiles' situation in specifically addressing how God will respond to their dispiritedness:

> He gives power to the faint,
>   and strengthens the powerless.
> . . . .
> those who wait for the Lord shall renew their strength,
>   they shall mount up with wings like eagles,
> they shall run and not be weary,
>   they shall walk and not faint. (40:29-31)

(See also 54:6; 57:15; 59:21.) This claim regarding what God is going to do is introduced by strong creation themes (40:28). To speak of such a renewed human spirit will take *a new act of creation* (42:5; 44:3; 48:16)! The interweaving of language about the creation of the world and the creation of Israel throughout Isaiah 40–55 is deliberate and compelling:

just as God created and continues to create the cosmos, so God is committed to bring newness to Israel's spirit and life. Even more, God's commitments to Israel are as sure as God's commitments to the creation itself (see 54:9-10; cf. Jer 31:35-37).[73]

Creation and Exile in a Foreign Land

Israel was being held captive in a land far from home, under the heel of the most powerful world empire of its day and most any other. The exiles certainly had no resources of their own that could bring them freedom; no Israelite armies were available to challenge the hegemony of the Babylonians. In addition, the exiles were confronted with the fact that this nation worshiped gods other than Yahweh. Both the Babylonians and their gods needed attention in such a desperate situation, and a word about creation could get at those issues very well.

The Gods. An argument from creation is important in asserting that there are no gods besides Yahweh, a repeated claim (e.g., 41:21-29; 43:10-13; 44:6-8; 45:5-6, 14, 18, 20-22; 46:9; cf. 47:8, 10). Such a universal claim about God assumes that more than Israel's own idolatry is in mind; the gods of all peoples come into view and are dismissed (40:18-20; 41:21-29; 42:15-17; 43:8-13; 44:9-20; 45:16, 20; 46:1-2, 5-7). It takes a creation-wide perspective in order to make that comprehensive claim. And so the introductory chapter opens the book with interwoven statements about the Creator God and other gods (40:12, 22, 26, 28 with 40:18-20, 25). Various rhetorical questions and imperatives are addressed to the gods (and their adherents), with links to creational themes, to draw out their weakness and falseness (40:12; 41:1-7, 21-29; 44:10-11; 45:9-11, 20-21; 47:12-13; 48:14). Israel's God is not a local god, locked in uncertain competition with the gods of other nations. Yahweh is the God of all creation and hence the claims of other gods and their adherents can be dismissed.

The Nations. Liberation from Babylonian exile can only come from outside of Israel; Cyrus and the Persians are the vehicles presently available to God. In the wake of the rise of the Persian Empire, the vaunted Babylonians, who exceeded the divine mandate (47:1-15), will have no future. The assumption behind the divine declarations about Cyrus in 44:24–45:8 is that of a Creator God, as the explicit creation language beginning and ending this text indicates (44:23-24; 45:7-8).[74] An explicit link between God as Creator of the world and the emergence of Cyrus is also drawn in 45:12-13: "I made the earth / I have aroused Cyrus." A creation theology is necessary in order to make the claim that God is working in and through Cyrus for the deliverance of Israel. That is to say, such a claim necessitates having a God who is active out and about in the world outside Israel, indeed in a world claimed by other gods. God was engaged on behalf of Israel in and through Cyrus and Persians, even though they did not realize it (45:4).[75] And other nations will respond to this new worldwide activity of God and be subservient to God's own people (e.g., 45:14; 49:22-23; cf. 60:4-16; 61:5-6). In Ben C. Ollenburger's words, Isaiah's creation theology "places *all* particular histories within the universal framework of God's good and just creation . . . [and] places the liberation of Israel within the context of God's cosmic plan—within a universal 'world order.' "[76]

That this claim about creation and the nations is foundational for Isaiah 40–55 is evident in the introductory chapter (40:12-31). Images of nature have been used to speak of the transience and weakness of humankind (40:6-8). Then repeated declarations about God as the Creator of the world (40:12, 22, 26, 28) are interwoven with strong statements about the place of all the nations/peoples/princes of the world (40:15-17, 22-24). These nations may constitute a huge obstacle in Israel's eyes as it contemplates its own future, but to God they are negligible, "small-time stuff." The litany is remarkable; compared to God (40:25) they are nothing, even less than nothing, a drop in the bucket, dust on the scales, grasshoppers, and stubble (40:15-24). This assessment is grounded in claims about God as the Creator, who both originates the world and its creatures and continues the creative task. This claim is generalized elsewhere: Yahweh, the redeemer of Israel, is the "God of the whole earth" (54:5) and the "Maker" of all peoples (45:11-12). It is this Creator God to whom the exiles can look in confidence, for God is not just their God; God is the God of all. And hence, given God's publicly stated commitments to the Israelites, God will be at work among the nations to see to a glorious future for them. Isaiah has to hold together conquests of Cyrus and restoration to Zion—what keeps them together is a theology of creation.

Creation and Power? Does this creational emphasis of Second Isaiah constitute an effort to speak to the exiles regarding the *power* of God? In effect, because the power of the nations (including Babylon and Persia) and the gods is nothing compared to the power of the Creator God, the future of God's people is assured; God has the power to release them from exile and bring them home.[77]

Scholars have certainly often stressed that the key question is: *can* God deliver on these promises (40:1-11)? Thomas W. Mann, for example, states that "The cumulative metaphors of immensity produce a sense of awesome power, a power infinitely greater than that of nations, rulers, and even rival deities."[78] Given God's power as Creator, God will *be able* to be Israel's redeemer. Brevard S. Childs states that "The issue at stake lies in the credibility of God in the eyes of his exiled and disheartened people. What are the grounds for believing in the promise of new things and a glorious future?" Most basically an appeal is made to God's power. "Because God is the creator God who brought the world into being, who sustains it by his power, who establishes it in justice, he *is able* to execute his new promise of salvation to Israel in which the entire universe participates."[79] While this is a helpful interpretation in a general way, is the stress to be placed on a God who "is able"? Walter Brueggemann lifts up this theme of divine power as well,[80] and goes on to speak of cosmic creation as an invitation to Israel to be confident in Yahweh. "Creation faith is the summons and invitation to trust the Subject of these verbs . . . [God] can be trusted in the midst of any chaos, even that of exile and finally that of death."[81]

Israel can certainly trust this Creator God, but a straightforward link between power and trust is problematic, as if a demonstration of sheer power on God's part can elicit Israel's trust in any genuine way. The argument is not "that Yahweh had a monopoly on violent political power and that the gods had none. Who among the exiles could buy that argument? . . . It would have been impossible to argue for the ascendancy of the exiles' God on the basis of power politics."[82] This is the case not least because of Israel's recent experience of immense power at the hands of the Babylonians. In such a discussion, definitions of *power* are exceedingly important. Is the issue essentially that of the power of muscles and armies? My God has got more muscles than your God has![83] Such an understanding of power is deeply problematic, especially in a text that gives such a central role to the suffering servant (42:1-7; 49:1-6; 50:4-9; 52:13–53:12). What kind of power is that? Do these texts, finally, make a claim for power more defined in terms of suffering than our usual definitions of power allow?

Another approach seems to be more in tune with the texts. The primary issue at stake for the exiles is not the power of God, at least in the sense of force and muscular demonstration. Certainly claims are made regarding the power of God to accomplish marvelous things in the world's history (e.g., Isa 40:10, 25-26), and the use of power in the leadership of Cyrus will take violent forms (45:1-2). It is not that issues of such power are irrelevant for that divine activity, but are they central?[84] Isaiah 40–55 considers sheer force inadequate for speaking of the ways in which God is at work in the present situation. The assumption is that God the Creator once again will do marvelous things in the next stages of Israel's journey; at the same time, this action will not only release them from the clutches of powerful peoples, it will also transform their spirit and their life. What *kind* of "power" can bring into being the renewal of the spirit that is hymned in 40:29-31 and elsewhere in these texts (see above)? An action by God that moves beyond the kind of power it takes to free the exiles from Babylon will be needed.

Does the stress on the creation themes not have more to do with issues of newness and creativity as God's way of working in the world? What God is doing in Israel's present situation will have to connect with those deeper human issues; hence, images of birthing a renewed people come into play (42:14; 49:14-21; see 66:7-14) and the suffering that is necessary to bear away their sin (43:24-25; 53:5-6, 8, 11-12). These oracles speak to the revitalization of the weak and the weary (40:28-31; 50:4), the deep healing of those who despair (53:4), and the forgiveness that is needed to get to the heart of the issues they face (40:2; 43:24-25; 44:22). The power of armies would prove to be remarkably insufficient for such a purpose. God has called Cyrus to be his messiah (44:28–45:7, 13), and his work will have violent dimensions (45:1-2), but Israel's future is not fundamentally shaped by such armed activity. That future is finally shaped by the forgiveness that can come only in and through the suffering of God and the servant (43:24-25; 53:1-12). The basic understanding of the power of God in Isaiah 40–55 will finally be shown in 53:1: Who would have believed that the arm (power) of God would be revealed in such a one as this (the suffering servant)? Kings won't believe it (52:15).

Creation and Israel's Vocation

Creation language is also used in Isaiah 40–55 to speak of Israel's vocation in the world. God formed Israel for a purpose; God did not create this people to be nothing or to loll in the lap of the divine blessings. This vocation responds to wonderments among the exiles as to whether they had any continuing role in God's purposes in and for the world. God's response, permeating these texts, is a resounding Yes! That what they do and say makes a difference in the divine economy is an especially important word for dispirited exiles to hear. At the same time, the nature of the vocation may have exceeded the expectations of the exiles. Two perspectives come to mind.

One, Israel's vocation encompasses all the nations of the world. While this vocation to which Israel is called is not radically different from the tradition (see Gen 12:3), it is stated in terms that break open new images and formulations (e.g., "I have given you as a covenant to the people, / a light to the nations," Isa 42:6). It is precisely the universal character of that vocation that calls on the support of creational perspectives. And so strong claims about God as creator of the cosmos (42:5) are a key element in the first of the calls to Israel to be "a light to the nations" (42:1-6; see also 50:2-3 as a preface to 50:4-9). Israel has been created to declare God's praise to all (43:21; 48:20).

Moreover, the servant songs are oriented not toward Israel but toward the nations (42:1, 4; 49:1-6; 52:13-15; 53:11-12). The introduction to the second of the calls to be a light to the nations lifts up the creational gifts of the one who is called (49:1-2; see 50:4). Such gifts enable the proclamation of the salvation of "the God of the whole earth" (54:5) to reach "to the end of the earth" (Isa 49:6; 52:10). God "the Creator of the ends of the earth" (40:28) calls upon "all the ends of the earth" (45:22; cf. 42:10) to turn and be saved, and God anticipates that "To me every knee shall bow, / every tongue shall swear" (45:23) and make confession of God alone (45:14; cf. 2:2-4). Justice will be established "in the *earth*" (42:4, emphasis mine). For such a proclamation to make sense and to realize such universal effects, it must function within a universal frame of reference, undergirded by creational perspectives.

Two, this God-shaped vocation invites Israel to be about the task in a certain way—not through conquest and empire, but by speaking clearly and entering deeply into the suffering life of the world and making it their own—for the sake of the many.[85] For all of Israel's mortal status (40:6-8) and deep suffering, its special vocation is to be pursued not merely in the face of such suffering but somehow in and through it (42:1-9; 49:4-9; 50:4-9; 52:13–53:12).

The language of Israel being "created" is a part of this argument. That is to say, God's creative actions with respect to Israel are not, finally, limited to Israel; rather, they have a fundamental continuity with God's purposes with respect to the rest of God's created ones. That is to say,

God's initially exclusive move was for the sake of a maximally inclusive end. To speak, then, of God *creating* Israel is to think about Israel in these more comprehensive terms. God creates Israel for the sake of the entire creation. The nations of the world seem to have their place in God's economy only in and through their relationship with Israel. Though Isa 19:18-25 seems to break out of that mold to some degree, the basic word is that Zion remains the center for the salvation of all (Isa 2:2-4).

Creation, Redemption, and Salvation

The relationship of these three themes—creation, redemption, and salvation—has occasioned considerable scholarly reflection.[86] In the words of P. B. Harner: "How is the belief that Yahweh is the Creator of all the ends of the earth related to the conviction that he is the Redeemer" who has acted in the past on Israel's behalf and is about to act anew for the deliverance of his people?[87] His discussion of this question engages the seminal essay of Gerhard von Rad (and those following in his train), who concluded that "at no point in the whole of Deutero-Isaiah does the doctrine of creation appear in its own right . . . it performs only an ancillary function. . . . It is but a magnificent foil for the message of salvation, which thus appears the more powerful and the more worthy of confidence."[88] Creation is entirely incorporated into the dynamic of the prophet's salvation faith.[89] But Harner and others show correctly that creation faith is not simply absorbed into the structure of salvation faith in Isaiah 40–55.[90] Indeed, it is now common to say that "faith in God the Creator was perceived and experienced as the all-embracing framework, as the fundamental, all-underlying premise for any talk about God, the world, Israel, and the individual."[91] Thomas W. Mann lifts up Isa 40:12-31 as key for interpretation of this matter in Second Isaiah; this introduction "suggests that whatever actions in history may be attributed to Yahweh, they are grounded in a theology of Yahweh as 'creator of the ends of the earth.' In this sense, a theology of creation is prior to and foundational for a theology of history."[92]

Our discussion to this point has shown that von Rad's perspective regarding the role of creation in Isaiah 40–55 is much too narrow. We here continue our own response by noting that Isaiah 40–55 appeals to God's cosmic creation, both in the sense of originating creation—"I am the LORD, who made all things" (44:24; see 45:12, 18; 48:13; 51:13, 16)—and continuing creation (40:22, 26, 28; 42:5; 48:13; 50:2). Many of these texts weave originating creation and continuing creation together into a single fabric: "the LORD,"

> who created the heavens and stretched them out
> . . . .
> who gives breath to the people upon it
> and spirit to those who walk in it. (42:5)

(See 40:26, 28-31; 44:24-28; 45:12-13; 48:13; 51:13-16.) These same verbs are also used for God's creating Israel so that God is both "the Creator of the ends of the earth" (40:28) and "the Creator of Israel" (43:15, a formulation unique to Second Isaiah); at times these divine creations are immediately juxtaposed (44:24; 45:11-13; 51:13, 16). Because God's continuing creation work occurs over the course of history (e.g., the history of nature), Isaiah 40–55 can use creation language for God's *specific* historical activity, whether in the history of Israel—past, present, and future: "the LORD who made you, / who formed you in the womb" (44:2; see 41:20; 43:1, 7, 15, 21; 44:21, 24-28; 48:7) or the history of the nations: "I . . . created the ravager to destroy" (54:16; see 45:7-8). These creational actions of God over the course of history may issue in such effects as election, redemption, judgment, or salvation.

At the same time, "redemption" language (*gā'al*) is used only for Israel; God is "the Redeemer of Israel" (49:7), but *not* of other peoples. In addition, "salvation" language (*yāša'*) is used for God's action on behalf of Israel: "I am . . . your Savior" (43:3; see 45:17; 46:13; 49:8; 52:7); that is to say, the redemption of Israel is an act of salvation (49:26). At the same time, salvation is a more comprehensive reality than redemption. In other words, God's salvation is both redemptive act and the *effects* of that act over time on Israel and the entire creation. God's creative work is active *in everything*; salvation is perhaps the most prominent effect of that creative activity. And so "salvation" language is also used with respect to the nations: "Turn to me and be saved, / all the ends of the earth!" (45:22-23; 49:6; 51:5-6, 8; 52:10). But that salvation is represented as an outgrowth of God's salvation of Israel (45:8; 51:5; 52:10) and largely depicted as a future reality associated with Israel's assuming the vocation to be a "light to the nations" (42:6; 49:6). God's objective is "salvation" for all the ends of earth (52:10) for all time to come (51:6, 8). The formulations in Isa 51:6, "the heavens will vanish like smoke, / the earth will wear out like a garment," could suggest that salvation ("forever") will "outlast" the creation, but Israel never conceived of a bodiless and earthless future. It is probable that Isa 65:17-25 (cf. Isaiah 24–27) fills out this theme in its proclamation of God's creating "new heavens and a new earth." God's redemptive activity on behalf of Israel is the means to such a universal salvific end for all; at the same time, a new creative action of cosmic proportions on God's part will finally be necessary.

Another question arises: does the prophet use the terms *creator* and *redeemer* (or *savior*) as "virtual synonyms," as some suggest?[93] In view of the discussion to this point, I believe the appropriate answer is: yes and no, depending on the context. On the one hand, creation in the *originating* sense is not collapsed into salvation/redemption; *no* salvation/redemption language is used in Isaiah 40–55 for God's creative activity such as that depicted in Genesis 1–2. To collapse originating creation and salvation/redemption would be to claim that God's creative activity in the beginning was already compromised by sin and evil and needed salvation; but, in the language of 45:18, God "did not create it a chaos."[94] Second Isaiah thus does not use redemption/salvation language for *all* creative activity. On the other hand, some contexts do present God's redemptive activity on behalf of Israel as an experience of God's creational activity (e.g., 41:17-20; 43:1-7, 14-21).[95] But, given the more comprehensive use of creation language we have noted, creation language is used to interpret redemptive events and not the other way around. This more focused use of creation language probably has to do with the nature of the redemptive activity: the fundamentally new and life-giving activity of God that has deep and broad effects not only on Israel but on all of creation.

Creation language thus serves to give to Israel's redemptive experience a cosmic cast with universal implications. Second Isaiah is not the first to link redemption and creation themes in the interests of such a purpose. This linkage is especially evident in Exodus 15, a song sung upon the deliverance of the Israelites from Pharaoh and his armies in which creational language is drawn upon to describe what has occurred (see Exod 15:4-5, 8-12, 14-16). Ronald A. Simkins has put it well: "Cosmic metaphors are applied to a historical account in order to attribute cosmic meaning to the historic events. . . . The cosmic metaphors in Exod 15:1-18 place God's deliverance of Israel from Egypt at the sea within the context of God's activity in creation."[96] But it is not just that "Israel's redemption is *compared* to a new creation."[97] The creational language is used to give recognition to an actual new state of affairs; the redemptive act of God is more than a local event; it has cosmic depth and significance.

"It is precisely because what happens here is cosmic that it has universal effects."[98] God's redemptive acts are not narrowly conceived, as if only Israel benefited from what happened; God acts in specific redemptive ways finally for the sake of the salvation of the world.

Isaiah 40–55 makes several references to the exodus/wilderness wandering events—presented as a single event-complex; this cross referencing suggests that the deliverance from exile is to be understood in comparable ways. For example, 55:9-11 draws together the crossing through the sea in Exodus 14–15 with the exiles returning home and links them through the use of creation language (see also Isa 43:2, 14-17; 52:4-6, 11-12). The post-exodus journey through the wilderness (Exod 15:21–18:27), eventually to the land of promise, is also drawn on for its parallels with the journey across deserts from Babylon to Israel (Isa 40:3-5; 41:17-20; 42:13-17; 43:19-21; 48:20-21; 49:8-12; 51:3). Creation language is used throughout in reflecting upon their commonalities as redemptive events. At the same time, creation not only bridges "the gap between the Exodus tradition and the expectation of the imminent restoration of Israel,"[99] it also invites the interpretation of the latter in terms of the former. That is to say, just as the sea crossing was interpreted in cosmic and universal terms, so also the return from exile should be so understood. The creation material once again gives cosmic range to what is about to occur; the effect will not simply be the redemption of Israel, but the entire cosmos is affected in such a way that salvation shall spring forth and embrace every creature. God has launched a universal work of salvation and hence the history of Israel is no longer sufficient basis for grounding such a universal proclamation; creation must be brought into the picture in a decisive way.[100]

Both exodus/wilderness wanderings and deliverance from Babylon are understood as redemptive events, forging the identity of the people of God. But the relationship is not so simple as to say: just as God acted back then, so God is acting now. The exodus is also *contrasted* with what God is now about to do in returning the exiles home and planting them in the land: "Do not remember the former things. . . . I am about to do a new thing" (Isa 43:18-19; see 41:22-23; 42:9; 46:8-11; 48:3, 6); Jer 16:14-16 (= 23:7-8) claims a comparable contrast between the exodus and the return from exile.[101] The "old" exodus event no longer stands on its own as a redemptive and cosmic event; indeed, it is sharply reduced in importance compared to the new. God is now creating something genuinely new; not only will Israel be newly constituted as a people of God but also the cosmic significance of the event will be more wide-ranging in its effects.

In addition, that long-ago action of God in the exodus was no longer capable of speaking a clear word of God to the dispirited exilic community. Given the horror of recent events, a new creation-based word from God was needed. Hence, some of the most straightforward proclamations of good news to the exiles in Isaiah 40–55 are shaped by statements about God as Creator (40:27-31; 44:24-28; 45:11-17; 50:1-3; 51:12-16; 54:4-10). The last-noted text makes an especially strong statement: God, the Maker of Israel and of "the whole earth" stands behind the promises now to be made. God's "everlasting love" and "covenant of peace" will be extended to the people in exile, and they can be as certain of this promise as was God's promise following the flood (Gen 8:21-22; 9:8-17). As it was after the flood, so it will be after the destruction of Jerusalem and exile; yet, the new creation is much more clearly in view now compared to then.

Brevard S. Childs argues that "The prophetic emphasis upon the creation of the new heavens and new earth . . . forcibly *illustrates* the one redemptive will of God from the beginning to the end."[102] To this James K. Bruckner properly responds:

> Creation is more than an "illustration" of the redemptive will of God. In the overarching story of redemption, creation is the necessary reality from which redemption emerges, and for the sake of which redemption history is even necessary. . . . It is, after all, creation that must be redeemed. . . . Creation's explicit development in relation to redemption in Isaiah ought not be viewed as an exception, but the manifestation of an implied norm that is so deeply embedded that its articulation only became necessary in the most fundamental theological crisis.[103]

For Isaiah 40–55, creation is the beginning, middle, and end of God's work with the world. God originated the cosmos, has continued creative work all through the course of the world's history, and will one day bring a new heaven and new earth into being. In linking redemption and creation, Isaiah 40–55 shows that redemption is not something extracreational or extrahuman, something different from what God gives in creation; redemption makes ordinary human life in creation possible once again. At the same time, creation and redemption, though integrally related, are not to be equated with each other. Redemption as well as distinguishable continuing acts of creation (e.g., healing) are the means;

a new creation is the end, ultimately a new heaven and a new earth. God's redemptive activity is in the service of that new creation; indeed, because of sin, creation must be redeemed or the end would not be what God intends. Redemption is the divine act in and through which the forces that threaten life and creation are overcome. The word *salvation* is to be distinguished from *redemption* in that it refers to the *effects* of *both* God's redemptive activity and God's continuing creative activity.[104] Without redemption, there would be no new creation; but it is a new creation, not a new redemption. And in the end, salvation will be *the* characteristic of that new creation.

Creation, New Creation, and the Natural Order

God has a future in store for the entire created order, not just human beings. For the sake of that future—a new heaven and a new earth—God's *salvific* activity catches up every creature.[105] The need for such a comprehensive divine activity is, most fundamentally, to be laid at the door of human decisions and actions.[106] While human faithfulness could lead to blessing for the natural order (e.g., Lev 26:3-6), human sin has had a deeply negative effect upon all creatures, as is clear from the beginning of the Bible (Gen 3:17-19; 9:2-3). As we have seen, the close interrelatedness of human and cosmic orders is characteristic of the entire Old Testament, not least the prophets, sometimes explicitly associated with judgment (Isaiah 24–27; Jer 4:23-28; Amos 4:6-11), sometimes not (Hos 4:1-3).[107] Judgment on Israel and the nations may be specifically designed as a divine action on behalf of the land (e.g., Lev 26:32-43).

While there is no indication that every "disruption" in the natural world is the effect of human sin (including earthquakes, famines, and wild animals; see below),[108] human sin has resulted in the degradation of the environment. Given this link between moral order and cosmic order, human redemption must be accomplished in order for this destructive cycle to be stopped. And then, in turn, human redemption will be accompanied by a healing, indeed the salvation, of the natural order. Even more, given the close interrelationship of human beings and environment, *only when the natural order has been healed will human salvation be fully realized*. We look more closely at the effect of God's redemption of Israel on the natural order, on human beings, and on their relationship with one another.

God's salvation is not conceived in a narrowly human sense, as if only people will be affected by God's work. All nonhuman creatures will participate in a universal salvation, envisaged most fundamentally in terms of a renewal of nature (see Isa 35:1-10; 41:18-19; 51:3; 55:12-13; cf. 11:6-9; 42:15-16; 51:4-6; 65:17-25). "The divinely created new thing is described primarily in terms of botanical growth."[109] A rejuvenated wilderness and a land that is filled with thriving plant life become a key image for God's promised deliverance of Israel (Isa 44:1-5; see Hos 14:4-7). At the same time, these texts cannot be reduced to poetic imagery, as if they were not emblematic of actual change on the part of the natural order. The images from the realm of botany do not simply image what God will do for the people; the rejuvenation of the natural realm is real in itself.[110] A cosmic change is in view, not simply God's actions on Israel's behalf. The language of "comfort" is even used for the natural order (51:3), wherein joy shall be as characteristic of nonhuman creatures as human (35:1-2), as all break forth in singing (44:23; 49:13; 55:12). To make such claims, a creational perspective is essential. What God is doing in these momentous events, while catching up Israel in a special way, has salvific effects on every creature, human and nonhuman.

Notably, as nature is renewed, so also will the human body be restored to wholeness from disabilities and sicknesses (Isa 29:17-18; 35:3-6; 53:4; cf. 33:24; 42:7, 16; 65:20; 66:14; see Jer 30:12-17; 33:6; Ezek 34:16) and food and water made readily available (Isa 41:17-18; 43:20; 49:9-10; Joel 2:19-27; 3:18; Zech 8:12; 9:17). Salvation is as much bodily as it is spiritual, extending even to population growth and the perpetuation of the generations (Isa 49:19-21; 54:1-3; see Jer 30:19; Ezek 34:8-12).[111] God's creative deed will also affect the spirit of the people, as God

> gives power to the faint,
> and strengthens the powerless.
> . . . .
> [They] shall renew their strength,
> they shall mount up with wings like eagles,
> they shall run and not be weary,
> they shall walk and not faint. (Isa 40:29-31)

(See 29:19; 52:7-10; 61:1-3; Jer 31:12-13.) Indeed, the re-creation of the human *heart* (or will) is brought to expression in several texts. In Second Isaiah, the emphasis of God's work is placed on the forgiveness of sins (43:25; 44:22; 53:5-6, 10-12; cf. 33:24). Jeremiah and Ezekiel link forgiveness with the gift of a new heart (Jer 31:31-34; 32:39-40; 33:8; Ezek 36:24-33). These promises have a plural reference, first and foremost; this new creation will not consist of isolated individuals. Though individuals will no doubt be caught up in this creational change, the *community* will be given a new heart and new spirit.[112] Then the relationship between God and people will be what God intended: "they shall be my people and I will be their God" (Jer 24:7; 30:22; 32:38; Ezek 11:20; 34:30-31; 36:28).

That work of God with human beings will also positively affect the estranged relationship between human beings, the animals, and the natural order more generally. Indeed, as we have said, *human* salvation will only then be realized. The close links between this human change and positive effects in the natural order are evident in Ezek 36:29-36, where the removal of Israel's uncleanness is accompanied by natural abundance and a new day for the land and its various creatures (see Ezek 36:8-12; 34:25-31; 47:7-12). Even more, a "covenant of peace" will be established between human beings and the animals (Ezek 34:25-29).[113] Other prophets envision this changed relationship. Hosea 2:18-23 speaks of a future that includes such a covenant; indeed, it catches up all of creation that has been estranged (domestic animals are not included).[114] Including even creeping things! A communicating relationship among God, human, and nonhuman becomes sharply enhanced. In Amos 9:11-15 (see Isa 30:23-26), the restoration of the Davidic monarchy is accompanied by a renewal of the productivity of the fields. Israel will live so harmoniously with the land that, rather than bring forth thorns and thistles (see Gen 3:17-19), it will produce crops in such abundance that the farmers will not be able to keep up with the growth (see Jer 31:1-6, 10-14; Ezek 36:8-12).

Isaiah 11:6-9 is especially striking in this regard (see 65:25).[115] On the one hand, the relationship of human beings and animals will be positively affected:

> a little child shall lead them.
>
> . . . .
>
> The nursing child shall play over the hole of the asp,
> and the weaned child shall put its hand on the adder's den. (11:6-8)

On the other hand, apparently, even animals that are natural "enemies" will be so no more:

> The wolf shall live with the lamb,
> the leopard shall lie down with the kid,
> the calf and the lion and the fatling together.
> . . . .
> The cow and the bear shall graze,
> their young shall lie down together;
> and the lion shall eat straw like the ox. (11:6-7)

It may be important to note that the weak animals do not reside in the home of the strong but the strong in the weak, suggesting maximal security for the weak in their own domicile.

The text seems straightforward, but interpreters disagree on several features of the text.[116] Ronald A. Simkins is representative of those who think that the images speak to violence directed against the human world, *not* violence among animals. The domestic animals mentioned (lamb, goat, cow) were considered a part of the human world (often living in the same household) and so mesh well with the children mentioned. Hence, an attack against the domestic animals by the wild animals is an attack on the human world. No evidence exists that "violence among animals was deemed contrary to the created order. . . . The Bible is not concerned about violence within the animal world."[117] And so, no transformation of the animal world to exclude interanimal violence is in view; nature, "red in tooth and claw," will remain in this new creation. The point that the text makes, perhaps somewhat utopian, is that human beings (Israel) will not be threatened by the wild animals that continue to exist. This interpretation would correlate well with other texts that speak of the new creation as being protected from wild animals (see Ezek 34:25, 28; Isa 35:9). Donald E. Gowan, on the other hand, calls attention to lions eating straw and bears grazing (11:7). What concerns the prophet is not new digestive systems for animals, but "violence of any kind, even in the animal world, for he cannot accept that as being a rightful part of God's good world, and so he dreams of a day when there will no longer be any need for any living thing to kill another."[118] This perspective, which has some continuity with the vegetarian diet for both human beings and animals in Gen 1:29-31, may be correct. At the same time, a common vision of the new heaven and new earth does include death (Isa 65:20), and that would be continuous with an ongoing world in which violence among animals does not end.

It is important to be clear, however, that this text does not speak of a return to Eden.[119] The most fundamental difference from Eden is that this new covenant does not have the possibility of being undercut by human failure; that cycle will never be repeated.[120] The new creation will be much greater than Eden ever was. This new day will come when the words of Isa 32:15-18, 20 will forever describe that new creation:

> a spirit from on high is poured out on us,
>   and the wilderness becomes a fruitful field,
>
> . . . .
>
> Then justice will dwell in the wilderness,
>   and righteousness abide in the fruitful field.
> The effect of righteousness will be peace,
>   and the result of righteousness, quietness and trust forever.
> My people will abide in a peaceful habitation,
>   in secure dwellings, and in quiet resting places.
>
> . . . .
>
> Happy will you be who sow beside every stream,
>   who let the ox and the donkey range freely.

CHAPTER SEVEN

WISDOM AND CREATION

This chapter seeks to address the relationship of wisdom to creation, with special attention to Proverbs 8 and Job 38–41.[1]

Creation and Wisdom Literature

Wisdom is an inexact term that is commonly used to refer to knowledge regarding life that God has built into the infrastructure of the natural and social worlds, the search for those understandings in everyday experience, and the transmission of the results of that search. God has created wisdom in the first place and continues to mediate God's will and ways in and through that reality; at the same time, wisdom functions as a creature allowed to be itself apart from specific divine management. As such a reality, the wisdom embedded in the world makes itself available to human beings; wisdom has a certain drawing power, but the process of human discovery and discernment is crucial for the proper shaping of human life. The gathering and transmission of wisdom is an intellectual exercise and accumulation of knowledge not simply for its own sake but to enable the best human life possible in God's world, both individual and communal. The heart of wisdom is what is done with that knowledge in the daily round, the discernment of the appropriate relationship between what individuals have come to know and how they live.

Many results from this discernment process, often used in Israel for teaching those in the preparatory stages of life, have been gathered into literary collections, typically called Wisdom literature. The literature usually included in this collection are Job, Proverbs, Ecclesiastes, and several psalms (e.g., Pss 1; 34; 37; 49; 73; 127–28). Two books from the larger Old Testament canon, Ecclesiasticus and Wisdom (of Solomon), also belong to this genre of literature. In addition, wisdom materials of various sorts have found their way into many corners of the canon (e.g., Isa 28:23-29; Jer 17:5-11). We focus here on Proverbs and Job. This literature was neglected for generations in church and academy, not least because it has no specific interest in Israel's historical traditions and, with its emphasis upon daily experience, cannot be made to relate easily to the traditional perspectives of special revelation or "salvation history." Only in the last generation or so has Wisdom literature begun to receive the attention it deserves. Much remains to be done.

It could be said that wisdom's centering in creation is a corollary of the interest of other traditions in divine action in historical events; that is, wisdom has to do with everyday experience as a context and medium of revelation regarding God and God's will for the relationship of human beings to the natural and social worlds of which they were a part. The result of the canonical decision to place these differing traditions side by side in the Old Testament is a much more balanced approach to the issues of divine revelation and activity than one without the other. Both creation and redemption, both everyday life and special historical events are seen to be crucial in understanding God and the nature of God's work in the world.

While Israel's particular story is of no apparent interest to the earlier wisdom teachers and writers, Israel's God is basic to their reflections: "The fear of the LORD is the beginning of knowledge [wisdom]" (Prov 1:7; 9:10). If the fear of the Lord is the beginning of wisdom, then wisdom proceeds from God, indeed is a gift from God; but that is not the end of the story, for the fear of the Lord is only the *beginning* of the acquisition and application of wisdom. Human study and reflection are necessary in the right development of that wisdom for use in daily life.[2] Wisdom "affirms the importance of the role of reason and human experience in the analysis and critique of faith," and, I would add, in the very formulations of faith for the witness of the community to the larger world.[3]

The most basic source of wisdom is the created order, broadly conceived to include both natural and social spheres. In view of the distinctions regarding creation made in chapter 1—originating creation, continuous creation, completing creation—only the first two have any place in the Wisdom literature. Even then, issues of origin are on the edges of wisdom discussions; the focus is the existing creation. Proverbs 8:22-31 is among the exceptions, but that interest seems to have more to do with the implications of origins for the authority of wisdom than creational origins in and of themselves.

Scholarly studies in Wisdom literature tend to work with matters of creation in two differing, but related ways.[4] On the one hand, the interest is primarily historical; creation is seen as a *construct* of wisdom, developing from an idea with ancient roots into the mature reflection of the later sages. On the other hand, creation may be understood as "the premise of all sapiential speech. . . . wisdom is a 'word' about creation. Or, to use the metaphor of artistry, creation is the canvas of wisdom's art. . . . a substantive reality that is the basis of wisdom's appeal . . . creation functions as more than a subcategory of wisdom; indeed, it is the ground upon which the house of wisdom is built (Prov. 9.1)."[5] As such, creation is not secondary or subordinate to, say, salvation history (or justice).[6] This substantive understanding of creation seems evident in Walther Zimmerli's seminal article: "Wisdom thinks resolutely within the framework of a theology of creation."[7] This approach has been carried through by Roland E. Murphy,[8] and especially Leo G. Perdue: "Each of the wisdom texts finds its theological center in creation." This means that "creation integrates all other dimensions of God-talk" and other theological topics of consequence.[9] God has to do with every creature, and every creature has to do with God, whether they recognize it or not; "God is the God of the world, not only of a specific people."[10]

From wisdom's creational perspective, human beings are given a specific vocation in the world (Gen 1:28, "subdue the earth," may be appropriate in specifying this task canonically). They are called not to be passive recipients of God-given blessings but to be engaged in discerning the wisdom made available in daily experience and to give shape to their *entire* life in such a way as to be in tune with creation (physically, morally, socially). The wise person is "one who both *creates* order and brings his life into harmony with the *established* order of the universe."[11] This implies a strong emphasis on God's expressed confidence in human beings, entrusting them with responsibility to discern the character of the social and natural orders, their interrelationship, and the implications for daily life.[12]

Several other features of wisdom are revealing of its creational grounding:

The Universality of Wisdom

Wisdom writings and reflections, in both form and content, are not unique to Israel and its Bible but were common in the ancient Near East. Moreover, it is evident that the wisdom writers in Israel knew of this material and drew upon it for their own reflections. An often cited example is a passage from the Egyptian wisdom book *The Instruction of Amenemope* that has been adapted and included in Prov 22:17–23:11.[13] That Israel integrated material of this sort, both directly and indirectly, into its own traditions is witness to its understanding that God the Creator was actively engaged in the everyday experiences and reflections of other peoples who had thereby gained many valuable insights into the nature of life and the world. God is not a God who restricts the divine activity to the chosen few; God is present and active among all people everywhere. Indeed, all creatures—human and nonhuman—are the recipients of God's continuing care, concern, and insight. As Prov 8:31 puts it, Woman Wisdom is active in the entire "inhabited world." The wisdom writers were stimulated by such insights and were prompted to probe even more deeply into that larger creation of which they were a part.

The "Secularity" of Wisdom

Given such parallels and other aspects of Israel's wisdom thought, Gerhard von Rad is able to say that the "experiences of community life are understood in a predominantly 'secular' way or, to be more precise . . . as a secular entity governed by Yahweh." God is spoken of in several contexts, but "in the vast majority of the sentences [in Proverbs], the order which is discovered is set down as a kind of neutral pattern immanent in the world."[14] Colin E. Gunton expresses this point in more systematic terms:

> There is something about the biblical God which enables a "secular" account of human life to be given. . . . By secular here I do not mean non-theological, but an account which enables the created world to be considered in its relative independence from the Creator: as distinctively creation. When the Wisdom Literature describes human life in the context of the created world, it has things to say comparable with the parallel literature of other cultures.[15]

In so understanding the creation as "secular," wisdom does not fall into a deistic perspective; God is a lively reality for the wisdom teachers. God enables the wise to "connect the dots," to discern the connections within the world that best contribute to life and well-being. At the same time, God allows the creation to be itself, which includes both being and becoming. That is, creatures are able to be what they were created to be; at the same time, because the creation is not a fixed reality, creatures are in the process of becoming. In this complex and ongoing process, God honors the createdness of the creatures, while not removing the divine self from their lives. Over time wisdom will become increasingly more explicit in its "theological expression: Later wisdom brought its theological questions, bringing the world and man back once again into the centre of God's sphere of activity."[16] But they only make explicit what was implicit in the earlier wisdom; a *theology* of creation is evident throughout the Wisdom literature, and that reality should not be discounted.

The Interrelationality of Wisdom

In the words of von Rad: "the most characteristic feature of [Israel's] understanding of reality lay . . . in the fact that she believed man to stand in a quite specific, highly dynamic, existential *relationship* with his environment."[17] God created both a natural order and a social order—including family, clan, people, nation (related with each other and within themselves). The major spheres of life in creation are thoroughly integrated—the natural order, the social order, and the individual human life, with each being able to affect the other positively or negatively. "*Israel only knew a related man*, related to other men, to his environment and, not least, to God."[18] To discern the character of these "orders" of creation and all of their interrelationships was considered crucial for the good life. Life's experiences are not objectified in wisdom or made into philosophical or abstract principles but have to do with life's specific, concrete relationships and contingent events. "Israel took great pains to learn from experience."[19]

We recall that *creation* in wisdom, as in the Old Testament as a whole, does not refer simply to "nature" or the physical or nonhuman world, but also to the community of human beings and their everyday life experience within the world.[20] This means that explicit reference to the Creator is not necessary for the link to creation to be clear. Specific references to God as Creator do occur here and there, including general claims about all creatures ("The LORD has made everything for its purpose," Prov 16:4) or all human beings (God made "the hearing ear and the seeing eye," Prov 20:12). "The rich and the poor have this in common: / the LORD is the maker of them all" (Prov 22:2; cf. 29:13). This text does not mean that God created individuals to be rich or poor but that they have a common maker. In addition, God is understood to be the sustainer of basic societal orders, from rulers (Prov 8:15-16; 16:13-15) to slaves and their respective places in society (Prov 19:10; 30:22; cf. Eccl 10:5-7). By implication, such orders would include nations and families, in and through which life and well-being can be enhanced in the human community. At the same time, these social orders are not absolutely fixed or inviolate. Slaves can become members of the family (Prov 17:2), kings can conduct themselves so as to bring their status into disrepute (Prov 16:12), and persons in authority "who oppress [or mock] the poor insult their Maker" (Prov 14:31; 17:5).

Wisdom promotes virtues such as prudence and justice and avoidance of vices such as contentiousness, indolence, and disregard for the poor and needy; all are grounded in a creational perspective. Such conduct either is or is not attuned to the wise structures of the creation; as a result, the effects on everyday life, both individual and communal, may be sharply positive or negative. Negatively, certain behaviors that do not conform to creational structures can bring individual lives to ruin and severely harm the social fabric. Positively, creational blessings follow upon wise conduct, including "long life, riches, a family with many children, health," and other less tangible blessings such as "contentment, peace, joy, and respect."[21]

The link between cosmic order and social order may be seen more indirectly in proverbs that, for example, claim that "honest balances and scales are the LORD's" (Prov 16:11; cf. 11:1; 20:10); the assumption is that balanced scales are in tune with a well-ordered world more generally, and God is responsible for the orders of society. More generally, realities in the natural world could be correlated with realities in the human sphere, either negatively or positively (30:15-19, 24-33; see Job 12:7-9). For example, human beings are compared and contrasted with animals, such as ants (6:6-11), birds (27:8), dogs (26:11), and lions and bears (28:1, 15); other realities are also drawn on for comparison, such as green leaves (11:28), honeycomb (16:24), fire (16:27), charcoal and wood (26:20-21), dripping rain, wind, iron, fruit trees, and water (27:15-19). The assumption here is that God has created a world in which significant correlations between the natural and human worlds are evident; hence, it is possible to discern implications for the order of sociohistorical life from the natural order.[22] Hans-Jürgen Hermisson puts it well, if with insufficient attention to irregularities in creation: "As is well known, wisdom searches for the knowledge of . . . a certain regularity within the diversity of the phenomena of the world. This world, however, is *unitary*. . . . Ancient wisdom starts from the conviction that the regularities within the human and the historical-social realm are not in principle different from the ones within the realm of non-human phenomena."[23] These texts show the remarkable levels of the interrelatedness of the social and cosmic spheres.

An important parallel text regarding wisdom and creation is Isa 28:23-29; it may illustrate the way in which wisdom is linked to creation. Herein lies explicit instruction from God regarding how best to be a farmer. Albert Wolters states the point very well:

> The Lord teaches the farmer his business. There is a right way to plow, to sow, and to thresh, depending on the kind of grain he is growing. Dill, cumin, wheat and spelt must all be treated differently. A good farmer knows that, and this knowledge too is from the Lord, for the Lord teaches him. This is not a teaching through the revelation of Moses and the Prophets, but a teaching through the revelation of creation—the soil, the seeds, and the tools of his daily experience. It is by listening to the voice of God in the work of his hands that the farmer finds the way of agricultural wisdom.[24]

Readers are therein invited to substitute for farming any other human endeavor or vocation.

Woman Wisdom in Proverbs 8

Female figures bracket the book of Proverbs. Proverbs 1–9 introduces readers to Woman Stranger (2:16-19), who is equated with Woman Folly (9:13-18), and she is contrasted with Woman Wisdom, who speaks with divine authority (e.g., 1:20-33; 8:1–9:6). The book concludes with a poem in praise of the "Woman/Wife of worth," a specific embodiment of what it means to be wise (31:10-31), and thereby linked to Woman Wisdom.[25] I focus on the Woman Wisdom text in 8:22-31 (anticipated in 3:19-20); it speaks of creation in especially striking ways.

This literary unit is a part of the larger body of poems in Proverbs 1–9 that are concerned to lift up wisdom, goodness, and life in contrast to folly, evil, and death. Proverbs 1–9, in turn, provides an introduction to the "proverbs of Solomon," beginning in 10:1, proverbs of insight that Woman Wisdom invites her readers and listeners to consider. These proverbs "deal largely with the practical wisdom necessary for everyday life, born of a God-fearing sensitivity to the created order in family life, farming, commerce, and administration. *The wisdom of Proverbs is the fruit of God's revelation in creation*."[26] Creation is here properly seen to move beyond any narrow reference to matters of origination or the natural world to encompass a concern for the ongoing well-being of the world, including its social institutions.

Initially, we take a brief look at Prov 8:22-31 in its immediate context. In the surrounding verses (8:1-21, 32-36; cf. 1:20-33), Woman Wisdom speaks in the first person.[27] Describing herself in a praiseworthy manner, she makes extraordinary claims. She speaks in the secular, public sphere amid the busyness of life, competing with other ideas but claiming priority for her own. She calls to all human beings, declaring herself to be the source of precious and truthful words of wisdom for everyone, even kings and nobles. She presents herself as one who hates evil and loves what is good, offering the best in life for all who would attend to her call (8:4-21).

Then, in 8:22-31, Woman Wisdom provides her credentials. As if anticipating challenges to her claims, she gives reasons as to why her assertions are valid. We summarize the key points, returning to some details below. Woman Wisdom owes her very existence and basic characteristics to God, coming into being independent of human thought. Unlike other creatures, she was birthed by God before even the foundational infrastructure of the world came into being (vv. 23-29; heaven and earth; mountains and deeps). All other creatures are dependent upon this infrastructure for their very life; Woman Wisdom is not dependent in the same way. Yet, once that world comes into existence, she is shaped in new ways by her experience with that world; indeed, *Wisdom needs a world to be truly wisdom*. Even more, Woman Wisdom was present and involved with God in creating the world; indeed, she was the necessary precondition for a well-constructed world; without her the creation would not be what God intended it to be or what it has become. And wisdom continues to be engaged with that creation, interacting with both God and human and nonhuman creation (vv. 30-31). With respect to God's ways with the world, she has an inside track; she has been in on everything (see Wis 9:9-11). And so, when she speaks, people are, in effect, listening to God through her, staying in close touch with the will and ways of God.

With that said, Woman Wisdom reiterates her call to all people (8:32), specifying that her teachings have a promise at their core—life and well-being—for all who follow her ways (8:33-35; cf. 1:33). At the same time, neglect of them will lead to death (8:36).[28] The issue as framed in Proverbs 1–9 is that an alternative way is available to humankind—that of Woman Folly (see 9:13-18)—and so the effects of the choices of human beings are sharply stated: life or death.

This context of 8:22-31 is significant; it demonstrates that the content and skills of the moral life (e.g., 8:13) are linked closely with Woman Wisdom's place in the creation of the world. Wisdom, therefore, has to do with both moral order and cosmic order and is related to every dimension of each. The "house" built by Woman Wisdom (9:1; cf. 14:1; 24:3-4) may be a reference to both orders, into which she invites everyone to "walk in the way of insight" (9:6). Woman Wisdom, in effect, is the "glue" that holds everything together in a stable and harmonious whole. The text thus speaks of a highly interrelated world—a spiderweb, if you will—in which all things are woven together and each creature affects every other, positively or negatively.[29] An enduring effect of such interrelatedness is that a careful study of the wisely structured creation can generate important insights for the moral life, while a proper discernment of the will of God for the moral life can keep one appropriately attuned to the cosmic order. To such study and discernment Woman Wisdom calls—for the sake of life. Human beings, however, can deeply disrupt this harmony and wreak havoc in the moral order, which can in turn have a negative effect on the cosmic order (e.g., Prov 12:10-11; 13:23; 14:4). How human beings respond to the wisdom that is made available is a matter of life and death for *all* creatures, human and nonhuman.

The identification of Woman Wisdom is a much debated issue.[30] The lack of precision may be intentional, but the text invites us to explore the impressionistic image. Several (overlapping) options have been suggested, including: a literary device to vivify and prioritize the wisdom that God used in creating the world and conveyed to the wise; the personification of an attribute of God; a being independent of Yahweh (hypostasis); the personification of a reality that has been divinely embedded in the creation and suffuses its structures and life. The latter seems most likely; wisdom is a dynamic, relational reality within creation that is personified. We will explore further dimensions of this issue as we move through the following discussion.[31]

Proverbs 3:19-20 ("The LORD by wisdom founded the earth; . . . by his knowledge the deeps broke open") could suggest that wisdom is a divine attribute.[32] But more likely this text *assumes* that God is wise and its language refers to God's specific employment of wisdom in establishing and stabilizing the infrastructure of the creation. In 8:22-31 this idea is extended, with the wisdom God has employed being portrayed as a *creature* birthed by God before all other creations, who then decisively shapes all the creative work that follows.[33] Wisdom is not "a principle or a rationality in the world, but of something created which is as real as other works of creation."[34] In addition, because *God* births this daughter (uniquely so), must she not also be understood to be divine? *So wisdom is likely presented as both divine and a creature*. As such, wisdom is uniquely capable of revealing both divine and creaturely worlds.

Later literature develops the idea of wisdom still further, with created Wisdom becoming an independent preexistent figure (Sirach 24; Wisdom 6–9; Bar 3:9–4:4; *1 En*. 42:1-3; cf. Job 28:12-28). At times wisdom is aligned with Torah (see Sirach 24). In such a linkage, whoever understands Torah understands creation's wisdom; to live life in accordance with Torah is to be in tune with creation.[35] A related development is that wisdom, which God is said to *speak* (Prov 2:6; Sir 24:3), comes to be identified with the *logos* in post–Old Testament times (cf. Philo), and the New Testament identifies the *logos* with the Christ (John 1:1; cf. 1 Cor 1:24, 30; Luke 11:49).[36]

Wisdom as Human and Female

Two distinguishable questions arise regarding Wisdom as a woman: why is this figure depicted as a human being and, given that, why a woman and not a man? The imaging of wisdom as a woman may be considered the most pressing question, but a prior issue pertains to the imaging of wisdom as a human being.

Wisdom imaged as a human being. Presumably any creature could have been used to depict wisdom, but the human being has attributes that more accurately describe its character. Claudia V. Camp's language is helpful: "the most fundamental point made by these poems is that wisdom is *not* an abstract concept but a way of being that is at its heart relational and holistic."[37] In order to be true to the lively character of wisdom, suffusing every dimension of the creation, it must be imaged as one who is personal and relational. The fundamental characteristic of this creational reality is relatedness; it is foundational to the way in which the world works. All creatures are related to every other creature and in such a way that they coexist in a way beneficial to all. Wisdom is a way of speaking of this interrelational dynamic. Perhaps one could speak of Woman Wisdom as the "relational infrastructure" of creation.[38] In other words, there is something basic about the very structures of creation—social as well as cosmic—that can be properly understood only in relational terms, indeed in personal terms. In and through a discernment of the many and various interrelationships that God has built into the created order, one may be more closely attuned to God's will for that world and act accordingly.

Given this focus on relatedness, the language of "order"—so often used in studies about wisdom—in and of itself does not do justice to wisdom's identity.[39] Woman Wisdom is not the order of creation as such, though issues of order are not irrelevant.[40] The word *order* can imply something that is static, never changing, forever fixed. But wisdom is imaged as a person precisely to prevent such understandings.[41] The language of "rationality" for wisdom can be misleading as well, as if wisdom were simply a matter of the mind.[42] A strong level of comprehensibility is indeed characteristic of the created order; much about the creation can be worked through with the use of the mind. But the emphasis on the personal element in the figure of wisdom means that the complexities of the human personality must be more fully taken into account than the language of reason allows. The word and will of God made available through wisdom pertains to all dimensions of what it means to be a person. If we do speak of "order," whether natural or social order, it must include characteristics such as these: dynamic, creative, developing, truly interactive, full of life, and genuinely relational with every other creature. Moreover, disorderly elements are inherent in wisdom (as with persons); such disorder is essential for creativity, growth, and the emergence of genuine novelty.[43] As such, elements of disorder are necessary for wisdom's ways to be truly benevolent. That continuing elements of disorder exist also carries the potential of a negative effect on human life; the sea has boundaries, it is not eliminated.[44] Yet, God's creative activity means that the cosmos is basically friend, not enemy; the creator has given us a trustworthy and benevolent environment within which to live and work.

These elements of disorder, as well as the dynamic character of wisdom, mean that one can never get a "fix" on wisdom, for, as with any person, it is a being that is always in the process of becoming. Wisdom can be observed, studied, and characterized but always within limits (see Job 28), and one must stay alert to keep track of where wisdom might be found, where it might show up next. Those in search of wisdom will always be finding ever new dimensions of reality to be studied and will always be at least one step behind. As with persons, wisdom is forever inexhaustible. At the same time, insight into the immensely varied life of creation is made available, indeed calls out for our attention; and, guided thereby, human life can be lived reasonably attuned to God's creational designs. This personal character of wisdom is likely the reason why it has been difficult for readers to bring the figure of wisdom into precise definition; one can never get a "fix" on a person.

Even more, to present wisdom as a human being is to link wisdom to human bodily form, which enhances the relational dimension of wisdom.[45] Wisdom's relationships, like those of human beings, are conceived as more than mental, intellectual, spiritual, or psychological in nature. These relationships are tangible, tactile, earthly, and bodily. And so, again, Wisdom is characterized by reference to every dimension of human life. Even more, Wisdom thereby has significant continuity with forms of creation (in all of their interrelatedness) that are not human yet "embodied." Wisdom has been built into the being and becoming of the nonhuman creation (see Job 38–41); God's purposes for the world have to do with the life and well-being of all creatures. Given this way of being for all creatures enables human beings, who experience such a world, to access its wisdom for the purposes of the fullest life possible within that interrelated creation. But they are to do so not only for their own sake but for the sake of all creatures. More generally, wisdom may be imaged as a human being because it is human beings who can most fully embody wisdom.

Wisdom imaged as a woman.[46] Woman Wisdom is a striking image, not least given Israel's patriarchal structures. While the generally human dimension of wisdom is important to observe, imaging wisdom as a woman suggests that there is something in what it means to be female that is especially characteristic of wisdom. In working on that issue, it has been helpfully suggested that Woman Wisdom is modeled after the everyday roles of Israelite women in their families and societal roles, such as teacher and homemaker. The role of women underlies "every important personal, social and religious experience familiar to the ancient Israelite."[47] Even more, it may also be the case that the often "powerless," behind-the-scenes way in which women worked within that culture is an essential element in how wisdom is to be characterized. The image of the "Woman/Wife of worth" in Prov 31:10-31 is a supreme embodiment of such wisdom. Might a right definition of power be at stake in the use of female imagery for wisdom? The power of wisdom is a power in, with, and under rather than power over; it is a power that is committed to the dynamics of genuine relationship. That Woman Wisdom plays such an important continuing role in a way that exceeds male images says something important about the continuing use of such images in the life of religious communities.

Another feature of the female dimension of the Prov 8:22-31 passage is evident in the birthing language. A translation difficulty immediately presents itself to the reader.[48] NRSV translates 8:22-23 as follows:

> The LORD created me at the beginning of his work,
> the first of his acts of long ago.
> Ages ago I was set up,
> at the first, before the beginning of the earth.

The word *created (qānānî)* could also be translated as "beget" or "acquire." Given the language of "brought forth" in verses 24-25 (see Deut 32:18), birthing imagery for God and creation seems preferable,[49] though one can acquire things by various means, including begetting.[50] The image is that of God as a mother, giving birth to wisdom (the verb, *qānānî*, is also used for Eve giving birth to Cain in Gen 4:1; and for God in Gen 14:19, 22). The word in verse 23 translated "set up" *(nāsak)* could also be translated "woven."[51] The latter translation seems likely, particularly in view of other texts that link birthing and the work of a seamstress (Job 10:11; Ps 139:13);[52] this translation also continues the female image for God. The use of female images for God is especially common in Second Isaiah (42:14; 66:12-13), and Woman Wisdom may have been drawn from that trajectory of reflection about God. These images make it clear that wisdom is birthed because God willed it so; wisdom is a divine *decision* for the sake of the creation.

Because birthing language is used for wisdom, but not for other creations of God in this text, wisdom's relationship with God is established as a unique one.[53] Inasmuch as wisdom is God's daughter, she is divine in some fundamental sense, not only creature.[54] In thinking this through, transcendence should not be set over against immanence. The God who is transcendent is at the same time a God who is in relationship to the world.[55] Other texts such as Job 38:28-29 and Isaiah 40–66 will use birthing imagery for God's more comprehensive creational work, both originating and continuing creation. But the point made in Prov 8:22-31 is to distinguish the place of wisdom among God's creations. The effect is that the birthing image used of God's creation of wisdom parallels the unique birthing work of women. Having been birthed, Woman Wisdom in turn becomes one who has birthing *potential* and as such she is used to image the *ongoing* creational process. Wisdom's continuing role in the creation would thus be seen as a bringing to birth of ever new life, especially in the human community (see 4:13, "she is your life"; 4:22-23; 8:35, "whoever finds me finds life"; 16:22, "Wisdom is a fountain of life").[56]

The use of birthing language may also speak to the "newness" of the divine experience. As with any mother, the birthing of wisdom presents a new situation to God, as does the creation of the world. God has never been Creator before; inasmuch as Woman Wisdom is the first of God's creations, God's experience as Creator begins with her. For the first time, God has an Other with which to relate. Given that this relationship is ongoing and catches up other creatures along the way, ever new experiences for God present themselves. Such experiences for God would certainly have an effect on God (see on "delighting" below). For example, to be faithful to this relationship with these new creatures, God now has to move over and allow them to be themselves, to be what they were created to be without divine micromanagement. While "Yahweh assured that the world would be fully permeated with an intentionality for life . . . Proverbs 8 imagines and articulates a way of God with the world that is not intrusive and occasional, but that is constant in its nurturing, sustaining propensity."[57]

The significance of the birthing imagery may be drawn out even further. We have noted that wisdom, while creature, is a member of God's family and hence also a divine figure (though not God). Hence, a divine community is in view in the creating that now occurs (recall the "us" in Gen 1:26).[58] This means that the God who proceeds to create the world, with wisdom "beside him," is not a solitary figure in that creative task. God does not create in isolation, but works with that which is not God in creating the cosmos. For God to be in a precreation relationship with wisdom *within the divine realm* entails an understanding that relationship is basic to the divine identity.[59] This God in relationship creates a world with which the divine community is in continuing relationship (cf. the divine council). Moreover, by virtue of the creaturely identity of wisdom that suffuses the creation, the interrelated character of that world is assured. Even more, by virtue of the divine identity of wisdom, the will and ways of God become available for the best possible life in the world.

Wisdom as Created Cocreator

God is imaged as creator in Prov 8:25-29 primarily in terms of the building trades: shaping, establishing, setting foundations, stabilizing, and boundary marking.[60] The resultant heavens, earth, mountains, water, and soil are the necessary elements of the world's infrastructure for the provision of living spaces and resources, making it possible for creatures to live and thrive. A key interpretive issue that arises is how Woman Wisdom, existent throughout these creations, is related to this creative activity of God. Her claims are: "I was there" (v. 27); "I was beside him" (v. 30).[61]

Wherever and whenever God was creating—no exceptions—Woman Wisdom was there; her presence was an all-pervading presence. This claim seems to imply more than that she was simply present. At the least, by being with God, Wisdom has carefully observed God's creation come into being. Such observation on Woman Wisdom's part would certainly result in a detailed understanding of how the world works; this would entail knowledge of what today would be called "scientific." Wisdom "not only knows all the particulars and individual quirks revealed in the history of humankind from the beginning, but . . . she also knows equally the basic structures, components, patterns, and functions of reality."[62]

Even more, such observation on Woman Wisdom's part would yield more than knowledge of the "facts" about the creation. It would also entail gaining knowledge of God's will/purposes for the world; Wisdom, shaping the divine design for the creation, knows what God's purposes for human and nonhuman life in such a world are. This understanding of Wisdom's comprehensive knowledge is more fully supported by the likelihood that Woman Wisdom's presence with the creating God entailed interaction and communication between them, as the delighting on the part of both God and Wisdom in verses 30-31 implies. For human beings to respond to Woman Wisdom's call to seek wisdom, then, is to seek to discern what Wisdom knows, both knowledge about the world and the underlying will of God for the world and each creature within it. Those who seek this wisdom and take it to heart will be in tune with the creation as God intended it.

But a key question remains: was Wisdom only observing and listening, or was she also engaged with God in creative activity? In thinking about this question, a key translation difficulty looms (*'āmôn*; v. 30). When Woman Wisdom was "beside" God, was she "a master worker" (NRSV; see Song 7:1) or a "little child"?[63] Several scholars argue for the latter translation and discount the former by appealing to the birthing imagery, the playfulness suggested by the delighting and rejoicing (vv. 30-31), and "the absence of any hint of creative role assigned to Wisdom."[64] William P. Brown refers to God's creation as "essentially Wisdom's playhouse, the formative context and setting in which Wisdom matures as player and moral agent."[65]

But must not interpreters claim more for Woman Wisdom? It seems best to understand *'āmôn* in terms of an artisan or skilled worker, with attributes such as wisdom, practical skill, and expertise.[66] For Woman Wisdom to say "I was beside him" implies more than presence and observation (notably, no explicit reference to observation is present either). Wisdom's communicating presence with God while God is creatively active suggests that such a presence entails *effect*; the "product" of God's work is infused by Wisdom's very presence.

The issue of maturation is also problematic. For Woman Wisdom to be an astute witness to God's creative activity suggests greater maturity than that of a "little child."[67] In any case, the image of birthing does not necessarily entail the image of growing up. Indeed, the text contains no explicit language regarding Wisdom's maturation.[68] Even if maturation does occur, it is unlikely that Woman Wisdom would remain a child over the entire time that is implied between "beginning" (vv. 22-23) and "inhabited world" (v. 31), as some interpretations suggest?[69] Given God's creation of full-blown mountains and fountains, it seems more likely that Wisdom was a mature woman from birth.[70] This would not mean that Wisdom could not "play" or would not continually surpass that knowledge over time in view of ever new experience. In addition, one might note that the delighting and rejoicing (or play) have no necessary reference to the activity of children; in fact, "delight" is infrequently used with children, while adults can "play" (see Job 41:5; 2 Sam 2:14; the adult David in 2 Sam 6:5).

Moreover, if Wisdom's role is simply that of witness, recounting "its story to her audience," then the link between Woman Wisdom and creation would only be indirect.[71] Texts such as Prov 3:19 (cf. Ps 104:24; Jer 10:12) certainly connect *God's* wisdom directly with creation; the obvious continuities between God's wisdom and the character and attributes of Woman Wisdom suggest a close link between her and creative activity. That Woman Wisdom is also the subject of building metaphors in Prov 9:1 (cf. 14:1), as God is, may also be pertinent for claiming an active role for Wisdom throughout.[72] It should also be noted that, in the early history of the interpretation of this text, Wisdom's creative role is clearly recognized. For example, Wisdom of Solomon (7:22; 8:6; 14:2; cf. 9:2) clearly understands Woman Wisdom to be an artisan.

If the translation, "master worker," is retained,[73] then the theme of Woman Wisdom as "created cocreator" is the likely interpretation; this translation would lift up the skill, intelligence, and purposefulness of wisdom's activity in the creative process.[74] The focus is clearly on what *God* has done, but God has not created the world apart from Wisdom; she has a special place "beside him" throughout the process. This understanding would involve genuine creative activity on the part of Woman Wisdom; indeed, God would then be *dependent* upon Wisdom's creativity in establishing the world.

Further elucidation of this point is available. To say that wisdom was with God is also to say that *God was with wisdom*. The presence of God with Woman Wisdom implies a significant relationship between them, to which God would be fully and appropriately attentive. Indeed, Woman Wisdom was a daily delight to God (v. 30); this would mean that Wisdom does have an effect on God and, by implication, what God is doing. One might ask then how Woman Wisdom *could* be a neutral or passive reality, present but having no influence on God's creative activity. Woman Wisdom's presence is not a neutral matter for God; she makes a difference to God, for what God is about in creation. The point made is not simply that Wisdom was the first of God's creations but that Wisdom became an integral dimension of God's further creations and hence *necessarily participant* in what they had become.

The effect of such an understanding would be that God does not create in an unmediated way but works in and through Wisdom in bringing the creation into being. Wisdom is thus appropriately described as a created cocreator. This role for Wisdom in creation would be parallel with the way in which creation is sometimes depicted in Genesis 1, where among the "modes" of God's creating is that of acting through already existent creatures, such as the earth (1:11-13) but especially the "us," the divine council, in 1:26.[75] This understanding fits with the relational model of creation we have noted; God chooses not simply to be independent in creative activity.[76] God chooses to be dependent upon wisdom, not only in creating the world but in continuing the relationship with that world. To be an observant and discerning member of such an interdependent creation will then entail hearing both the voice of Wisdom and the voice of God in and to that world—but then proceeding to act on what they hear. The goal for human beings is to be caught up in the task of cocreating, participating creatively in the continuing becoming of the world.[77]

Rejoicing and Delighting

What then of the delighting and rejoicing that is reported in verses 30-31? The fourfold reference to these themes in four successive lines is striking and emphatic. The two words seem to be used as synonyms, with the basic idea of "taking pleasure in" (see Jer 31:20; 31:4, "merrymakers"). These words imply an evaluative stance, thinking so highly of what is happening or has happened that delight is the only proper response (such as parents being delighted at the birth of a baby).[78] Delighting may refer to an internal pleasure, while rejoicing (usually the verb *sāhaq* is translated "laugh" or "play" [e.g., 2 Sam 6:5; Zech 8:5] for both adults and children) may designate more external indications that one is pleased. These words have reference to joy and wonder both with respect to the creative process itself and to the effects of that process (see Job 38:7). Basic to this responsiveness is the ongoing close relationship among all involved: God, wisdom, and the creation itself, especially humanity.[79]

To speak of wisdom being God's daily delight is, most fundamentally, to make a claim about *God*. God is not passive or aloof to the daughter who has been birthed but so enters into this relationship that it has a dynamic and interactive character. God's relationship to that which is other than God is genuine. Integral to such a relationship is a delighting in the other; wisdom is a source of pleasure to God. Wisdom 8:2-3 sharpens the point: "The Lord of all loves her" (for God's pleasure, see Isa 5:7; Jer 31:20). Inasmuch as *delight* is an evaluative word, it is parallel to God's evaluating of the creation as "good, very good" in Genesis 1.[80] Woman Wisdom does not introduce joy and delight into the creative process; God does. But Wisdom as the offspring of God continues that divine commitment and response.

From another angle, God delights in Woman Wisdom because Wisdom has *enabled* God to make the world such a dynamic place. God's creating would not have had such extraordinary effects without Woman Wisdom. Then, evincing the genuine character of the relationship, Wisdom delights in God and what God is creating (see Job 38:7; Ps 104:31). Notably, their mutual delighting does not take place simply at the completion of the "construction" of the creation; delight is a "*daily*" matter, occurring all along the way as the creation comes into being.[81] Together God and Wisdom take pleasure in each other, in what has been created, and in what continues to be created.

This mutual delight is taken a step further in verse 31, perhaps climactically so. Here Wisdom's delighting no longer simply relates to God as Creator; it relates also to the *effects* of God's creative work, namely *God's* "inhabited world," human beings in particular. Even more, as human beings live out their proper role in the world, Wisdom delights in who they are and what they are doing; she has the best interests, the good pleasure of human beings at heart. Then, as verses 32-36 make clear in the repeated reference to human happiness, Wisdom's delighting in humanity will be matched by the delight of human beings in keeping Wisdom's ways. God, wisdom, and humanity, interrelated as they are, are each represented as delighting (cf. Ps 104:31-34). When this happens, God's purposes for the creation are being realized: The world is a delight!

More can be said about the mutuality of delight. Delight is not amusement in the sense of an activity different from work but a dimension of the relationship itself, including work and all participants—God, wisdom, and creation. Pleasure and playfulness are built into the very structure of things, enabling all of life, including God's own life, to be what God intended it to be.[82] The pleasure evident in the God-Wisdom relationship becomes a dimension of all of creation, dancing into every creature's life as they are brought into being over time.[83] Inasmuch as Woman Wisdom delights both before God and before humankind in an *ongoing* relationship, there is a sense in which "wisdom functions as an intermediary between God and man, between God and his world."[84] Wisdom belongs both in the world and with God; as we have noted, Wisdom is both creature and divine. It is not simply a quality "immanent in creation" or "an attribute of the world"; it remains alongside God.[85] Wisdom delighting with human beings carries the implication of divine immanence—direct presence and involvement in creation. The idea is that God not only created the world but, in and through the figure of Wisdom, chooses to dwell among the creatures in terms that are described as delightful.

Because delighting and rejoicing demonstrate the dynamic character of this relationship, this text "excludes any theological view that the universe is a closed system operating according to fixed laws, of either nature or human destiny, which determine every occurrence."[86] That wisdom is not a fixed order will become evident in Proverbs 10–31 by the way individual proverbs sometimes contradict themselves depending on the life situation. Hans-Jürgen Hermisson also points out that, given the nature of the proverbial literature and its varied contents, "creation did not only happen at the beginning of the world, but takes place continuously; therefore, the orders have not become rigid, but necessarily remain flexible."[87] Wisdom does not set absolute standards or norms; Wisdom does not fix life in place; the wise and discerning human response may, indeed must, vary from situation to situation if it would be true to Wisdom's intention. The authority of Wisdom, and the limits of which one might speak, are of such a nature that much freedom of life and expression is allowed. That means that Woman Wisdom opens up the world rather than closes it down; she is always ready to take new experience into account, recognizing that God may be about new things for new times and places. Such is the life of a genuine Creator.

In addition, the presence of irregularities and ambiguities in the order of things means that discernment has to be open to new perceptions and shifts in understanding regarding what is wise. Wisdom is more dynamic than static in view of such changes and perceptions of reality. "These relationships, however, were always extremely variable and could certainly never be evaluated unambiguously. Behind the teachings of the wise men there lies, therefore, a profound conviction of the ambivalence of phenomena and events."[88] Close attention to actual experience means learning to live with ambiguity.

Revelation—Words to the Wise

Along the way in our discussion we have spoken of wisdom being a vehicle for divine revelation.[89] A few gathered remarks conclude this section. The reality of wisdom's relationship with creation means that God is not interested in keeping people ignorant regarding the world and God's ways within it. While God may not be obvious, indeed is hidden from view, God has not left human beings without resources and the resourcefulness to use them well in charting a course for their lives.

Wisdom assumes that God did not bring the world into being as a chaos but as a creation (see Isa 45:18-19), while not eliminating all traces of disorder. The very idea of creation assumes a certain ordering of spaces and creatures (human and nonhuman) *and* a certain disorder, as we have seen. Given Wisdom's experience "beside" God in creating such a world, Wisdom is uniquely positioned to "communicate to her clients the secrets of how the world works," as well as provide insight into God and God's ways.[90] The communicating relationship between Wisdom and God becomes a communicating relationship between Wisdom and creation, humankind in particular. Wisdom's role with respect to human beings is mediatory and revelatory, that is, she mediates God's communication regarding God's will for life and well-being—which Wisdom has heard—to humankind.[91] For the wise, God is known most basically in and through the experience of all of the forms of natural and social life integral to creation. That is, wisdom is so built into the infrastructure of the creation that God's character and purposes for the world can be reasonably, if not fully discernible to human probing and reflection. "Everything that happened in this life that was granted by Yahweh was at the disposal of Israel's search for knowledge."[92] It is a reality, which, surrounding humankind, "was possessed of a highly developed declaratory power. Creation not only exists, it also discharges truth."[93] "The world has something to say; she actually dispenses truth."[94]

In sum, in calling human beings (not just Israel) to dance to her rhythms and harmonies, Wisdom reveals *God's* dynamic intentions for life.[95] The human being, in turn, can hear this call and discern wisdom in, with, and under that which is created. The world is open to human probing and yields insight to those who ask appropriate questions and consider issues in a discriminating way. To be educated in the ways of the world by God through Woman Wisdom is to become a wise person.

God and Creation in the Book of Job

Echoing the scholarly consensus, J. Gerald Janzen states that "it is commonly recognized, of course, that creation themes abound in Job."[96] James L. Crenshaw lifts up a key thematic link: "The question of theodicy lies at the heart of the book of Job; so does creation theology."[97] Indeed, creational perspectives, especially evident in the God speeches in Job 38–41, are the primary theological matrix within which the book responds to issues raised by Job's suffering. The *nature of the world* as created and sustained by God is a key to interpreting both Job's complaint and God's response, as is the place of the human in this divine economy. Creational themes throughout the book contribute to this discussion, especially in Job 3:3-9; 7:16-19; 9:4-24; 10:8-13; 12:13-25; 25:1-6; 26:5-14; 36:24–37:24.[98] We will focus on the God speeches in Job 38–41 as a response to creation issues raised in the prior dialogue.

I begin by raising questions regarding the *kind of God* the book of Job portrays.[99] Job begins with a question about human piety (1:9), but that is almost immediately transmuted to include a question about the character of God, which the book pursues until the very end. A straightforward reading of Job lifts up several problematic portraits of God, including:

1. God sets Job up for suffering by bragging about him to "the *satan*" (1:8).
2. God is manipulated (NRSV, "incited"!) by "the *satan*" (= an accusing voice in the heavenly council, not the later devil) to allow him virtually free reign in visiting Job with suffering "for no reason" (!) one more time (2:3).
3. God is perfectly willing to sacrifice Job's children in order to score a debating point with "the *satan*" (1:12, 18-19).
4. God is confident in Job, but God does not know for sure how Job will respond under pressure. Otherwise, God could have overridden "the *satan's*" challenge on the basis of exceptional knowledge, or "the *satan*" would have so understood (1:11-12).
5. Everything that happens comes from God (monism). God gives, and God takes away; good and bad come from the Lord (1:21; 2:10).
6. For Job, throughout the dialogue, God is hostile and cruel, but inaccessible.
7. For Job's friends (and Job in the dialogue), God is a distant, aloof, heavenly accountant who only reacts within a retributive structure to which God is bound.
8. God responds to a suffering Job with two long-winded speeches (38–41) that, rightly or wrongly, would provoke a failing grade in most pastoral counseling classes.

This portrayal of God is troublesome for many Bible readers, and rightly so. Can God be trusted? Manipulated? Does God bet on the best horses? Does God send suffering "for no reason"? Is God insensitive to suffering people? Do God's ends justify *any* means? Is God responsible for everything that happens, good or evil? Does God know the future less than absolutely (whether Job can take the pressure)? I look into several of these questions. Initially, I note that it soon becomes clear that a theological reading must take into account certain rhetorical strategies that have been used in this sophisticated piece of literature.

The Genre and Rhetorical Strategy of Job

Most scholars think that the prose framework of Job is a didactic tale (1:1–2:13; 42:7-17; the poetic body of the book is drawn into this genre in a general way).[100] The tale is set in an ancestral era in an unidentifiable place called Uz. Job is "once upon a time" literature (1:1). The depiction of Job may well reflect an experience of deep suffering, and Job may be a legendary pious man, but the book is neither historical literature nor (auto)biography. Neither Israel nor its story is mentioned in the book. One rhetorical strategy of Job may be to create a setting at some distance from the readers' time/place/familiar traditions.

The lament/complaint is given a prominent place in Job's speeches; readers will recognize this genre from Psalms and elsewhere. The lament serves the broader purpose of disputation, between Job and both friends and God. From another angle, the issue of suffering is considered entirely from within a theology of creation (including the *gō'ēl*, "redeemer," theme) and eternal life is only a question (e.g., 14:14), in spite of Handel's use of 19:25-26 (a text never cited in the New Testament). As Wisdom literature, the book's purpose is certainly didactic. In this vein, a basic rhetorical strategy of the book is to offer a theological construct (even if several different perspectives are presented). That is, focused on the issue of suffering, Job is a what-if book, a let's-suppose-for-the-sake-of-argument book. Whatever the origins of the prose framework, its presence makes the book much more complex, creating many tensions with what follows, not least regarding the changes in the characterization of Job, his friends, and God.

The interpretation of Job is shaped to a great degree by decisions made regarding genre and rhetorical strategy. Generally speaking, many interpreters highlight the didactic element and consider the book an effort to consider the topic of suffering from various points of view, including the prologue, Job, Job's friends, Elihu, God, and the epilogue. Carol A. Newsom, for example, reads Job "as a polyphonic text in which a variety of different voice-ideas, embodied not only in characters but also in genres, engage one another without privilege."[101] But is "without privilege" too strong? Does the author think equally highly of each of the perspectives presented? Does the author not commend the perspectives of one or more of these segments more than others? Given the diversity of perspectives on suffering that the book presents, it seems unlikely that the author is so evenhanded or honors no theological move more than another.

Such an evaluative angle of vision seems to me to be suggested by Job 42:7. God therein evaluates the speeches of the friends of Job with their strict retributive understandings—major portions of the book's content—in negative terms. God also repeatedly evaluates Job's words as "right" (42:7-8). Does that evaluation include *everything* that Job and his friends have spoken? Or, is the evaluation to be understood only in general terms? Inasmuch as Job at times agrees with the theological perspective of the friends (e.g., their basic understanding of retribution), does not God's evaluation of Job need to be understood with some qualification? Is this suggested by 38:2, wherein God charges Job of speaking "without knowledge"? Is this ambiguous divine evaluation (38:2 with 42:7-8) an authorial way of not simply speaking in general terms but also calling for the reader's discriminating capacities in sorting out the yes and the no? If so, God's evaluations of Job and the friends entail something other than a *wholesale* acceptance/rejection of their point of view.[102]

When 42:7-8 are added to the common evaluations of Job's words by the friends and the friends' words by Job (see also Job 28 and Elihu), *evaluation of the perspectives of others* becomes a key thread in the book. They constitute an evaluative dialogue into which the reader is invited. Evaluation is integral to a proper dialogue and this would include discernment regarding the relative value of the options presented. The process of negative evaluation in particular entails having some kind of perspective to which one is committed, even if tenuously so. These innertextual evaluations seem to me to alert the reader that the book as a whole does not commend every point of view it considers or at least not every viewpoint equally. Readers of Job are thereby invited to engage in a hermeneutics of evaluation (not necessarily suspicion) as they seek to interpret the book. How might God's evaluations be made more explicit? Might there be points of view in the book that deserve the reader's critique besides those about which the book is explicitly evaluative? The book raises the evaluative question again and again for the reader; while the book does not sort the process, it invites choices among options. Generally, with respect to God issues, I agree with Norman C. Habel that

> the God of the prologue is too arbitrary and selfish, intervening at will in human lives. . . . The God of the friends is too mechanical, reacting according to a rigid code of reward and retribution. . . . The God of Job in his anguish is too violent, harassing humans and creating anarchy. . . . The God of the poet's commentary in Job 28 is too remote and inaccessible.[103]

I will contend that the God speeches (chs. 38–41) carry the most basic (if not the only) perspective regarding God (and suffering) that is commended to readers. I look at some detail.

The Prologue (1:1–2:13)

Given the genre of the book of Job, the God-*satan* wager should not be interpreted as if it actually happened.[104] At the same time, the reader could claim that this portrayal of God is sufficiently realistic so that it portrays the kind of God that God actually is. This direction for interpretation has been common. For example, in seeking to draw out the God imagery in the prologue, some interpreters highlight the parental images in Job; God is a proud parent confident of his child's integrity.[105] Perhaps so. But what loving parent would put their child through such abuse "for no reason" and, after a reprieve, turn around and inflict him again even more severely (2:3)?[106]

Or, from another perspective, God is testing Job and hence this divine move is parallel to other divine testings. Perhaps so. But it should be recognized that this linkage to the testing tradition carries with it some uncomfortable theological assumptions. Without the heavenly dispute, there would have been no test (v. 9: Is Job in it only for what he can get out of it?—an important question in its own right). Given the "wager," the test is for *God's* sake, not Job's, so that God can show "the *satan*" that he is wrong, that God's confidence in Job is well placed. At one level, this "testing" does link up with other divine testings. For example, God tests Abraham and Israel so that *God* may know what is in their hearts (Gen 22:12; Deut 8:2); so, the issue of God's knowledge does ring true to these types of texts. God knows all there is to know, but there is a future that is not yet there to know (will Job's faith be able to withstand the pressure?). Yet, "testing" does not seem adequate language to describe the settling of a *celestial* dispute. For God to be proved right in this argument among "adults," Job must lose, treated as a pawn and visited by suffering. The end, apparently, justifies the means.[107]

Still other interpreters take a different tack. The prologue is a means by which one "answer" to the problem of suffering (perhaps current among readers) is put forth: suffering is due to arbitrary heavenly decisions. The reader of the book is invited to consider this explanation of Job's suffering as a serious proposal, among others. For some scholars, this "answer" is not directly disputed in the book, but is simply set alongside others for the reader to consider. In fact, one dimension of Job's own perspective in the ensuing dialogue is similar to this view. While he disputes the friends' view that he suffers because he has sinned, Job does not dispute their view that God is the one responsible (or that he would have deserved suffering had he sinned). The issue, for Job, is that this divine action is arbitrary; even more, and especially, it is evidence of a divine failure in the managing of the creation. As such, this view would be parallel to the way in which God's relationship to suffering is portrayed in the prologue. This seems to me to be an unlikely interpretation, but further evidence from the book will be necessary to support such a decision.

Still another proposal, the most convincing to me, has been suggested. For this reading of Job, the prologue presents an "outrageous premise" or a "deliberate provocation."[108] As such, the prologue serves as a rhetorical strategy for the book as a whole, which could function in different though not necessarily exclusive ways. For example, the prologue is designed to grab the attention of readers who may not have been familiar with this imaging of God's ways. The idea of a divine wager is unparalleled in the Old Testament, as is the idea that God would be manipulated or incited by "the *satan*." As such, the prologue would serve to create theological distance from the typical readers' point of view. Or, the rhetorical strategy would seek to maximize the readers' sympathies toward Job rather than God, who is finally more responsible for Job's suffering than "the *satan*" (in this respect, Job's later complaints against God are on target). Or, the prologue sets up an image of a micromanaging God, which the book proceeds to subvert by providing an alternative view.

If the reader moves with one or more of these (or related) rhetorical strategies, then the prologue's portrayal of God should be treated just as suspiciously as, say, the theology of Job's friends. The appropriateness of such a perspective may be signaled by the disappearance of "the *satan*" figure and the wager in the rest of the book; they were both part of this rhetorical setup. It might be suggested that "the *satan*" figure in the prologue is essentially a symbol for the way in which God lets the creation work; in effect, giving "the *satan*" permission to let moral and natural evil loose on Job is emblematic of God letting the creation be what it has the potential of being and becoming, including the experience of suffering.

Such a perspective regarding the prologue may be supported by Job's "confessions of faith" in 1:21 and 2:10. These verses are often thought to stand at odds with the impatient Job of the dialogue; but other scholars have shown that this impatience is anticipated in subtle ways in Job's statements.[109] Uttered in deep suffering, these words reflect Job's point of view that God is responsible for what he is going through. In terms of the prologue's setup, this conviction proves to be basically accurate, though there is some development in Job's point of view.

But, the question then arises: do these words of Job also express the "whence" of suffering from the narrator's point of view, or at least one commendable option? This is probably not the case, in view of several considerations. One, Job's "confessions" claim that God is responsible for both good and evil (monism); that this point of view is also held by Job's friends makes it suspect in view of God's evaluation of their speaking (42:7). The words of 1:21 and 2:10 probably portray Job's reflexive falling back on a conventional piety—a common human response at such times.[110] Later (42:5), Job will stand in judgment over his prior piety, declaring it hearsay; this development provides another clue regarding the evaluation of Job's "confessions" in the prologue. The God speeches will finally present a more nuanced understanding of divine responsibility for a world in which one may be deeply hurt; God will be presented as *ultimately* responsible.

Two, the reader is invited to distinguish between the two confessions. While the first (1:21) is conventional piety, the second (2:10) is more ambiguous. A careful comparison of 1:21 and 2:10 reveals important differences:[111] the initial declarative statement becomes a question, the first-person singular becomes plural, Yahweh becomes the generic "God," and the second verse concludes with the minimalist "Job did not sin with his lips."[112] Job's second response begins to break away from the piety of 1:21 and moves toward the complaints of the dialogue. Job's wife's remarks (2:9) may encourage Job in this important move to lament/complaint, and hence it may be said that her challenge to Job to "curse God, and die" sets up the rest of the book.

Three, if the prologue is read in a straightforward manner, it would present an "answer" to the *why* of Job's suffering. Though Job is never informed of the reason (he experiences both moral evil and natural evil), the reader is given access to the mind of God (!) regarding the matter. Readers now have an "explanation." This interpretation of the prologue has spawned many attempts to "explain" instances of human suffering in comparable terms. God likes to bet on the best horses; if you're one of them, watch out! Or, more generally, God sends sufferings directly upon specific individuals. But, if our reading of the prologue is near the mark, then the "explanation" is in fact no explanation; it is simply "outrageous" or "provocative," setting up the rest of the book. Job's friends will continue in the prologue's "explaining" mode, but God's speeches will make clear, in support of Job's protest, that there is, for those who suffer like Job, no "answer" or "explanation." At the same time, silence is not the only other alternative.

Job experiences both moral evil and natural evil, but the only instance of moral evil is the attack of the foreigners; the strong emphasis is on natural evil. From Job's perspective, at least, the immediate source of his suffering is not otherworldly (e.g., "direct hits" from "the *satan*" or even God), but observable "natural evil" (fire and lightning, windstorm, disease). God is understood to mediate the suffering through such phenomena. Some "moral evil" is experienced, but its source is external to Job himself and his social world, namely, seminomadic peoples (Sabeans; Chaldeans) from the wilderness areas (where the wild animals are at home). The strong emphasis on natural evil links up with the God speeches in an important way. The issue, finally, will have to do with *the nature of the creation* that God brought into being.

The Words of Job and His Friends (3–37)

The interaction between Job and his friends consists of a remarkable series of disputatious theological conversations, initiated by Job's angry lament (Job 3). Job continues to press his case in the face of his friends' disapproving responses, and he brings the dialogue to a climax by building a strong case for his own innocence in the face of God's irresponsible work *as Creator* (Job 29–31); God has not tended to the created moral order as he ought to. Generally speaking, the three friends' responses to Job (each in turn) finally drop away altogether without completing the normal cycle; Bildad's response in Job 25 is brief and Zophar's is missing altogether (cf. Elihu in chs. 32–37). Job's speeches, however, generally get more intense as he leaves the friends' arguments behind and, more and more, challenges God directly.

It is important to say that, despite the rigor and harshness of his charges against friends and God, Job retains his faith in God throughout his speaking. Job understands that his relationship with God is of such a nature that he can speak his mind without having to worry about the rupture of the relationship from the divine side (this is at least one of the reasons for the divine evaluation in 42:7-8). Job spells out the history of his relationship with God and the way in which that has worked itself out in his daily life (chs. 29–31). The issue for Job, given what has happened to him, is that God's relationships to creation (and to him as a creature) have not been faithful. In any case, Job is an example of remarkable faithfulness in the midst of horrendous personal tragedy. And Job will finally come to see (42:1-6) that, in spite of appearances, God has been faithful, and that has been shown in chapters 38–41 by the way in which God has related to the created order, perhaps especially in letting the creation be what it was created to be, even with all the suffering that has entailed.

A related issue to be tracked through the dialogue is that of silence and being silenced. Initially, the friends sit with Job for seven days, silent and weeping (2:11-13); Job asks his friends to teach him and he will be silent (6:24); but they talk and talk with "windy words" so that Job complains of being silenced. "If you would only keep silent!" and listen to me speak (13:5-6, 13; 21:2-3), "for then I would be silent and die" (13:19). But his voiced experience cannot break into their theological system (16:2-5). Elihu pleads with Job to be silent and listen to him (33:31-33), but he is only full of wind. Finally, Job cries out to be heard by God, who has been silent to this point (31:35). Finally, God does speak; Job is silent and is taught by God himself (38–41), but Job is not silenced and is given the last word (42:1-6) before the epilogue.

Job sets the dialogue in terms of creation (ch. 3) and it becomes the most common and intense theme that occurs throughout, most explicitly in Job 3:3-9; 7:16-19; 9:4-24; 10:8-13; 12:13-25; 25:1-6; 26:5-14; 36:24–37:24. This choice of themes is no doubt prompted by the fact that Job's most personal experiences of suffering are due to natural evil (fire and windstorm and the loss of his children, 1:16-19; disease and its toll on himself, 2:7-8). More generally, Job is absolutely right in centering his words on creational matters; Job's suffering most fundamentally *does* have to do with issues regarding the nature of God's creation and God's continuing relationship to it. *The most fundamental issue for Job is theological*, more specifically, *a certain theology of creation*, and that is where the crux of the matter lies for him. This kind of concern is one of the most basic reasons why God responds with creation imagery and why that response is eminently appropriate for Job in his suffering (Job 38–41). God's positive evaluation of Job's words (42:7-8) may in part be grounded in *Job's choice of creation* (which the friends pick up on) as the *heart* of the matter at stake between them.

Job's argument with both friends and God has to do with the nature of God's created order and God's activity, or the absence thereof, within that order. For the friends, that created moral order is rigidly fixed. For them, "Justice is a guaranteed system of reward and retribution, of God *reacting* to the good or ill that mortals do."[113] In effect, the world runs like a machine, so God does not act in freedom, but only reacts within a tightly woven creational system. The striking thing is that Job in essence agrees with his friends, and the very nature of that understanding leads him to have explicit expectations regarding how God will act within that created order. This conception of creation will need sharp challenge and correction, finally by God. For God, on the other hand, as the God speeches will make clear, the creation is not so rigidly fixed and God's relationship to that creation is not that of a micromanager. The nature of the creation and God's relationship to it are of such a nature that (innocent) suffering can happen. As noted, the *satan* figure in the prologue may essentially be emblematic for the way in which God lets the creation work; in effect, giving "the *satan*" permission to let moral and natural evil loose on Job is an illustration more generally of God letting the creation be what it has the potential of being and becoming, including the experience of suffering.

Again and again, Job blames God for what he has gone through (6:4; 30:20-21; 23:6). In the language of James L. Crenshaw, Job levels two basic charges against his God: "First, God fails to govern the universe properly, that is, in such a manner that virtuous people thrive and wicked individuals come to grief. Second, at the very least God is guilty of criminal negligence."[114] Job places this fundamentally creational issue in a judicial context, demanding that God appear in court so that he might bring charges against God. He seems to assume that God has no defense: God is guilty as charged, not being the kind of Creator that God ought to be. I take a brief look at several texts that feature the creational argument at stake in the dialogue.[115]

Job's lament in chapter 3 seems to be addressed to no one but himself and his own history, though Eliphaz will respond (4:1). Job draws correlations between his own creation (conception and birthing) and that of the creation as a whole (3:3-10; many links to Gen 1:1–2:4 have been noted; see also Jer 20:14-18). This link between the creation of Job and the universe suggests that God's "randomness and injustice toward him is simply one more instance of God's randomness and injustice toward the world."[116] In other words, Job links his own integrity and the (lack of) integrity of the created order.

Job's lament does not seek to place a retroactive curse on a birthday very much in the past, nor does he seek somehow to "uncreate" the world, to bring about a reversal of creation or speak chaos into being, in the interests of bringing about the end of his own life. Rather, he focuses on his "day" of creation, the day (and night) he was born; the day of his creation seems to be universalized: all days in such a creation are *actually* like the day of his birth. Given Job's experience, his very birth demonstrates that this world is not a just order; his birth was the result of a creation in disarray and his own personal "day" and night participated in that disorder. *God's creation was complicit* in what he had become as a suffering one, and given the nature of a created order that makes possible such suffering, its very status as creation should be recognized as cursed. He declares his own life to be like that world, having the *ongoing* status of being cursed, filled with darkness and death rather than life, like the precreation situation in Gen 1:2.

For Job, God's creation is out of whack, a disorderly place within which nothing of importance can be truly counted on. God will respond (in chs. 38–41) and claim, among other things, that such disorderly elements and random events are an integral part of "the warp and woof of the cosmic fabric" (e.g., darkness, unruly waters, Behemoth, Leviathan).[117] But Job's viewpoint must be openly and thoroughly voiced before that divine response can be appreciated.

In Eliphaz's response to Job (4–5), the creation is wonderfully and precisely ordered and, contrary to what Job thinks, it can be counted on. As an example, the innocent finally do not perish while those who sow trouble will reap trouble (4:7-9; 5:1-16). Eliphaz notes that if Job will but repent, like other innocent ones he will live long with many descendants, with a peaceful rather than terrifying relationship with all of nature (5:22-23; cf. Hos 2:18-25; Ezek 34:25; 37:26). In his reply, Job claims that God as Creator has brought human beings into the world for hard service and "months of emptiness, / and nights of misery" (7:1-6). He is being treated as a disorderly element in a disorderly creation. He parodies Psalm 8 in 7:17-18; humans are not actually called to such a vocation in God's world but to be the object of God's relentless control. Bildad responds (8:1-22) that if he would turn to God, he would experience creation as a good creation, unlike the wicked who experience it as a threat.

Job 9–10 reports Job's anguished reply, with direct queries about justice and God's creative purpose. "Job sees creation as a violent and careless manipulation of things and living beings" (9:5-13; 10:8-13; see 12:13-25).[118] In 9:4-15, Job parodies creation hymnody by mocking God's control over the entire created order but (by implication) has no control over what has caused his suffering. God's world is in fact a mess, so disorderly that the innocent life one may live has no relationship to whether or not he is visited with suffering; it makes no sense. In 9:16-24 Job contests any claims that justice is an integral part of the created order of things; justice has been given over to the power of the wicked (9:24). If God's creative purpose is in doubt, then claims concerning redemption and covenant are likewise in jeopardy. The striking thing is that Job is basically right about the creational order; as the God speeches will later show, God has not created a machine, a tightly woven cosmic order. But Job faults God for not creating an order which makes sense in direct correspondence to human behaviors.

Job continues his response by lifting up his own creation as a human being (10:3-13, 18-19; cf. Ps 139:13-15). Job 10:8-12 parodies Ps 139:13 ("you knit me together in my mother's womb"); but unlike the latter, he uses God's creating of him as an individual created for trouble. For Job, there is an absence of praise and wonder, with complaint and even self-loathing (10:1) filling the room about what God has done with his creation.[119] References to creation (10:3*a*, 8-12, 18*a*) alternate with juridical references (10:3*a*, 3*b*, 6-7, 13-17) with reflections on both birth and death. For Job, God is acting in ways that are not in tune with God's acts of creation and God's purposes related thereto. God's knowledge of his origins, and indeed participation in his gestation and birthing, should tell God that he is innocent. Given the breadth of the divine knowledge, God is hiding all the positive evidence. Zophar's response (11:1-20) essentially claims that God's ways in the creation are inscrutable and hence Job is wrong to take God to task for the kind of world he has created.

Job 12:13-25 may be another parody of a hymn. Based on Job's own experience, he launches into a defense against the accusations of the friends. God's governance is entirely arbitrary and does not have the best interests of the creatures at heart. God's wisdom as a creator is admitted, as is God's power, but they are used arbitrarily against people like himself. God's creation is poorly designed, because retribution does not function very well and hence justice is skewed and creation is anarchic. God is finally responsible for this descent of the creation into chaos. Job insists, in the face of the friends' contrariness, that the world of nature is an important source of knowledge about God and world, indeed the natural world is imaged as a teacher of human beings (12:7-9, the only use of Yahweh in the dialogue; 13:1-2), but in this context it is a teacher with respect to God's abuse of the suffering Job. Eliphaz accuses Job of arrogance in thinking he knows what he knows about the creation (15:7-8). Skipping ahead to 25:1-6; 26:5-24,[120] Bildad lifts up the orderly design of God's creation; he is awed by it and submissive before it (25:4-6; 26:14). Job's response in 29–31 is designed to lift up the incongruity that Job sees between the exemplary ways in which he has lived out his life and the way he has been treated by the Creator God. Job seeks to bring God into court to answer the charges regarding the poor divine design and administration of the created order. Elihu's intervening speeches (32–37) conclude on this creational theme in detail (36:24–37:24) and as such appropriately introduce the God speeches.

Creation is the primary issue between Job and his friends, and God will respond directly to those important creational dimensions that have surfaced again and again in that dialogue. Before taking a close look at the God speeches, we briefly consider the epilogue and Job's response to the words of God.

Job's Response to God and the Epilogue (42:1-6, 7-17)

The place of the epilogue (42:7-17) within the book is difficult to assess. This is so not least because it portrays a seemingly idyllic ending, in which Job supposedly can forget all the children he has lost in view of the new ones he has been given. It is important to remember that the epilogue belongs together with the prologue in its genre, and hence should be interpreted in comparable terms as part of a what-if construction. The epilogue is no more "real" or reflective of historical reality than the prologue.

Several interpretations are possible. The epilogue could invite the reader into thinking of the time beyond any suffering, perhaps even a new heaven and a new earth, when God will be at work in both wrath/judgment (the friends) and healing. On the far side of suffering a future will be put in place that is shaped by goodness, life, and giftedness (see Rom 5:3-5). Such a view of the future could be generative of hope in the midst of suffering. The epilogue could also present one more point of view of suffering to be considered alongside others in the book. For example, it might support one dimension of the view of Job's friends: the righteous will receive rewards. They might have to be disciplined before they do, but it will be worth the wait!

A more attractive interpretation to my way of thinking would start from God's *evaluation* (see above) of the words of Job and his friends (42:7), strategically placed at the beginning of the epilogue. The friends thought that Job was blasphemous in his God-talk and hence would be punished further. God, by pronouncing the rightness of Job's words and condemning theirs, *in a public way* affirms that Job's suffering, contrary to their way of thinking, was innocent and that his complaints did not jeopardize his standing with God (demonstrated by the restoration of his fortunes). Even more, God, though filled with wrath, provides a sacrificial means by which the wrongs of the friends can be atoned for; contrary to their own retributive perspective, they will not suffer the consequences of their "folly." Ironically, though the friends judged Job's words so harshly, Job's *words* (his prayers) will prove to be life-giving for them (42:8-9).[121]

Job's response to the God speeches (42:1-6) provides the transition between God's speeches and the epilogue. How the reader interprets Job's response in 42:1-6 will shape the understanding of the book of Job as a whole. Unfortunately, there is widespread disagreement on the translation of verse 6.[122] The translation tradition of RSV/NRSV, "therefore I despise myself, / and repent in dust and ashes," is usually regarded as misleading. The object ("myself") is not explicit in Hebrew, and the word translated "repent" *(niḥām)* is not the usual word for repentance of sin (*šûb*); in fact, it may never be so used.[123] The verb *niḥām* normally carries the sense of reversal and often has God as the subject (e.g., Jer 18:8-10). The Tanakh gives an alternate sense, "I recant and relent, / Being but dust and ashes." Still another is given by J. Gerald Janzen: "Therefore I recant and change my mind concerning dust and ashes."[124] The last-noted translation best catches the basic sense of the verb in this context. But, what or whom is Job repudiating? Probably he is setting aside his case against God, withdrawing his words against God's governance of the creation and recognizing that what he had known about God and God's world was inadequate (42:5). The speeches of God have given him new insight into his place within the complexities and ambiguities of the created order.

The God Speeches, Job's Responses, and Importance of Creation (38:1–42:7)

God's response to Job (and, indirectly, Job's friends) is a verbal recreation of an amazingly diverse universe.[125] The reader is taken up into a literary spacecraft, as it were, and shown a splendid creation. The type of verbal journey on which God takes Job is noteworthy. God does not take Job into the temple or into the depths of his own soul or insist on some ancient equivalent of clinical pastoral education (CPE). God takes him to the zoo, or better, out to "where the wild things are." That God's creation is both good and wild is an important dimension of these speeches and provides a clue to the nature of God's response to Job in his suffering. By appearing in the whirlwind, God discloses God's self to Job within the natural order of things, as the God of creation not the God of Israel or the God of redemption or the God who intervenes to make sure that nothing goes wrong.

This wild world of God's good creation is the context for interpreting the "whirlwind" within which God appears (38:1). It is important to note that this appearance of God to Job is a theophany, a common means by which God reveals God's self to individuals and to Israel.[126] That God so reveals the divine self outside of Israelite channels immediately says something about God the Creator, whose revealing is not confined to "salvation history" contexts. This appearance to Job in the whirlwind does not signal a destructive or judgmental mode,[127] but corresponds to other theophanies of God as Bearer of the Word wherein God's speaking is accompanied by meteorological phenomena (e.g., Ezek 1:4, "stormy" wind). God's revelatory mode connects with the content of the word that God now speaks; that is, the whirlwind constitutes an example of creation's chaotic elements. Far from providing a critique of ways of gathering wisdom from experience, so typical of Wisdom literature more generally, the divine voice is specifically set within the natural order and brings knowledge regarding that creation.[128] Such knowledge would be available to human beings properly attentive to experience; the implication is that Job has not been as attentive to the creation as he might have been. God appears, "clothed" by elements of God's good creation. God "wears" a creaturely form in order to be as concretely, persuasively, and intensely present to Job as possible. God assumes this mode so that Job may be moved to discover God and God's ways embodied within the world itself. Job should understand the focus on creation as revealing of God's ways in the world more generally. At least some insight into suffering is thereby made available.

But readers have often wondered whether these speeches of God are relevant to Job in his suffering. Many interpreters would claim that God is revealed as insensitive to Job in his suffering (and, by implication, all suffering), one who "skirts the profound questions being explored," and does not "own up" to the divine complicity in Job's suffering.[129] Gerhard von Rad puts the matter in these terms: "All commentators find the divine speech highly scandalous, in so far as it bypasses completely Job's particular concerns, and because in it Yahweh in no way condescends to any kind of self-interpretation."[130] Crenshaw calls the God speeches "sublime irrelevance" with regard to any insight into Job's suffering.[131] I would challenge this direction for interpretation; the speeches do in fact speak to Job in his suffering and about his suffering.

The God speeches belong to the disputation speech genre; they are particularly concerned to challenge Job's accusations; at the same time, they also affirm a key dimension of Job's claim about the creation. God's world does indeed have significant "chaotic" elements, but Job's negative interpretation of that disorder needs to be challenged and recharacterized. Yet, given the "awesome" theophany within which God speaks, the reader may well expect a severe indictment of Job, with a guilty as charged result. But is this what happens? In thinking about this question, it has been pointed out that the two God speeches may be correspondent to the two basic charges Job has brought before God, charges of faulty creational design and inept and unjust governance (in our terms, originating creation and continuing creation, though they overlap).[132]

The first speech (38:1–39:30) focuses on the issue of the "design" of creation (38:2).[133] Job is questioned by God not because he really has sinned after all but because he has interpreted his suffering in terms of a wrongheaded understanding of the way in which God's world works. He has, like his friends, bought into a strict retributive orthodoxy where there are, or should be, no "loose ends" to God's creation and where all suffering is rooted in sinful behaviors. Inasmuch as he has not sinned (this entails no claim that he is sinless), the problem lies with God, who has designed this creational "system" in the first place. God's counter-questions in effect deny Job's accusations regarding God's design of the creation and way of caring for it, laying out evidence from the animal world that God is not cruel but provides bountifully for the creation. But, even more basically, God's questions demonstrate that in order to understand his personal suffering Job must revise his evaluation of the nature of the creation and the way in which God works in and through it. Job's claims regarding a world that does not function in a precisely ordered way are largely accurate (e.g., 12:1-25), but how he interprets this disorderliness is faulty, for that is precisely the kind of world God intended. In effect, human suffering, even suffering such as Job's, may indeed occur in a good, well-ordered, and reliable creation, for that world is not a risk-free world! Indeed, being a part of such a world means that suffering can take place quite apart from sin and evil.[134] This point may be linked with the primary cause of Job's suffering in Job 1–2, namely, natural evil. God's directive to Job to "gird up" his loins (38:3; 40:7) is a call for him to probe his experience of suffering more deeply in terms of God's complex design of the creation and his own place within it.

The second speech (40:6–41:34) continues the theme of the first speech and adds issues of divine justice and governance with a focus on the enigmatic figures, Behemoth and Leviathan.[135] The scholarly interpretation of these figures varies from actual animals (hippopotamus and crocodile) to mythic figures to symbolic forces of evil.[136] I agree with those who see these creatures as animals, though their "reputation" in that world has drawn them into the realm of fantasy and myth (cf. the dragon in our own culture).[137] It is doubtful that these figures have any reference to evil or to chaos as an evil force; any correlations they may have to ancient Near Eastern themes are literary not substantive. If one insists on thinking of these creatures in terms of "chaos," that does not make them evil any more than Gen 1:2 is a reference to evil.[138] That they are created by God (40:15, 19; 41:33, "creature") strongly suggests that however strange and atypical they might be they are good creatures, not evil. They are a part of the diverse and wonderful world that God has created. At the same time, these creatures are revealing of the kind of good creation wherein human beings can be hurt and suffer, not least because they are certainly beyond any human control. At the same time, it is not helpful to suggest that these creatures are fully within divine control; God has set creational limits (e.g., 38:8-11), but within those limits there is no sense of divine micromanagement.

One major point seems to be, again, that God did not create a risk-free world, and that world included animals, though majestic in their own right, that could harm human beings. God's creation is filled with good creatures that entail risks for human beings quite apart from questions of evil. Human beings are created as finite, with limits of strength, intelligence, and agility, including an inability to bring under their control every creature that God has made any more than they could bring all the wicked in the world to their just end (40:10-14).

Even "all who are proud" (40:11-12) cannot bring these creatures to heel; indeed these creatures rule over "all who are proud" (41:34). Additionally, 40:10-14 might be linked to one of the mediators of suffering to Job (1:13-17); there are wicked human beings in God's world who can bring suffering to human beings, but God's approach is not to intervene and annihilate every wicked person; "true royalty engages 'proud' power otherwise than by brute force."[139] And so, these creatures that contribute to disorder in God's creation, whether human or non-human, are part of life and God will not "fix" things by "uncreating" them.

We turn again to Behemoth and Leviathan. The goodness of God's creation includes water, which is both gift and danger; the law of gravity is a great blessing, but it works every time and hence is potentially a very dangerous reality for human beings. One also thinks of earthquakes, storms, bacteria, and viruses; human beings can suffer deeply from an encounter with such creatures, which are good in themselves, not evil (but can become so in their effects, hence, "natural evil"). Such a great diversity of creatures makes the world so much more interesting, not least because they are not under human control. Yet, these creatures do not threaten God's good creation; God made them an integral part of that wondrous creation.[140] God is not engaged in a battle with them;[141] though God could conquer them if God so chose (40:19),[142] this is not God's way with God's own creation. Indeed, God's hymn in praise of Leviathan (41:12-34), anticipated by the praise of the heavenly beings (38:7), shows that God delights in these creatures; they are creatures that have a significant part in making the creation good.

These creatures, then, may be termed "chaos," though, contrary to its usual usage not because they are evil or "hostile to human life"[143] but because they constitute elements of God's good creation that are not neat and tidy, and human beings can get hurt in just such a world. These creatures constitute an element of complexity, ambiguity, and even disorder in God's creation.[144] And that kind of world is necessary for it to be a good world. To say that the creation is good, as we have seen, is not to say that it is perfect;[145] at the same time, to say that creation is not perfect is not to say that evil makes it so. For Job to understand his suffering, then, would be to recognize that God neither created a risk-free world nor provided danger-free zones for the pious to be kept free from any harm. And God will not micromanage such a world to make sure no one gets hurt; God will let the creatures be what they were created to be. Such a world is necessary if it would be other than a drab, monotonous, and ever-the-same world. Such a world is necessary for there to be genuine novelty and new creative ventures on the part of both God and creatures. And so God will sustain such an ordered and open-ended creation even in the face of the suffering ones who wish that God would have created a world wherein human beings could be free from suffering. That is a price, sometimes a horrendous price, which creatures pay for the sake of having such a world; but it is also a price that God pays, for God will not remove the divine self from that suffering and will enter deeply into it for the sake of the future of just such a world.

God's parading of animals before Job is no doubt intended to remind the reader of Gen 2:19-20, where God brings each animal before Adam for naming. This action is deeply ironic. In such naming, the human once brought a certain order to God's creation, but, God suggests, the creatures that the human being has named include such creatures as Behemoth and Leviathan. And so the human has been participant in shaping just such a world that God brings before Job. By implication, Job should link himself more closely with Adam and recognize that God's creation, filled with disorderly elements, has in part been shaped by that human naming and that such a creation is good.[146]

In sum, both speeches address Job's charge that God's world is chaotic, but *not* by showing that the creation can only be described as wonderfully ordered and secure. Job has been right in his basic claim about a disorderly world, but Job draws the wrong conclusion. To have elements of such disorder and insecurity is precisely the kind of world God wanted, for God did not intend the world to be a machine. God challenges Job so that he realizes the proper nature of that creation, that suffering may be experienced in just such a world, and so that he can learn what his place within it properly is, even in the midst of suffering.

Interpreters differ, however, in working out what these divine responses entail regarding (1) the relationship between God and world and (2) the implications that the nature of God's world has for thinking through the issue of suffering. James L. Crenshaw represents one point of view. The emphasis of the speeches falls on the divine control, with chaos virtually no threat; "Nothing is left to chance here."[147] Yahweh is in "complete control."[148] Human beings are "incidental—mainly an important foil to God."[149] The speeches of God do respond "after a fashion" to Job's charges, but God is basically silent regarding the issues of suffering with which Job has been confronted. But, another point of view is in fact available to interpreters, and I raise two issues to that end.

First, whether Job's suffering has been directly addressed by God. The various speeches in Job 3–37 have offered several options regarding the "whence" of suffering: punishing sin; God sending suffering "for no reason"; disciplining; warning; testing; shaping of character; refining fire; producing insight into life; being temporary rather than final. God does give a general evaluation of these speeches in the epilogue (42:7-8), but given the fact that God neither explicitly affirms nor negates any of these options in the God speeches, does this constitute a divine admission that there are no other options in thinking about the question of suffering?[150] Or, that they are all equally valid?

In an initial response to such a question, God's speeches are certainly no "answer" to the suffering of Job, but that constitutes their strength. The danger is that we will fall into the trap of thinking that God's (our!) only options in the face of suffering are either an "answer/explanation" or silence—sitting on the mourning bench with nothing to say. God recognizes an option for understanding suffering that the speeches in Job 3–37 have *not* offered and proceeds to address that option in chapters 38–41. God was silent for a period of time (as are the friends, and admirably so, 2:11-13); this could be named a divine strategy to get the various options "on the table." But, there comes a time to speak, and God does speak. Indeed, God *appears* and speaks, and in such a way that Job is not silenced, even in the face of a whirlwind and God's extensive speaking. God may even consider Job's initial response (40:3-5) much too self-effacing, and so God continues to speak until Job responds in more direct, less self-negating ways. God does offer a deeply relevant, even pastorally sensitive response to this suffering one and, indirectly, regarding the suffering of any individual. This option for understanding suffering has to do with the nature of the world that God has created.

Second, regarding the design of God's world and issues relating to divine "control" and "chance." In these speeches, Job is introduced to a remarkable range of matters having to do with zoology, meteorology, and cosmology. Readers are, for one thing, introduced to images of boundary and law and rule; this world proves to be a well-ordered and basically coherent world. Readers also are given images of care and nurture, especially for the animals, whose unmanaged freedom is celebrated. At the same time—and this is very important, images of wildness and strangeness are present, including the wild seas, wild animals, wild weather (rain, hail, ice, snow, lightning), the uncertainties of the night, and Behemoth and Leviathan, the inhabitants of an ancient Jurassic Park. For all the world's order and coherence, it doesn't run like a machine; a certain randomness, ambiguity, unpredictability, and play characterize its complex life. The proverb of Eccl 9:11 would apply to this kind of world: "time and chance happen to them all." Lifting up this dimension of the speeches of God is absolutely crucial, for it provides the fundamental context for God's response to Job's suffering. This is the case not least because natural evil is a basic feature of the causes of Job's suffering.

Ellen F. Davis sees this complex and ambiguous dimension of the God speeches. She notes that the speeches reveal that God has aesthetic preferences, not just moral preferences.[151] God's way of creating the world is of such a nature that it has elements of the extraordinary, the beautiful, the bizarre, and the irregular. Davis cites Annie Dillard's *Pilgrim at Tinker Creek* in this connection; this work is a beautiful reflection on this kind of work on the part of the Creator:

> The world is full of creatures that for some reasons seem stranger to us than others, and libraries are full of books describing them—hagfish, platypuses, lizardlike pangolins four feet long with bright green, lapped scales like umbrella-tree leaves on a bush hut roof, butterflies emerging from anthills, spiderlings wafting through the air clutching tiny silken balloons, horseshoe crabs . . . the creator creates. Does he stoop, does he speak, does he save, succor, prevail? Maybe. But he creates; he creates everything and anything. The creator goes off on one wild, specific tangent after another, or millions simultaneously, with an exuberance that would seem to be unwarranted, and with an abandoned energy sprung from an unfathomable font. What is going on here? The point of the dragonfly's terrible lip, the giant water bug, birdsong, or the beautiful dazzle and flash of sunlighted minnows, is not that it all fits together like clockwork—for it doesn't, not even inside the goldfish bowl—but that it all flows so freely wild, like the creek, that it all surges in such a free, fringed tangle. Freedom is the world's water and weather, the world's nourishment freely given, its soil and sap; and the creator loves pizzazz.[152]

God the Creator loves pizzazz! That is one key dimension of God's work in the world that Job has not observed or, better, has not considered a positive dimension of God's world; it will be an important word for him to hear in the midst of his suffering. In fact, it will be this word more than any other that moves him toward further understanding of his suffering and God's relationship to it.

I look at the God speeches from another angle of vision. If they are approached in terms of the God images that scholars bring to their reading of the text, most interpretations can be placed under one of three umbrellas (perhaps not altogether fairly).

1. *God as lord, warrior, judge.* I use James L. Crenshaw's work as an example. Job has been presumptuous to raise the questions he has. God's response is a put-down, a "badgering," a debasement of Job, in "a spirit of mockery,"[153] through an accompanying display of divine power.[154] God simply overwhelms the challenging Job, emphasizing his utter helplessness when faced with the workings of the world. And, when faced with the wild animals, Job is a lightweight, out of his league, unable to control them, and unknowing regarding their ways in God's world. In the face of this divine barrage, Job, in acts and words of self-negation, gives up on his quest for justice.[155] Crenshaw will speak of some positive notes. Job is addressed by the creator and God refuses to give "simple solutions to complex questions" (the only option available to God?); God allows each creature to develop according to its own nature.[156] But Crenshaw will even generalize to ask: "Must the 'greater glory of God' always require a belittling of human beings."[157]

In response, this approach tends to understand the God speeches as designed fundamentally to make a negative point, and it is difficult to believe that four chapters of Job would be needed to do so. God's positive evaluation of Job's words in 42:7 also tends to be neglected in this view.[158] Elements of this perspective may be present, but they stand in the service of a more positive point. Some further comments on the disputation genre may also be helpful here. It is common to suggest that God's speeches do challenge Job, but do they debase him or condemn him? For all the formal characteristics of disputation in the God speeches, the effect given in the epilogue is quite different: vindication for Job rather than condemnation (see 42:7-8).[159] Samuel E. Balentine is convincing when he says: "God's review of creation's design serves primarily to confront and challenge Job, not to condemn or silence him."[160] Job's dispute with God is resolved in the epilogue, wherein both Job and God state that they have learned from this encounter and journey into a new future. William P. Brown gets at the issue in a balanced way: "Yahweh's discourse is as much a didactic treatise and source of resolution for Job as it is a deposition against him." God "effectively silences Job's contentious discourse yet somehow confirms Job's innocence is a true coup de grace, a final blow and a 'stroke of grace.'"[161] It is important to add that, while God's speeches do silence Job's accusations, they do not silence him (42:1-6) nor suggest that questions in themselves are somehow inappropriate to address to God (as God's evaluation claims, 42:7).

2. *God as parent.* God's relationship to Job in the midst of his suffering is what truly counts. Job's questions are basically appropriate, especially in challenging the retributive orthodoxy of the friends, but he is insufficiently aware of the range of God's parenting work in the larger creation (note the parental images in 38:8-11, 28-29). God's response is disciplinary, but fundamentally nurturing in character and encouraging of freedom, rather than interventionist and controlling. God comes to Job and is present with him in love.

William P. Brown articulates well this particular image; at the same time, his comments move toward the next image, that of creator and sage.[162]

> Like a proud parent who proudly displays the pictures of her children . . . Yahweh has recharacterized creation for Job. . . . There are no puppets or tools employed by a capricious God. . . . Yahweh is characterized ultimately by creativity, self-restraint, and gratuitous pride. . . . It is out of gratuitous delight that Yahweh steps back and lets creation run its course, allowing the citizens of the cosmos the freedom to maneuver and negotiate their respective domains and lives. Far from being a divine tyrant, Yahweh is the gentle parent whose care extends beyond the maintenance of order and structure. Yahweh's love embraces each creature's individuality and unique role within the wonderfully complex network of life.

This approach has many virtues, but it is insufficiently attentive to the creational and vocational dimensions of these speeches of God. Moreover, this approach tends to suggest that, given the resolution, Job will have no more questions about suffering that need to be asked.

3. *God as creator and sage.* Job's questioning was appropriate, but he did not sufficiently recognize the complexity, ambiguity, and goodness of the creation. God's questions are rhetorical and ironic and/or "challenge questions."[163] As they reveal Job's lack of breadth and depth in wisdom and strength, they *recharacterize* Job's understanding in two ways.

First, they reorient for Job what it means to be a human created in the image of God. Job's status as a human being and his vocation of "dominion" in the tradition of Gen 1:28 are affirmed not merely in the face of such suffering but somehow in and through it.[164] Job is to "gird up" his loins (38:1; 40:6) and "be the man" he was created to be, acting relative to the nonhuman world in ways that God intended in creation. In Janzen's words:

> Yahweh parades before Job a realm of nonhuman creatures wild as at the day of their creation, or perhaps we should say wild as at the day of their original presentation to human view for domination. Against the background of Genesis 1 and 2, and of Psalm 8, Job is invited (like the reader) to take this parade as a re-presentation of the human vocation to royal function, in the face of Job's experience of the "wildness" present in creation in the form of inexplicable suffering.[165]

God's questions provide for Job a recharacterization of his identity in God's creation and challenge him to engage more deeply in his vocation on behalf of God's creatures of great worth and value. This focus on vocation relative to the nonhuman creation best explains the lack of attention to human beings in the God speeches.[166]

Second, the speeches of God enable a new understanding of the created order and the way it functions in all of its complexity, its order and disorder. Norman C. Habel helpfully states that in the God speeches,

> God offers a defense by challenging Job, and any who would listen, to discern God as the sage who designed a world of rhythms and paradoxes, of balanced opposites and controlled extremes, of mysterious order and ever-changing patterns, of freedom and limits, of life and death. Within this complex universe, God functions freely to monitor the intricacies of the system, to modulate its ebb and flow and to balance its conflicting needs. Here there is no El Gibbor, no hero king performing mighty acts of intervention, no swift administration of justice. To know this God is to live in the cosmic system, discern its flow, and explore its governing principles. This God is no indulgent father but a shrewd sage who confronts Job with tough questions and tantalizing clues that will exercise the mind and test the spirit of those who would be wise. God's cosmic design is to be explored, not obscured.[167]

Finally, I move back to the question of the "new" option regarding the interpretation of suffering that the God speeches offer. It is common to suggest that the answers to God's questions are obvious in that they emphasize what Job cannot know or do. But God's point is neither to belabor the obvious nor to set Job up for failure. The point of God's questioning is not Job's faith or his personal conduct but basically his knowledge (recognized by Job in 42:3-5). And then the stated issue is not so much *what* Job *could* not know or do but *that* he *does* not know or act with sufficient vision regarding God's "design" (38:2; 42:3) for the creation.[168] God's questions (Who are you? Where are you? What do you know? Are you able?) challenge Job to probe the creation more deeply than he has already, but this time with a greater appreciation for the grand design.[169]

Job's descendants have done precisely that, challenged by the seemingly impossible questions regarding the knowing and the doing. If God were to appear in the early part of the twenty-first century and ask these questions, a scientifically sophisticated Job could answer many of them. Job, have you walked on the floor of the ocean? Yes, parts of it. Job, have you any idea how big the world is? Yes, I've got a sense of that, but I'm learning more every day. Job, do you know where the light comes from? As a matter of fact, I do. Job, who is the mother of the ice and frost, which turn the waters to stone and freeze the face of the earth? God, I live in Minnesota; it runs something like this. Job, who is wise enough to count the clouds and tilt them over to pour out the rain? Well, we're working on that one; there are some lively possibilities. Job, do you know when the mountain goats are born? Yes. Have you watched wild deer give birth? Yes. Do you know how long they carry their young? Yes, God, I do. The more recent conversations between religion and science, especially the new physics, have been engaged in explorations that touch on the issue of creational "design" raised by the God speeches, with important implications for the problem of suffering.[170] Job's descendants will be working on some of God's questions forever, but they have come a long way in furthering their understanding of creation.

From Job's perspective, the primary source of his suffering was not otherworldly (e.g., direct hits from "the *satan*") but observable "natural evil" (fire and lightning, windstorm, disease). Some "moral evil" was experienced, but its source was external to Job himself and his social world, namely, seminomadic peoples (Sabeans; Chaldeans) from the wilderness areas (where the wild animals are at home). This may explain why, though Job tends to couch the issue in terms of justice, God focuses on matters of creation: "Who is this that darkens my (creational) design?" (cf. JB and NEB). Job's questions were not attentive to those dimensions of the created order most directly related to the sources of Job's actual suffering (mostly "natural evil").[171] That is where, given his experience, he should have probed in his questioning. Job had tended to reduce the issue of suffering to his own guilt and innocence (as had his friends) and the issue of God's justice.

Yet, the design issues that God addresses are at least indirectly concerned about matters of justice. There is no morality to the way the law of gravity functions or to the range and efficacy of storms, earthquakes, and viruses. God's creation is good, but in being what it was created to be (and has become), it has the potential of adversely affecting human beings, quite apart from the state of their relationship with God (hence, "natural evil"). Once again, God's good world is not a risk-free world.

This creational being and becoming is well ordered, but the world does not run like a machine, with a tight causal weave; it has elements of randomness and chaos, of strangeness and wildness. Amid the order there is room for chance. The world has ostriches and eagles, raging seas and predictable sunrises, wild weather and stars that stay their courses. God creates space for creaturely freedom at varying levels of complexity. Given the communal character of the cosmos—its basic interrelatedness—every creature will be touched by the movement of every other. While this has negative potential, it also has its positive side, for only then is there genuine possibility for growth, creativity, novelty, surprise, and serendipity. Legal categories and justice-oriented thinking are not adequate for thinking about this complex world or its suffering.

So, Job's world is not a static world; it is a dynamic and interconnected world in the process of becoming. God has a committed relationship to that world to let it be what it was created to be (Gen 8:22). Rather than God taking the mode of control and intervention, such a commitment means divine constraint and restraint (even regards to "moral evil" evident in the nomadic marauders and in 40:10-14). They provide an image of the way in which God relates to the creation, not as one "who intervenes or reacts, but one who modulates and constrains."[172]

And so God takes responsibility for Job's suffering by having created, and still sustaining, a world that is not risk-free and in which people can suffer undeservedly. The divine relationship to this world is such that God no longer acts with complete freedom, but from within a committed relationship to the structures of creation to which God will be faithful. Hence, unlike the provocations of the prologue, instances of suffering are not a matter of divine arbitrariness but of a creation wherein it rains on the just and the unjust. The speeches reveal that God's well-ordered world does not have a tight causal weave; there is room for ambiguity and randomness that may occasion suffering. At the same time, the speeches speak of God's creation as having a basic stability and reliability and so they can contribute to an orienting vision for a time when everything is flying apart and the center no longer holds. This point has been very well made by J. Gerald Janzen.[173]

> At once with freedom and fidelity, justice and generosity, Yahweh makes a world whose dependable orders breathe with flexibility, willing for freedom to exist as the condition for worth to arise. In the world Yahweh has created, it is possible for a righteous, innocent person such as Job to suffer terribly. . . . To participate with God in a world whose life arises from generosity and issues in ordered freedom, leaves one open to undeserved suffering. That suffering arises as part of the price of participating in a world ordered by the power of persuasive address [Gen 1].

I highlight two further ways in which the God speeches reveal a divine responsiveness to Job in his suffering and, in the process, give him a renewed vision of God and of his vocation in the world.

1. *Job and the Lament Tradition.* Job's primary mode of speech throughout the dialogue has been that of lament. Characteristic of these laments (e.g., in the psalms) is the use of images from the world of creation, which also populate God's words to Job, especially the wild animals and the raging sea.

Take the wild animals. Job's laments often voice a deep sense of isolation, often imaged in terms of inhabiting desolate or dangerous places (such as the wilderness) or the animals that inhabit them. Take Ps 102:6-11, "I am like an owl of the wilderness, / like a little owl in the waste places." Job's lament is comparable, "I am a brother of jackals, / and a companion of ostriches" (30:29). Thus God's word to him becomes: If all the wild animals of the wilderness are embraced by God's care and nurture, then so also is Job embraced in his disconnectedness from friends and family. The God speeches highlight themes of creaturely interconnectedness at a time when feelings of isolation hold sway; in effect, all these creatures in God's review provide a community that can surround the suffering one and help to absorb his sorrow. With this God, there are no alien creatures, no outsiders. God even visits the wilderness with rain, and you should see the flowers in the spring![174] Another image is threat from unruly water (e.g., Ps 69:1-3). God has created the sea, and it is not tightly controlled, but its raging has boundaries (Job 38:8-11).

And so the God speeches connect with the images of God that bespeak care, nurture, and community, willing the best for every creature, no matter how unusual or untamed, whether clean or unclean; they enable the one who suffers to get beyond a debilitating focus on his own troubles (and in view of chs. 19, 29–31, his own family and neighborhood) and to see a larger world in which God works in caring ways beyond his knowing.

2. *Questions to and from God.* Job is a book filled with questions and so are its readers. God's positive words regarding Job's lamenting (42:7-8) give human beings permission to voice their deepest laments and sharpest accusations, even if they do not turn out to be strictly orthodox in their expression. Job has the capacity to help readers speak and hear questions in a time of suffering, questions both to God—even shrill ones—and from God (through intermediaries or more directly). God's questions are addressed to the suffering one who has voiced questions, inviting him into a wider cosmic vision within which individual suffering takes place; the persistent question from God constitutes an invitation to seek understanding.

If questions are encouraged when things are going well, and pastoral and other leaders are honest about sharing their own questions, then questions during a time of trauma will be more freely voiced and be more direct and probing. God's strategy with Job might be compared to that of counselors in certain situations: questions responding to questions. But if we don't already have questions humming; if we deny or paper over the experience of suffering; if we have a ready compartment or explanation for all our questions, then the whirlwind, if and when it comes, may be experienced only as stillness. And God will then be silent, because we have no ear to hear God pressing us, challenging us with even further questions.

In the end God is more honored by the impatient probing of Job than by the friends who place certain questions off limits. Job gives voice to those who dare not raise unconventional questions for fear of treading on existing orthodoxies, or being shushed up by those who think it improper to explore the edges of the faith. Job gives voice to those who have indeed experienced great suffering, but who cannot find their voices in the midst of a clamor that suggests that such questions are impertinent. Job gives voice to those who do not have the courage or the theological moxie or the articulateness to raise their deepest questions. Job gives hope that rest and healing may come, but perhaps only on the far side of the probing and the questions; but then the healing will have touched some of the deepest recesses of minds and hearts. Finally, the descendants of Job can have hope in the midst of their most probing questions: they will be caught up into the whirl of the wisdom, the strength, and the infinite resourcefulness of God.

CHAPTER EIGHT

NATURE'S PRAISE OF GOD

Creation is often associated with the praise of God in the Old Testament, especially in the book of Psalms.[1] These hymnic materials are voiced by both human beings and nonhuman creatures; they participate in a mutuality of the praise of God, and their praises are interdependent.[2] With respect to human praise, Psalms 8, 33, 104, and 147 are especially to be noted.[3] In this chapter I focus on the praise of the nonhuman creatures; this theme occurs some fifty times in twenty-five contexts (including fourteen psalms).[4] According to H. Paul Santmire, nature's praise of God is "one of the least understood themes in the Old Testament."[5] The following discussion of the language of nonhuman praise can also be associated with the character of the praise voiced by human beings in more general ways. I give special attention to Psalm 148, wherein an amazing array of nonhuman creatures are called upon to praise God (vv. 3-10):

> Praise him, sun and moon;
>   praise him, all you shining stars!
> Praise him, you highest heavens,
>   and you waters above the heavens!
> Let them praise the name of the LORD,
>   for he commanded and they were created.
> He established them forever and ever;
>   he fixed their bounds, which cannot be passed.
> Praise the LORD from the earth,
>   you sea monsters and all deeps,

fire and hail, snow and frost,
  stormy wind fulfilling his command!
Mountains and all hills,
  fruit trees and all cedars!
Wild animals and all cattle,
  creeping things and flying birds!

Another example, from Isa 44:23:

Sing, O heavens, for the LORD has done it;
  shout, O depths of the earth;
break forth into singing, O mountains,
  O forest, and every tree in it!
For the LORD has redeemed Jacob,
  and will be glorified in Israel.

Initially in this chapter, I track elements of the history of interpretation of nature's praise of God and then move to considerations of genre, metaphor, and tradition, with some theological reflections along the way. Overall, the most basic questions will be: what kind of thinking about God and what kind of thinking about nature would have occasioned this kind of language?

One fundamental issue associated with the interpretation of these texts has certainly been a preoccupation with the human as the center of the universe. In Psalm 148, readers are no doubt pleased to be listed among the angels in the call to praise God and perhaps not so thrilled to be included among creeping, crawling things and crab apple trees. Our anthropocentric sensibilities may be offended to be on a list with hills, horses, and hurricanes. Certainly human praise to God means more to God than the clatter of hail on tin roofs or the clapping of the musically inclined leaves of the aspen trees! Perhaps, but not as much as human beings would like to think.

This anthropocentrism is evident in a salvation history that is focused on human beings, or an existentialism that sees all of reality from the perspective of human existence, or a political theology centered on the liberation of the human, or a theology of the word that includes only human beings within its purview. In such views, nature has often come to be seen as having only an instrumental value, to be used for the enhancement of human life. Emil Brunner illustrates much thinking on this matter: "The cosmic element in the Bible is never anything more than the scenery in which the history of mankind takes place."[6] Often accompanying one or more of these perspectives is an understanding of God in terms of a radical transcendence, often voiced in a spatial sense, that has tended to remove God from too close a brush with the world.[7]

Often accompanying such perspectives has been an emphasis upon Israel's "desacralization" of creation, which in many formulations entails a secularization, indeed a profanation of nature.[8] A distinction should be made between the desacralization of nature and the biblical claim that no creature is divine. The language of desacralization is not helpful because it suggests that God is removed from the natural order, indeed suggests a separation of the spiritual and the material, which opens the way to a misuse of nature. What is needed is a unifying view of worldly reality that brings God, the human, and the natural order together in an interconnected whole. It is precisely this to which these texts testify (as do other texts such as Genesis 1).[9] No aspect of the natural order exists in which God is not intimately involved. God is to be distinguished from the world of nature but not separated from it. God is a factor in every aspect of the life of the natural world, albeit not all-determining. Such claims will be given flesh and blood from Old Testament texts in what follows.

In order to speak properly of Psalm 148 and related passages, readers need to be converted into a mode of perceiving reality that, at the least, is less anthropocentric and more inclusive of the value of the nonhuman for the world and for God. Such a conversion is easier now than it was a generation or so ago. For one thing, such a perspective is more in tune with contemporary scientific perspectives, where the universe is understood to consist not of isolated elements but of a complex set of interrelationships that fit together into a unified whole.[10] Moreover, we are living in a time when increasing numbers of people have an ecological consciousness, a new sense and experience of the oneness of all things, a recognition that there are continuities across the spectrum of all created things that call for new images regarding creaturely relationships. Creation is a seamless web. If this is the case among the creatures, then it is more so between Creator and creatures; for the oneness of creation and the oneness of the Creator are inextricably interconnected, or polytheism is very near at hand. To speak of desacralization can mean a return to Baalism in a different form; to remove God from intimate involvement with the world invites the introduction of other divine powers at the earthly level (Mother Nature?). Or, more drastically, the radical transcendence of God may lead to the death of God in the life of the world.

History of Interpretation

The history of interpretation of passages of this sort, however, does not often reflect such an environmental consciousness.[11] Francis of Assisi stands out because his sensitivities are comparatively rare; he belongs to a very thin tradition. In fact, his reflections find greater sympathies among interpreters today than during any other period since he claimed a creation-wide family of creatures that included the human. One could perhaps cite certain aspects of the Elizabethan worldview with its sense of the music of the spheres and John Dryden's heavenly harmonies. The following are other examples; while not strictly an interpretation of these texts, they are almost certainly informed by them in direct or indirect ways.

First, a passage from Hildegard of Bingen, a twelfth-century prophetess who speaks of the Holy Spirit in this way:

> I am that living and fiery essence of the divine substance that flows in the beauty of the fields. I shine in the water; I burn in the sun and the moon and the stars. The mysterious force of the invisible world is mine. I sustain the breath of all living beings. I breathe in the grass and in the flowers; and when the waters flow like living things, it is I . . . I am the force that lies hidden in the winds; they take their source from me, as a man may move because he breathes; fire burns by my blast. All these live because I am in them and am their life. I am Wisdom. The blaring thunder of the Word by which all things were made is mine. I permeate all things that they may not die, I am life.[12]

Second, from Martin Luther, sixteenth century, in a treatise on the sacraments:

> God is substantially present, everywhere, in and through all creatures, in all their parts and places, so that the world is full of God and he fills all, but without being encompassed and surrounded by it. He is at the same time outside and above all creatures. These are exceedingly incomprehensible matters; yet they are articles of faith and are attested clearly and mightily in Holy Writ. . . . For how can reason tolerate it that the Divine majesty is so small that it can be substantially present in a grain [of wheat], on a grain, over a grain, through a grain; within and without, and that, although it is a single majesty, it nevertheless is entirely in each grain separately, no matter how immeasurably numerous these grains may be? . . . His own divine essence can be in all crea-

> tures collectively and in each one individually more profoundly, more intimately, more present than the creature is in itself.[13]

Other directions in interpretation have more commonly been taken, however. Surprisingly, an allegorical interpretation of these passages has not been especially common. One occasionally finds such an approach among medieval commentators.[14] Some examples: The fruit trees are those who are zealous in good works; the cedars, those who are lofty in contemplation; the wild beasts, those who live a solitary life; the creeping things, those who quietly and steadily busy themselves; the birds, those who rise on high in heavenly meditation; and the hail are the great preachers who pour down stern and lashing rebukes on sinners! Occasionally, one finds a christological interpretation where the various natural elements are seen as "emblems of Christ."

A tendency toward a rationalistic interpretation of these verses is also evident, with not a little touch of arrogance in some formulations. W. O. E. Oesterley's views of Psalm 148 illustrate how this view lurks around the edges: "However much there may be in the psalm which, in view of the advanced knowledge of later ages, cannot be accepted, such as the idea of the inanimate world and of animals praising God, we can appreciate the psalmist's conception, even though erroneous, of the instinct of worship as innate in the whole of created matter."[15]

More common among older commentators is an eschatological interpretation: such a responsiveness on the part of nature will be integral to the new heaven and earth, when all of nature takes on human characteristics (which in some formulations arrogantly seems finally to be a humanization of nature). The presence of nature's praise in Second Isaiah and in the Enthronement Psalms (93–99), texts that are often interpreted eschatologically, has been one factor prompting this approach; the new role for the animal kingdom in passages such as Isa 11:6-9 and 65:25 contributes to this direction in interpretation. Also to be noted in this connection is the expanded version of Psalm 148 in the Song of the Three Young Men in the Additions to Daniel as well as 4 *Ezra* (5:5): In that day "the trees will drip blood and stones will speak" (cf. *2 Baruch* 73; *1 En.* 69:16-24). The only direct occurrences of this motif in the New Testament are in the book of Revelation (5:13; 12:12; 18:20; cf. also Rom 8:19-22).[16] These references prompt one commentator to speak of Psalm 148 as "a song of liberty because all creation is loosed from bondage at last and is invited to sing forth."[17] But whatever the truth in an eschatological interpretation, it occurs often enough in noneschatological materials to warrant the claim that nature's praise is understood to be characteristic of present reality.

Another perspective views these texts as polemical.[18] What are gods elsewhere are here reduced to elements of the natural order in praise of Yahweh; these entities praise God, they are not themselves objects of worship. Aside from the fact that this gives a negative cast to a highly positive, even celebrative text and context, readers must be careful in overstressing the distinctions between Israel and other ancient Near Eastern religions on the relationship between nature and the divine. James Barr claims that already in Akkadian myths the gods have ceased to be aspects of nature.[19] One can certainly find ideas that "divinity was in nature or that nature was in harmony with the divine," but it is not so clear that there is always or often an explicit identification. One must distinguish between the animation of natural phenomena, a common idea, and their supernaturalization.

A more recent development is much more difficult to assess: the natural order and the human are incorporated in a "psychic whole" in which all of nature is permeated by a diffused awareness. To use the language of Luis I. J. Stadelmann, nature is understood to have a "psychic affinity" with the human, and natural elements such as stars (cf. Job 38:7) are understood as "beings prodded with consciousness."[20] "The universe is thoroughly alive, and therefore, the more capable of sympathy with man and of response to the rule of its Creator. . . . Certainly we have here more than a mere poetical personification of the cosmos when it is invited to rejoice."[21] To assess this panpsychical interpretation (along with the closely related vitalism) is difficult because the sources and argumentation for this perspective are not carefully documented in Old Testament studies. One form of this perspective can be traced back at least to Gunkel, who states in his Psalms commentary: "Such exhortation of creatures to praise of God was not simply a 'poetic figure' in Israel; the concept of nature as animate still was lodged" in human consciousness in that time.[22]

One of the more influential studies on this theme has been that of H. Wheeler Robinson.[23] He claims that "objects of nature were conceived as having a psychical life of their own." Natural objects have "a diffused consciousness with [their] own psychical . . . possibilities, and [their] own capacity to be indwelt or made instrumental by yet higher powers, and finally by the activity of Yahweh himself."[24] Another work that has popularized this kind of thinking about nature are the essays edited by Henri and H. A. Frankfort.[25] The fundamental difference between ancient and modern thought regarding nature is that for moderns "the phenomenal world is primarily an 'It'; for ancient—and also for primitive—man it is a 'Thou.'"[26] This does not mean that primitives personified the inanimate world; they simply did not know of such a lifeless world.[27] In the same volume, Thorkild Jacobsen also states that the ancients regarded the natural world as possessing individual will and qualities.[28] "They are somehow alive; they have wills of their own; each is a definite personality." "Any phenomena which the Mesopotamian met in the world around him was thus alive, had its own personality and will, its distinct self." "To understand nature was to understand the personalities in these phenomena, to know their character, the directions of their wills, and also the range of their powers. It was a task not different from that of understanding other" people.[29] G. Ernest Wright continues in the train of the Frankforts' perspective, noting that "Israel did not conceive of an inanimate nature any more than did polytheists . . . [but] continued to think of the elements of nature as possessing a psychic life of their own." He cites Isa 1:2 and Mic 6:2.[30]

In anticipation of our later discussion, it may be said here that the truth in this perspective is that natural phenomena must be of such a nature that God is able to sustain the close relationship with them that the biblical evidence implies. This relationship suggests that these creatures have a certain inwardness or interiority such that more than external relationships are possible. To speak in this way does not necessarily lead to panpsychism or vitalism, but it certainly suggests a greater continuity between the animate and the inanimate than moderns have commonly been willing to claim. At the least, the possibilities for an *internal* relationship between God and all created things must be left open. This issue deserves further exploration.

Genre and Metaphor

The praise of God on the part of nature is a theme that never occurs in narrative material. Found only in poetry, it is almost exclusively associated with hymnic literature, primarily in the Psalter and Second Isaiah. This genre specificity gives no little credence to the often suggested notion that we have here to do with poetic license or poetic fancy or "highly poetic language." Or, the language of personification is used, "a rhetorical figure by which an inanimate or abstract thing is represented as a person, or with personal characteristics."[31] Leslie C. Allen speaks of "rhetorical calls to creation to praise its God" and metaphorical personifications.[32] Moreover, the fact that these texts have to do with Israel's worship life has suggested to interpreters that in the exuberance of the worship of God a certain extravagance has taken control of the language, with little if any correspondence to reality.

How does one evaluate such directions in the interpretation of these texts? I am convinced they are quite inadequate, but it is difficult to demonstrate the point directly. Certainly one avenue to pursue is to speak about the nature of language, particularly metaphoric language as well as the language of worship. Another approach is to set these materials alongside other Old Testament texts that relate God to the natural order and see whether this pushes us toward another interpretation, to which I will return.

First of all, the issue of language. To use the language of poetic license, literary figure or personification suggests that we are dealing with a fictive matter or a matter of some artificiality that does not in fact correspond with reality. But, "Such a classification of the sense of the text may domesticate it too quickly, assimilating it to a ready-made static catalogue of rhetorical figures drawn up from non-religious materials. . . . No one is more unimaginative than an interpreter who speaks so neatly and readily of the imagination."[33] That is to say, in designating these texts as poetic license (or the like) the reader has closed off several interpretive possibilities. The depth of these texts, their expressive thickness, is not given its full range.

One important factor to be considered is the use of nature metaphors for God. For example, God is light, water, rock, fire, wind, as well as a few animals, such as the eagle. While language used to speak of God is drawn primarily from human relationships, the use of nature metaphors opens up new avenues in considering Israel's way of thinking about God. If God is a rock or a mother eagle, for example, rocks and mother eagles are reflective in some sense of the identity of God. That is to say, there are continuities between rocks and eagles and the reality of God. In view of this correspondence, certain divine attributes are elucidated by reference to the natural order. For example; God's righteousness is like the mountains (Ps 36:6) or God's faithfulness is like the fixed orders of creation (Jer 31:35-36).

As always with metaphor, an "is" and an "is not" must be recognized in the use of nature language for God. *Rock* and *mother eagle* are descriptive of God in some ways; in some ways they are not. Certain other qualifying metaphors need to be drawn into the discussion in order to discern where the continuities and discontinuities lie.[34] Nonetheless the point is still made: if rock and eagle and other natural metaphors for God are in some ways descriptive of God, then they reflect in their very existence, in their being what they are, the reality which is God. It is in view of this point that nature's praise of God is to be understood and explicated.

In other words, it is basically in terms of their intrinsic rather than their instrumental value that nonhuman creatures function as such metaphors. In themselves they are capable of showing forth the strength, care, glory, faithfulness, or the majesty of God. Such a use of natural metaphors serves to temper a certain anthropocentricity in our talk about God. In fact (and this is an ironic point, given the common understanding of the God-nature relationship), it could be said that God's transcendence is given a special lift by the use of such natural metaphors, for among other things they evoke wonder and awe in human beings; God's strength and majesty are commonly emphasized. Generally speaking, the use of natural metaphors for God opens up the entire created order as a resource for depth and variety in our God language.

In view of these considerations, a closer look at some of the details of Psalm 148 is in order. The structure of the psalm follows that of a typical hymn of praise, except that the call to praise is much more extensive. The calls begin in the heavenly sphere (vv. 1-4) and move to the earth (vv. 7-12), with heaven and earth brought together in verse 13*c*, with a final note on praise centered on Israel in verse 14. The calls to praise are followed by *kî* ("for") clauses in verses 5*b*-6, 13 (see also Ps 69:34-36; Isa 43:20; 44:23; 49:13; Jer 51:48; Joel 2:21).

First of all, the calls to praise. These serve to express praise; they call attention to the range of God's creative work and hence God's praiseworthiness.[35] Also, the listing together of the creatures suggests both individuality and complementarity in praising. Each entity has its own distinctiveness in its praising according to its intrinsic capacity and fitness, with varying degrees of complexity. But each is also part of the one world of God contributing to the whole. The model of the symphony orchestra comes to mind. Environmental considerations are immediately present, for if one member of the orchestra is incapacitated or missing altogether, the scope, complexity, and intensity of the praise will be less than what it might be. Environmental sensitivity in every age is for the sake of the praise of God and the witness it entails; indeed, it has implications for God's own possibilities in the world.

Moreover, the calls to worship suggest that there may well be differing possibilities of response. Indeed, would it be possible to suggest that the call to praise implies the possibility of refusal? Such refusal is certainly a reality for the human beings, but for the other creatures? Such possibilities could simply have reference to the fact that for some creatures (e.g., stormy wind and hail) praising is occasional, not constant. Beyond that, as we shall see, readers of these texts should consider whether the responsiveness of the nonhuman creatures is drawn out or called forth by the divine work with and within them. In this interaction with God, the creatures become more of what they are or have the potential of becoming. Without the call to praise some possibilities for praise might not be realized.

The reasons for praise are expressed in the two *kî* clauses of Ps 148:5*b*-6, 13. In verses 5*b*-6, the reason given is the fact of creation by God and being given a particular place within the created order for all time. The praise expressed is thus praise for being what they are. This is echoed in verse 8*b* (cf. Ps 107:25) with reference to the stormy wind fulfilling God's command. Praise occurs when the creature fulfills the task for which it was created.[36] In verse 13 the reason is expressed in terms of God's name being above all others. The concern is witness, making known the name of Yahweh, especially among all those who do not honor Yahweh or who honor other gods. It is not just Israel that hears the witness of nature; all peoples hear this testimony (cf. Ps 97:6). In Isa 42:10-12 nature and all peoples join together in a praise that is universal. It might be suggested that the call for all peoples/lands/nations/earth to praise God that is present in so many psalms (47:1; 49:1; 66:1; 96:1, 9; 97:1; 98:4; 99:1; 100:1; 117:1) is made possible because of the witness of the natural order.

This witness element in the hymns of praise makes for decisive continuities with the songs of thanksgiving. In these psalms (and in the vow commonly spoken at the end of the laments) gratitude is expressed not only to God, as important as that is, but gratitude is also to be expressed in the presence of others (see Ps 22:22; 109:30). Gratitude is giving testimony to others regarding what God has done (Pss 34:11; 40:9-10; 66:16). Indeed, the whole world is in view as the object of such witness (Pss 18:49; 22:27; 57:9).

Together then, the reasons for praise relate specifically to God for what God has done and then beyond God to God's relationship with those who do not honor Yahweh. These are the two central facets of praise: the honor of God and the witness to others (cf. Ps 119:171-72). The one always entails the other.[37] These come together in a phrase such as "praise magnifies God,"[38] or to use Mowinckel's remarkably modern language, the song of praise "increases God's power and renown"; it "gives power" to God (see Ps 22:3).[39] *God* is affected by praise, not simply those who (speak) praise or respond to it.

Tradition

What fund of understandings in Israel about the relationship between God and nature contributes to the development of this theme? Nature's praise would not have sounded strange to Israel's ears. First, parallels in the ancient Near East should be noted. Delbert Hillers[40] effectively refutes von Rad's thesis that the prehistory of this material is to be found in ancient Egyptian onomastica, encyclopedic lists that bear some similarity to the listings in Psalm 148 and Job 38.[41] Hillers clearly demonstrates that the idea of nature's praise of God is to be traced back to pre-Israelite Mesopotamian and Egyptian hymnic materials. Among his many examples, the following Egyptian hymn to the sun god from the Ramesside period might be cited:

> The gods jump up before you in praise,
> Mankind awakens, to adore your beauty;
> Beasts dance before you in the wilderness,
> . . . .
> Earth [trembles] before the holiness of his name,
> Egypt gathers, the wilderness rises early,
> To behold his appearance in the morning.[42]

Walter Beyerlin notes another special parallel to Psalm 148, the Egyptian "Hymn of a 1000 strophes."[43] He notes that this hymn to Amun from the post-Amarna period "depicts a response in which all the world, along with nature, offers the praise of God":

> All trees rise before his countenance,
> they turn towards his eye,
> and their leaves unfold.

The scaly creatures leap in the water,
they come out from their pools, for love of him.
The sheep and cattle skip before his presence.
The birds dance with their wings.
They (all) observe that he is in his good time.
They live by seeing him as their daily need.
They are in his hand, sealed with his seal,
and no god can open them but his majesty.[44]

Moving to the Old Testament itself, a variety of materials are related to this theme, most notably the theophany (e.g., Hab 3:1-15).[45] The language used to speak of God's appearances is not unlike that used for nature's praise. This language is bursting at the seams. Moreover, the theophany brings God and the natural order closely together; they act in concert with one another. The degree to which one should speak of literary convention or historical reality or liturgical simulation, or a combination thereof, is often raised in this connection. It is probably a combination, with one or another emphasized, depending on the theophany being studied. The theophanies, however, do commonly involve more than internal sight, as do the praises of the elements of the natural order. One might speak of an inarticulate, yet visible praise. Moreover, the language for nature in these contexts suggests a certain perception regarding possibilities for nature in relationship to God.

The responses of nature to God's appearance in various psalms serve well as examples. Look at what happens to nature in response to the presence of God! The earth quakes and the heavens rain down (68:8); the sea looks and flees and the mountains and hills skip like young animals (114:3-7); the cedars are broken and the oaks whirl (29:5-9); the mountains melt like wax (97:5); the waters are afraid and the deep trembles (77:16). While occasionally the language used is unusual, it is not unnatural; as in the praise passages, a certain correspondence with natural activity is present. The sea roars, the waters are troubled, and the hills skip. The storms are no more stormy than other storms and the earthquakes could have been measured on a Richter scale. No telltale trail of God tracks could be detected in the response of nature that would unambiguously reveal God. Yet, the intensity and magnitude of the language that is used to depict the experience are such that special attention from the reader is invited.

From another perspective, the God who appears is clothed in elements of the natural orders. Smoke and fire emanate from God; darkness and clouds cover God; wings of the wind support God; lightning surrounds

God (Ps 18:8-15). Light envelops God like a garment and the clouds are the divine chariots (104:2-4). What does it mean for natural phenomena to be considered the clothing or the companion of Yahweh? Certainly it means a fundamental compatibility between God and the natural order; they are not like oil and water in relationship to each another. The *finitum capax infiniti* could be cited here; the finite is capable of bearing the infinite.[46] As such, nonhuman creatures are considered to be in the service of Yahweh (Pss 104:2-4; 119:91); they serve God's purposes of revelation, salvation, judgment, and instruction (cf. Amos 4:6-13; Exod 14:21; Jonah 4). To see nature so closely bound to God indicates that God is internally rather than externally related to it; nature does bear Yahweh. *The fact that theophanies function as revelatory events means that the function of nature in theophany is only an intensification of what is true of nature otherwise.* Ample material is present in these theophanies to provide the basis for an understanding of God's relationship to nature; nature's praise would be but another dimension of a widespread interresponsiveness between God and nature in the Old Testament.

This understanding can be extended by reference to other passages that speak of God's close relationship to elements of the natural order. The valuation of the nonhuman creation by God in Genesis 1 ("and God saw that it was good") occurs independently of the creation and valuation of the human. In fact, both the human and the nonhuman are spoken of in the same language of evaluation, yet without denying important differences regarding their place in the divine economy (see Gen 1:28). All creatures were considered by God to have intrinsic value. It is striking that the valuation by God of the goodness of the creation is a valuation returned to God in praise: "O give thanks to the LORD, for he is good" (Ps 106:1; 107:1; 118:1; 136:1). In other words, the creatures reflect the goodness of their createdness back to God and become a witness to God, reflecting that created goodness toward the entire world.

Moreover, all of the creatures of the natural order are considered to be members of God's own family.

> For every wild animal of the forest is mine,
>   the cattle on a thousand hills.
> I know all the birds of the air,
>   and all that moves in the field is mine.
> (Ps 50:10-11; cf. Ps. 24:1-2; 1 Chr 29:11)

God is not only a God of history; God is also a God of nature. Or, to put it in other terms, God is as active in the history of nature as God is in the history of humankind; from God's perspective we have to do with one history and one world.

Moreover, God's relationship with the nonhuman is such that God can draw the creatures out or call them forth, with the understanding that they can be responsive to God's work with them or within them in some sense. God's call to the waters and the earth to participate in the creative activity (Gen 1:11, 20, 24) suggests that a response is expected; and, indeed, that response is forthcoming (see Gen 1:13).[47] God and these natural elements have the kind of relationship where mutual interaction is possible. This phenomenon is not uncommon elsewhere. God calls to the earth (Ps 50:4; Hag 1:11) and addresses natural entities (Isa 45:8; Job 37:6). They in turn respond to God (Job 38:35; Ps 145:10) and look or cry to God (Ps 104:21; 145:15-16; Job 38:39-41; Joel 1:20) and even possess a kind of knowledge regarding God's activity (Job 12:7-9); God in turn responds with care and sustenance (Ps 147:9; Deut 10:12). God's closeness to creation is evident in that God calls them by name (Isa 40:26; Ps 147:4; see also God's naming of nonhuman creatures in Gen 1:5-10); readers should recall the full significance of naming for Israel to capture the sense of this. Salvation language is used for the animal world as well as for humankind, from the story of the flood (Gen 6:19; 9:10) to everyday activity ("you save humans and animals alike, O LORD," Ps 36:6) to the new heaven and earth (Isa 11:6-9; 65:25). God is as concerned with the liberation of the animals as with human beings.[48] Moreover, God rejoices and delights in God's relationship with the nonhuman order of things (see Ps 104:31; Job 38–39; see Prov 8:30-31 on rejoicing).[49]

In this connection, Klaus Koch has an interesting, if brief study of Hos 2:21-22: "On that day I will answer, says the Lord, I will answer the heavens and they shall answer the earth; and the earth shall answer the grain, the wine, and the oil."[50] In what might be called a "sociology of nature" he suggests that the Hebrew verb *'ānāh*, while having the basic meaning of "answer," may also have the sense of "to respond in a discussion," and it may, in this context, have reference to nonverbal reactions, to the providing of new impulses by one subject to another within a given relationship. Hosea appears to be "thinking of a coherent chain in which God is the initiator, but an initiator who acts in interdependence with earth, man, and nation . . . nowhere does the Old Testament offer such a pregnant description of natural process as in this sentence of Hosea." The world of nature is a world of interrelated creatures, held together by divine interaction with the creatures.

Koch goes on to speak of a dynamic interrelationship between Aelohim, Adamah, and Adam, a "triangle" in which there is movement every which way within the triangle, except from the earth to God. Why Koch stops short at this point is not certain, but his move seems unnecessary. In any case, Koch's emphasis on a nonverbal relationship between God and the nonhuman is important. Nonverbal praise or witness would simply be one aspect of such an understanding. Inarticulateness does not disqualify one from praise. At the human level one thinks of praise offered by those who dance or play musical instruments or are disabled.

If one says that God is truly present in, with, and under every aspect of the created order, what does it mean to speak of the presence of God? Is it only external, a presence *with* or a presence *to*? The texts suggest that God is able really to *relate to* every creature. There seems to be implied, as we have suggested, a certain inwardness characteristic of these creatures, or at least a nature that enables a relationship of consequence with God to exist. Given the relationships that human beings often have to pets and even trees and other natural elements,[51] we dare not suggest that God is incapable of such relationships.[52] If a human being can speak this way about the natural order, given the alienation that exists, how much more should God be able so to speak.[53]

Finally, we ask about the historical function of this material. The usage in Second Isaiah seems to be reasonably clear.[54] Because the salvific deed God is about to accomplish is cosmic in its effects, the response of praise must be comparably cosmic. Because nature, too, participates in God's act of salvation, it too responds in praise. The interconnectedness of nature and history in God's redeeming activity is demonstrated in the response of both. Whenever this theme occurs, it seems to be in the service of kerygmatic or doxological claims regarding the cosmic dimensions of God's work and, hence, may speak to narrower visions of God's work in the world that were current in Israel or in our own time.[55]

Concluding Reflections

Because nature is not fallen as human beings are, though human sin has disrupted the natural order, it still witnesses to the reality of God in ways more constant than human beings do.[56] The heavens do proclaim the glory of God (Ps 19:1). The praise called for in Psalm 148 *is* the revelation spoken of in Psalm 19 and elsewhere.[57] The fact that human beings do not recognize this revelation as often as they should roots the problem of recognition more in human beings than in the natural order. The problem is in human seeing and hearing and, perhaps most of all, in our alienation from the nonhuman. This greater constancy prompts some comment on the nonhuman world as models for human behaviors. In Isa 1:2 and Jer 8:7 we find animals conforming to the will of God for their existence in ways not true of human beings. The nonhuman world may also be thought of as models of praise. As these creatures are what they were created to be, so should we offer our praise to God.[58] The integration of the human and nonhuman in Psalm 148 may well carry some of this understanding. Human beings should be praising as nonhuman creatures do.

But more needs to be said about the relationship between the human condition and the natural orders. *No* human history is independent of the history of nature, and this for both good and ill. This reality suggests a symbiosis in praise; every element in all of God's creation is called to praise together, and given the depth of their interrelatedness, the response of one will affect the response of the other.

First, a look at this symbiosis from a positive angle. From the perspective of Gen 1:28, the earth needs to be subdued and hence, as created, would not witness to God with pristine clarity. Positively, the human being is needed to bring at least the earthly orders to their fullest possible potential, and that would entail their fullest possible potential for praise. There remains work to be done in the natural world by human beings in order for this potential to be more fully realized (see Gen 2:5).

Another way of speaking of the symbiosis of human and nonhuman in praise is to speak of their mutual support of each other in praising. From the side of nature, the natural order provides raw material for human praise. Without the natural order, the praising metaphors at the disposal of the human would be fewer in number. Without the praise of nature, secondary human forms of praise would be much more meager, that is, we would be without much praise-full painting, music, and literature inspired by nature. In George Herbert's language, human beings have been made the secretaries of the praise of nature.[59] Without the praise of the nonhuman, the witness of the human would not be what it has the potential of becoming. From the human side, human beings give voice to nonhuman praise; they make articulate what is inchoate in nonhuman praise. One could perhaps speak of the praise of the nonhuman in terms of the old Simon and Garfunkel song, "The Sound of Silence." Human beings participate with the nonhuman by giving voice to silent praise. We live in a world highly charged with wonder and praise; it is up to human beings to give it clearer voice.

Second, from a negative perspective, what human beings do in their sinfulness affects adversely the possibilities for praise on the part of the nonhuman creatures. Human sinfulness can have an adverse effect on the ability of the natural orders truly to be themselves. Many biblical examples have been cited in the previous chapters (e.g., Hos 4:1-3; Isa 24:4-7; Jer 12:4; Joel 1:18; Zeph 1:3). Genesis 3 sets the biblical pattern: the sin of humankind lessens the productive possibilities of the earth and, hence, reduces its praising possibilities. To use a modern illustration, the heavens proclaim the glory of God with less clarity on a smoggy day than on other days.

The integration of heavenly, human, and nonhuman language in Psalm 148 may well recognize this interconnectedness of praise possibilities. That is, only as all creatures of God together join in the chorus of praise do the elements of the natural order or human beings witness to God as they ought to. Hence, to call upon the elements of the natural order to praise God within a *human* worship context ("Praise the Lord," in Psalm 148 implies the call of a worship leader) contains an implicit call to human beings to relate to the natural orders in such a way that nature's praise might show forth with greater clarity. As noted above, environmental activity is directly related to nature's praise possibilities. That is, by the way in which human beings relate to environmental matters they can enhance or inhibit nature's response to God's call.

This brings the discussion back to the truth in the eschatological interpretation of these materials; in the new heaven and earth (and the totality of this language ought not to be lost), nature's praise of God will have a clarity and a perfection unknown this side of the eschaton. In that future world, nature will no longer lament and groan but simply praise. In the new heaven and new earth, the earth shall be full of the knowledge of the Lord as the waters cover the sea (Isa 11:9; 65:25). In the present, God fills heaven and earth (Jer 23:25), but not yet the knowledge of God. The steadfast love of God and God's faithfulness fills the universe (Pss 33:5; 36:5; 57:10; 85:10-12; 119:64) but not yet the knowledge of that love and faithfulness.[60] The symbiosis of human and nonhuman in the praise of God is intended to fill the universe with the knowledge of God, with the knowledge of God's love and faithfulness.

To speak of nature's praise from God's perspective, God needs both the human and the nonhuman for the fullest possible witness to God in the world. Without praise, mission is muted. Moreover, because God is Lord of the universe and not just Lord of the earth or of human beings, then praise too must be universal. Without the witness of the nonhuman, mission is muted in vast stretches of the universe: God is enthroned not only on the praises of Israel (Ps 22:3); God is enthroned on the praises of all God's creatures. The realization of the praiseworthiness of God in the universe is dependent upon this creation-wide praise.

This point may be recognized in Ps 148:14: God has made God's people strong, indeed has made them a praise in the earth, for the purposes of the universal praise of God. Whereas the prior mention of human praise (vv. 11-12) is generic, having reference to all people everywhere, verse 14 makes a historical reference to Israel as the embodiment of praise. Just as the various other creatures show forth the praise of God by being what they are as God's creatures, so Israel, having been made what it now is by God, shows forth God's praise by being who they are: the redeemed people of God. The wonder of God and God's work can be seen in what has become of them, that they have become the redeemed people of God.[61] If verse 14 also suggests that *Israel* shares in the praise that is voiced to God, it would not be for its own self-glorification, but for the purpose of witness. Just so, the praise of God is not just for God's sake but, finally, also for the sake of other creatures. God's people are called upon to continue showing forth the praise of God because of what they have been made by God. As new creatures, they will join with that vast chorus of God's nonhuman creatures in honor of God and in witness to God.

These lines from "God's Grandeur" by Gerard Manley Hopkins capture the essence of nature's praise of God in the Old Testament:

> The world is charged with the grandeur of God.
>   It will flame out, like shining from shook foil;
>   It gathers to a greatness, like the ooze of oil
> Crushed.
> . . . .
> There lives the dearest freshness deep down things;
> . . . .
> Because the Holy Ghost over the bent
> World broods with warm breast and with ah! bright wings.[62]

Nature's Praise of God in the Old Testament

Text	*Genre*	*Subject*	*Activity*
Job 38:7	theophany	morning stars	sing together *(rnn)*
Ps 19:1	hymn	heavens	tell glory *(spr)*
Ps 19:1	hymn	firmament	proclaim *(ngd)*
Ps 19:2	hymn	day	pours forth speech *(nbʻ)*
Ps 19:2	hymn	night	declare *(ḥwh)*
Ps 50:6	theophany	heavens	declare *(ngd)*
Ps 65:8	thanksgiving	morning/evening	shout for joy *(rnn)*
Ps 65:12	thanksgiving	hills	girded with joy *(gîl)*
Ps 65:13	thanksgiving	meadows/valleys	shout for joy *(šîr)*
Ps 69:34	lament (end)	heaven/earth/seas	praise *(ḥll)*
Ps 89:5	lament	heavens	praise wonders *(ydh)*
Ps 89:12	lament	mountains; Tabor/ Hermon	praise name *(rnn)*
Ps 93:3	hymn	floods	lift up voice/roaring
Ps 96:11	hymn	heavens	be glad *(śmḥ)*
Ps 96:11	hymn	earth	rejoice *(gîl)*
Ps 96:12	hymn	field/inhabitants	exult *(ʻlz)*
Ps 96:12*	hymn	trees of wood	sing for joy *(rnn)*
Ps 97:6	hymn	heavens	proclaim *(ngd)*
Ps 98:7	hymn	sea/inhabitants	roar *(rʻm)*
Ps 98:8	hymn	floods	clap hands *(mḥʼ)*
Ps 98:8	hymn	hills	sing for joy *(rnn)*
Ps 99:1	hymn	earth	quake *(nûṭ)*
Ps 103:22	thanksgiving	God's works	bless Lord *(brk)*
Ps 145:10	hymn	God's works	give thanks *(ydh)*
Ps 145:11	hymn	God's works	speak/tell glory/power
Ps 148:3	hymn	sun/moon/stars	praise *(ḥll)*
Ps 148:4	hymn	high heavens/ its waters	praise *(ḥll)*
Ps 148:7	hymn	sea monsters/deeps	praise *(ḥll)*
Ps 148:8	hymn	fire/hail/snow/frost/ wind	praise *(ḥll)*
Ps 148:9	hymn	mtns/hills/fruit trees/cedars	praise *(ḥll)*
Ps 148:10	hymn	beasts/cattle/ creepers/birds	praise *(ḥll)*
Ps 150:6	hymn	all that breathe	praise *(ḥll)*
Isa 35:1	hymnic	wilderness/dry land	be glad *(śûś)*

Text	*Genre*	*Subject*	*Activity*
Isa 35:1	hymnic	desert	rejoice (*gil*)
Isa 35:2	hymnic	desert	rejoice with joy (*rnn*)
Isa 42:10	hymn	sea/coastlands' inhabitants	roar (*r'm*)
Isa 42:11	hymn	desert	lift up voice
Isa 42:12	hymn	the ends of the earth	give glory
Isa 42:12	hymn	the ends of the earth	declare (*ngd*)
Isa 43:20	hymn	wild beasts/jackals/ ostriches	honor God (*kbd*)
Isa 44:23	hymn	heavens	sing (*rnn*)
Isa 44:23	hymn	depths of earth	shout (*rû'*)
Isa 44:23	hymn	mountains/forest/ trees	sing (*pṣḥ*)
Isa 49:13	hymn	heavens	break/sing (*rnn*)
Isa 49:13	hymn	earth	exult (*gîl*)
Isa 49:13	hymn	mountains	break/sing (*pṣḥ*)
Isa 55:12	hymn	mountains/hills	break/sing (*pṣḥ*)
Isa 55:12	hymn	trees of field	clap hands (*mḥ'*)
Isa 66:23	oracle	all flesh	worship (*sḥh*)
Jer 51:48	oracle	heavens/earth inhabitants	sing for joy (*rnn*)
Joel 2:21	oracle	land (*'adamah*)	be glad/rejoice (*śmḥ/gîl*)
Hab 3:3**	hymn	earth	full of praise

* = Chr 16:31-33

** Cf. Rev. 5:13; 12:12; 18:20

CONCLUSION

IMPLICATIONS OF A RELATIONAL THEOLOGY OF CREATION: HUMAN VOCATION AND NONHUMAN VOCATION

Much of the conversation about matters environmental, both within and without the religious community, seems to be centered on human activity, on what human beings can do to care for the earth and its creatures. In these formulations, the earth's creatures often become the *object* of human activity. In this concluding chapter, I draw on some biblical texts that relate to this human vocation, but I think it is finally important to speak of a mutuality of human vocation and nonhuman vocation. Human vocation in isolation is too limiting, insufficiently fundamental, and does not take adequate account of the character of the relationship of the nonhuman, the human, and God. In this interrelated community—and the word *community* is important—issues of dependence, independence, and interdependence become more complex than we often realize and are applicable in varying ways to both human and nonhuman.[1]

A Relational Model of Creation

The texts under discussion throughout this volume contribute to what might be called *a relational model of creation*. That is, both God and the creatures have an important role in the creative enterprise, and their spheres of activity are interrelated in terms of function and effect. Traditionally, God is seen as one who is independent, with the creatures only and absolutely dependent upon God not only with respect to origins but also regarding their continuing life.[2] The various Old Testament texts regarding creation, however, want to speak in a more complex way about what is entailed in this relationship.[3]

It seems clear from the texts that God is not only independent and the creatures only dependent. All creatures, of course, are *deeply dependent* upon God for their existence and continuing life. At the same time, God has freely chosen to establish an *interdependent* relationship with the creation, with respect to both origins and continuation and with overlapping spheres of responsibility. Indeed, God has freely chosen to be *dependent* upon both human and nonhuman in the furtherance of God's purposes in the world.[4] All creatures have a God-given vocation within God's creation-wide purposes; in other words, God has freely chosen to rely upon that which is not God to engage those purposes.

This perspective is evident already in Genesis 1–2. Michael Welker formulates the point in a helpful way:

> Where the conventional guiding conceptions [of creation] focus upon division and hierarchical arrangement, the classical creation accounts [in Genesis] emphasize the connectedness and cooperation of creator and that which is creaturely. In no way do the creation accounts of Genesis offer only a gloomy picture of sheer dependence. God's creative action does not confront that which is created with completely finished facts. The creature's own activity as a constitutive element in the process of creation is seen in harmony with God's action.[5]

The nature of the interrelationships among the creatures is also important: while being relatively independent, they are dependent on other creatures and interdependent among themselves. Both human beings and animals are given an independent role (1:22, 28; 2:24). At the same time, human beings and animals are keenly dependent upon the ground (along with the trees, 2:9, 16) not only for their sustenance and livelihood but also for their very being (1:29-30; 2:5-7, 19). At the same time, the ground is dependent upon the human for its proper development (2:5, 15), as well as upon the rain (2:5). Moreover, that which is nonhuman is made dependent upon varying forms of "dominion" exercised by the human (1:28). And both human and nonhuman creatures are caught up in the task of continuing creation (Gen 1:11-13; 2:18-25). Such an understanding stands over against a perspective wherein God is understood to stand in a totally external relationship to the creation and to act in unmediated ways in the ongoing creation and governance of the world.[6]

Within this relational model, it is important to speak of both distinctions and commonalities among the principals. On the one hand, God is God and freely brings into being that which is not God. A deep dependence of the creatures upon the Creator for their existence and continuing life is apparent. As we have seen, Genesis 1 stresses this divine initiative, imagination, transcendence, and power in a way that Genesis 2 does not. The placement of Genesis 1 suggests that these divine characteristics should stand at the beginning and in the foreground in any discussion of creation. Yet, no simple or static hierarchy emerges, as there is already a leaning toward Genesis 2 in some features of Genesis 1. Moreover, chapter 2 lifts up several dimensions of creation in a way that chapter 1 does not. For example, God's creative acts in chapter 2 are presented as a *deeply personal* divine action. This God carefully shapes the first human being from the dust of the ground with God's own hands and breath; this Creator works in remarkable close range with the *'ādām* in discerning which creations will best serve as his partner; this God puts the *'ādām* to sleep and personally designs and constructs the woman from the side of the *'ādām* (not head or feet, and hence on the same level). Such a down-to-earth God is portrayed here! Engaged in such intricate work at close personal range!

Creation here is presented in relational terms, both in terms of origin and in terms of God's continuing work with the *'ādām* in developing the creation into a more welcoming and gracious place. If one takes this understanding of Genesis 2 and then reads Genesis 1 in light of it, then the latter's language of divine word is seen as highly relational in character—a communicating with (the earth and the waters, the members of the divine council, the newly created human beings) and not simply a talking to. God's word invites a response. God works in and through that which is not God in bringing the world into being—a highly relational way of proceeding. Only Genesis 1 and 2 taken together, and qualifying each other, give readers an adequate portrayal of God's relationship to the creation.

The realm of the divine and the realm of the creature are seen not to be two radically unrelated spheres; there are overlapping powers, roles, and responsibilities, to which "image of God" language testifies (1:26-27; 5:3; 9:6). God is not powerful and the creatures powerless; we need constantly to be reminded that the Godness of God cannot be bought at the expense of creaturely diminishment. In the very act of creating, God gives to that which is other than God an assured independence and freedom. God has created an Other alongside the divine self with whom God chooses to be in an ongoing relationship (see Prov 8:30, for Woman Wisdom who is "beside him"; see ch. 7). That God in creating gives space to the creatures to be what they were created to be means that, in some sense, God moves over and makes room for the Other. The result is an ordered freedom in the creation, a degree of openness and unpredictability wherein God leaves room for the nonhuman creatures to develop in less than fully determined ways and for genuine decisions on the part of human beings as they exercise their God-given power.

But, even more, God gives human beings powers and responsibilities in a way that *commits God* to a certain kind of relationship with them. This commitment entails a divine constraint and restraint in the exercise of power within the creation. For example, God will not do the procreating of animals or the bearing of fruit seeds in any unmediated way. More ominously, human beings have been given the freedom to destroy themselves, though this stands against the will of God for them. This commitment to give power and responsibility over to the creature results in an ongoing divine dependence upon creatures in and through whom God will work in the life of the world.

Even more, what creatures do with the gifts they have been given will *make a difference to God*. God's actions are not fixed for every conceivable future moment; they will be shaped to some extent by the actions of the creatures (see, e.g., Jer 22:1-5). Another way of moving into this theme would be to say that God does not have a final and solitary will in place from the beginning regarding every aspect of the created order. God makes adjustments in the divine will for the world in view of God's ongoing interaction with the world. At the same time, these divine moves will always be in tune with God's absolute will regarding life and salvation for all humankind, indeed for every creature.

In sum, this relational perspective means that God's sovereignty is understood, not in terms of absolute divine control, but as a sovereignty that gives power over to the created for the sake of a relationship of integrity.[7] This move is risky for God, for it entails the possibility that the creatures will misuse the power they have been given, which is in fact what occurs.[8] A reclamation of creation will be needed. While God will finally bring that new heaven and earth into being, what the creatures, especially human beings, do between now and that certain future will make a difference with respect to the shape of that future.

Human and Nonhuman Vocation

We have suggested that it is a mistake to consider creation as an activity that moves in only one direction: from God to creature. Creatures are also involved in creative activity—*for God's sake*. It is also a mistake to think that vocation moves only in one direction: from the human to the nonhuman. The net effect of such an understanding, however environmentally sensitive one may be, is to diminish the place and value of the nonhuman. In some formulations, the nonhuman is almost a "basket case," as if these creatures did not possess significant capacities both to care for themselves and to be drawn into God's larger purposes for the entire creation, as if they did not have a vocational role to play within God's world. I want to claim that vocation also moves from the nonhuman to the human.[9] Thus I speak of *a mutuality of vocation*; both humans and nonhumans are called to a vocation on behalf of each other in the furtherance of God's purposes for the creation. We consider, in turn, the human vocation and the vocation of all other creatures.

Human Vocation

The question has arisen with respect to the proper language to speak of the vocation of the human relative to the nonhuman world. Should it be *steward* or *partner* or *servant* or *custodian* or something else? Stewardship is the traditional language, and will probably remain for some time the dominant lens for reflection on this issue.[10] I take a brief look at some of the options. I think, finally, that no metaphor will be completely satisfactory. In addition, there should be a comparable search for the best language to speak of the vocation of the nonhuman.

Several scholars have raised questions regarding the adequacy of stewardship language, with which I agree.[11] The idea of stewardship too easily feeds into a pyramidal or hierarchical structure of valuation that is finally anthropocentric (God, humans, and nonhumans), or into a moralistic and functional list of dos and don'ts, or into a managing-our-own-resources (especially money!) mentality. Rather, our environmental considerations must be grounded in the relationship that *God* has with the animals and other creatures.[12] It is because of *God's relationship to the nonhuman* that our relationship to the earth and all of its creatures becomes such an important theological and ethical issue for Christians.

H. Paul Santmire in particular has promoted the use of the word *partnership* instead of *stewardship*.[13] He seeks to develop a "theology of partnership" at some length, grounded primarily in biblical reflection. He includes the following emphases: creative intervention in nature (e.g., Noah), sensitive care for nature (e.g., Genesis 2), and awestruck contemplation of nature (e.g., Job).[14] His understanding is important in recognizing that the language used needs to cut across the relationships involved: "That God has a partnership *with us humans*, and we *with one another*, is a thought that most students of the Bible in our time will take for granted. That God has a partnership *with nature*, and humans *with nature* likewise" may need to be introduced to many.[15]

Whether this language will prove to be satisfactory is uncertain. In 1980 Odil Hannes Steck objected to its usage, preferring words such as *representative*, *steward*, and even *executive*. Though these words will not do, is he right in saying that *partnership* (also *cooperation*) is inadequate because it encourages "a pseudo-personalization of the relation between" human beings and nature and denies the God-human relationship as the "only" determining *personal* relationship? For Steck, the human being "*is not nature's partner*."[16] I do not think these objections are adequate to set the language of partnership aside altogether, but they raise appropriate questions that need a response. I wonder whether the word insufficiently differentiates between human and nonhuman; would *partner* entail being "equal partners"?

The language of "servanthood" has also been suggested. Among others, Ellen F. Davis picks up on the verb *'ābad* used in Gen 2:5, 15, and notes its more common meaning of "serve" (not "till"). Neither of the verbs used in 2:15 are words drawn from the fields of horticulture and agriculture; only rarely are they used for land cultivation. The words are primarily related to human activity in relationship to God—to work on behalf of or to worship (e.g., Exod 9:1, 13).[17] She concludes: to "serve" the land would thus imply "that we are to see ourselves in a relation of *subordination* to the land on which we live . . . deferring to the soil. The needs of the land take clear precedence over our own immediate preferences."[18]

This language stresses that human beings are dependent upon the land for their very life. She also notes that the verb *šāmar* ("keep") has primary reference to keeping Torah (e.g., Exod 13:10; 20:6). To keep the commandments has both positive and negative dimensions: to promote the well-being of others and to restrain violence and the misuse of others. And so to "keep" the land is to promote its well-being and keep it from being violated through human misuse.[19]

As with the other words, the language of servanthood has advantages and disadvantages. The latter might become evident if the emphasis on service becomes associated with self-denigration or inappropriate self-sacrifice (cf. the feminist critique). I worry, too, about the language of "subordination"; that language could skew the meaning and reality of dependence, which is common to all creatures (and even God, as we have noted). Among the advantages to be cited include, especially, the strong scriptural emphasis generally on being a servant. Moreover, and not often noted, the verb *serve* is used for the animals' relationship to human beings (Jer 27:6; see below).[20] Servanthood is thus not a uniquely human vocation. One could possibly speak of a mutual servanthood.

The language of stewardship, partnership, and servanthood can be more or less helpful; as with all metaphors, we need to speak a yes and a no with respect to each. In this conversation, it is important to remember a key foundation point: the "co-creatureliness"[21] of human and nonhuman, each of which, without distinction, is "good," has inherent value, is a focus for moral concern, and stands in a unique relationship with God. Every creature begins here; there is no difference among us in these respects; that all creatures receive the same textual valuation ("good") insists on these points of commonality. One significant point of difference, of course, is that human beings are responsible for the pervasive misuse of creatures other than themselves.

Once the language of calling or vocation is introduced, the role of the human relative to the nonhuman is given another point of distinction, at least in Gen 1:28, though what that language entails is not as straightforward as it might seem.[22] At the least it means "a special responsibility to foster a world in which all receive their due as God's creatures."[23] At the same time, and often forgotten, the testimony of Genesis 1 and many other Old Testament texts will speak, in effect, of the vocation of the nonhuman. Human and nonhuman have a commonality in that each is called to a vocation. We need to keep these two vocations in appropriate interaction in what might be called *an interdependent mutuality of vocation*.

I summarize some previous reflections on Genesis 1–2 as a way of lifting up the human vocation. In Gen 1:26-27, God declares that the human being, both male and female, is created "in the image of God." The content of the word *God* at this point in the text has fundamentally to do with God's *creative* activity; so the human vocation to be in God's image is modeled on the creative actions of God. If the God portrayed in this chapter is understood only or fundamentally in terms of overwhelming power, absolute control, and independent, unilateral activity, then human beings, created in the image of this God, *rightfully* understand their relationship to the nonhuman world as one of power over, absolute control, and independence. Hence, by definition, the natural world becomes available for human manipulation and exploitation. The human tendency over the years to dominate the nonhuman creatures and treat them as passive putty has been an effort, recognized or not, to act in the image of the dominating God so often thought to be portrayed in Genesis 1. Readers may ask whether it is not more an understanding of God than of humanity that has been the most basic problem for the environment. On the other hand, if God is imaged more as sharer of power in Genesis 1–2, then the way in which the image of God exercises dominion is to be shaped by that model.[24]

As we have seen, the "let us" rhetoric in Gen 1:26 is testimony to mutuality within the divine realm. God shares the creative process with that which is not God. Human beings are created in the image of a God who shares power, who has a dialogical relationship with those who are not God. This language implicitly extends the mutuality of the creative process to those who are created in the image of this kind of God. God's word, "have dominion" (Gen 1:28), means that God thereby chooses not to retain all power. That the divine command, "subdue the earth," is needed at all means that the evaluative word *good* does not mean perfect; the creation is not a static reality, forever fixed just as God initially created it. For human beings to subdue the earth means that, in time, creation would look other than what it did on the seventh day. Somewhat ironically, God gives human beings this "natural law" so that the created order would not remain the same. And, in fact, we know that the created order has not remained the same. Development and change are what God intends for the creation. God creates a paradise, but not a static paradise.

Hence, the two creation accounts do not present the world as a finished product. The commands to the human beings in 1:28 are to be linked to 2:5 (cf. 2:15), where the presence of a human being to till/serve (*'ābad*) the ground is considered just as indispensable as the rain for the development of the creation. Human beings are given responsibility for intracreational development, bringing the world along to its fullest possible potential. The creation is a highly dynamic reality in which the future is open to a number of possibilities and creaturely activity is crucial for the becoming of the creation. Creative capacities have been given to the created ones for the task of continuing creation.

This theme is explicitly developed in 2:18-25. God evaluates the creational situation and announces (to the divine council) that it is "not [yet] good." This link back to 1:26 correlates God's "let us" to the divine council with God's relationship with *'ādām*. In the divine actions that follow, God implicitly speaks a "let us" to the first human being, inviting the *'ādām* to participate in the creative process. God places various creative possibilities before the *'ādām*. The initially negative human response to God's presentation of the animals sends God back to the drawing boards. Human decisions are honored and valued by God in moving into new stages of creaturely development.

In the process of looking for "a helper as his partner," the *'ādām* names the animals and the woman. That naming is explicitly creative is shown by the fact that in Genesis 1 it is *God* who names the creatures on the first three days of creation (1:5-10). Naming is an act of discerning the nature of intracreaturely relationships, and that is a creative act. *Whatever* the human being called each animal, that was its name (2:19). The evaluative words that the man speaks about the woman (2:23) parallel the evaluations of God in Genesis 1. The human words recognize that the creation has moved from not good to good. God has thereby involved human beings in the creation of the world.

Human beings do not do so well in their exercise of power in the chapters (and centuries!) that follow. But even in the face of human sin—no minimizing this—God treats human beings with integrity and honor and does not renege on the original entrusting of humans with creational and future-shaping responsibilities as 3:23 shows (and Psalm 8). The story of Noah, the one human being named as righteous in Genesis 1–11 (6:9), testifies that not all post-sin human behavior is a betrayal of that trust. In exemplary obedience to the divine command, and that is stressed in the narrative, he makes sure that the animals get taken into the ark and are thereby preserved.

In conclusion, God's way into the future with this creation is dependent at least in part on what human beings do and say. This state of affairs brings human responsibility to the forefront of the conversation. Many of us would just as soon leave everything up to God, and God can then be blamed when things go wrong, tragically or otherwise. A way between pessimism in the face of the difficulties on the one hand and a Messiah complex on the other will not always be easy to locate. But God calls human beings to take up these God-given tasks with insight and energy—for the sake of God's world and all of its creatures, indeed for God's sake. Some comfort can be found in the assurance that in this effort we do not act alone, that God will remain faithful to commitments made and will be present on every occasion and active in every event.

The Vocation of the Nonhuman

God's presence and activity in the life of the world must be conceived in relation to the history of the nonhuman as well as that of the human. In fact, the Old Testament thoroughly integrates these histories from the creation story to apocalyptic visions.

From the creation on, God's relationship with nonhuman creatures is extensive.[25] The nonhuman creatures belong to God; God addresses them by name and delights in them. These creatures in turn respond to God and look to God for their food. God in turn responds with care and sustenance. The relationship of God to the animal world and other nonhuman creatures evident in these texts is not simply an external one. These passages suggest a more complex relationship, so that the nonhuman creatures, at least the animals, have an interiority that is of such a nature that they can come into a relationship with God that is more than objective. Given the close relationship that human beings often have with animals, God would certainly be capable of such relationships. In fact, given human sin, would not God's relationship with them be closer and more intense?

Given this relationship, the issue of vocation on the part of nonhuman creatures calls for discussion. At one level, this is a truism, given the kind of dependence of human beings on, say, the ground and its vegetation. What I have in mind is a more complex and comprehensive role for the nonhuman in the interconnected life of the world.

We return to Genesis 1–2.[26] Genesis 1 invites a perspective on creation that is not simply God-generated. Several times God invites the earth and the waters to be involved in creative acts. In these cases, God speaks *with* that which has *already* been created and involves them in further creative activity. This is mediate rather than immediate creation; it is creation from within rather than creation from without; God's creating is not unilateral, it is multilateral. The nonhuman creatures have a genuine vocational role. Perhaps a distinction between primary and secondary action is present, but the waters and earth do actually participate with God in acts of creation.

Genesis 1 also reports that two activities usually ascribed to God—separating and ruling—are given over to the creatures.[27] Moreover, it is not only human beings that are blessed and invited to be fruitful, multiply, and fill the earth but also the birds and the fish are called to do the same (1:22). Such creative capacities are thus not a distinctively human prerogative; God gives power over to the nonhuman to propagate their own kind, and implicitly God thereby chooses to exercise an ongoing restraint and constraint in relationship to their future. God will not suspend the created orders and relieve creatures of these "responsibilities."

The role of the nonhuman becomes more specifically vocational as we move into further texts. From within our understanding of interrelatedness and interdependence, the animals and other nonhuman creatures are given a servant role by God with respect to human life. The animals play an explicitly stated servant role in Jeremiah, as they called by God to "serve" the king of Babylon in his judgmental work against Israel: "I have given him even the wild animals of the field to serve him" (Jer 27:6; 28:14). God calls the wild animals to come against Jerusalem to devour it (Jer 12:9; 15:3). While animals are used in Jeremiah as metaphors for the Babylonians (e.g., 4:7), these texts speak of the agency of the animals themselves in helping to carry out God's judgment. Other prophetic texts will put another twist on the agency of the nonhuman creatures. The desolation of the land and its animals may be considered an effect of human iniquity (e.g., Hos 4:1-3), but it is important not to think of the environment as a victim, or at least simply as a victim, for God uses this very environmental degradation as an instrument of judgment (e.g., Jer 3:2-3; 5:24-25; 14:2-12). Simply using victim language for the land and its animals in these judgment texts insufficiently recognizes a vocation to which God calls them in the service of the divine purposes; at the least we could speak of the nonhuman as both victim and vehicle. Moreover, God, in using the nonhuman for the divine purposes, including judgment, calls the nonhuman to a servant vocation that may entail suffering (see Jer. 9:10-11). Given that servant language is explicitly used for the nonhuman in Jeremiah, can we not speak even of a call to suffering on the part of these nonhuman creatures in the furtherance of God's purposes?

Nonhuman creatures are also used in salvation contexts. At the Red Sea, the nonhuman creatures—wind, waves, sea, clouds, and darkness—are key divine means in and through which the Egyptians are immobilized and destroyed in the process of Israel's redemption. It is not too much to say that, at the Red Sea, the nonhuman is the savior of the human! In a way parallel to God's use of human beings to, say, proclaim the gospel and feed the hungry, so the nonhuman becomes a medium in and through which God works salvation on behalf of the oppressed.

The wilderness narratives witness to the role of the nonhuman in continuing creation.[28] In Exod 15:25, the Israelites, desperately in need of water, found only the bitter waters of Marah. In order to resolve the problem, God showed Moses a piece of wood; Moses threw it into the water and the water became sweet. No miraculous claim is made; rather, God provides a means for Moses to resolve the water problem from the world of nature, namely, a piece of wood, which had certain properties that enabled it to sweeten water. God here works in and through human knowledge and the healing properties of certain elements in the natural order. God's providence is here shown in leading Moses to help that is already available in the world of nature for the health of the wilderness community. Similar understandings of the providential role of the nonhuman are evident in other wilderness narratives, from manna and quail (Exod 16:4-21; Num 11:7-9, 31-32) to water in rock formations (Exod 17:1-7; Num 20:2-13). The wilderness, for all its discontinuity from creation as God intended it, is not without resources. And God (with Moses) uses those natural resources in order to sustain the human community in the midst of hardship. The wilderness narratives witness to *nature's God-given potentialities as a vehicle for the healing of the human community*. Several other such texts might be cited in this connection, from the ravens feeding Elijah (1 Kgs 17:1-7), to the fish saving Jonah from drowning in the sea (Jonah 2:1-10), to Israelites winning battles because the sun stayed its course (Josh 10:12-14).[29] One might even speak of animal sacrifices as a divinely given means in and through which Israel's sin can be forgiven (Leviticus 1–7).

I pause to reflect briefly on the agency of both God and the nonhuman order, what we might call *dual agency*.[30] For example, while Ps 104:14 testifies to God's making the grass and plants grow, Hag 1:10-11 speaks of the ground itself bringing forth such vegetation and of the earth withholding its produce. The latter passage also speaks of the *heavens* withholding the rains, while Job 37:6 makes it clear that God is responsible for *every* shower or snowfall. Other texts also make clear that blessings are due not solely to divine activity but to a sharing of that creative power with the created order itself (e.g., Deut 28:4; Ps 65:9-13).[31]

In the natural order, then, there is neither a "letting go" of the creation on God's part nor a divine retention of all such powers.[32] Creative powers are shared, with the context determining where the emphasis ought to be placed. Both God and the creation are involved in every such ongoing creative act, though God always relates to this order in ways that are appropriate to its nature. Thus it is clear that while God's ongoing creative activity is efficacious, there is a significant element of indeterminacy.[33]

Continuing the look at the vocation of the nonhuman, texts that speak of God's appearances are remarkable in the extent to which God's coming is accompanied by activity in the nonhuman sphere: the earth quakes and the heavens rain down (Ps 68:8), the mountains and hills skip like young animals (Ps 114:3-7), the cedars are broken and the oaks whirl (Ps 29:5-9), the mountains melt like wax (Ps 97:5), and the waters are afraid and the deep trembles (Ps 77:16). Or, God is accompanied by fire and smoke, covered by darkness and clouds, supported by the wings of the wind, surrounded by lightning, and enveloped by the clouds—God's own chariot (Pss 18:8-15; 104:2-4). There is no telltale trail of God tracks in these responses of nature, which unambiguously reveal God. Yet, in accompanying the presence of God, these nonhuman entities *serve* to enhance and intensify the divine revelation.

The God speeches in Job 38–41 are also revealing of a significant vocational role for the nonhuman. While it has been common to speak of the God speeches and the human vocation with respect to the environment, the role of the nonhuman creatures as God's agents in Job's healing (and potentially the suffering of others) has been less frequently noted. Interpreters have read these speeches of God to a suffering Job and wondered about God's pastoral counseling skills. By drawing on the significant place of the nonhuman in Job's world, the healing possibilities for Job are enhanced.[34]

Job responds to his suffering with remarkably sharp laments, typical for an ancient Israelite. Job compares himself to the wild animals, which inhabit desolate places (30:29; cf. Ps 102:6-11). God in response introduces many wild creatures of the wilderness, noting that they are encompassed within the care and nurture of God. One implication for Job is that, in his feelings of isolation and dislocatedness, he is comparably embraced. Job, who feels that he is an outcast, thrust out into the margins of his society, rejected by family, friends, and God as well, is here assured that with God there are no alien creatures, no outsiders. Such a vision can counter the isolation that catastrophe brings—particularly if accompanied by a sense of divine rejection or forsaking; it can give one a sense of connectedness to an all encompassing created order. Job can see in this vision of the nonhuman world a God-cared-for community to which he belongs.

In addition, the sea and its raging waters that threaten boats and shorelines, are often presented as an image of personal distress in the laments (e.g., Ps 69:1-3). These are chaotic elements of the earth's becoming, and they are often parallel to life in human society; God's assurance is that, finally, they have divinely constrained limits in their ability to destroy (Job 38:8-11). Though Job may feel rejected and tossed about in the desolate places of the earth, he can be assured that God visits even those places with life-giving rain (Job 38:22-27). Even in those wilderness areas, you should see the flowers in the spring!

In the midst of Job's turmoil and loss, the issue of trust in the fundamental orders of creation, however marked by randomness, will be important. At the heart of the world's structures, one may observe a God who cares and nurtures and desires the best for every creature. And if every creature, then certainly human beings! In the face of experienced chaos in one's life, there is considerable value to an orienting vision that claims coherence, reliability, and graciousness for God's good creation. Moreover, such a vision can contribute to a kind of dispersion of one's suffering and grief out into the larger world, where it dissipates and is absorbed. It is almost as if the trees, the sky, the mountains, the sea, the animals, all silent and accepting, take our pain into them and bring us relief from the burden. This focus on creation in God's speeches suggests that one important word of God to such a suffering situation is a renewed vision of God's caring presence throughout the creation and of a larger creational design of which Job is a part. Perhaps above all, this vision of the nonhuman creation can enable him to get beyond the debilitating focus on his own troubles, to see that larger nonhuman world in which God works in caring ways beyond his knowing.

Several years ago, in teaching a course on God and suffering in the Old Testament, the class got to thinking through some of these creation texts.

A woman in the class shared an experience that had been crucial to her well-being. She reported that her husband had killed himself several years earlier, and she reflected on the various ways in which she had coped with that experience. She had drawn on the various consolations that her pastor and congregation offered, and she testified that they had been helpful. But, she said, the breakthrough in her recovery came when her sons had taken her canoeing in the wilderness areas of northern Minnesota. This close touch with God's majestic creation had enabled a new sense of the goodness of God's work in the world. This renewed sense of God's wonder-filled creation proved to be a crucial means in and through which God brought healing to her.

This perspective may assist us in speaking in more balanced ways regarding various issues relating to the nonhuman world in our own time. Take an issue such as animal rights. If we are working with a genuinely relational and interdependent model of the creation, animals are called to contribute to the life of the human not just the other way around; they can be a medium in and through which God gets things done in the world on behalf of human beings. One thinks of the use of plants and animals in medical research, as scientists seek to find new forms of medicine for human beings. *Time Magazine*, in a section on the future of drugs, carried an article entitled, "Potions from Poisons."[35] It was reported that modern medicine is filled with life-enhancing drugs derived from poisonous snakes, spiders, scorpions, plants, frogs, and other poisonous creatures. Can one not speak of a servant role that such animals have, serving human beings in particular? How researchers handle such animals in assisting them in this role is of crucial importance, so that cruelty does not become the order of the day. But that seems to me to be an issue of how, not whether, animals may be so used in the service of the life of others. One might also note the many caring services that animals provide for human beings. This would include their presence in nursing homes or among the sick and lonely; the animals can function as "best friend" and bring comfort and even promote healing among human beings.[36]

I move, finally, to a role that nonhuman creatures play in our theological vocation. Animals and other nonhuman creatures assist us in the tasks of preaching, teaching, theological formulation, and hymn-singing in more ways than we normally think. Several animals are used, in both Old Testament and New Testament, as metaphors to speak of the ways in which God relates to the world. God is light, water, rock, fire, wind, as well as a few birds and animals, such as the eagle and the lion. If God is a rock or a mother eagle, then rocks and eagles are in some sense reflective of the very identity of God. Moreover, certain divine attributes are elucidated by reference to such nonhuman entities. For example, God's righteousness is like the mountains (Ps 36:6) or God's faithfulness is like the enduringness of the sun, moon, and stars (Jer 31:35-36). These nonhuman creatures, in their very existence, in their being what they are, reflect the reality that is God. Such metaphors, drawn from the sphere of the nonhuman, can assist us in remarkably relational ways to speak of the God in whom we believe. The vocation of nonhumans can enhance the vocation of human beings.

In view of these relationships between God and the nonhuman, another level of the vocation of the nonhuman is evident, namely, the praise of God.[37] The natural order provides raw material for human praise. Without the nonhuman creatures, the praising metaphors at the disposal of the human would be far fewer in number. Without the praise of nature, secondary human forms of praise would be much more meager; we would be without much praise-full painting, music, and literature. Human beings give voice to nonhuman praise, to a world highly charged with wonder and praise. On the other hand, our sinfulness may adversely affect the ability of the world of nature to voice their praise in being themselves. The heavens, for example, will proclaim the glory of God with less clarity on a smoggy day in one of our cities than on other days. Human sins lessen the productive possibilities of the earth, and hence lessen its praise potential. In other words, our environmental activity is directly related to the praise possibilities of nature. We can enhance or inhibit the vocation to which it has been called.

Abbreviations

ABD	*Anchor Bible Dictionary*. Edited by D. N. Freedman. 6 vols. New York, 1992
ANQ	*Andover Newton Quarterly*
BA	*Biblical Archaeologist*
BJRL	*Bulletin of the John Rylands University Library of Manchester*
BZAW	Beihefte zur Zeitschrift für die alttestamentliche Wissenschaft
CBQ	*Catholic Biblical Quarterly*
CC	*Continental Commentaries*
CSR	*Christian Scholar's Review*
CurTM	*Currents in Theology and Mission*
Di	*Dialog*
ExpTim	*Expository Times*
ExAud	*Ex Auditu*
HBT	*Horizons in Biblical Theology*
HTR	*Harvard Theological Review*
Int	*Interpretation*
JNES	*Journal of Near Eastern Studies*
JBL	*Journal of Biblical Literature*
JETS	*Journal of the Evangelical Theological Society*
JQR	*Jewish Quarterly Review*
JR	*Journal of Religion*
JSOT	*Journal for the Study of the Old Testament*
JSOTSup	Journal for the Study of the Old Testament: Supplement Series
JTS	*Journal of Theological Studies*
OtSt	*Oudtestamentische studiën*
PSB	*Princeton Seminary Bulletin*

SBLDS	Society of Biblical Literature Dissertation Series
SJT	*Scottish Journal of Theology*
TD	*Theology Digest*
ThTo	*Theology Today*
TS	*Theological Studies*
TZ	*Theologische Zeitschrift*
USQR	*Union Seminary Quarterly Review*
VT	*Vetus Testamentum*
WMANT	Wissenschaftliche Monographien zum Alten und Neuen Testament
WW	*Word and World*
ZAW	*Zeitschrift für die alttestamentliche Wissenschaft*

NOTES

Introduction

1. Walter Brueggemann, "The Loss and Recovery of Creation in Old Testament Theology," *ThTo* 53 (1997): 177-90; see also his summary in *Theology of the Old Testament: Testimony, Dispute, Advocacy* (Minneapolis: Fortress, 1997), 159-64; Henning Graf Reventlow, "Creation as a Topic in Biblical Theology," in *Creation in Jewish and Christian Tradition* (ed. Henning Graf Reventlow and Yair Hoffman; London: Sheffield Academic Press, 2002), 153-71; Ronald A. Simkins, *Creator and Creation: Nature in the Worldview of Ancient Israel* (Peabody, Mass.: Hendrickson, 1994), 15-40; Theodore Hiebert, "Re-Imaging Nature: Shifts in Biblical Interpretation," *Int* 50 (1996): 36-46; idem, *The Yahwist's Landscape: Nature and Religion in Early Israel* (New York: Oxford University Press, 1996); Leo G. Perdue, *The Collapse of History: Reconstructing Old Testament Theology* (Minneapolis: Fortress, 1994), 113-50; Rolf P. Knierim, "Cosmos and History in Israel's Theology," *HBT* 3 (1981): 64-74. For a somewhat earlier perspective, see George S. Hendry, "Eclipse of Creation," *ThTo* 28 (1971–1972): 406-25. Cf. already the 1934 sermon by Rudolf Bultmann, "Faith in God the Creator," in *Existence and Faith: Shorter Writings of Rudolf Bultmann* (ed. Schubert M. Ogden; London: Hodder and Stoughton, 1960), 172.

2. Gerhard von Rad's article, originally published in 1936, assigned a secondary status for creation thought in Old Testament theology (*The Problem of the Hexateuch and Other Essays* [trans. E. W. Trueman Dicken; Edinburgh: Oliver & Boyd, 1966], 131-43). For a thorough assessment of von Rad's work on creation, see Rolf Rendtorff, *Canon and Theology: Overtures to an Old Testament Theology* (ed. and trans. Margaret Kohl; Overtures to Biblical Theology, ed. Walter Brueggemann, et al.; Minneapolis: Fortress, 1993), 92-113. See the summary of these developments in Brueggemann, "Loss and Recovery," 177-79. See also Norbert Lohfink, *Theology of the Pentateuch: Themes of the Priestly Narrative and Deuteronomy* (trans. Linda M. Maloney; Minneapolis: Fortress, 1994), 117-18; Reventlow, "Creation as a Topic," in Reventlow and Hoffman, *Creation in Jewish and Christian Tradition*, 157-60.

3. See von Rad, "The Theological Problem": Israel's faith is "primarily concerned with redemption" (p. 131). His *Theology of the Old Testament* subsumes the discussion of creation to that of history. While he does consider creation before redemption in his *Theology*, it seems to have had little impact on his discussion of either. Reventlow, "Creation as a Topic," 159-60, documents less than fully developed changes in von Rad's later work ("Some Aspects of the Old Testament Worldview," in *Problem of the Hexateuch*, 144-65, and *Wisdom in Israel* [trans. James D. Martin; Nashville: Abingdon, 1972] are often cited). See also Reventlow's survey in *Problems of Old Testament Theology in the Twentieth Century* (trans. J. Bowden; London: SCM, 1985), 134-86. See the review of this point in Knierim, "Cosmos and History," 66-70. The work of G. Ernest Wright, extending certain emphases of von Rad, has been influential in this respect, especially in the United States, seen not least in his sharp separation of history and nature (out of a concern to set Israel's historical faith over against Canaanite myth and religion). See especially his *God Who Acts: Biblical Theology as Recital* (London: SCM, 1952); *The Old Testament against Its Environment* (Studies in Biblical Theology; London: SCM, 1950). A quotation from the latter work illustrates the point: "Israel was little interested in nature" (*Old Testament Against*, 17). Lohfink speaks of "a traditional Christian system of values in which words like salvation and redemption are writ large, but where other words like earthly reality, humanity, and creation appear seldom or only in the margins" (*Theology of the Pentateuch*, 117).

4. A point well made by Claus Westermann, "Biblical Reflection on Creator-Creation," in *Creation in the Old Testament* (ed. Bernhard W. Anderson; Issues in Religion and Theology 6, ed. Douglas Knight and Robert Morgan; Philadelphia: Fortress, 1984), 92.

5. So Brueggemann, "Loss and Recovery," 188-89. He quotes Phyllis Trible on this point: "Creation theology undercuts patriarchy" ("Treasures Old and New: Biblical Theology and the Challenge of Feminism," in *The Open Text: New Directions for Biblical Studies?* [ed. Francis Watson; London: SCM, 1993], 47).

6. Northrop Frye, *The Great Code: The Bible and Literature* (London: Routledge & Kegan Paul, 1982), 112-13.

7. On these developments, with bibliography, see Simkins, *Creator and Creation*, 1-14; Hiebert, *Yahwist's Landscape*, 3-29. Both have helpful assessments of the work of von Rad and others, with their continuing effect on the study of Israel's understanding of creation. These studies are basic for further reflection regarding the Bible's perspectives on nature. Also fundamental for a broader look at this topic is H. Paul Santmire, who traces the history of the understanding of nature in Christian thought in *The Travail of Nature: The Ambiguous Ecological Promise of Christian Theology* (Philadelphia: Fortress, 1985); idem, "Toward a New Theology of Nature," *Di* 25 (1986): 43-50; see also his recent "Partnership with Nature according to the Scriptures: Beyond the Theology of Stewardship," *CSR* 32 (2003): 381-412. For further bibliography and a discussion of several features of a theology of nature, see ch. 8.

8. Simkins has argued that Lynn White, whose controversial 1967 article "The Historic Roots of Our Ecological Crisis" (*Science* 155 [1967]: 1203-7) sharply blamed biblical perspectives on nature for the environmental crisis, "stands as a watershed figure in the history of biblical interpretation because his attack on the biblical tradition forced scholars to examine the Bible's view of the natural world and especially its presentation of humankind's relationship to nature." At the same time, he notes that biblical scholars have "failed to articulate adequately the biblical writers' attitudes toward the natural world" (*Creator and Creation*, 7). Thankfully, that has begun to fade.

9. Brevard S. Childs essentially follows von Rad in stating, "Israel's faith developed historically from its initial encounter with God as redeemer from Egypt, and only secondarily from this centre was a theology of creation incorporated into its faith" (*Biblical Theology of the Old and New Testaments: Theological Reflection on the Christian Bible* [London: SCM, 1992], 110). See also n. 41 of this chapter.

10. Horst Dietrich Preuss, *Old Testament Theology* (2 vols.; trans. Leo G. Perdue; The Old Testament Library, ed. James L. Mays, Carol A. Newsom, and David L. Petersen; Louisville: Westminster John Knox, 1995). Preuss's brief discussion of creation concludes that creation has "no central theological significance for the Old Testament" (1:226-39). Following a common pattern, he subsumes creation under history as "a historical act" or "the extension of salvation history" (pp. 236-37).

11. Bernhard W. Anderson, *Contours of Old Testament Theology* (Minneapolis: Fortress, 1999). Anderson has written several important and helpful works on creation that help break the discussion out of traditional categories, including *Creation Versus Chaos: The Reinterpretation of Mythical Symbolism in the Bible* (New York: Association, 1967); *From Creation to New Creation: Old Testament Perspectives* (Overtures to Biblical Theology, ed. Walter Brueggemann, et al.; Minneapolis: Fortress, 1994). But in *Contours of Old Testament Theology*, he largely subsumes his consideration of creation under the Abrahamic covenant, to which the covenant with Noah has standing only as a "preface."

12. Erhard Gerstenberger, *Theologies in the Old Testament* (Minneapolis: Fortress, 2002). Gerstenberger's ecological sensitivities are made clear early on (pp. 7-12), but little sustained reflection on creational themes occurs in the volume, admittedly focused on a historical approach (pp. 242-44; see also pp. 224, 287, 300, 317).

13. Walter Brueggemann, *Theology of the Old Testament*, esp. 145-64, 333-58, 528-51. Brueggemann's work on creation has been more positively developed in recent years, and this is also the case in his *Theology*, where he begins his segment on Israel's verbal testimony with verbs for God's creating. Yet, for all the space devoted to creation, the material in the volume is somewhat scattered, leaving the impression that it is less than fully integrated into the whole. Brueggemann's perspective has shifted not least in light of his interchange with J. Richard Middleton,

"Is Creation Theology Inherently Conservative? A Dialogue with Walter Brueggemann," *HTR* 87 (1994): 257-77. Brueggemann's response follows (pp. 279-89). For a more recent helpful study by Middleton, see his "Creation Founded in Love: Breaking Rhetorical Expectations in Genesis 1:1–2:3," in *Sacred Text, Secular Times: The Hebrew Bible in the Modern World* (ed. Leonard Jay Greenspoon and Bryan F. LeBeau; Studies in Jewish Civilization 10; Omaha: Creighton University Press, 2000), 47-85.

14. John Goldingay, *Israel's Gospel* (vol. 1 of *Old Testament Theology*; Downer's Grove, Ill.: InterVarsity, 2003). Pages 42-192 are devoted to a discussion of Genesis 1–11 and related texts (primarily Psalms, but all explicit texts that reference originating creation). It is not clear to me, however, that creation forms an important or integrating theme for him in the balance of the volume, not least because he gives no place to continuing creation (pp. 126-28).

15. Rolf Rendtorff, "Some Reflections on Creation as a Topic of Old Testament Theology," in *Priests, Prophets, and Scribes: Essays on the Formation and Heritage of Second Temple Judaism in Honour of Joseph Blenkinsopp* (ed. Eugene Ulrich et al.; JSOTSup 149; Sheffield: JSOT Press, 1992), 204.

16. Claus Westermann, *Creation* (trans. John J. Scullion; Philadelphia: Fortress, 1974); idem, *Blessing in the Bible and in the Life of the Church* (trans. Keith R. Crim; Philadelphia: Fortress, 1978).

17. H. H. Schmid's work has been especially influential ("Creation, Righteousness, and Salvation: 'Creation Theology' as the Broad Horizon of Biblical Theology," in Anderson, *Creation in the Old Testament*, 102-17). This collection of essays also contains important articles by Anderson; Hermann Gunkel; von Rad; Walther Eichrodt; Dennis J. McCarthy; Westermann; Hans-Jürgen Hermisson; and George M. Landes. Also deserving of mention in this connection is Klaus Koch, "Is There a Doctrine of Retribution in the Old Testament?" in *Theodicy in the Old Testament* (ed. James L. Crenshaw; Philadelphia: Fortress, 1983), 57-87; his focus on an understanding of justice in the context of creation has important links to Schmid's work.

18. Knierim, in an important series of essays (*The Task of Old Testament Theology: Substance, Method, and Cases* [Grand Rapids: Eerdmans, 1995]), was an early proponent of the centrality of creation in Old Testament theology; see also his "The Task of Old Testament Theology," *HBT* 6 (1984): 25-57: "Yahweh's relationship to universal reality as expressed in the theology of creation can be discerned in the final analysis as what is at issue in the Old Testament" (p. 43).

19. Odil Hannes Steck, *World and Environment* (Nashville: Abingdon, 1980). An "early" work that lifted up environmental issues and helped chart the way for others.

20. For Anderson's key works, see n. 11.

21. Jon D. Levenson's learned work has been and remains deeply influential across the discipline (*Creation and the Persistence of Evil: The Jewish Drama of Divine Omnipotence* [San Francisco: Harper & Row, 1988]).

22. James Barr, *Biblical Faith and Natural Theology* (Oxford: Clarendon, 1993). This work is especially helpful in cutting against theological objections to "natural theology" and grounding such an understanding in the biblical texts themselves.

23. Simkins (*Creator and Creation*) exhibits considerable range in his analysis of biblical and ancient Near Eastern texts regarding Israel's view of nature.

24. Leo G. Perdue, *Wisdom and Creation: The Theology of Wisdom Literature* (Nashville: Abingon, 1994). A thorough analytical and constructive examination of the place of creation in Wisdom literature.

25. William P. Brown, *The Ethos of the Cosmos: The Genesis of Moral Imagination in the Bible* (Grand Rapids: Eerdmans, 1999). Arguably the finest current study of creation in the Old Testament, focusing on the Yahwist, the Priestly writer, Second Isaiah, Proverbs, and Job. Theologically and ethically sophisticated, Brown's work is marked by thoughtful exegesis and an imaginative use of language.

26. Karl Löning and Erich Zenger, *To Begin with, God Created . . . : Biblical Theologies of Creation* (trans. Omar Kaste; Collegeville, Minn.: Liturgical Press, 2000). Unusual in its effort to cover the understanding of creation in both Testaments, this study constitutes a wide-ranging exegetical and theological analysis of key texts and includes thoughtful portrayals of ancient Near Eastern parallels.

27. Stefan Paas, *Creation and Judgement: Creation Texts in Some Eighth Century Prophets* (Leiden: Brill, 2003). An extensive analysis of creation texts in the early prophets, with much helpful discussion of exegetical and historical issues.

28. W. Randall Garr, *In His Own Image and Likeness: Humanity, Divinity, and Monotheism* (Leiden: Brill, 2003). A detailed and sophisticated historical study, focused on the Priestly account of creation, especially Gen 1:26-27, and biblical and ancient Near Eastern parallels.

29. Five volumes were published between 2000 and 2002: Introduction, Genesis, Wisdom Literature, Psalms and Prophets, and the New Testament (New York: Sheffield Academic Press). Shirley Wurst was the coeditor of two volumes. An extensive examination of numerous biblical texts from the perspective of an ecojustice hermeneutic; the study is concerned especially with whether the Earth is treated unjustly in the text, working from the angle of "the Earth as a subject rather than an object." The basic aims and approach are outlined by editor Habel in the introductory volume, *Readings from the Perspective of Earth*, 25-53.

30. Among the many that might be mentioned, the volumes edited by Dieter T. Hessel should especially be noted, including *After Nature's Revolt: Ecojustice and Theology* (Minneapolis: Fortress, 1992); *Theology for Earth Community: A Field Guide* (Maryknoll, N.Y.: Orbis, 1996); with Rosemary Radford Ruether, *Christianity and Ecology: Seeking the Well-Being of Earth and Humans* (Cambridge: Harvard Center for the Study of World Religions, 2000); with Larry Rasmussen, *Earth Habitat: Eco-Injustice and the Church's Response* (Minneapolis: Fortress,

2001). Feminist scholarship has also been influential in this discussion (e.g., Rosemary Radford Ruether, Heather Eaton). More generally, the works of Thomas Berry and Holmes Rolston have been enormously influential.

31. Important studies by systematic theologians include those of Michael Welker, Jürgen Moltmann, Douglas John Hall, Keith Ward, Langdon Gilkey, Colin E. Gunton, Catherine Keller, Kathryn Tanner, Francis Watson, Philip Clayton, and Paul R. Sponheim. Also significant for these discussions are those scholars who have pursued the interface of science and theology, including John Polkinghorne, Ian Barbour, Arthur R. Peacocke, Ted Peters, Robert Russell, and Nancey Murphy. Occasional reference to the work of these scholars will be made as links to the biblical material seem pertinent. An especially important contributor that crosses biblical, theological, and historical disciplines is H. Paul Santmire (see n. 7).

32. See especially *Creation*; *Blessing in the Bible*; *Elements of Old Testament Theology* (Atlanta: John Knox, 1982); "Creation and History in the Old Testament," in *The Gospel and Human Destiny* (ed. Vilmos Vajta; Minneapolis: Augsburg, 1971), 11-38.

33. My colleague Frederick Gaiser, a student of both von Rad and Westermann, refers to the latter's work as a "Yes, but" response to von Rad.

34. Westermann, *Elements*, 86.

35. Reventlow, "Creation as a Topic," in Reventlow and Hoffman, *Creation in Jewish and Christian Tradition*, 161. We consider continuous creation in the next chapter.

36. We pick up this conversation in the next chapter.

37. A helpful critique of Westermann is made by Paas, *Creation and Judgement*, 17-18.

38. H. H. Schmid, *Gerechtigkeit als Weltordnung* (Tubingen: Mohr Siebeck, 1968); idem, "Creation, Righteousness, and Salvation," in Anderson, *Creation in the Old Testament*.

39. The judgment of Brueggemann, *Theology of the Old Testament*, 161.

40. See the discussion of law in ch. 5.

41. Schmid, "Creation, Righteousness, and Salvation," in Anderson, *Creation in the Old Testament*, 105. In postbiblical creedal terms, these kinds of matters are commonly understood as "first article" issues. For critical comment on Schmid's work, see Childs, *Biblical Theology*, 109, 490-91. While Childs is appreciative, Schmid is thought to be too dependent upon the ancient Near Eastern material and insufficiently attentive to its adaptation by Israel as well as to "Yahweh's fully sovereign intervention in redemptive acts of surprise and wonder in restoring his own creation" (*Biblical Theology*, 490). This criticism is important to consider, though the world order and God's continuing activity need not be pulled apart, and just how to conceive of God's actions within such an order will need careful attention (e.g., what would be entailed in a "fully sovereign intervention"?).

42. Brown, *Ethos*, 25.

43. Knierim, "The Task of Old Testament Theology," 40.
44. Ibid., 42.
45. I have sought to make this point in "The Reclamation of Creation: Redemption and Law in Exodus," *Int* 45 (1991): 354-65.
46. See the discussion in Childs, *Biblical Theology*, 107-18.
47. So Paas, *Creation and Judgement*, 18.
48. For a discussion of this issue, see next chapter.
49. James Barr, "Biblical Law and the Question of Natural Theology," in *The Law in the Bible and in Its Environment* (ed. Timo Veijola; Publications of the Finnish Exegetical Society 51; Göttingen: Vandenhoeck & Ruprecht, 1989), 21; see also his *Biblical Faith and Natural Theology*. Such an understanding need not be set over against divine revelation; see the discussion of natural law in ch. 5.
50. For a brief survey of these ancient Near Eastern texts, see Excursus in ch. 2.
51. See also the discussion in Rendtorff, *Canon and Theology*. In view of Rendtorff's concern about the "center of the faith," it is important for me to state that, if one were to speak of such a center (to Israel's faith, not to Old Testament theology), it would be God's redemptive actions. See my comments about generalizing genres (e.g., Exod 34:6-7) in "The God Who Acts: An Old Testament Perspective," *ThTo* 54 (1997): 16-18.
52. See especially the work of Westermann, *Blessing in the Bible*.
53. See Childs: "Israel's faith developed historically from its initial encounter with God as redeemer from Egypt, and only secondarily from this centre was a theology of creation incorporated into its faith" (*Biblical Theology*, 110). See Anderson, *From Creation to New Creation*, 3-7, 22-25. Such a perspective can be seen in the claim that the natural element in the story of the exodus was "the servant of Yahweh's *historical* purpose" (p. 5, emphasis mine).
54. For detail, see Terence E. Fretheim, *Exodus* (Interpretation: A Bible Commentary for Teaching and Preaching, ed. James Luther Mays; Louisville: Westminster John Knox, 1991), 12-14. On the exodus events and creation, see ch. 4.
55. George M. Landes puts it this way: "Cosmic creation, though not in itself an activity of liberation, was nonetheless the crucial supposition of God's liberating work in history, which was also a form of creation" ("Creation and Liberation," in Anderson, *Creation in the Old Testament*, 139).
56. Rendtorff, *Canon and Theology*, 107-8 (emphasis mine). Cf. Langdon Gilkey: "The idea that God is the Creator of all things is the indispensable foundation on which the other beliefs of the Christian faith are based" (*Maker of Heaven and Earth: A Study of the Christian Doctrine of Creation* [Garden City, N.Y.: Doubleday, 1959], 15).
57. See Paas, *Creation and Judgement*, 38-53, for a brief survey of a possible chronology for the development of creation thought in Israel. Paas also disputes, correctly in my estimation, the effort by Rainer Albertz to claim different points

of origin for traditions regarding the creation of the individual and the creation of the world (*Weltschopfung und Menschenschopfung untersucht bei Deuterojesaja, Hiob und in den Psalmen* [Stuttgart: Calwer, 1974]). Albertz's views are also contested by Richard J. Clifford, *Creation Accounts in the Ancient Near East and in the Bible* (Catholic Biblical Quarterly Series 26; Washington, D.C.: Catholic Biblical Association of America, 1994), 5-6, 152-53.

58. See, for example, the conclusion of Anderson, *Creation Versus Chaos*: "The Jerusalem cult, then, was undoubtedly a crucible for the fusion of the creation-faith with the faith based upon Israel's sacred history" (p. 68). See also his discussion of "Creation and Worship" (pp. 78-109).

1. *Theological Perspectives*

1. For a discussion of these terms, see Stefan Paas, *Creation and Judgement: Creation Texts in Some Eighth Century Prophets* (Leiden: Brill, 2003); see also the verbs treated by Walter Brueggemann, *Theology of the Old Testament: Testimony, Dispute, Advocacy* (Minneapolis: Fortress, 1997), 146-49; John Goldingay, *Israel's Gospel* (vol. 1 of *Old Testament Theology*; Downer's Grove, Ill.: InterVarsity, 2003), 42-130; Theodore Ludwig, "The Traditions of the Establishing of the Earth in Deutero-Isaiah," *JBL* 92 (1973): 345-57.

2. Contexts in which these and other words appear will be discussed throughout the volume.

3. Ronald A. Simkins, *Creator and Creation: Nature in the Worldview of Ancient Israel* (Peabody, Mass.: Hendrickson, 1994), 91.

4. See Margaret L. Hammer, *Giving Birth: Reclaiming Biblical Metaphor for Pastoral Practice* (Louisville: Westminster/John Knox, 1994), 28-81; Phyllis Trible, *God and the Rhetoric of Sexuality* (Overtures to Biblical Theology, ed. Walter Brueggemann and John R. Donahue; Philadelphia: Fortress, 1978); Goldingay, *Israel's Gospel*, 61-62; William P. Brown, "*Creatio Corporis* and the Rhetoric of Defense in Job 10 and Psalm 139," in *God Who Creates: Essays in Honor of W. Sibley Towner* (ed. William P. Brown and S. Dean McBride Jr.; Grand Rapids: Eerdmans, 2000), 107-24; Paas, *Creation and Judgement*, 65-69.

5. See ch. 7 for detail on the Proverbs and Job texts.

6. William P. Brown has an extensive treatment of the botanical imagery in Second Isaiah; see *The Ethos of the Cosmos: The Genesis of Moral Imagination in the Bible* (Grand Rapids: Eerdmans, 1999), 229-69.

7. See Leo G. Perdue, *Wisdom and Creation: The Theology of Wisdom Literature* (Nashville: Abingdon, 1994), 82-83; Ludwig, "Traditions."

8. For further reflection on the conflict motif, see next chapter.

9. On the use of *'āsāh* with *bārā'* in Genesis 1, see next chapter.

10. See David L. Petersen, "The World of Creation in the Book of the Twelve," in Brown and McBride, *God Who Creates*, 204-14.

11. See discussion in the next chapter.

12. For examples, see the essays in *The Vitality of Old Testament Traditions* (2nd ed.; ed. Walter Brueggemann and Hans Walter Wolff; Atlanta: John Knox, 1982); Goldingay, *Israel's Gospel*, 81.

13. See, e.g., Dennis J. McCarthy, "'Creation' Motifs in Ancient Hebrew Poetry," in *Creation in the Old Testament* (ed. Bernhard W. Anderson; Issues in Religion and Theology 6, ed. Douglas Knight and Robert Morgan; Philadelphia: Fortress, 1984), 75. On the theology of nature, see Simkins, *Creator and Creation*; Gerhard von Rad, *The Problem of the Hexateuch and Other Essays* (New York: McGraw-Hill, 1966), 144-65. Notably, *creation* is not a common word outside of religious communities. For other works on nature, see ch. 8.

14. McCarthy, "'Creation' Motifs," 79.

15. The work of Paas is helpful on this point (*Creation and Judgement*, 55-107).

16. Claus Westermann, *Genesis 1–11: A Commentary* (Minneapolis: Augsburg, 1984), 175; similarly, Goldingay denies "continuous creation" and considers the creation "finished" (*Israel's Gospel*, 126-28). His concern for stability need not include such ideas.

17. For a recent effort, see Francis Watson, *Text and Truth: Redefining Biblical Theology* (Grand Rapids: Eerdmans, 1997), 225-27. Not unlike Westermann, he wishes to consider all such divine activity under the rubric of preservation (268 n. 7), reserving the word *creation* for what happened "in the beginning." Watson, however, in the distinction he makes between creation and covenant (defined as "the entire complex history that begins with the call of Abraham and that culminates in the story of the life, death and resurrection of Jesus" [*Text and Truth*, 232]), essentially reduces God's work in the world subsequent to the creation to a salvation history. At the same time, Watson will speak of "the continuing divine *creative* activity in the present" (p. 262, emphasis mine), so his distinctions are not cleanly carried through. Colin E. Gunton, somewhat more tentatively (see pp. 88-89), wants to restrict the language of creation to the beginning, for only then can one speak of creation out of nothing; everything since "the beginning" is only a rearrangement of what is given in Genesis 1 (*The Triune Creator: A Historical and Systematic Study* [Edinburgh: Edinburgh University Press, 1998], 88-89).

18. Ben C. Ollenburger, "Isaiah's Creation Theology," *ExAud* 3 (1987): 60. For Patrick D. Miller, creation in Psalm 104 is "a process of past and present. Indeed, the poetry does not set neat distinctions between these temporal dimensions or between creation and providence" ("The Poetry of Creation: Psalm 104," in Brown and McBride, *God Who Creates*, 97).

19. Hans-Jürgen Hermisson's statement about wisdom applies generally to the Old Testament: "Creation did not only happen at the beginning of the world, but takes place continuously; *therefore*, the orders have not become rigid, but necessarily remain flexible" ("Observations on the Creation Theology in Wisdom," in Anderson, *Creation in the Old Testament*, 122, emphasis mine).

20. For details on Isa 40–55, see ch. 6. For a discussion from the perspective of

systematic theology, see Jürgen Moltmann, *God in Creation: An Ecological Doctrine of Creation* (trans. Margaret Kohl; London: SCM, 1985), 206-14.

21. See next chapter for further details.

22. See, e.g., *Cosmos as Creation: Theology and Science in Consonance* (ed. Ted Peters; Nashville: Abingdon, 1989), 18-21 (and the related essays in the volume). For a succinct statement of the issues at stake here, see also Philip Clayton, "Emerging God: Theology for a Complex Universe," CC 121 (2004): 26-30.

23. See Peters, *Cosmos as Creation*, 85.

24. See next chapter.

25. Cf. the discussion in Jon D. Levenson, *Creation and the Persistence of Evil: The Jewish Drama of Divine Omnipotence* (San Francisco: Harper & Row, 1988), 117-18.

26. For a thoughtful reflection on the range of creation thought, using biblical resources, see Paul R. Sponheim, *The Pulse of Creation: God and the Transformation of the World* (Minneapolis: Fortress, 1999), 18-21.

27. See discussion of Wisdom in ch. 7.

28. Claus Westermann, *Creation* (trans. John J. Scullion; Philadelphia: Fortress, 1978), 120; see Paul Tillich: "The doctrine of creation is not the story of an event which took place 'once upon a time.' It is the basic description of the relation between God and the world" (*Systematic Theology* [Chicago: University of Chicago Press, 1951], 1:252).

29. Bernhard W. Anderson, *From Creation to New Creation: Old Testment Perspectives* (Overtures to Biblical Theology, ed. Walter Brueggemann, et al.; Minneapolis: Fortress, 1994), 101; see also 117.

30. See next chapter for details.

31. On the links between creation and tabernacle, see ch. 4.

32. See ch. 5 on law.

33. Richard J. Clifford, *Creation in the Biblical Traditions* (ed. Richard J. Clifford and John J. Collins; The Catholic Biblical Monograph Series 24; Washington, D.C.: Catholic Biblical Association of America, 1992), 8; so also Levenson, *Persistence of Evil*, 12.

34. Anderson, *From Creation to New Creation*, 89. See also Brevard S. Childs: "God . . . is not a static being, but is engaged in constant creative activity" (*Biblical Theology of the Old and New Testaments: Theological Reflection on the Christian Bible* [Minneapolis: Fortress, 1993], 397).

35. Anderson, *From Creation to New Creation*, 7; see 9, 117.

36. See ch. 3 for details. Note the clear affirmation of Goldingay: "Creation is an act of commitment on God's part" (*Israel's Gospel*, 56). Goldingay notes that Psalm 33 fills a gap in the creation accounts in explicitly stating that creation is an act of divine steadfast love (p. 57).

37. Anderson speaks of "moment by moment" (*From Creation to New Creation*, 10).

38. Goldingay's formulation is helpful: "God is not a micromanager who seeks

to make every decision for the company, but the wiser kind of executive who formulates clear goals but involves the work force in determining how to implement them, and also recognizes that the failure of members of the work force will require an ongoing flexibility in pursuing these goals" (*Israel's Gospel*, 60).

39. See the discussion of natural law in ch. 5.

40. Moltmann speaks of continuing creation "as an activity that both preserves and innovates. God's preserving activity manifests hope, and his innovating activity, his faithfulness" (*God in Creation*, 209).

41. Anderson, *From Creation to New Creation*, 105.

42. See ch. 6 for discussion of creation in Second Isaiah.

43. See Anderson, *From Creation to New Creation*, 179-94; see also Phyllis Trible, "The Gift of a Poem: A Rhetorical Study of Jeremiah 31:15-22," *ANQ* 17 (1977): 271-80.

44. Walther Zimmerli speaks about the "world-orientation" of the Old Testament in *The Old Testament and the World* (trans. John J. Scullion; London: SPCK, 1976), 13-14.

45. See Jürgen Moltmann: "Creation at the beginning is the creation of conditions for the potentialities of creation's history . . . of constructive and destructive possibilities. . . . We cannot see in initial creation the invariant nature of history, but we can see the beginning of nature's history" (*The Future of Creation: Collected Essays* [Philadelphia: Fortress, 1979], 120).

46. See ch. 6 on prophets and salvation.

47. On the following matters, see my "Reclamation of Creation: Redemption and Law in Exodus," *Int* 45 (1991): 354-65.

48. As noted in ch. 6, salvation is a much more comprehensive word than *redemption*; redemptive events are saving events, but not all saving events are properly called redemptive. On salvation, see Terence E. Fretheim, "Salvation in the Bible vs. Salvation in the Church," *WW* 13 (1993): 363-72.

49. Karl Löning and Erich Zenger, *To Begin with, God Created . . . : Biblical Theologies of Creation* (trans. Omar Kaste; Collegeville, Minn.: Liturgical Press, 2000), 3-4.

50. Christians will draw connections with the New Testament and the Christ event at this point, especially cosmic Christology (see Col 1:15-20).

51. Gerhard von Rad, for example states that "the doctrine of creation has been fully incorporated into the dynamic of the prophet's doctrine of redemption" (*Hexateuch*, 136). He is followed by Thomas W. Mann, "Stars, Sprouts, and Streams: The Creative Redeemer of Second Isaiah," in Brown and McBride, *God Who Creates*, 137; so also Brown, *Ethos*, 264. Cf. Claus Westermann: Creation and redemption are "very closely connected; however, this must never be taken as meaning that, in whole or in part, the two merge" (*Isaiah 40-66: A Commentary* [The Old Testament Library, ed. Peter Ackroyd, et al.; Philadelphia: Westminster, 1969], 25).

52. For a discussion of Isa 45:7 as a reference to *historical* rather than cosmic

events, see my "Divine Dependence upon the Human: An Old Testament Perspective," *ExAud* 13 (1997): 6-7; see also ch. 6 n. 27.

53. Temporal distinctions in the use of creation language for Israel seem to be present in, say, 43:1, where the God "who created you" and "formed you" has now redeemed Israel.

54. For details, see ch. 2.

55. Knierim, *Task of Old Testament Theology* (Grand Rapids: Eerdmans, 1995), 209-10. This statement is quoted approvingly in connection with Psalm 74 by Goldingay (*Israel's Gospel*, 67) and assumed more generally, e.g., in speaking of "metaphysical conflict" or "supernatural evil," he states that "God won a victory at the Beginning" (pp. 74-75).

56. See the discussion of God as Victor in the next chapter.

57. George M. Landes, "Creation and Liberation," in Anderson, *Creation in the Old Testament*, 138.

58. In ch. 3 we will seek to show that the Genesis texts make this point, namely, that there is a temporal distinction between creation and the entrance of sin into the life of the world.

59. To opt for an eternal dualism is to claim that something comes into being without God, and the claim that God is the Creator of all is a compromised confession. Moreover, because sin and evil always stand against God, God would not be their ultimate author (God's use of evil, such as in Isa 45:7, will be taken up later). Though a precreation (but not eternal) dualism—an angelic fall—is argued by some, it seems too much of a stretch to ascribe such a view to Old Testament texts. The temporal emergence of systemic evil, a buildup of anti-God forces over time, is probably a reality to be reckoned with (personalized as Satan only in post–Old Testament texts, except possibly 1 Chr 21:1). For a discussion of these issues from the perspective of historical and systematic theology, see Paul R. Sponheim, "Sin and Evil," in *Christian Dogmatics* (ed. Carl E. Braaten and Robert W. Jenson; Philadelphia: Fortress, 1984), 1:385-403.

60. See my "To Say Something—About God, Suffering, and Evil," *WW* 19 (1999): 339, 346-50.

61. See Samuel E. Balentine, *Prayer in the Hebrew Bible: The Drama of Divine-Human Dialogue* (Minneapolis: Fortress, 1993), esp. 33-47; Douglas John Hall, *Imaging God: Dominion as Stewardship* (Grand Rapids: Eerdmans, 1986), 113-39; Moltmann understands relationship as basic to God's creation and to his own work on creation: "Life is communication in communion. . . . Isolation and lack of relationship means death. . . . So if we want to understand what is real as real, and what is living as living, we have to know it in its own primal and individual community, in its relationships, interconnections and surroundings" (*God in Creation*, 3). See also his remarkable paragraph on p. 11, part of which reads: "The existence, the life, and the warp and weft of interrelationships subsist in the Spirit. . . . But that means that the interrelations of the world cannot be traced back to any components, or universal foundations. . . . But in reality relationships are just as primal as the things

themselves. . . . 'In the beginning was relation,' writes Martin Buber." See also Paul R. Sponheim, *Faith and the Other: A Relational Theology* (Minneapolis: Fortress, 1993); Keith Ward, *Religion and Creation* (Oxford: Clarendon, 1996); Carol J. Dempsey, *Hope Amid the Ruins: The Ethics of Israel's Prophets* (St. Louis: Chalice, 2000). Dempsey has a helpful opening chapter on the importance of relationality for Israel's prophets (pp. 19-34) though she unnecessarily elides covenant and relationship: for Israel, "covenant was relationship" (p. 20).

62. Hall, *Imaging God*, 113-14.

63. This biblical theme also connects well with the contemporary world, wherein words such as *relationship*, *relationality*, *sociality*, *community*, etc., pepper our conversation. The use of this language has been driven by several realities, but especially, it seems to me, by the increased recognition, indeed experience, of the connectedness of our life together, as well as by renewed studies on various theological issues, especially Trinitarian reflections. Still, the word *relationship* is often used in ways that do not connect very well with the usual understanding that people have regarding their interpersonal relationships. When we use the word *relationship* for the God-human encounter, people will be thinking primarily in terms of interhuman relationships, and they are encouraged by the Bible to do so. In other words, the relationship with God of which we speak may not look very much like other relationships in which we participate. The upshot may be that people will experience such a disjunction between their interhuman experience and the way in which God is portrayed that, when used of God, the word relationship is meaningless or incoherent.

64. Walther Eichrodt, *Theology of the Old Testament* (trans. J. A. Baker; The Old Testament Library, ed. G. Ernest Wright, et al.; Philadelphia: Westminster, 1961), 1:36. For recent studies of covenant, see Norbert Lohfink, "The Concept of 'Covenant' in Biblical Theology," in *The God of Israel and the Nations: Studies in Isaiah and the Psalms* (ed. Norbert Lohfink and Erich Zenger; Collegeville, Minn.: Liturgical Press, 2000), 11-31. Ernest W. Nicholson, *God and His People: Covenant and Theology in the Old Testament* (Oxford: Clarendon, 1986). These scholars recognize the complexity in the use of this word over the course of the Hebrew Bible, with the effect that no single word or phrase will convey the meaning in specific contexts. For a survey of the history of the study of covenant, see Robert A. Oden, Jr., "The Place of Covenant in the Religion of Israel," in *Ancient Israelite Religion: Essays in Honor of Frank Moore Cross* (ed. Patrick D. Miller, et al.; Philadelphia: Fortress, 1987), 429-47.

65. Brueggemann, *Theology of the Old Testament*, 297; see also 417-21. While Brueggemann often seems to regard covenant and relationship as synonyms, at times he will speak of "relatedness that we subsume under covenant"; see "Theology of the Old Testament: A Prompt Retrospect," in *God in the Fray: A Tribute to Walter Brueggemann* (ed. Tod Linafelt and Timothy K. Beal; Minneapolis: Fortress, 1998), 312; this formulation would seem to make relatedness a narrower category than covenant (so also his *Theology of the Old Testament*, 453-54).

66. Brueggemann, "A Prompt Retrospect," 312.

67. Eichrodt, *Theology*, 1:68, 1:52. Several scholars have more recently argued that covenant cannot simply be equated with the God-human or God-Israel relationship. See the studies of Lothar Perlitt, *Bundestheologie im Alten Testament* (WMANT 36; Neukirchen-Vluyn: Neukirchener Verlag, 1969); Ernst Kutsch, *Verheissung und Gesetz: Untersuchungen zum sogenannten Bund im Alten Testament* (BZAW 131; Berlin: Walter de Gruyter, 1973).

68. See Löning and Zenger, *To Begin with*, 17.

69. For a development of this theme, see Terence E. Fretheim, *Exodus* (Interpretation: A Bible Commentary for Teaching and Preaching, ed. James Luther Mays; Louisville: Westminster John Knox, 1991), 255-61.

70. See Terence E. Fretheim, *The Pentateuch* (Interpreting Biblical Texts, ed. Gene M. Tucker and Charles B. Cousar; Nashville: Abingdon, 1996), 48.

71. Eichrodt, *Theology*, 1:51-52.

72. Nicholson, *God and His People*, 81. This is true even in Nicholson's work: "In the Old Testament Yahweh is creator but radically transcends his creation. The distance between [God] and the human world is polarized" (p. 200). God "stands outside his creation confronting it with his righteous will" (pp. 207-8). Nicholson goes on to speak of Yahweh as "partner" to the covenant, but how can a God who stands outside the creation and radically transcends it be a partner in any genuine sense? Brueggemann (*Theology of the Old Testament*, 416-564) also uses the language of "partner," and the results are not dissimilar.

73. See Rolf Rendtorff, who states that "in defining the relationship of God and Israel more precisely, it is not useful to fix one's gaze one-sidedly on particular terms, since no one of them taken by itself expresses, or can express, the whole of that relationship" (*The Covenant Formula: An Exegetical and Theological Investigation* [Old Testament Studies, ed. David J. Reimer; trans. Margaret Kohl; Edinburgh: T&T Clark, 1998], 45; cf. 3-4, 65). But certainly the covenant formula ("I will be your God and you shall be my people"), which interprets the word *covenant* (p. 83) or is an "explication of the actual content of the covenant" (p. 87), is one key way of expressing the fundamental relationship between God and Israel, a relationship that is mutual. The "essential concept" of the covenant is "the mutual relationship between God and Israel" (p. 88). Rendtorff will regularly use the phrase "covenant relationship," though he doesn't seek to define the word *relationship*.

74. Abraham J. Heschel, *The Prophets* (New York: Harper & Row, 1982), 486; see Terence E. Fretheim, *The Suffering of God: An Old Testament Perspective* (Overtures to Biblical Theology, ed. Walter Brueggemann and John R. Donahue; Minneapolis: Augsburg Fortress, 1984), 71.

75. The language is that of Paul R. Sponheim, "Transcendent in Relationship," *Di* 12 (1973): 264-71.

76. So John D. Zizioulas, *Being as Communion: Studies in Personhood and the Church* (London: Darton, Longman, and Todd, 1985), 17.

77. See Terence E. Fretheim, "Christology and the Old Testament," in *Who Do You Say That I Am? Essays on Christology* (ed. Mark Allan Powell and David R. Bauer; Louisville: Westminster/John Knox, 2000), 201-15. These Old Testament perspectives on the social nature of God provided understandings that laid the groundwork for later theological developments. For example, early Christian reflections about God that led to Trinitarian thought were not just grounded in New Testament claims about Jesus and the Spirit.

78. It might be noted that if we do not use genuinely relational language in our talk about God, then that may adversely affect how we think about the human. A high view of human responsibility and human relationality may be subverted and diminished, indeed made incoherent, by an understanding of God who is relational only in a perfunctory sense.

79. Moltmann puts it this way: "If the Creator is himself present in his creation by virtue of the Spirit, then his relationship to creation must rather be viewed as an intricate web of unilateral, reciprocal and many-sided relationships" (*God in Creation*, 14).

80. Brueggemann, *Theology of the Old Testament*, 453. Brueggemann introduces the category of relationship relatively late in his *Theology*, with the effect that it does not have the import for theological reflection that it might have (see pp. 296-303 and 409-12, introducing the sections on "Partner").

81. It is ironic that Christians have at times had difficulty with this language, for, in Jesus Christ, God has acted anthropomorphically in a most supreme way.

82. For the New Testament to use this language for Jesus (e.g., Col 1:15) is testimony to him, not only as the supreme exemplification of humanity but also as one who reveals the relational God most fully and decisively.

83. See ch. 4.

84. For helpful comments on "a relational, dynamic notion of personhood" in a discussion regarding the human being in the Old Testament, see Brueggemann, *Theology of the Old Testament*, 451-54.

85. For details, see ch. 6.

86. For a brief and clear statement of how biblical insights and modern physics can come together on such matters, see John Polkinghorne, *Quarks, Chaos, and Christianity: Questions to Science and Religion* (New York: Crossroad, 1994).

87. See ch. 7 on Job.

88. See Fretheim, *Suffering of God*, 71-78.

89. See Terence E. Fretheim, "The God Who Acts: An Old Testament Perspective," *ThTo* 54 (1997): 6-18.

90. Brueggemann, *Theology of the Old Testament*, 410. Yet, it must be said, Yahweh's basic character and purpose will not change.

91. Ibid. I do not understand the balance of this sentence, where Brueggemann states that such mutuality speaks "insistently against any notion that Yahweh is transcendent beyond Israel" (p. 410). This sounds like God's transcendence (elsewhere affirmed by Brueggemann) can be turned on and off, and it is turned

off when God engages in this relationship. It must be insisted, as we have noted, that God remains transcendent in relationship.

92. Ibid.

93. Ibid., 411. In this connection, Brueggemann cites Jürgen Moltmann, *The Crucified God: The Cross of Christ as the Foundation and Criticism of Christian Theology* (New York: Harper & Row, 1974).

94. Brueggemann, *Theology of the Old Testament*, 410-11. This theme becomes a virtual refrain on pp. 297-313, though he seeks to qualify the point by suggesting that Yahweh "found . . . new measures and depths of positive passion for Israel that were not available to Yahweh" until the moment of crisis, in the midst of which "Yahweh redecides . . . how to be Yahweh and who to be as Yahweh" (pp. 299, 302). God can even "withdraw fidelity" in view of human response and leave the relationship (*A Commentary on Jeremiah: Exile and Homecoming* [Grand Rapids: Eerdmans, 1998], 121, 152). It seems to me that the language of commitment and fidelity is not suitable for such a mercurial God, who is so unsure of the divine identity that he waits upon events to decide. Brueggemann's use of the preface to the flood story (Gen 6:5-13) as an illustration is unfortunate (p. 411), for God commits the divine self to never do that again (8:21-22; 9:8-17). Or, can God choose to withdraw that promise as well (see pp. 363, 544-46)?

95. See my critique of these issues in "Some Reflections on Brueggemann's God," in Linafelt and Beal, *God in the Fray*, 30.

96. For an earlier development of these points, see Terence E. Fretheim, "Old Testament Foundations for an Environmental Theology," in *Currents in Biblical and Theological Dialogue* (ed. John Stafford; Winnipeg: St. John's College, 2001), 58-68.

97. For an earlier development of this point, see Fretheim, *Exodus*, 52-53.

98. On issues of divine limitation in the exercise of power in view of commitments to relationship, see Fretheim, *Suffering of God*, 71-78.

99. See Fretheim, *Suffering of God*, on the affectivity of God; idem, "The Earth Story in Jeremiah 12," in *Readings from the Perspective of Earth* (ed. Norman Habel; Sheffield: Sheffield Academic Press, 2000), 96-110.

100. For possible resistance on the part of the nonhuman, see Isa 24:20 (see ch. 3).

101. The Incarnation could be said to be on this relational trajectory, being the exemplification of this kind of divine relatedness and its irrevocability.

102. Erhard Gerstenberger says it well: "A learned insistence on the remote revelations of God has stunted our capacity to perceive the God who is present" (*Theologies of the Old Testament* [Minneapolis: Fortress, 2002], 304). For a fuller delineation of Israel's understanding of divine presence, see my *Suffering of God*, 60-78; idem, "Where in the World Is God? Reflections on Divine Presence in the Old Testament," *Lutheran Theological Journal* 25 (1992): 6-13.

103. The influence of G. Ernest Wright has been considerable; see *The Old Testament against Its Environment* (London: SCM, 1950).

104. Von Rad, *Hexateuch*, 150.

105. Fretheim, *Suffering of God*, 71.

106. Von Rad, *Hexateuch*, 151-52. Westermann also adopts a divine pancausality reading: "each and every thing created, each and every event that happens, light and darkness, weal and woe, are attributable to [God]," and to God alone (*Isaiah 40-66*, 161-62). For a contrary view, see Fredrik Lindstrom, *God and the Origin of Evil: A Textual Analysis of Alleged Monistic Evidence in the Old Testament* (Lund: Gleerup, 1983), 178-99.

107. See ch. 4.

108. That this language is used to speak of Jesus Christ (e.g., John 1:14; 2 Cor 4:4-6) catches him up in a trajectory of divine movement toward more intensified forms of presence in the life of the world.

109. See Fretheim, *Suffering of God*, 39-44. Neither timelessness nor the simultaneity of past, present, and future, would represent the view of any biblical tradition. Goldingay speaks clearly of a God who "lives in time" (*Israel's Gospel*, 64).

110. See ch. 2. To suggest that God first entered into time and history in the Christ event is to ignore this wide swath of Old Testament material.

111. For these reflections, see especially Moltmann, *Future of Creation*, 115-30.

112. This verse in Isaiah prompted Jürgen Moltmann to speak of the ecological implications of the fact that the heavens and the earth together are God's home and God's environment. To care for the environment is not simply to care for our home and the home of other creatures; to care for the environment is to care for the home of God ("Reconciliation with Nature," *WW* 11 [1991]: 118). Goldingay also speaks of the creation as "God's Home" (*Israel's Gospel*, 85-86).

113. See Fretheim, *Suffering of God*, 37-39.

114. I develop this direction of reflection further in the concluding chapter in view of the intervening discussion.

115. Inasmuch as Israel was a kind of "traffic stop" for those on journeys between Egypt and countries north and east of Israel, in addition to the travels of Israelites, meant that literature and thought from the larger ancient Near East readily found its way into Israel's life.

116. Peters excludes four "popular blind alleys" in seeking to discern the proper relationship between science and theology: scientism, ecclesiastical authoritarianism, scientific creationism, and the two-language theory (that is, two distinct domains of knowing). He opts instead for the idea of "hypothetical consonance," wherein "knowledge gained from theological resources will actually contribute to scientific knowledge and, conversely, one in which scientific inquiry makes a substantive contribution to the theologian's knowledge of God's relation to the world." Hence, for example, it is important to keep *why* questions, *that* questions, and *how* questions together in our study of the Genesis texts; these questions can overlap (*Cosmos as Creation*, 14-17). Anderson (*From Creation to New Creation*, 1-4, 9, 97-110) and others seem to exclude the idea that the

biblical writers were interested in *how* questions and were disinterested in more speculative issues. Part of the narrowness of this approach can also be seen in Anderson's claim that these Genesis accounts, rather, "[affirm] something about *human* existence itself" (p. 3, emphasis mine). Westermann explicitly excludes the idea that the question of *how* could be "an article of faith" (which is quite different from it being a question of knowledge) (*Creation*, 5).

117. One of the most helpful authors is Polkinghorne, *Quarks,Chaos, and Christianity*. See also the essays in Peters, *Cosmos as Creation*.

2. The Creation Accounts in Genesis

1. This chapter is dependent on several of my earlier writings, including "Genesis" (vol. 1 of *The New Interpreter's Bible*; Nashville: Abingdon, 1994); *The Pentateuch* (Interpreting Biblical Texts, ed. Gene M. Tucker and Charles B. Cousar; Nashville: Abingdon, 1996); "Creator, Creature, and Co-Creation in Genesis 1–2," in *All Things New: Essays in Honor of Roy A. Harrisville* (ed. Arland J. Hultgren, Donald H. Juel, and Jack Dean Kingsbury; Word and World Supplement Series 1; St. Paul: Word and World, 1992), 11-20.

2. Karl Löning and Erich Zenger put this point well, "The creation is a beginning that alters and determines God's own life history" (*To Begin with, God Created . . . : Biblical Theologies of Creation* [trans. Omar Kaste; Collegeville, Minn.: Liturgical Press, 2000], 10).

3. An important article that surveys current scholarship, addresses contemporary issues, and considers Gen 1:1–2:3 in detail is J. Richard Middleton, "Creation Founded in Love: Breaking Rhetroical Expectations in Genesis 1:1–2:3," in *Sacred Text, Secular Times: The Hebrew Bible in the Modern World* (ed. Leonard Jay Greenspoon and Bryan F. LeBeau; Studies in Jewish Civilization 10; Omaha: Creighton University Press, 2000), 47-85.

4. See Excursus, ch. 1.

5. For further reflections regarding my understanding of the authority of the Bible, see Terence E. Fretheim and Karlfried Froehlich, *The Bible as Word of God: In a Postmodern Age* (Minneapolis: Fortress, 1998), 81-126.

6. For surveys, see R. Norman Whybray, *The Making of the Pentateuch* (Sheffield: JSOT Press, 1987); Joseph Blenkinsopp, *The Pentateuch: An Introduction to the First Five Books of the Bible* (New York: Doubleday, 1992).

7. Genesis 1–11 consists of an admixture of genealogy and story. I use the word *story* because no precise designation has been agreed upon. *Saga, legend, myth, folktale, etiology, story*, and *theological narrative* have all been candidates. The designation *story* (or story of the past) is perhaps most commonly used.

8. See below regarding the seven days of Gen 1:1–2:3.

9. Claus Westermann claims that the opening chapters of Genesis are not interested in the question of origins; the concern evident in these texts is an existential, not an intellectual problem (*Creation* [trans. John J. Scullion;

Philadelphia: Fortress, 1974], 11). See the brief survey of the issue in Henning Graf Reventlow, *Problems of Old Testament Theology in the Twentieth Century* (trans. J. Bowden; London: SCM, 1985), 163-67. See also Dennis T. Olson ("God the Creator: Bible, Creation, Vocation," *Di* 36 [1997]: 172): "the two primary creation stories in the Bible begin at some point *after* the very beginnings of the cosmos."

10. See Westermann, *Creation*, 109.

11. See the helpful discussion of Samuel E. Balentine, *The Torah's Vision of Worship* (Minneapolis: Fortress, 1999), 81-95.

12. See Balentine, *Torah's Vision*, 67-68; Jon D. Levenson, *Creation and the Persistence of Evil: The Jewish Drama of Divine Omnipotence* (San Francisco: Harper & Row, 1988), 66-99.

13. Walter Brueggemann, *Theology of the Old Testament: Testimony, Dispute, Advocacy* (Minneapolis: Fortress, 1997), 154.

14. Ibid., 153.

15. Odil Hannes Steck, *World and Environment* (Nashville: Abingdon, 1980), 75.

16. Ibid., 67.

17. See especially Middleton, "Creation Founded in Love." For detail, see n. 25 of this chapter.

18. S. Dean McBride Jr. works with Gen 1:1–2:3 largely in isolation from Gen 2:4-25 and places particularly strong emphasis on the sovereignty of God and human dependence in Genesis 1 ("Divine Protocol: Genesis 1:1–2:3 as Prologue to the Pentateuch," in *God Who Creates: Essays in Honor of W. Sibley Towner* [ed. William P. Brown and S. Dean McBride Jr.; Grand Rapids: Eerdmans, 2000], 7-11, 16-18). See also the chapter "Genesis and Power," in Dale Patrick and Allen Scult, *Rhetoric and Biblical Interpretation* (Sheffield: Almond Press, 1990), 123-25.

19. Michael Welker, "What Is Creation? Rereading Genesis 1 and 2," *ThTo* (1991): 56-71.

20. See, e.g., David M. Carr, *Reading the Fractures of Genesis: Historical and Literary Approaches* (Louisville: Westminster/John Knox, 1996), 317-19; Middleton, "Creation Founded in Love," 53-57, gives several examples of this kind of interpretation of these chapters, by both biblical and systematic theologians, and draws out the ethical implications in particular of such a perspective.

21. See Frank Moore Cross, *Canaanite Myth and Hebrew Epic: Essays in the History of Religion* (Cambridge: Harvard University Press, 1973), 293-325.

22. William P. Brown follows traditional source analysis in his two long chapters that treat Priestly and Yahwistic creation accounts separately. Such a sharp source distinction becomes highly speculative, not least because we have no assurance that these two accounts ever stood alone in their present form. The canonical presentation of creation in Genesis 1–2 receives only scattered points of attention in his presentation (*The Ethos of the Cosmos: The Genesis of Moral Imagination in the Bible* [Grand Rapids: Eerdmans, 1999]).

23. See the discussion in Löning and Zenger, *To Begin with*, 99-117.

24. Cf. the listing in Westermann: creation by birth or succession of births; creation through struggle; creation as fashioning, making or forming; creation through utterance (*Genesis 1–11: A Commentary* [Minneapolis: Augsburg, 1984], 26). Francis Watson speaks of three "models," namely, speech-act, fabrication, and mediation. His more limited, threefold listing is shaped overly much by Trinitarian considerations. See his *Text, Church, and World: Biblical Interpretation in Theological Perspective* (Grand Rapids: Eerdmans, 1994), 140-43.

25. Levenson considers it possible that the seven-day structure of creation is drawn from the seven-day autumn and spring New Year's festivals (*Persistence of Evil*, 66-77). Middleton is especially helpful in showing the importance of the considerable variation that exists within this structure. For example, eight creative acts over six days; "and it was so" is missing from day five; "And God saw that it was good" is missing from day two; and both are missing from the creation of humanity on day six. "That is, whereas the world rhetorically depicted in Genesis 1 is certainly ordered, patterned, and purposive . . . this world is not mechanistically determined. . . . The God who is artisan and maker, reflected rhetorically in the literary artistry of the text, does not over-determine the order of the cosmos" ("Creation Founded in Love," 57-63, esp. 59, 61-62). He suggests some parallels with contemporary chaos theory.

26. For this outline, see Fretheim, "Genesis," 342. Cf. the outline in James Barr, "Was Everything that God Created Really Good? A Question in the First Verse of the Bible," in *God in the Fray: A Tribute to Walter Brueggemann* (ed. Tod Linafelt and Timothy K. Beal; Minneapolis: Fortress, 1998), 55-65.

27. Cf. Löning and Zenger, who suggest the translation, "As a beginning" or "To begin with" God created heaven and earth (*To Begin with*, 21).

28. For other arguments that v. 1 is a summary statement, see Barr, "Was Everything that God Created Really Good?"

29. Any theological claim for *creatio ex nihilo* would have to be based on other arguments and texts, see 2 Macc 7:28; Rom 4:17; Heb 11:3. Löning and Zenger have an interesting formulation: "What fascinates the biblical narrators about creation is not that there is something there that was not there earlier, but that something new is underway that was not there—nor could have been—before the creation. . . . The contrast is not between nothing and something, but between the hideous and the wonderful" (*To Begin with*, 10).

30. The formlessness and emptiness (void) of v. 2 are dealt with in turn over the six days: the first three days have to do with the creation of environments (light/darkness, sky and separation of waters, land/vegetation) and the next three days their occupants (luminaries, sea creatures/birds, land animals/human beings).

31. On God's abode within the created order, see Terence E. Fretheim, *The Suffering of God: An Old Testament Perspective* (Overtures to Biblical Theology,

ed. Walter Breuggemann and John R. Donahue; Minneapolis: Augsburg Fortress, 1984), 37-39.

32. See Watson, *Text, Church, and World*, 144. Löning and Zenger speak of the spirit as "the divine energy and creativity that then becomes reality in creation . . . the motherly, creative life power the creator God breathes into his creation 'to begin with'" (*To Begin with*, 19). On chaos, see below.

33. The point made by Jürgen Moltmann that *bārā'* is only used for creation as a whole and not particular creations is mistaken (*bārā'* is used in 1:21, 26 for particular creations) and hence cannot be used to establish his point that God's creative activity is without analogy. See *God in Creation: An Ecological Doctrine of Creation* (trans. Margaret Kohl; London: SCM, 1985), 73.

34. See ch. 1 for this distinction.

35. The verb may have originally had a concrete meaning (to split or cut apart) with human subjects (see the use of the *pi'el* in Josh 17:15, 18); if so, then this verb, too, might have been understood as an analogy drawn from the human sphere.

36. See Levenson, who considers the language of "cocreator" or "partner in creation" inaccurate because *bārā'* only has God for a subject (*Persistence of Evil*, 117). He makes no mention of the use of *'āsāh* in this context. I have no particular stake in the specific language of "cocreator," but Levenson makes an insufficient argument against its use. The phrase "created cocreator" has also been used to make the distinction between Creator and creature clear. This is the formulation of Philip J. Hefner in *Christian Dogmatics* (ed. Carl E. Braaten and Robert W. Jenson; Philadelphia: Fortress, 1984), 1:325-28. Levenson does speak of "a certain subordinate role that humanity is to play in the cosmogonic process" (*Persistence of Evil*, 117). But this is largely related to cultic matters and seems not to be descriptive of the creation accounts themselves.

37. Paas says that *bārā'* "is a theological 'umbrella' term . . . within which very diverse forms of creation can be included" (*Creation and Judgement: Creation Texts in Some Eighth Century Prophets* [Leiden: Brill, 2003], 64).

38. For the literature see Paas, *Creation and Judgement*, 77 n. 119. It is not clear why Paas considers word to be "the least human-like manner of creation and, therefore, the most theologically developed" (p. 77). Speaking words, even performative words, is a key analogy from the human sphere.

39. See ch. 1.

40. Sometimes "and it was so" occurs as a kind of summary; sometimes it occurs between speaking and acting. See J. Rogerson, *Genesis 1–11* (Old Testament Guides; Sheffield: JSOT Press, 1991), 58-60.

41. The mediation of creation through already existing creatures has recently been emphasized by Welker, "What Is Creation?" and myself, "Creator, Creature," but was noted much earlier by Walther Zimmerli, *The Old Testament and the World* (trans. John J. Sculllion; London: SPCK, 1976), 29. This idea is also now stressed by Watson (*Text, Church, and World*, 142) and Colin E.

Gunton, who finds a comparable theme already in Basil of Caesarea (*The Triune Creator: A Historical and Systematic Study* [Edinburgh: Edinburgh University Press, 1998], 61, 71). Note also the "let [the firmament] separate" in 1:6 (cf. also 1:18); the task of separation is assumed by God in 1:4, 7. Also, the "let" used in 1:14-18 for the "rule" of the heavenly luminaries, gives to the created a task commonly assumed by God in other Old Testament texts.

42. See Paas, *Creation and Judgement*, 73. The formation of the human from the dirt/dust/clay is found in many cultures; see Excursus.

43. One might also cite those texts that use God as the subject of the verb *yṣr*, "to form, shape" (e.g., Gen 2:8; Isa 45:18), which assumes working with existing material. This may be linked with those texts that speak of laying foundations and "establishing the earth" in Second Isaiah (Ps 24:2; Job 38:4 and other texts). See Paas, *Creation and Judgement*, 71-72; Theodore Ludwig, "The Traditions of Establishing the Earth in Deutero-Isaiah," *JBL* 92 (1973): 345-57.

44. Dexter E. Callender Jr. speaks of the garden (and temple) as a place for "unmediated" encounter with God. This is at best an overstatement; for God to appear in human form is in itself a form of mediation. The encounter with God may be direct, but the divine presence is mediated by the human form that God assumes for the encounter (*Adam in Myth and History: Ancient Israelite Perspectives on the Primal Human* [Winona Lake, Ind.: Eisenbrauns, 2000], 42-50).

45. For an extended study of the theological import of the theophanic texts, see Fretheim, *Suffering of God*, 79-106. For Christians, the link between divine word (Genesis 1) and divine flesh (Genesis 2–4) is sharply evident in New Testament claims regarding the Incarnation (John 1:14).

46. See Watson: "God indwells her creation, not in the form of a passive, static presence but in an active, dynamic, self-transcending movement towards the emergence and reproduction of life and breath" (*Text, Church, and World*, 144).

47. Dietrich Bonhoeffer puts it well: "God breathes the spirit of God into the body of the human being. And this spirit is life; it brings the human being to life. Other life is created through God's word, but in the case of human life God gives of God's own life, of God's own spirit" (*Creation and Fall: A Theological Exposition of Genesis 1–3* [vol. 3 of Dietrich Bonhoeffer Works; trans. Douglas Stephen Bax; Minneapolis: Fortress, 1997], 78).

48. See, e.g., Colin E. Gunton, ed., *The Doctrine of Creation: Essays in Doctrine, History and Philosophy* (Edinburgh: T&T Clark, 1997), 47-82.

49. Watson, *Text, Church, and World*, 146-47.

50. For a helpful assessment of these dimensions of the creation story, see Welker, "What Is Creation?"

51. Childs, *Biblical Theology of the Old and New Testaments: Theological Reflection on the Christian Bible* (London: SCM, 1992), 385.

52. See Robert E. Brown, "On the Necessary Imperfection of Creation: Irenaeus' *Adversus Haereses* iv, 38," *SJT* 28 (1975): 17-25. He notes that, for Irenaeus, creation was unqualifiedly good, but imperfect.

53. See Claus Westermann, *Blessing in the Bible and in the Life of the Church* (trans. Keith R. Crim; Philadelphia: Fortress, 1978).

54. On the image of God as a consultant, see, e.g., Gen 18:17-22. For a study of these texts, see Fretheim, *Suffering of God*, 49-53. Levenson claims "that Genesis 1:26 relates a consultation of God the king with his cabinet has been suggested since Talmudic times" (*Persistence of Evil*, 173 n. 18). He cites *Bereshit Rabbah* 8:4. Implications of this suggestion for an understanding of God seem not to be developed by Levenson (see below on God as King).

55. Other interpretations of the plural are not convincing; the plural of *majesty* is without parallel, and the plural of *deliberation* does not account for the use of the plural in 3:22 (see 11:7; Isa 6:8). On this issue, see the compelling study of W. Randall Garr, *In His Own Image and Likeness: Humanity, Divinity, and Monotheism* (Leiden: Brill, 2003); Patrick D. Miller, *Genesis 1–11: Studies in Structure and Theme* (Sheffield: JSOT Press, 1978), 9-26; E. Theodore Mullen, *The Divine Council in Canaanite and Early Hebrew Literature* (Harvard Semitic Monographs; Chico: Scholars Press, 1980); idem, "Divine Assembly," in *ABD*, 2:214-17. On the import of this text for the relationality of God, see ch. 1.

56. For example, Bernard F. Batto, *Slaying the Dragon: Mythmaking in the Biblical Tradition* (Louisville: Westminster John Knox, 1992); in a more nuanced way, John Day, *God's Conflict with the Dragon and the Sea: Echoes of a Canaanite Myth in the Old Testament* (Cambridge: Cambridge University Press, 1985). Cf. also Garr, *In His Own Image*, 201-40. The work of Hermann Gunkel is basic to this discussion; see his "Influence of Babylonian Mythology upon the Biblical Creation Story," in *Creation in the Old Testament* (ed. Bernhard W. Anderson; Philadelphia: Fortress, 1984), 25-52.

57. The most helpful analysis of "creation as a violent act," together with compelling arguments against such an interpretation, is that of Middleton, "Creation Founded in Love." Middleton's article includes a thoughtful critique of Catherine Keller's reading of Genesis 1 in terms of divine violence, which, she claims, has legitimated violence and oppression, especially against women (*From a Broken Web: Separation, Sexism, and Self* [Boston: Beacon, 1986]). Keller is right to discern the clear link between the imaging of God in this creational chapter and the behaviors of its readers. Paas, *Creation and Judgement*, doubts that "a developed myth of the *Chaoskampf* was ever known or functioning in Israel" (p. 79). He also notes that this theme occurs in relatively late texts, and is not "the basis for the history of creation belief in Israel" (p. 80). Also important for denying a violent perspective to Genesis 1 is the work of David Toshio Tsumura, *The Earth and the Waters in Genesis 1 and 2: A Linguistic Investigation* (JSOTSup 83, ed. David J. A. Clines and Philip R. Davies; Sheffield: JSOT Press, 1989).

58. Tsumura, *Earth and the Waters*, 65.

59. Ibid., 43. See also Norman Habel, who gives some possible reasons why the chaos motif has been commonly accepted in the face of minimal evidence ("Geophany: The Earth Story in Genesis 1," in *The Earth Story in Genesis* [ed.

Norman Habel and Shirley Wurst; Sheffield: Sheffield Academic Press, 2000], 38-39); see also Middleton, "Creation Founded in Love," 79 n. 59. More briefly, see Mark G. Brett, "Earthing the Human in Genesis 1–3," in Habel and Wurst, *Earth Story in Genesis*, 74 n. 1; Ellen van Wolde, "Facing the Earth: Primeval History in a New Perspective," in *The World of Genesis: Persons, Places, Perspectives* (ed. Philip R. Davies and David J. A. Clines; JSOTSup 257; Sheffield: Sheffield Academic Press, 1998), 25.

60. Brown, *Ethos*, 46. The word *nothingness* could be misinterpreted and be thought to claim a "creation out of nothing" viewpoint for the entire chapter. It is not unimportant that the earth is a reality in v. 2 and just appears in v. 9. George M. Landes states: "The primordial waters . . . are not thought of as intrinsically evil or threatening" ("Creation and Liberation," in Anderson, *Creation in the Old Testament*, 138). Brown says further: "As God is no divine warrior who slays the forces of chaos to construct a viable domain for life, so human beings are not ruthless tyrants, wreaking violence upon the land that is their home. By dint of command rather than brute force, the elements of creation are enlisted to fulfill the Deity's creative purposes" (*Ethos*, 45).

61. Brueggemann apparently thinks of the chaos of v. 2 in terms of forces of evil: God "imposes a will on destructive, recalcitrant forces and energies" (*Theology of the Old Testament*, 529). He also speaks of "*an enduring force of chaos in [Israel's] life*" (p. 534; he entitles the subsection "Dualism-in-Creation") in affirming the conclusions of Levenson, who thinks that "the primordial chaos" continues to be a reality; God has "only limited it" (*Persistence of Evil*, 123). Indeed, for Brueggemann, some texts claim that "Yahweh's absolute sovereignty is in jeopardy" (*Theology of the Old Testament*, 535), while other texts claim God's complete mastery of these forces and the capacity to unleash these forces as a medium of judgment (pp. 537-43). The one specific element of the chaos that Levenson discusses (darkness) is to be interpreted as "a malign power." Earlier, he claims that God has "transformed" the "primordial chaos" of v. 2 (p. 122). If it has been "transformed," then what has been "limited" becomes something different from the realities of v. 2 with which God worked in creating the world. There is no indication (in Genesis 1 or elsewhere in the OT) that the "darkness" which now alternates with light to create day and night was or is "a malign power," though darkness is often associated with divine judgment (Lam 3:2, 6) or with death (Job 3:4-6). Levenson cites Isa 45:7 in this connection, believing it to be a step beyond Genesis 1, with God now being the creator of darkness (and evil). On this, see ch. 6. Cf. also Löning and Zenger, *To Begin with*, 20-21.

62. Levenson, *Persistence of Evil*, 122; cf. Goldingay, *Israel's Gospel*, 67-75, 82.

63. Ibid., 123, 127.

64. Ibid., 127 (emphasis mine).

65. Levenson seems to collapse creation and redemption. He speaks of creation climaxing in the divine rest as "an act of redemption" (Ibid., 119) and, with the exodus, as "two great acts of deliverance" (p. 105) or "Creation is a vic-

tory and an act of liberation" (p. 106). His closer definition, "cosmogony and redemption . . . work[ing] in tandem and not independently of one another" (p. 105), seems to stop short of a simple collapse. Yet, if the same end is accomplished by both creative and redemptive acts, then finally there is no important distinction in basic meaning. See also Garr, *In His Own Image*, 198-99.

66. Levenson seems to assume this from his discussion of other texts that seem to speak of a combat, e.g., Ps 74:12-17.

67. We consider Gen 1:28 below.

68. W. Sibley Towner, *Genesis* (Louisville: Westminster/John Knox, 2001), 21.

69. See Towner, *Genesis*, 18-21; see also the survey in Brown, *Ethos*, 12-17; Middleton uses "chaos" language (and illustrations) to refer to the literary variation in Genesis 1 ("Creation Founded in Love"). John Polkinghorne (and others) has been especially effective in considering the interface of scientific and theological reflection regarding this matter (e.g, *Quarks, Chaos, and Christianity: Questions to Science and Religion* [New York: Crossroad, 1994]).

70. This rendition of Everett Fox is preferable to "corrupted," not least because it links up with the same Hebrew verb in v. 13 commonly translated "destroy" (Fox, "bring to ruin"). See Everett Fox, *Genesis and Exodus* (New York: Schocken, 1998), 32.

71. See Fretheim, "Genesis," 356. At times, the historical embodiment of sin and its effects is so profound that only the word *evil* tells it like it is; hence, pharaoh is an embodiment of such forces.

72. See the discussion in Day, *God's Conflict*, 288-89. Day wonders whether these images would have been taken literally by those who worshiped the gods of Canaan or a syncretistic form of Yahwism. He asks whether there is any polemic in these texts against those who would hold such a view. If so, this is an argument for an interpretation of these texts that is not literal in any straightforward sense.

73. The description of McCarthy's position is that of Paas, *Creation and Judgement*, 80. A comparable position is that of Roland de Vaux, *The Bible and the Ancient Near East* (New York: Doubleday, 1971), 133-34. Compare also the discussion of H. W. F. Saggs, *The Encounter with the Divine in Mesopotamia and Israel* (London: Athlone, 1978), 54-62.

74. So, for example, Rahab is Egypt in Ezek 29:3-5; 32:3; in Job they are probably actual animals (Job 41).

75. Dennis J. McCarthy, "'Creation' Motifs in Ancient Hebrew Poetry," in Anderson, *Creation in the Old Testament*, 75, 79; "the point is always political or social order" (p. 83).

76. Terence E. Fretheim, *Exodus* (Interpretation: A Bible Commentary for Teaching and Preaching, ed. James Luther Mays; Louisville: Westminster John Knox, 1991), 161-70; cited with approval and further argumentation by Ronald A. Simkins, *Creator and Creation: Nature in the Worldview of Ancient Israel* (Peabody, Mass.: Hendrickson, 1994), 107-17. See ch. 4 for further discussion.

77. See, e.g., Moshe Weinfeld, "Sabbath, Temple, and the Enthronement of the Lord—The Problem of the *Sitz im Leben* of Genesis 1:1–2:2," in *Melanges bibliques et orientaux en l'honneur de M. Henri Cazelles* (ed. A. Caquot and M. Delcor; Neukirchen-Vluyn: Neukirchener, 1981), 501-12; in Löning and Zenger (*To Begin with*) this royal imaging of God is pervasive, and at times at odds with some of their most basic claims about God; Brown, *Ethos*, 46-52; Callender, *Adam in Myth and History*; Paas, *Creation and Judgement*, 85; Garr, *In His Own Image*, 191-200, 212-19; more cautiously, Marc Zvi Brettler, *God Is King: Understanding an Israelite Metaphor* (Sheffield: JSOT Press, 1989); Bernhard W. Anderson, *From Creation to New Creation: Old Testament Perspectives* (Overtures to Biblical Theology, ed. Walter Brueggemann, et al.; Minneapolis: Fortress, 1994), 119-28. John Macquarrie assumes the dominance of this metaphor when he claims that "the relation of God to the world in the Old Testament is what we may call the monarchical model . . . But . . . there are at least traces of an alternative model, which we may call the organic model" ("Creation and Environment," *ExpTim* 83 [1971–1972]: 6). Macquarrie also notes that such a monarchial model of God was also accompanied by anthropocentricity and a lower estimate of the nonhuman world.

78. See Brettler, *God Is King*, 117. See also Anderson, *From Creation to New Creation*, 121-22, who considers Psalm 8 to speak of Yahweh "elevating humankind to a royal position" in view of the phrase "crowned with glory and honor" (Ps 8:5; cf. the "glory and honor" ascribed to Yahweh in Ps 29:1; 104:1) and the language of ruling and putting others under their feet (8:6; cf. Ps 2:8). Anderson understands the royal language to be "used more openly" in this psalm than in Genesis 1.

79. For Paas, royal metaphors are central, even in several contexts where they are not explicit (*Creation and Judgement*, 69-72, 86-88). And so "architectonic metaphors" (*bānāh*, "build"; *yāsad* and *qûm*, "establish") not only relate to creation but are also royal metaphors (because kings were builders in that culture). He does not consider that these metaphors may be related to more general human roles in architecture and construction (pp. 73-76). For Paas, wherever royal metaphors are used, creation is likely assumed. An attempt to see royal links in the use of verb *bārā'* is made by S. Lee, "Power Not Novelty: The Connections of BR' in the Hebrew Bible" (ed. A. G. Auld; *Understanding Poets and Prophets: Essays in Honor of G. W. Anderson* [Sheffield: JSOT Press, 1992], 199-212). The following sentence is quoted approvingly by Paas (*Creation and Judgement*, 85): "when YHWH is portrayed as Israel's creator, it indicates not so much a special relationship but YHWH's sovereign control over everything happening to his people" ("Power Not Novelty," 211).

80. See H. Wildberger, "Das Abbild Gottes, Genesis 1:26-30," *TZ* 21 (1965): 245-59, 481-501. See also Werner H. Schmidt, who considers the idea of the image of God in his section on the *monarchy* (*The Faith of the Old Testament: A History* [Oxford: Oxford University Press, 1986]).

81. See Weinfeld, "Sabbath, Temple, and Enthronement," 501-12. For further reflection on the links between creation and tabernacle, see ch. 4.

82. On this text, see especially Callender, *Adam in Myth and History*. See the brief survey in Anderson, *From Creation to New Creation*, 122-23. Callender also calls attention to images associated with royal gardens in ancient Near Eastern literature. See also J. van Seters, "The Creation of Man and the Creation of the King," *ZAW* 101 (1989): 333-42.

83. For an argument that distances Ezekiel 28 from Genesis 2–3, see James Barr, " 'Thou Art the Cherub': Ezekiel 28:14 and the Post-Ezekiel Understanding of Genesis 2–3," in *Priests, Prophets, and Scribes* (ed. Eugene Ulrich, et al.; JSOTSup 149; Sheffield: JSOT Press, 1992), 213-23.

84. See the extensive discussion of Eden in Callender, *Adam in Myth and History*, 39-84; Brown uses the garden as a key motif for interpreting the Yahwist's account of creation (and other texts); see *Ethos*, 133-228.

85. As the clean distinction between heaven and earth in 1:1; 2:4*a*; 2:4*b* would seem to indicate.

86. Links to the tabernacle (and temple) texts are important in this connection (see ch. 4). Callender considers Eden an "archetype for the temple as the place where divine and human meet" (*Adam in Myth and History*, 50). Perhaps so, but neither the garden nor the tabernacle (temple) are places of unmediated encounters between human beings and God; moreover, Eden, made inaccessible to human beings (3:24), does not somehow once again become available in tabernacle and temple. Brown (*Ethos*, 219-28) speaks too easily, if not unqualifiedly, about a "return to the Genesis garden" (p. 226) or "back to Eden" (p. 227) or "*tôrâ* offers an entrance into the garden that can be crossed only through a life of obedience . . . the opportunity to unlock the garden's entrance" (p. 224). For all the "echoes of Eden," it is not unimportant that the word *Eden* itself is rarely used to describe the prophetic future ("*like* Eden," Isa 51:3; Ezek 36:35) and is never mentioned in the New Testament (cf. T. Stordalen, *Echoes of Eden: Genesis 2–3 and Symbolism of the Eden Garden in Biblical Hebrew Literature* [Contributions to Biblical Exegesis and Theology 25; Leuven: Peeters, 2000]). Not only is there no return to Eden, it would be unfortunate if it were a desideratum; to use the vision of Jer 31:31-34, the future will, thankfully, move beyond the possibilities of Eden, beyond the contingencies of Gen 2:16-17. Moreover, given that the creation of Genesis 1–2 is not a "finished product," Eden does not begin to image what God has in store in the new creation. Note that Goldingay does think creation is a finished product and that the language of "continuous creation" is not appropriate (*Israel's Gospel*, 127-28).

87. See Mark G. Brett, "Motives and Intentions in Genesis 1," *JTS* 42 (1991): 11-12. Such a perspective might be illustrated by this sentence from Callender: "Having seen that other ancient Near Eastern literatures use the language of image and likeness in royal contexts, we *must* then recognize that within its present context in Genesis 1, this 'royal' imagery applies to the primal human

and to humanity in general" (*Adam in Myth and History*, 29, emphasis mine). Callender's work is a strong defense for seeing royal imagery in the creation accounts (and elsewhere).

88. See Westermann, *Genesis 1–11*, 153-54.

89. See discussion below.

90. So also H. Paul Santmire, "Partnership with Nature according to the Scriptures: Beyond the Theology of Stewardship," *CSR* 32 (2003): 394-95.

91. See Mark G. Brett, *Genesis: Procreation and the Politics of Identity* (London: Routledge, 2000), 24-35.

92. I worry, for example, that William P. Brown, who uses royal language for the God of Genesis 1, speaks too readily about God's "control over and in creation," so that creatures who "share a level of power" entail no risk for God. He speaks of "an arresting paradox," but that seems to me to be too easy an appeal with respect to what is likely a problematic formulation (*Ethos*, 47-48).

93. John Macquarrie, *The Humility of God* (London: SCM, 1978), 4.

94. For a survey, see Gunnlaugur A. Jónsson, *The Image of God: Genesis 1:26-28 in a Century of Old Testament Research* (trans. Lorraine Svendsen; Lund: Gleerup, 1988); David J. A. Clines, "The Image of God in Man," *Tyndale Bulletin* 19 (1968): 53-103; see now Garr, *In His Own Image*. See also Hall (*Imaging God*, 113-39) for a strong statement on interpreting the image of God in relational terms.

95. Or, more precisely, inasmuch as human beings are created in "our" image, the entire divine realm comes into view. The plural includes the divine council; human beings were created "to be a terrestrial counterpart to God's heavenly entourage" (S. Dean McBride Jr., "Divine Protocol: Genesis 1:1–2:3 as Prologue to the Pentateuch," in Brown and McBride, *God Who Creates*, 16). See also Patrick D. Miller (*Genesis 1–11*, 14), who notes that the move back and forth between singular and plural in the divine world is matched by the same language for the human world ("him . . . them," v. 27).

96. This point has been forcefully made by Jürgen Moltmann, "Reconciliation with Nature," *WW* 11 (1991): 118. See also his *God in Creation*. See also Kathryn Tanner, "Creation, Environmental Crisis, and Ecological Justice," in *Reconstructing Christian Theology* (ed. R. Chopp and M. Taylor; Minneapolis: Fortress, 1994), 99-123.

97. See Steck, *World and Environment*, 105. The focus on the *human* vocation is unfortunate; see my concluding chapter.

98. See Bonhoeffer: "It is humankind's whole empirical existence that is blessed here, its creatureliness, its worldliness, its earthliness" (*Creation and Fall*, 68).

99. It is not clear to me from Brown why *blessing*, as a word spoken to already existing creatures, entails divine power-sharing but not empowerment (*Ethos*, 47).

100. For basic understandings, see Westermann, *Blessing in the Bible*, 54-55.

101. David Heyd, "Divine Creation and Human Procreation: Reflections on Genesis in the Light of Genesis," in *Contingent Future Persons: On the Ethics of*

Deciding Who Will Live, or Not, in the Future (ed. Nick Fotion and Jan C. Heller; Theology and Medicine 8; London: Kluwer Academic Publishers, 1997), 57-70.

102. See Heyd, "Divine Creation," 60. Citing the parallel in 1:22 (but without the "to them"), Heyd claims: "In its instinctive, purely sexual manifestation, reproduction is just a natural process like any other. What provides it with an ethical nature is the choice involved, the understanding of its meaning, the significance of the intentional perpetuation of the conditions of value in the world" (p. 61). Human beings are the only creatures capable of being evaluators like God has been throughout Genesis 1, continuing to invest value in the world like God has done.

103. Phyllis Bird thinks of this divine move in polemical terms, as undercutting the importance of the fertility cult activities; no activity of the gods is needed for perpetuating the agricultural year or the species (*Missing Persons and Mistaken Identities: Women and Gender in Ancient Israel* [Overtures to Biblical Theology; Minneapolis: Fortress, 1997], 137-38).

104. Compare the "responsibility" given to the luminaries as part of their creation (Gen 1:14-16); they are to "rule" and to distinguish days and seasons for the sake of "the earth" (1:15, 17).

105. Heyd states: "The image of God, human reproduction, and the uniqueness of the value of human life are all tied together conceptually and theologically" ("Divine Creation," 66).

106. Heyd, "Divine Creation," 65-66.

107. Many studies could be cited. See, e.g., Anderson's chapter "Human Dominion over Nature," in *From Creation to New Creation*, 111-31. James Limburg interprets the text in terms of royal images: "The Responsibility of Royalty: Genesis 1–11 and the Care of the Earth," *WW* 11(1991): 124-30.

108. See the helpful discussion in Löning and Zenger, *To Begin with*, 114-15.

109. Brown speaks helpfully of several factors that contribute to a "softer" interpretation of dominion, and eliminates the warrior imagery, but he still retains monarchial imagery (e.g., "Lord over" and "royal office"; *Ethos*, 45). Theodore Hiebert speaks of "the human domestication and use of animals and plants and the human struggle to make the soil serve its farmers" ("Re-Imaging Nature: Shifts in Biblical Interpretation," *Int* 50 [1996]: 42).

110. Bonhoeffer, *Creation and Fall*, 66. Moreover: "The reason why we fail to rule, however, is because we do not know the world as God's creation and do not accept the dominion we have as God-given but seize hold of it for ourselves" (p. 67). See Hall, *Imaging God*; Santmire, "Partnership with Nature."

111. Norbert Lohfink, *Theology of the Pentateuch: Themes of the Priestly Narrative and Deuteronomy* (trans. Linda M. Maloney; Minneapolis: Fortress, 1994), 10; Löning and Zenger think that the verb refers to taking possession of the earth/land (see Josh 18:1). Yet, that activity would seem to be covered by the command to fill the earth. Löning and Zenger add the ideas of protection and defense, but the word is used in contexts (e.g., Num 32:22, 29) with respect to

taking the offensive against others rather than defending what one is charged to defend (*To Begin with*, 110).

112. Gen 2:5, 15; 3:23 also assume that the earth "needs work"; it is not fully able to take care of itself.

113. See Gunton, *Triune Creator*. Gunton works with Irenaeus in particular in developing this idea.

114. Santmire makes a helpful point: "It is almost as if God Himself were the premiere gardener! . . . Yahweh Himself 'planted a garden in Eden,' . . . [and] 'made to grow every tree that is pleasant.' . . . The strong implication seems to be that Yahweh Himself is involved in the care and the protection of this garden, setting the stage for the human creature to do likewise" ("Partnership with Nature," 402).

115. Ellen F. Davis, *Getting Involved with God: Rediscovering the Old Testament* (Cambridge, Mass.: Cowley, 2001), 192.

116. Ibid., 193.

117. Ibid., 194.

118. Note also the continuity in work as integral to human vocation; 3:17-19 recognizes that work has *become* toil, not that there was no work prefall.

119. Theodore Hiebert thinks that irrigation farming is in view (*The Yahwist's Landscape: Nature and Religion in Early Israel* [Oxford: Oxford University Press, 1996], 36-37).

120. So Gerhard von Rad, *The Theology of Israel's Historical Traditions* (vol. 1 of *Old Testament Theology*; trans. D. M. G. Stalker; New York: Harper & Row, 1962), 1:146.

121. Gunton, *Triune Creator*, 205. He goes on to say that "any notion of the image of God which spiritualises it, in the sense of dematerialising it, misses its meaning." So also Dietrich Bonhoeffer: humankind "is the image of God not in spite of but precisely in its bodily nature" (*Creation and Fall*, 79).

122. Bonhoeffer, *Creation and Fall*, 76-77.

123. On theophanies, see Fretheim, *Suffering of God*, 79-106. So also Moltmann, *God in Creation*, 239-40, 245; Francis Watson links this understanding to christological material; see *Text and Truth: Redefining Biblical Theology* (Grand Rapids, Mich.: Eerdmans, 1997), 291.

124. See Moltmann, *God in Creation*, 234-43; Hall, *Imaging God*, 113-39. It has been maintained that God's creation of "humankind" has reference to human beings collectively (as with the plants, birds, and animals), hence many men and women, and not to the first man and woman. But this is difficult to maintain in view of 5:1-3; moreover, 2:7 (NIV) actually reads, "the LORD God formed *the* man from the dust," suggesting a closer specification of the *'ādām* created in 1:26-27. It seems best also, especially in view of 5:2, to regard "humankind" in 1:26-27 as a *generic* reference to human beings. See David J. A. Clines, "*'ādām*, the Hebrew for 'Human, Humanity': A Response to James Barr," *VT* 53 (2003): 297-310: *'ādām* is a reference to "humanity without distinction of gender" except in the creation accounts (pp. 309-10).

125. On the history of a relational understanding of the image of God, Bonhoeffer is especially important (*Creation and Fall*, 3:65). Karl Barth develops the idea more fully, but acknowledges dependence on Bonhoeffer (*Church Dogmatics* [ed. G. W. Bromiley and Thomas F. Torrance; Edinburgh: T&T Clark, 1958], 3/1:228-30; 3/2:220-21). Bonhoeffer understands correctly that this relationship is not something potential or achieved; human beings are created with relationality as a given. See especially Hall, *Imaging God*, 113-39.

126. The REB translation more narrowly expresses the idea of purpose for image: "Let us make human beings in our image, after our likeness, [that they may have] dominion" (1:26). But it seems unlikely that the *purpose* of the image is the only sense the language carries.

127. It has been suggested that male and female are specified for the human (and not for other animals) so as to make it very clear that the image does not mean identity with God. See Phyllis Bird, "Genesis 1–3 as a Source for a Contemporary Theology of Sexuality," *ExAud* 3 (1987): 34-35.

128. See Gordon J. Wenham, *Genesis 1–15* (vol. 1 of the Word Biblical Commentary, ed. David A. Hubbard and Glenn W. Barker; Nashville: Thomas Nelson, 1987), 30-31; Brett, *Genesis*, 24-35; idem, "Earthing the Human," 77-78, 83-84; Santmire, "Partnership with Nature," 394-95. Walter Brueggemann thinks that the raising of the *'ādām* from dust is a royal symbol for the enthronement of the human on the basis of texts such as 1 Kgs 16:2 ("From Dust to Kingship," *ZAW* 84 [1972]: 1-18). Simkins shows that it is more likely that what was originally a royal tradition (see Ezek 28:12-19) has in Genesis 2 been divested of such a perspective, though traces remain (*Creator and Creation*, 181-82). The language of democratization is not new; see, e.g., Zimmerli, *Old Testament and World*, 40; Anderson, *From Creation to New Creation*, 125-29.

129. On this see Michael Welker, "What Is Creation?" Brown prefers to use the language of "finished product" (*Ethos*, 49).

130. For a thoughtful use of this text by a systematic theologian regarding the suffering of becoming, see Douglas John Hall, *God and Human Suffering* (Minneapolis: Augsburg, 1986), 53-62.

131. See Bruce Vawter, *On Genesis: A New Reading* (Garden City, N.Y.: Doubleday, 1977), 74.

132. It is likely that this text does not function with a notion of absolute divine foreknowledge. God does not seem finally to know just how the *'ādām* will respond until he in fact does (see Gen 22:12; Deut 8:2 for other such texts). God knows all there is to know, including all the possibilities or probabilities of the future (and hence omniscience is not the issue). For details, see Fretheim, *Suffering of God*, 45-59.

133. Walter Brueggemann, *Genesis* (Interpretation: A Bible Commentary for Teaching and Preaching, ed. James Luther Mays; Atlanta: John Knox, 1982), 47.

134. This text with its concern about human aloneness has more recently been seen as an important source for singles, both straight and gay.

135. Westermann, *Genesis 1–11*, 228.

136. Gerhard von Rad, *Genesis: A Commentary* (rev. ed.; Philadelphia: Westminster, 1971), 83.

137. Bonhoeffer notices: "It was Adam's first occasion of pain that these brothers and sisters whom Adam loved did not fulfill the human being's own expectation" (*Creation and Fall*, 96).

138. See Walther Zimmerli, "The Place and Limit of the Wisdom in the Framework of the Old Testament Theology," *SJT* 17 (1964): 146-58: "God empowers *['ādām]* with a striking independence" (p. 151).

139. Phyllis Trible, *God and the Rhetoric of Sexuality* (Overtures to Biblical Theology, ed. Walter Brueggemann and John R. Donahue; Philadelphia: Fortress, 1978), 93.

140. Is this much different from the present situation where, say, human environmental (in)sensitivity or the use of nuclear weapons may have a comparable import for the future of the world? Indeed, such decisions could put an end to the human race as decisively as the choice of the animals would have.

141. Fox, *Genesis and Exodus*, 18.

142. The sanction attached to the prohibition states: "in the day that [= when] you eat of it you shall die" (2:17). It seems clear that this language does not entail "you shall become mortal"; they already are mortal beings, as the presence of the tree of life assumes (see 3:9, 22).

143. Note also the claim of Eve in 4:1 that she has produced an *'îš*, that is, a man.

144. The discussion of Trible, *Rhetoric of Sexuality*, remains most helpful regarding these matters.

145. See David J. A. Clines, *What Does Eve Do to Help? and Other Readerly Questions to the Old Testament* (Sheffield: JSOT Press, 1990), 27-37.

146. See George W. Ramsey, "Is Name-Giving an Act of Domination in Genesis 2:23 and Elsewhere?" CBQ 50 (1988): 24-35. Clines may be right that discerning does not necessarily exclude domination, but it does not include it without some contextual marker either (*What Does Eve Do*, 39).

147. In 3:14-19, God announces what the effects of the sin are, which God mediates. Of course, those judgments are not intended to be eternal decrees; every effort should be made to overcome patriarchy just as efforts have been made to relieve pain in childbirth and the hardships associated with farming. On 3:16, see especially Carol L. Meyers, *Discovering Eve* (New York: Oxford University Press, 1988).

148. Trible suggests that the *'ādām* ought to be considered an "earth creature" without sexual identity until the creation of the woman. Yet, without an explicit linguistic marker for a change in the meaning of the word *'ādām*, it seems best to retain the translation "the man" or "the human being" in 2:7-22 (*Rhetoric of Sexuality*, 79-81). See the evaluation of this interpretation in Thomas L. Brodie, *Genesis as Dialogue: A Literary, Historical, and Theological Commentary* (Oxford:

Oxford University Press, 2001), 138. See also Brown (*Ethos*, 142), who speaks helpfully of the *'ādām* gaining "a new aspect of his identity." So also Julie Galambush, "'ĀDĀM from 'ĂDĀMÂ, 'IŠŠÂ from 'ÎŠ: Derivation and Subordination in Genesis 2:4b–3:24," in *History and Interpretation: Essays in Honor of John H. Hayes* (ed. M. P. Graham, et al.; Sheffield: Sheffield Academic Press, 1993), 36. That gender is meaningful in 2:7-22 may be assumed from the use of *male* and *female* in 1:27. At the same time, the use of *'ādām* as a generic noun for humankind (1:26-27; 2:5; 5:1-2) suggests that *'ādām* in these verses (see also 3:22-24) can be extended to refer to a *human* role. This might extend David J. A. Clines's argument that *'ādām* is ungendered, is extended even into these chapters ("Human, Humanity"). See n. 24.

149. See Ellen van Wolde, *Words Become Worlds: Semantic Studies of Genesis 1–11* (Leiden: Brill, 1994), 50.

150. See Callender, *Adam in Myth and History*, 32-33. Note: "image" and "likeness" are reversed from 1:26.

151. Ibid., 33. My concerns regarding Gen 5:1-3 are somewhat different from those of Callender, but his work is helpful in raising issues regarding the relationship between human and divine creativity. I would view the creativity of Adam as a statement about that which is typically human rather than any special interest in a primal human figure who intermediates between the divine and human worlds.

152. It may be important to note that the only specific namings that occur in the genealogy bracket the account (5:3, 29).

153. Brodie, *Genesis as Dialogue*, 137. It has often been noted that the theme of divine rest is present in other creation accounts (see Levenson, *Persistence of Evil*, 101-3). Though these verses contain no explicit reference to worship, some allusion to liturgical celebration may be present. Löning and Zenger cite the following from *Midrash Rabbah* on Genesis: "What was created on the seventh day? Composure, serenity, peace, and quiet" (*To Begin with*, 116). These creations do not stand over against human vocation but are a gift within that vocation. See also the discussion of sabbath in Balentine, *Torah's Vision*, 90-95.

154. According to Steck, time and life are the two major themes of the creation account. He speaks of environments for living, conditions favorable to life, including time, and living things for each of these favorable living spaces (*World and Environment*, 94-95).

155. This is not, however, to conclude with Childs, following Barth, that humankind "is invited to participate in God's rest, not in God's creative work" (*Biblical Theology*, 401). The pattern for those created in the image of God is work/rest, not just rest.

156. So von Rad, *Genesis*, 65. Steck speaks of "seven real days" (*World and Environment*, 99).

157. For details, see Terence E. Fretheim, "Were the Days of Creation Twenty-Four Hours Long?" in *The Genesis Debate: Persistent Questions about Creation and the Flood* (ed. Ronald Youngblood; Nashville: Thomas Nelson, 1986), 12-35.

158. Moltmann, *God in Creation*, 88.

159. Levenson, *Persistence of Evil*, 120.

160. For a full discussion of the Old Testament evidence for the temporality of God, see Fretheim, *Suffering of God*, 39-44. For a somewhat different look at the biblical evidence by a systematic theologian, see Alan G. Padgett, *God, Eternity, and the Nature of Time* (New York: St. Martin's Press, 1992).

161. Linkages between this divine rest and the divine resting theme associated with tabernacle and temple can be observed. Whether this divine act can be considered a (self-)*enthronement* is another question; quite apart from such an interpretation of divine rest, the character of the creation accounts makes it unlikely that rest would be associated in any particular way with monarchial images. For a contrary view, see Levenson, *Persistence of Evil*, 107-11. If one were to insist on rest as enthronement, then divine kingship would have to be radically redefined from its usual connotations.

162. See Gunton, *Triune Creator*, 83-84, 93.

163. Michael Welker, "Creation: Big Bang or the Work of Seven Days?" *ThTo* 52 (1995): 184.

164. Brown takes a different tack, with God and the Sabbath being "separate from the world" and inhabiting a "distinct domain" of holiness. For him, the Sabbath is correspondent to the tabernacle/temple as temporal and spatial divine dwelling places (*Ethos*, 49-50; see Ps 132:13-14 for a link between temple and divine rest), but this seems to "separate" God out from the actual world of times and places.

165. Moltmann, *God in Creation*, 279.

166. See, e.g., Levenson, *Persistence of Evil*, 117.

167. See the definition of *creation* in ch. 1.

168. Only some brief notes can be given here. For a helpful survey of creation myths and themes from the ancient Near East, see Simkins, *Creator and Creation*, 41-81. See also Richard J. Clifford, *Creation Accounts in the Ancient Near East and the Bible* (Washington, D.C.: Catholic Biblical Association, 1994); Dexter E. Callender Jr., *Adam in Myth and History*; see also the collection of essays in Richard S. Hess and David Toshio Tsumura, ed., *I Studied Inscriptions from before the Flood: Ancient Near Eastern, Literary, and Linguistic Approaches to Genesis 1–11* (Winona Lake, Ind.: Eisenbrauns, 1994). For an older study of biblical and extrabiblical creation accounts, indeed probably the first comprehensive study of them, see S. G. F. Brandon, *Creation Legends of the Ancient Near East* (London: Hodder and Stoughton, 1963); for a brief assessment, see Clifford, *Creation Accounts*, 3-4.

169. For discussion, see especially Levenson, *Persistence of Evil*, 101-3.

170. Cf. the listing in Simkins, *Creator and Creation*, 82.

171. Translation in *Ancient Near Eastern Texts Relating to the Old Testament* (ed. James B. Pritchard; 3rd ed.; Princeton: Princeton University Press, 1969), 60-61.

172. W. G. Lambert and A. R. Millard, *Atra-Hasis: The Babylonian Story of the Flood* (Oxford: Clarendon, 1969). See also Tikva Frymer-Kensky, "The Atrahasis Epic and Its Significance for Our Understanding of Genesis 1–9," *BA* 40 (1977): 147-55; Robert A. Oden, "Divine Aspirations in Atrahasis and Genesis 1–11," *ZAW* 93 (1981): 197-216.

173. See J. K. Hoffmeier, "Some Thoughts on Genesis 1 and 2 and Egyptian Cosmology," *JNES* 15 (1983): 39-49. For texts, see Miriam Lichtheim, *Ancient Egyptian Literature* (3 vols.; Berkeley: University of California Press, 1973, 1976, 1980).

174. For texts and discussion, see Levenson, *Persistence of Evil*, 53-65.

175. Lichtheim, *Ancient Egyptian Literature*, 3:54.

176. Simkins, *Creator and Creation*, 68.

177. Ibid., 70.

178. See Richard J. Clifford, "Cosmogonies in the Ugaritic Texts and in the Bible," *Orientalia* 63 (1984): 183-201; Day, *God's Conflict*. For comparisons between biblical accounts and ancient Near Eastern cosmogonies, see Richard J. Clifford, "The Hebrew Scriptures and the Theology of Creation," *TS* 46 (1985): 507-23.

179. See, e.g., Walther Eichrodt, *Theology of the Old Testament* (trans. J. A. Baker; Philadelphia: Westminster, 1967), 2:93-117.

180. See Bertil Albrektson, *History and the Gods* (Lund: Gleerup, 1967).

181. Simkins, *Creator and Creation*, passim, is particularly effective in demonstrating that this contrast has often been overdrawn.

182. Scholars have long pursued possible polemical interests in Genesis 1, the most commonly noted being a polemic against astrological reflection, most evident in the way the sun and moon are not named as such and are clearly understood as created by God (1:16), and against any combative role for the sea monster, demythologized in 1:21. For a list of such scholarly efforts, see J. Richard Middleton, "Creation Founded in Love," 77 n. 36; see also Levenson, *Persistence of Evil*, 54-55.

183. For a closer look at a "shared perception of reality" between Israel and ancient Near Eastern understandings of creation, see Simkins, *Creator and Creation*, 82-120.

3. Creation at Risk

1. T. Stordalen finds a number of allusions in the rest of the Old Testament. This may well be so, but it is not unimportant that references to Genesis 3 are never direct. *Echoes of Eden: Genesis 2–3 and the Symbolism of the Eden Garden in Biblical Hebrew Literature* (Leuven: Peeters, 2000).

2. The commentaries on Genesis 3 are numerous; I cite only a basic list here. The scholarly standards include the commentaries of Gerhard von Rad and Claus Westermann. More recent commentaries that are particularly concerned

to address theological issues include Walter Brueggemann, W. Sibley Towner, and Thomas L. Brodie. For issues of rhetoric and ideology, see Beverly J. Stratton, *Out of Eden: Reading, Rhetoric, and Ideology in Genesis 2–3* (Sheffield: Sheffield Academic Press, 1995). See also Phyllis Trible, *God and the Rhetoric of Sexuality* (Overtures to Biblical Theology, ed. Walter Brueggemann and John R. Donahue; Philadelphia: Fortress, 1978). For my own work, see "Genesis" (vol. 1 of *The New Interpreter's Bible*; Nashville: Abingdon, 1994), 357-70; "Is Genesis 3 a Fall Story," *WW* 14 (1994): 144-53.

3. See, e.g., Terence E. Fretheim, *Creation, Fall and Flood: Studies in Genesis 1–11* (Minneapolis: Augsburg, 1969), 93-94; Alan J. Hauser, "Linguistic and Thematic Links between Genesis 4:1-16 and Genesis 2–3," *JETS* 23 (1980): 297-305.

4. James Barr, *The Garden of Eden and the Hope of Immortality* (Minneapolis: Fortress, 1993), ix. Among others, he echoes Walter Brueggemann, "nothing could be more remote from the narrative" than the fall (*Genesis* [Interpretation: A Bible Commentary for Teaching and Preaching, ed. James Luther Mays; Atlanta: John Knox, 1982], 41); and Claus Westermann: "The narrative of Gen 2–3 does not speak of a fall," and these chapters know of no human being before sin (*Genesis 1–11: A Commentary* [Minneapolis: Augsburg, 1984], 276).

5. Claus Westermann, *Creation* (trans. John J. Scullion; Philadelphia: Fortress, 1974), 20.

6. Such a perspective, with its emphasis on sin as pride, thinking of yourself more highly than you ought to think, tends to neglect the sin of self-denigration, thinking of yourself less highly than you ought to think. The latter is a fundamental human problem that needs greater recognition. Catherine Keller makes the point clearly: "the traditional notions of sin as pride and self-assertion serve to reinforce the subordination of women, whose temptations *as* women lie in the realm of 'underdevelopment or negation of the self'" (*From a Broken Web: Separation, Sexism, and Self* [Boston: Beacon, 1986], 12).

7. For an initial effort on this developmental understanding, see Fretheim, "Is Genesis 3 a Fall Story?"

8. These references are found in *Near Eastern Religious Texts Relating to the Old Testament* (ed. Walter Beyerlin; The Old Testament Library, ed. Peter Ackroyd, et al.; Philadelphia: Westminster, 1978). See index under "sin."

9. NRSV's use of "wild" to describe the serpent in 3:1 has no explicit counterpart in the Hebrew text.

10. William P. Brown, along with many other commentators, considers the serpent a malevolent creature; a positive or neutral interpretation is not taken into account. Brown's claim that the serpent is a wild animal that has no rightful place in the garden has no basis in the text that I can discern (2:19 places all such animals within the garden). See William P. Brown, *The Ethos of the Cosmos: The Genesis of Moral Imagination in the Bible* (Grand Rapids: Eerdmans, 1999), 146-57.

11. In a way different from image and likeness in 1:26-27.

12. For example, Brown, *Ethos*, 160-61.

13. See Donald E. Gowan, *From Eden to Babel: A Commentary on the Book of Genesis 1–11* (Grand Rapids: Eerdmans, 1988).

14. For example, Westermann, *Creation*, 98-103; Trible, *God and the Rhetoric of Sexuality*, 123.

15. The expulsion from the garden mirrors later Israelite banishments from the land because of disloyalty to God (e.g., Leviticus 26).

16. See R. Moberly, "Did the Serpent Get It Right?" *JTS* 39 (1988): 1-27.

17. So also John Goldingay, *Israel's Gospel* (vol. 1 of *Old Testament Theology*; Downer's Grove, Ill.: InterVarsity, 2003), 120.

18. See the discussion of 4:1 in ch. 2.

19. The suggestion of several scholars that Cain's offering is rejected because it is the product of a cursed ground will not stand up under scrutiny. In such an argument, Abel's offering should have been rejected as well, for his offering had been sustained by eating from this cursed ground.

20. This anticipates our later discussion regarding the relation between creation and law in ch. 5.

21. For a review of negative and positive assessments of these developments, see Brown, *Ethos*, 170-74.

22. See the Excursus in ch. 2.

23. For a gathering of the arguments that "nature" is not "fallen," see H. Paul Santmire, *Brother Earth* (New York: Thomas Nelson, 1970), 192-200. For a traditional view of the cosmos as fallen, see John Milton, "On the Morning of Christ's Nativity," in *The Complete Poetical Works of John Milton* (Cambridge Edition; Boston: Houghton Mifflin, 1899), st. 2 of The Hymn, p. 7:

> Only with speeches fair
> She woos the gentle air
> To hide her guilty front with innocent snow,
> And on her naked shame,
> Pollute with sinful blame,
> The saintly veil of maiden white to throw;
> Confounded, that her Maker's eyes
> Should look so near upon her foul deformities.

24. Brown speaks of "an earth wiped clean of corruption" (*Ethos*, 60). But, the remarkable reticence of the text to make this point should be honored, not least given the continuing violence implicit in the divine commands of 9:1-7.

25. So Goldingay, *Israel's Gospel*, 170.

26. Karl Löning and Erich Zenger, *To Begin with, God Created . . . : Biblical Theologies of Creation* (trans. Omar Kaste; Collegeville, Minn.: Liturgical Press, 2000), 104.

27. See Löning and Zenger, *To Begin with*, 118-19.

28. Whether or not there was a specific event behind this story, it is *represented in the text as such an event* (on the typical and atypical in Genesis 1–11, see previous chapter). The promise is not that God would never send a flood but that God would never send another annihilating flood (see Löning and Zenger, *To Begin with*, 119-27). It is striking that Löning and Zenger consider the flood story mythical but speak as if it were not. (E.g., what does it mean to speak of a change in God, as they do, unless there is a real before and after?) For details on historical issues across the centuries, see Lloyd R. Bailey, *Noah, the Person and the Story in History and Tradition* (Columbia: University of South Carolina Press, 1989).

29. Westermann seeks to draw a correlation between "the catastrophe at the beginning" and "the catastrophe at the end" (*Creation*, 22), but this formulation does not take God's promise seriously enough.

30. For a discussion of this text, see Terence E. Fretheim, *Jeremiah* (Macon: Smyth & Helwys, 2002), 105-6.

31. Löning and Zenger agree (*To Begin with*, 124). Note the title they give to this section of their book: "The Creation of the World and the Creator God's Learning Process" (p. 122).

32. For details on this important Old Testament theme, see Terence E. Fretheim, *The Suffering of God: An Old Testament Perspective* (Philadelphia: Fortress, 1984), 45-59.

33. The view of Löning and Zenger—that the difference between 6:5-7 and 8:21 is that, in the former, God looked at himself, but, in the latter, God looked at the humans—cannot be sustained; 6:5-7 begins with a divine seeing of the human situation (*To Begin with*, 124).

34. Löning and Zenger, *To Begin with*, 100. They speak of this outline for Genesis 1–9: 1:1–2:3; 2:4–4:26; 5:1–9:29. Genesis 10–12 constitutes the beginning of the history of Israel. I agree that 9:29 (or better 9:1) constitutes a fundamental break, but the narrative does not then move to a history of Israel. Genesis 11:1, with its "whole earth" reference, still keeps readers in a life setting that is more like what precedes than what follows. Genesis 10:l (or 9:1) moves to a narrative about the *known* nations of the world (and hence different from preflood narrative), and the now reported division of the world into families, peoples, and nations constitutes one very important dimension of God's creative work in the world. World history would be a better designation for this last segment of Genesis 1–11. To consider this text a part of God's creative work recognizes that God's creation has to do not simply with the natural order but also the social order.

35. Brown draws a parallel between God's self-limitation in promising no more floods to the restriction of human violence in 9:1-7 (*Ethos*, 59-60). Divine judgment, however, will not disappear from the narrative; indeed, it is implicit in God's own potential actions that entail violence (9:6-7).

36. In ch. 5, I will pursue the importance of the idea that law is grounded in creation and not Israel's redemption. The law given at Sinai is a further particularization for Israel of the law given in creation and to Noah and his sons.

37. The importance of obedience to law is evident in 9:1-7, but is not said to condition the promise. That the promise includes animals precludes the idea that the promise is conditional.

38. Löning and Zenger, *To Begin with*, 119.

39. For a study of the relationship between covenant and creation, see Patrick D. Miller, "Creation and Covenant," in *Biblical Theology: Problems and Perspectives* (ed. Steven J. Kraftchick, Charles D. Meyers, Jr., Ben C. Ollenburger; Nashville: Abingdon, 1995), 155-68. See also Rolf Rendtorff, *Canon and Theology: Overtures to an Old Testament Theology* (ed. and trans. Margaret Kohl; Overtures to Biblical Theology, ed. Walter Brueggemann, et al.; Minneapolis: Fortress, 1993), 92-113, 125-34.

40. Contrary to Miller, "Creation," 162.

41. For covenant as primary, see Miller, "Creation," 162, and Rendtorff's articles, n. 39.

42. Francis Watson speaks of the "interdependence of covenant and creation" (*Text and Truth: Redefining Biblical Theology* [Grand Rapids: Eerdmans, 1997], 232), though this stands in the service of another point that I am making. Watson is concerned, properly, to deny any claim that redemption is more important than creation. His concern, however, to claim that the language of creation belongs only to matters "in the beginning" is belied by many texts and factors, as we have sought to show in ch. 1. What God is about in the "middle" is insufficiently grasped by the language of "preservation" (p. 168 n. 7).

43. Recall that chaos as evil is not an ontological reality that stands over against God in the Old Testament, except possibly in later texts.

44. Miller reflects Rendtorff's discussion ("Creation," in Kraftchick, et al., *Biblical Theology*, 162).

45. See ch. 6 for further discussion.

46. Contrary to Miller, it is not that "a restoration happens through God's covenant" of peace, but that the relationship between God and people on the far side of restoration will be *recharacterized* in such terms ("Creation," in Kraftchick, et al., *Biblical Theology*, 162).

47. It is important to note that the "new covenant" of Jer 31:31-34 is not "new" relative to the Noachic covenant (or the Abrahamic/Davidic covenants), but the Sinai covenant. At the same time, Jer 31:35-37 makes it clear that this new covenant is different from the original Sinai covenant; it is now just as firm and sure as is the covenant with Noah and all flesh.

4. Creation and the Foundation Narratives of Israel

1. James K. Bruckner, *Implied Law in the Abraham Narrative: A Literary and Theological Analysis* (JSOTSup 335; Sheffield: Sheffield Academic Press, 2001), 199.

2. See David J. A. Clines, *The Theme of the Pentateuch* (rev. ed.; Sheffield: JSOT Press, 1997); Brevard S. Childs, *Introduction to the Old Testament as Scripture* (Philadelphia: Fortress, 1979); B. Dahlberg, "On Recognizing the Unity of Genesis," *TD* 24 (1977): 360-67; Thomas W. Mann, "All the Families of the Earth: The Theological Unity of Genesis," *Int* 45 (1991): 341-53. For my own work, see "Genesis" (vol. 1 of *The New Interpreter's Bible*; Nashville: Abingdon, 1994); *The Pentateuch* (Interpreting Biblical Texts, ed. Gene M. Tucker and Charles B. Cousar; Nashville: Abingdon, 1996).

3. See Robert Cohn, "Negotiating (with) the Natives: Ancestors and Identity in Genesis," *HTR* 96 (2003): 147-66. He correctly notes that Genesis 12–50 presents Israel's ancestors as the "outsiders" in a land not yet their own. I use the word *outsiders* with reference to those not part of the chosen family.

4. See William P. Brown, *The Ethos of the Cosmos: The Genesis of Moral Imagination in the Bible* (Grand Rapids: Eerdmans, 1999), 65-66.

5. Cohn, "Negotiating," 150.

6. See, e.g., Gerhard von Rad's negative assessment of human activity in the story of Hagar (*Genesis: A Commentary* [rev. ed.; Philadelphia: Westminster, 1971], 196).

7. See Westermann, *Genesis 12–36: A Commentary* (trans. John J. Scullion; Minneapolis: Augsburg, 1985), 35-41.

8. For a recent consideration of these and other biblical women (with extensive bibliography), see Carol L. Meyers, ed. *Women in Scripture: A Dictionary of Named and Unnamed Women in the Hebrew Bible, the Aprocryphal/ Deuterocanonical Books, and the New Testament* (Grand Rapids: Eerdmans, 2000).

9. An important study of land in these and other texts is that of Norman C. Habel, *This Land Is Mine: Six Biblical Land Theologies* (Minneapolis: Fortress, 1995). Also to be noted is the series of five volumes edited by Habel known as *The Earth Bible*; they are marked by the treatment of land as a *subject*. See Introduction, n. 29.

10. See Frederick J. Gaiser, "Why Does It Rain? A Biblical Case Study in Divine Causality," *HBT* 25 (2003): 1-18. See also Terence E. Fretheim, "Divine Judgment and the Warming of the World: An Old Testament Perspective," in *God, Evil, and Suffering: Essays in Honor of Paul R. Sponheim* (Word and World Supplement Series 4; ed. Terence E. Fretheim and Curtis L. Thompson; St. Paul: Word and World, 2000), 21-32.

11. We will see in the prophets that military sieges, prompted by human wickedness, will include devastating effects upon the environment (e.g., Jer 4:23-26; Isaiah 24). The prophetic view of the future will include a kind of environmental cleanup, a re-creation of the wilderness (e.g., Isa 35:1-10).

12. See Bruckner, *Implied Law*.

13. This aspect of our discussion is also reflected in ch. 5, "Creation and Law."

14. Bruckner, *Implied Law*, 200. The essential point being made here is comparable to that which I make in my article, "The Plagues as Ecological Signs of Historical Disaster," *JBL* 110 (1991): 385-96.

15. Ibid., 200-201.

16. Bruckner's analysis of Genesis 20 is instructive: Abimelech "must rely on a prophet to restore his health, not because he is guilty, but because he is sick. He is sick, not because he is guilty, but because he has become the victim of a lie and has unwittingly participated in a violation of the created moral order" (Ibid., 204).

17. Ibid., 204.

18. For details on the created moral order in the prophets, see ch. 6.

19. Bruckner, *Implied Law*, 203. Bruckner cites the following creational motifs: danger/safety, fight/flight, blindness/sight, nightmares/dreams, famine/prosperity, barrenness/fertility, and health/sickness.

20. For further reflections on creation and law, see ch. 5.

21. For a fuller consideration of this matter, see below.

22. Beyond Genesis, one might note the story of Balaam in Numbers 22–24.

23. See John Goldingay's formulation: God's choice of Israel "is subordinate to a commitment to humankind as a whole" (*Israel's Gospel* [vol. 1 of *Old Testament Theology*; Downer's Grove, Ill.: InterVarsity, 2003], 101); one might add God's commitment to the nonhuman creation.

24. See Löning and Zenger: "The world of peoples and religions outside Israel and outside the Church is not simply a salvationless void" (*To Begin with, God Created . . . : Biblical Theologies of Creation* [trans. Omar Kaste; Collegeville, Minn.: Liturgical Press, 2000], 3-4).

25. Though circumcision as covenant includes *all* of Abraham's offspring, including foreign slaves in Abraham's household (Gen 17:9-14, 23-27).

26. These texts raise the issue of how the promises regarding Ishmael also pertain to his descendants, including modern Muslims. Have Muslims grown in such large numbers over the years because God has been faithful to promises made to Hagar and Ishmael? For further reflections on this issue, see Fretheim, "Genesis," 455, 490.

27. Brueggemann, *Genesis* (Interpretation: A Bible Commentary for Teaching and Preaching, ed. James Luther Mays; Atlanta: John Knox, 1982), 153.

28. Generally, see Claus Westermann, *Blessing in the Bible and the Life of the Church* (trans. Keith R. Crim; Philadelphia: Fortress, 1978). Westermann divides God's activity in the world into categories of saving and blessing. This is a useful distinction but should not be understood too strictly, for God's saving activity is also described in terms of blessing. Moreover, one should not translate these categories into a creation/redemption distinction or, for that matter, into a law/gospel distinction.

29. See Terence E. Fretheim, "Which Blessing Does Isaac Give Jacob?" in *Jews, Christians, and the Theology of the Hebrew Scriptures* (ed. Alice Ogden Bellis and Joel S. Kaminsky; Symposium; Atlanta: Society of Biblical Literature, 2000), 279-91.

30. One might also distinguish between communal promises (e.g., 28:13-14) and personal promises (28:15). Laurence Turner is right to criticize the distinction between "religious" promises and "earthly" promises (*Announcements of Plot in Genesis* [Sheffield: Sheffield Academic Press, 1990], 116); see Brueggemann, *Genesis*, 206-7. The last two phrases of 27:29 do refer to 12:3, but this is the only time it is recalled in Genesis and hence not integral to the "blessing of Abraham." It may be a more personal reference (cf. 28:15).

31. For details see my "Reclamation of Creation: Redemption and Law in Exodus," *Int* 45 (1991): 354-65.

32. Regarding divine judgment in the Abimelech story (Gen 20:3-7), see discussion of Bruckner's work above. In these texts, judgment is shown not to be an attribute of God; it is a contingent divine response to a creational situation that threatens that very creation. The God who judges is the kind of God who will be confessed in Exod 34:6-7. For detail on judgment and the created moral order, see ch. 6.

33. For example, Bernhard W. Anderson, *Understanding the Old Testament* (4th ed.; Englewood Cliffs, N.J.: Prentice-Hall, 1986). See his articulation of this rationale in his 1955 article "The Earth Is the Lord's" in his collection of essays, *From Creation to New Creation: Old Testament Perspectives* (Overtures to Biblical Theology, ed. Walter Brueggemann, et al.; Minneapolis: Fortress, 1994), 3-7.

34. For introductory issues, see Terence E. Fretheim, *Exodus* (Interpretation: A Bible Commentary for Teaching and Preaching, ed. James Luther Mays; Louisville: Westminster John Knox, 1991), 1-22; Brevard S. Childs, *The Book of Exodus: A Critical, Theological Commentary* (Philadelphia: Westminster, 1974); William H. C. Propp, *Exodus 1–18* (New York: Doubleday, 1999), 31-54. For a theological exposition, see Donald E. Gowan, *Theology in Exodus: Biblical Theology in the Form of a Commentary* (Louisville: Westminster/John Knox, 1994). The material in this chapter is often adapted from my Exodus commentary.

35. Some scholars, e.g., John Van Seters, call on a variety of data to place the Yahwist in the exilic period, not least because of the parallels the plague traditions have with other literature from that era ("The Plagues of Egypt: Ancient Tradition or Literary Invention?" *ZAW* 98 [1986]: 31-39). It is not my purpose to enter into this particular debate, only to note that the links to exilic Israel have been observed in some detail.

36. That Isaiah 40–55 draws on creation materials links the Exodus texts with an exilic setting (see ch. 6).

37. See Terence E. Fretheim, "Because the Whole Earth Is Mine: Narrative and Theme in Exodus," *Int* 50 (1996): 229-39.

38. That the phrase "the land was filled with them" (Exod 1:7) is intended as an explicit reference to Gen 1:28 and 9:1 is evident, given the absence of any reference to Egypt or Goshen, the mention of which would have blurred this link.

39. Among the many fine studies lifting up the role of these women, see J. Cheryl Exum, "You Shall Let Every Daughter Live: A Study of Ex. 1:8–2:10,"

Semeia 28 (1983): 63-82; "Second Thoughts about Secondary Characters: Women in Exodus 1:8–2:10," in *A Feminist Companion to Exodus to Deuteronomy* (ed. Athalya Brenner; A Feminist Companion to the Bible; Sheffield: Sheffield Academic Press, 1994), 75-87.

40. The following incorporates my article, "The Plagues as Ecological Signs of Historical Disaster," 385-96.

41. For a convenient summary, see Childs, *Book of Exodus*, 130-42.

42. The closest narrative parallel may be the flood story, another ecological disaster; see the use of *kōl* in Gen 7:21-23. For literary analyses of the narrative, see especially these two articles: David M. Gunn, "The 'Hardening of Pharaoh's Heart': Plot, Character and Theology in Exodus 1–14," in *Art and Meaning: Rhetoric in Biblical Literature* (ed. David J. A. Clines, David M. Gunn, and Alan J. Hauser; Sheffield: JSOT Press, 1982), 72-96; Ann Vater, "A Plague on Both Our Houses: Form- and Rhetorical-Critical Observations on Exodus 7–11," in Clines, et al., *Art and Meaning*, 62-71. Generally on structural matters, the caution of John Durham (*Exodus* [Waco: Word, 1987], 96) is appropriate: "Formulaic patterns can easily become as wildly speculative and as absurd as fragment-hypotheses."

43. Adapted from Childs, *Book of Exodus*, 57.

44. This present/future correspondence is more broadly evident when viewed in terms of the ways in which these natural phenomena function in divine judgment contexts, especially prophetic (see ch. 7). For a contrary view, see Gowan, *Theology in Exodus*, 133-40. My claim that the plagues are "judgment" (not punishment) for pharaonic deeds (6:6; 7:4; 12:12) does not deny that God uses these realities for God's particular purposes in this time and place. God always uses judgment, finally, for salvific purposes. See also the comments in Propp (*Exodus 1–18*, 345-54) questioning the links to creation.

45. H. H. Schmid, "Creation, Righteousness, and Salvation: 'Creation Theology' as the Broad Horizon of Biblical Theology," in *Creation in the Old Testament* (ed. Bernhard W. Anderson; Issues in Religion and Theology 6, ed. Douglas Knight and Robert Morgan; Philadelphia: Fortress, 1984).

46. That Exodus is informed generally by creation theology is developed in my *Exodus*; cf. also my "Suffering God and Sovereign God in Exodus," *HBT* 1 (1989): 31-56. Contemporary understandings of the links between human misuse of the environment and consequent ill effects upon the entire world order may be said to correspond to such ancient views in many ways.

47. See below for some of the evidence for such a view of Pharaoh, both in Exodus and elsewhere in the OT. It is important to say that Pharaoh is understood to be both a historical and a mythological figure in Exodus (on the latter, see 12:12; 15:11; 18:1).

48. The sign value of these narratives participates in a broad-based literary feature of the book of Exodus: early narratives prefigure or foreshadow later developments in the book. Michael Fishbane has noted some of these features in

the relationship between chs. 1–4 and 5–19 (*Text and Texture* [New York: Schocken Books, 1979], 63-76). Our study suggests a more comprehensive use of this stylistic feature in Exodus.

49. The episode in 7:8-13 is sometimes formally considered to be the first plague; see Dennis J. McCarthy, "Moses' Dealings with Pharaoh: Ex 7, 8–10, 27," *CBQ* 27 (1965): 336-47. Some structurally common elements have suggested this (cf. v. 13), to which this feature may now be added. While its scope and effect are somewhat limited, its value as a sign is certainly considerable. At the least, it sets the stage for the remaining signs and provides important clues for their interpretation.

50. The verb *nākāh*, "smite," in 7:17, 25 points forward to its use in 12:12-13, 29 (cf. 8:16-17; 9:15).

51. The texts use different words in speaking of a nondivine agent for the last plague: 11:1 speaks of *nega'*, a word commonly used for "disease"; 12:13 speaks of *nega'*, commonly used for "a blow" or "pestilence"; in 9:15 *deber* is used, as in 9:3, for the cattle epidemic; *mašît* occurs in 12:23, a word associated with destruction and pestilence (cf. 2 Sam 24:15-16; Isa 37:36). It seems best to think of a pestilence epidemic that kills quickly in a "hypernatural" way. As with the other plagues, the emphasis on "all" is intended to portray an aspect of creation gone berserk. The moral order has boomeranged in such a way that the order of nature (including epidemics) has gotten all out of whack.

52. That the origin of the boils is furnace ash may be a sign of fiery judgment (cf. the use of fire in Joel 2:3).

53. So also Ziony Zevit, "The Priestly Redaction and Interpretation of the Plague Narrative in Exodus," *JQR* 66 (1975–1976): 193-211. Zevit correctly sees the importance of the theme of creation in the plague narratives, but the focus on finding specific links with Genesis 1 is at times strained.

54. The fact that these extensive links are with both Passover and sea crossing may provide further data for the exploration of the relationship of these two traditions. For a discussion of the issues, see George W. Coats, "The Sea Tradition in the Wilderness Theme: A Review," *JSOT* 12 (1979): 2-8.

55. For further discussion of this creation-wide purpose for Israel, see Fretheim, "Because the Whole Earth Is Mine"; see also Moshe Greenberg, *Understanding Exodus* (New York: Behrman, 1969), 169-70. For the extensive correspondences between Exodus and Genesis 1–11, see above. The use of *'ereṣ* in the ancestral narratives also should be noted (e.g., Gen 18:18; 41:57; cf. 12:3; 28:14).

56. Cf. Gowan, *Theology in Exodus*, 133; Propp, *Exodus 1–18*, 399-400. See ch. 6 for details.

57. See John J. Collins, *Between Athens and Jerusalem: Jewish Identity in the Hellenistic Diaspora* (New York: Crossroad, 1983), 184. He cites Wis 12:27; 15:17; 16:24 in noting that for wisdom "the events in question are not ascribed to the direct intervention of God but to the constant activity of wisdom in the world. The experience of Israel and its enemies is expressed as an experience of the cos-

mos rather than a direct encounter with God." He cites A. T. S. Goodrick: "Even miracles are regarded by 'wisdom' not as a derangement of the universe but as a rearrangement of the harmony of it."

58. On this symbiotic relationship and God's relationship to the nonhuman in the Psalms and the prophets, see Terence E. Fretheim, "Nature's Praise of God in the Psalms," *ExAud* 3 (1987): 16-30; see ch. 8.

59. Cf. also the extensive use of the plague tradition in the book of Revelation.

60. This section is a summary of my interpretation in *Exodus*, 161-70; also see my "Reclamation of Creation." See the discussions in Walter Brueggemann, *Theology of the Old Testament: Testimony, Dispute, Advocacy* (Minneapolis: Fortress, 1997), 504-6, 536-43; Ronald A. Simkins, *Creator and Creation: Nature in the Worldview of Ancient Israel* (Peabody, Mass.: Hendrickson, 1994), 109-17; Frank Moore Cross, *Canaanite Myth and Hebrew Epic: Essays in the History of Religion* (Cambridge: Harvard University Press, 1973), 112-44; Cross's work is important for refusing an easy split between myth and history.

61. See Anderson, *From Creation to New Creation*, 79. See Michael Fishbane, *Biblical Interpretation in Ancient Israel* (Oxford: Oxford University Press, 1985), 357. See also the discussion of creational dimensions of this text and related ancient Near Eastern parallels in Propp, *Exodus 1–18*, 554-61.

62. Simkins, *Creator and Creation*, 110. Simkins also notes: "God's activity in creation . . . served as the paradigm of God's repeated acts of redemption for Israel" (p. 112). He cites Psalms 74 and 79 and Isa 51:9-11 at this point. It would be important not to "flatten out" all redemptive actions so that the exodus and the return from exile have no special level of historical and cosmic importance. We return to this discussion in connection with Second Isaiah.

63. For details regarding this segment of Exodus, see my *Exodus*, 133-36, 152-54, 161-70.

64. To use images from the Christian tradition, cross and resurrection are kept together. Exodus 15 is a long-standing Old Testament lesson for Easter Sunday.

65. The historical question is whether the sea crossing refers to the Red Sea or one of the smaller bodies in the Egyptian delta region. While the actual crossing may have taken place in the delta region, the context is decisive for retaining the Red Sea translation. Such a major body of water best serves as a vehicle for conveying the cosmic freight of God's victory. See my *Exodus*, 153, for details.

66. For the implications for the interpretation of God as a warrior (15:3), particularly the absence of a single instrument of human warfare, see my *Exodus*, 169.

67. George M. Landes, "Creation and Liberation," in Anderson, *Creation in the Old Testament*, 143.

68. A narrow definition of creation may complicate this discussion (see ch. 1).

69.The word *salvation* may be said to refer to the positive *effects* both of God's redemptive *and* creative activity (both deliverance and, say, healing). The word *soteriological*, though linguistically related to salvation, should be reserved for specific divine acts of redemption (or forgiveness). Note that the language of salvation, in both Testaments, is rarely used with sin as the object (cf. Matt 1:21); in such contexts sin is best understood as referring to the *effects* of sin.

70. See ch. 6 on the prophets for fuller discussion of the cosmic effects of God's redemptive activity.

71. Propp, *Exodus 1–18*, 579.

72. Ibid., 580, 600, 607. I am not certain how he defines *supernatural*; it commonly has reference to unmediated divine action. For discussion of the wilderness provisions, see Fretheim, *Exodus*, 177-78, 182, 190-91.

73. Certain extraordinary features of the manna story should be noted (a two-day supply, with its nonavailability on the Sabbath and the leveling of the provision according to the need). Yet, these features of the story are presented in a very matter-of-fact way, with no ascription to the activity of God and no amazement on the part of the people. The extraordinary is worked in and through the natural features, not in independence from them, without naming them as miraculous.

74. For a general discussion of the miraculous in Old Testament texts, see Terence E. Fretheim, "The God Who Acts: An Old Testament Perspective," *ThTo* 54 (1997): 13-15.

75. See P. J. Kearney, "Creation and Liturgy: The P Redaction of Ex. 25–40," *ZAW* 89 (1977): 375-77; Joseph Blenkinsopp, "The Structure of P," *CBQ* (1976): 275-92; Jon D. Levenson, *Creation and the Persistence of Evil: The Jewish Drama of Divine Omnipotence* (San Francisco: Harper & Row, 1988), 78-89; Samuel E. Balentine, *The Torah's Vision of Worship* (Minneapolis: Fortress, 1999), 63-77, 136-41; E. Elnes, "Creation and Tabernacle: The Priestly Writer's 'Environmentalism,'" *HBT* 16 (1994): 144-55.

76. Levenson, *Persistence of Evil*, 86.

77. See the study of Frank H. Gorman Jr., *The Ideology of Ritual: Time and Status in the Priestly Theology* (Sheffield: JSOT Press, 1990), 9, 18, 230-34. See also Walter Brueggemann, *Israel's Praise: Doxology against Idolatry* (Philadelphia: Fortress, 1988), 1-28; Balentine, *Torah's Vision*, 64-65, 74-76, 90-92.

78. The following are summaries of my *Exodus*, 268-72; for further details, see Balentine, *Torah's Vision*, 138-41.

79. So Balentine, *Torah's Vision*, 141 n. 53.

80. Readers are invited to recall the important role of the creature in creating the world in Genesis 1–2. Bezalel may be said to continue in that creational activity.

5. *Creation and Law*

1. This chapter is an expansion and reworking of my article, "Law in the Service of Life: A Dynamic Understanding of Law in Deuteronomy," in *A God so Near: Essays on Old Testament Theology in Honor of Patrick D. Miller* (ed. Brent A. Strawn and Nancy R. Bowen; Winona Lake, Ind.: Eisenbrauns, 2003), 183-200.

2. For these concerns that undergird Deuteronomy, see Patrick D. Miller, *Deuteronomy* (Louisville: Westminster/John Knox, 1988); Walter Brueggemann, *Deuteronomy* (Abingdon Old Testament Commentary, ed. Patrick D. Miller; Nashville: Abingdon, 2001); Samuel E. Balentine, *The Torah's Vision of Worship* (Minneapolis: Fortress, 1999), 177-211; Dennis T. Olson, *Deuteronomy and the Death of Moses: A Theological Reading* (Minneapolis: Fortress, 1994).

3. For introductory issues, see James Watts, *Reading Law: The Rhetorical Shaping of the Pentateuch* (Sheffield: Sheffield Academic Press, 1999); Dale Patrick, *Old Testament Law* (Atlanta: John Knox, 1985). For a helpful analysis of the development of the book of the covenant, showing that it is not "an immutable, timeless law," see Paul D. Hanson, "The Theological Significance of Contradiction within the Book of the Covenant," in *Canon and Authority* (ed. George W. Coats and Burke O. Long; Philadelphia: Fortress, 1977), 110-31; see also Balentine, *Torah's Vision*, 119-36.

4. An important book focusing on this issue relative to the book of Deuteronomy informs my discussion. See Bernard M. Levinson, *Deuteronomy and the Hermeneutics of Legal Innovation* (New York: Oxford University Press, 1997).

5. For a brief summary, see Terence E. Fretheim, *The Pentateuch* (Interpreting Biblical Texts, ed. Gene M. Tucker and Charles B. Cousar; Nashville: Abingdon, 1996), 56-58.

6. An example of the difficulties such an understanding can generate may be seen in this statement by Watts: "Because YHWH has done and will do these things for Israel, Israel *owes* YHWH obedience" (*Reading Law*, 95, emphasis mine); similarly, "the exodus has obligated Israel to YHWH" (p. 125). The word *owes* draws on imagery from the world of finance and suggests that Israel is in debt to God and, hence, is obligated to repay God for what God has done. But if God is truly gracious, as Israel's central confession states (Exod 34:6-7), the language that Israel has an obligation to pay God back for services rendered compromises the claim regarding grace.

7. B. D. Napier, "Community under Law: On Hebrew Law and Its Theological Presuppositions," *Int* 7 (1953): 413. Cf. Jon D. Levenson, "The Theologies of Commandment in Biblical Israel," *HTR* 73 (1980): 28-33. Important for these considerations generally is the work of Gustaf Wingren, especially his *Creation and Law* (Philadelphia: Muhlenberg Press, 1961).

8. H. H. Schmid, "Creation, Righteousness and Salvation," 104-5. He notes that Hammurabi's giving of the law occurs in a creation context, and "so does every ancient Near Eastern legal code with the same structure" (p. 105). See also Klaus Koch, "Is There a Doctrine of Retribution in the Old Testament?" in *Theodicy in the Old Testament* (ed. James L. Crenshaw; Philadelphia: Fortress, 1983).

9. See the discussion in ch. 4. On law, creation, and covenant, see James K. Bruckner, *Implied Law in the Abraham Narrative: A Literary and Theological Analysis* (Sheffield: Sheffield Academic Press, 2001), 206-11.

10. Terence E. Fretheim, "Genesis" (vol. 1 of *The New Interpreter's Bible*; Nashville: Abingdon, 1994), 529. Bruckner has developed this and related themes at some length in *Implied Law*; idem, "The Creational Context of Law Before Sinai: Law and Liberty in Pre-Sinai Narratives and Romans 7," *ExAud* 11 (1995): 91-110.

11. For Genesis 18–20 especially, see Bruckner, *Implied Law*, passim and pp. 218-21.

12. See Bruckner: "This implementation and administration of law is prior to the context of the covenant. It is presented as a part of God's creating and sustaining work for his non-covenanted people" (*Implied Law*, 215). Bruckner lays the groundwork for consideration of the significant links between Exodus 18 and 24; the juxtaposition of which demonstrates "that God's creative activity in the daily and transcultural administration of justice has an important place alongside the formation of Israel at Sinai" (p. 216). See also the discussion of James Barr, *Biblical Faith and Natural Theology* (Oxford: Clarendon, 1993), 98-99.

13. Terence E. Fretheim, *Exodus* (Interpretation: A Bible Commentary for Teaching and Preaching, ed. James Luther Mays; Louisville: Westminster John Knox, 1991), 200.

14. Terence E. Fretheim, "The Reclamation of Creation: Redemption and Law in Exodus," *Int* 45 (1991): 363.

15. Barr states helpfully: "the character of the laws of the Hebrew Bible . . . [supports] the idea of a rational, knowable, accessible foundation for moral judgments that was, at least in principle, available to all humanity. People wanted to say that the biblical laws, however absolute in themselves, had some grounding in knowable principles: they were not totally and absolutely arbitrary" (*Biblical Faith*, 100).

16. See the discussion in H. H. Schmid, "Creation, Righteousness, and Salvation," 102-17.

17. See John Barton, "Natural Law and Poetic Justice in the Old Testament," *JTS* 30 (1979): 1-14. A view characteristic of later Judaism was that the law of Moses was preexistent, serving as the pattern God used in making the world.

18. For a discussion of the relationship of rain and human conduct, see Frederick J. Gaiser, "Why Does It Rain? A Biblical Case Study in Divine Causality," *HBT* 25 (2003): 1-18.

19. John Barton, *Ethics and the Old Testament* (London: SCM, 1998), 42.

20. Barton, *Ethics*, 43; see also Jacob Milgrom, *Leviticus 1–16* (New York: Doubleday, 1991), 718-36.

21. Barton, *Ethics*, 44.

22. Ibid.

23. On the interpretation of these texts as witnessing to a creation in process, see Fretheim, "Genesis," 343-46, 352, 357. For this perspective, see Michael Welker, "What Is Creation? Rereading Genesis 1 and 2," *ThTo* (1991): 56-71.

24. For a brief survey of the discussion, see Bruckner, *Implied Law*, 44-48. For a discussion of the function of law in pre-Sinai narrative, see ch. 4 above.

25. For a helpful discussion of these issues from an Old Testament perspective, see Barton, *Ethics*, 58-76.

26. See the discussion regarding the oracles against the nations in the prophets in ch. 6.

27. John Barton appropriately considers the Noachic laws (Gen 9:1-7) to be a formulation of long-standing natural law, though formally presented as specifically God-declared laws ("Natural Law," 3).

28. Barton, *Ethics*, 61.

29. Traditionally, theological reflection has distinguished between general and special revelation. At the same time, such discussions have not always discerned the extent of the overlap between them.

30. James Barr, "Biblical Law and the Question of Natural Theology," in *The Law in the Bible and in Its Natural Environment* (ed. Timo Veijola; Publications of the Finnish Exegetical Society 51; Göttingen: Vandenhoeck & Ruprecht, 1990), 17. See also Barr, *Biblical Faith*, 98-99. See as well Bruckner, *Implied Law*, 44-50; Markus Bockmuehl, "Natural Law in Second Temple Judaism," *VT* 45 (1995): 17-44. Bockmuehl has an extensive consideration of natural law in the Apocrypha, Pseudepigrapha, Dead Sea Scrolls, Philo, and Josephus.

31. Barr, "Biblical Law," 9-10.

32. From this perspective, Bockmuehl claims that, strictly speaking, there is no "natural" law in second-temple Judaism ("Natural Law," 43-44).

33. John Barton, *Amos's Oracles against the Nations: A Study of Amos 1:3–2:5* (Cambridge: Cambridge University Press, 1980). The basic point for our purposes is summarized in Barton, *Ethics*, 61-63.

34. Barton, *Ethics*, 61.

35. For consideration of the oracles against the nations in the prophets and the issue of judgment, see ch. 6.

36. See the discussion of Bruckner, *Implied Law*, 224-35.

37. For a consideration of creation and wisdom, see ch. 7.

38. For the links between Psalms 19 and 119 (which also makes no mention of Israel's history), see Levenson, "Theologies of Commandment," 28-33. Levenson seeks to speak about law theologically without speaking necessarily about covenant.

39. For a close study of this psalm and a discussion of the various efforts to resolve this relationship, see the commentaries and Karl Löning and Erich Zenger, *To Begin with, God Created . . . : Biblical Theologies of Creation* (trans. Omar Kaste; Collegeville, Minn.: Liturgical Press, 2000), 133-42; Rolf P. Knierim, "On the Theology of Psalm 19," in *The Task of Old Testament Theology: Substance, Method, and Cases* (Grand Rapids: Eerdmans, 1955), 322-50.

40. Whether vv. 11-13 constitute a third part of the psalm is disputed, but I think these verses speak to a key function of the law. Verse 14 is a concluding prayer.

41. Löning and Zenger, *To Begin with*, 133.

42. On the correlation of significance of the sun in its ancient Near Eastern context and its links to law, see Löning and Zenger, *To Begin with*, 138-40.

43. Levenson, "Theologies of Commandment," 28-29.

44. For this point, see Barr, *Biblical Faith*, 85-89.

45. Jon D. Levenson, "The Sources of Torah: Psalm 119 and the Modes of Revelation in Second Temple Judaism," in *Ancient Israelite Religion* (ed. Patrick D. Miller, et al.; Philadelphia: Fortress, 1987), 569.

46. What follows is an adaptation of material from my "Reclamation of Creation," 364. Generally on this theme, see Balentine, *Torah's Vision*.

47. Frank H. Gorman Jr., *The Ideology of Ritual: Time and Status in the Priestly Theology* (Sheffield: JSOT Press, 1990), 9, 18, 230-34. See ch. 4 (nn. 75-80) for other references.

48. Gorman's conclusion that the incompleteness of the created order in Genesis 1 is understood by the Priestly writers to be "*fully* finished" in the ordering of *Israelite* society around the tabernacle is problematic (ibid., 230, emphasis mine). His discussion moves from Israel to the generally human without sufficient consideration of the relationship between Israel and the larger creation (pp. 230-32).

49. For an earlier formulation, see my "Reclamation of Creation," 354-65.

50. For the theological significance of this literary reality, see Fretheim, *Exodus*, 201-7

51. On explicit links between creation and the wilderness journeys, see ch. 4.

52. Hanson, "Theological Significance," is particularly forceful on this point.

53. For a brief, helpful survey of these motive clauses, see Watts, *Reading Law*, 65-67.

54. See Miller, *Deuteronomy*, 55.

55. James Watts claims that the primary metaphor for the God who gives the law is "just king" (*Reading Law*, 91-109). He draws this conclusion primarily on the basis of certain parallels with ancient Near Eastern law texts. He recognizes that kingship language for God in the Pentateuch is rare, but that recognition should have proved decisive in rejecting such a primary metaphor. If Israel did borrow legal ideas, conventions, genres, etc., it is remarkable that they did *not* bring the royal language along with it. The most likely reason is that Israel did not find royal images particularly helpful in thinking about their relationship with God. This is borne out by the uncommon use of this imagery in the rest of the Old Testament, where it is used primarily in contexts relating to other nations.

56. Ibid., 108.

57. See also the comments in n. 6 this chapter.

58. Bernard M. Levinson, "The Human Voice in Divine Revelation: The Problem of Authority in Biblical Law," in *Innovation in Religious Traditions* (ed. M. Williams, et al.; Berlin: de Gruyter, 1992), 45.

59. In many texts in the Hebrew Bible the divine will changes in view of changing human circumstances, especially regarding announcements of judgment (e.g., Exod 32:14; 2 Kgs 20:1-7; Jer 26:18-19).

60. For Levinson, the Deuteronomic authors assert their freedom to revise the canonical law but sense that they must do so "under the table," so to speak. They assume that their program would not be acceptable in Israel if presented in a straightforward way. Is it clear that they could not have done this more openly? Or, from another angle, who is fooling whom? In addition, if the Deuteronomists sensed that they could do this only in a subversive way, as Levinson claims, whence from within Israel came the understanding that this would be an appropriate thing to do? If God had spoken in a prior generation—and this was generally recognized in Israel—what gave them the theological moxie that made them feel as though they could *completely* abrogate that earlier divine word? Levinson skirts the danger of making the Deuteronomists into religious charlatans; they camouflage their innovations "by feigning a cunning piety with respect to the very authoritative texts that they had subverted" (*Deuteronomy*, 48). The Deuteronomists are "subversives," religiously intolerant and "tendentious" folk, who sought to "silence," indeed "eliminate" the opposition, defining their new vision as normative while regarding the existing legal traditions as "odious" and "deviant" (pp. 144-50). Such judgments on the prior tradition seem unlikely and, in any case, the final form of the canon declares otherwise.

61. Ibid., 149.

62. Ibid., 153 (cf. p. 94).

63. Patrick lists twenty-two instances (*Old Testament Law*, 97).

64. A case from the prophets may be available in Isa 56:1-8, where laws regarding eunuchs and foreigners (e.g., Deut 23:1-6; Lev 21:20-23) are practically, if not formally, set aside. On the issues here, see Frederick J. Gaiser, "A New Word on Homosexuality? Isaiah 56:1-8 as Case Study," *WW* 14 (1994): 280-93.

65. Watts, *Reading Law*, 119.

66. Ibid., 104.

67. Patrick D. Miller's reflections on this "trajectory" in his *Deuteronomy* have been important for my thinking about relationships between Old Testament and New on matters of law.

68. Comparable reflections of the law and its development have long been discussed in the Jewish community as it has sought to relate the Torah to postbiblical formulations and applications.

6. Creation, Judgment, and Salvation in the Prophets

1. To my knowledge, no monograph on creation in the prophetic corpus as a whole has been written.

2. I outline these and other perspectives in detail in "Divine Judgment and the Warming of the World: An Old Testament Perspective," in *God, Evil, and*

Suffering: Essays in Honor of Paul R. Sponheim (ed. Terence E. Fretheim and Curtis L. Thompson; Word and World Supplement Series 4; St. Paul: Word and World, 2000), 22-26. This outline is similar to an earlier article on salvation: Terence E. Fretheim, "Salvation in the Bible vs. Salvation in the Church," *WW* 13 (1993): 363-72. See also my "Theological Relections on the Wrath of God in the Old Testament," *HBT* 24 (2002): 1-26.

3. Helpful resources include Patrick D. Miller, *Sin and Judgment in the Prophets: A Stylistic and Theological Analysis* (Chico, Calif.: Scholars Press, 1982); Klaus Koch, "Is There a Doctrine of Retribution in the Old Testament?" in *Theodicy in the Old Testament* (ed. James L. Crenshaw; Philadelphia: Fortress, 1983), 57-87. More recently, see Gene M. Tucker, "Sin and 'Judgment' in the Prophets," in *Problems in Biblical Theology: Essays in Honor of Rolf Knierim* (ed. H. Sun, et al.; Grand Rapids: Eerdmans, 1997), 373-88. Tucker delineates several formulations: texts that are "dynamistic" and have no explicit reference to God (e.g., Isa 3:9-11; Hos 10:13-15), those in which God makes the connection between sin and consequence (e.g., Jer 6:19; 21:14), and, least common, those that have a juridical element (e.g., Amos 4:1-3). How these "judgment" texts are to be related is best seen in the work of H. H. Schmid, who places them under the comprehensive umbrella of creation theology ("Creation, Righteousness, and Salvation: Creation Theology as the Broad Horizon of Biblical Theology," in *Creation in the Old Testament* [ed. Bernhard W. Anderson; Issues in Religion and Theology 6, ed. Douglas Knight and Robert Morgan; Philadelphia: Fortress, 1984]). See also Walter Brueggemann, "The Uninflected Therefore of Hosea 4:1-3," in *Reading from This Place: Social Location and Biblical Interpretation in the United States* (ed. Fernando F. Segovia and Mary Ann Tolbert; Minneapolis: Fortress, 1995), 231-49.

4. For details, see Terence E. Fretheim, "The Repentance of God: A Key to Evaluating Old Testament God-Talk," *HBT* 10 (1988): 47-70; idem, "God and Violence in the Old Testament," *WW* 24 (2004): 18-28; idem, "'I Was Only a Little Angry': Divine Violence in the Prophets," *Int* 58 (2004): 365-75. God does not "control" or micromanage Nebuchadnezzar's judgmental activity, for he overreaches the divine mandate and is judged for it (Jer 25:11-14; Isa 47:5-7; Zech 1:15, "while I was only a little angry, they made the disaster worse"); he is no puppet in the hand of God.

5. Erich Zenger, *A God of Vengeance? Understanding the Psalms of Divine Wrath* (trans. Linda M. Maloney; Louisville: Westminster/John Knox, 1996), 73.

6. It remains a lively question whether it is helpful to continue to speak of "divine judgment" when its effects are so all-encompassing, but the biblical texts do so.

7. For details, see Fretheim, "Divine Judgment."

8. The faithful are promised deliverance from eschatological wrath (1 Thess 5:9), but they will certainly experience judgment in this life, both individual and communal, to a greater or lesser degree.

9. For a New Testament perspective, see Rom 8:18-22.

10. See the theologically sophisticated study of agency in Frederick J. Gaiser, "To Whom Then Will You Compare Me? Agency in Second Isaiah," *WW* 19 (1999): 141-52; its argument pertains to the prophets more generally. A surprisingly common scholarly claim images God as acting in an unmediated way. See, for example, Walter Brueggemann, *A Commentary on Jeremiah: Exile and Homecoming* (Grand Rapids: Eerdmans, 1998), 54, 70, 176, 193, 428, 430, 439, 460; Robert P. Carroll, *Jeremiah* (Old Testament Library; Philadelphia: Westminster, 1986), 294. Zenger reports the view of Jan Assmann, who draws a distinction between Egypt and Israel at a strange point: "in Egypt God . . . hands over governance, that is, the role of ruling and judging in the world, to the king, who represents God in this role, while in Israel it is God who exercises the role immediately and in person" (*A God of Vengeance?* 72). Whatever one might say about Egyptian perspectives, the latter view regarding Israel's portrayal of God is certainly insufficient. For Israel, God is directly involved *and* rules and judges through means.

11. See final chapter for issues of nonhuman vocation.

12. Contrary to Brueggemann, *Jeremiah*, 242.

13. On this theme, see Fretheim, "I Was Only a Little Angry."

14. See Terence E. Fretheim, "Is Anything too Hard for God? (Jeremiah 32:27)," *CBQ* 66 (2004): 231-36.

15. God (and other observers) knows from experience that these empires will act as kings and armies in that world are known to act. This portrayal of God is a kind of extreme realism regarding what is about to happen to the people. And when the people do experience the pillaging, burning, and raping by the Babylonian armies, readers can be sure that they were real agents. Jeremiah 39; 52 also make this witness in describing the actual destruction of Jerusalem in terms that hardly mention God.

16. See Terence E. Fretheim, *Jeremiah* (Macon: Smyth & Helwys, 2002), 36; idem, "The Character of God in Jeremiah," in *Character and Scripture: Moral Formation, Community and Biblical Interpretation* (ed. William P. Brown; Grand Rapids: Eerdmans, 2002), 211-30.

17. Exodus 3:8-10, where both God and Moses (often called "my servant") bring Israel out of Egypt, could function as a paradigm for such considerations. On issues of divine dependence on the human, see Terence E. Fretheim, "Divine Dependence upon the Human: An Old Testament Perspective," *ExAud* 13 (1997): 2-13. For Brueggemann's perspective, see *A Commentary on Jeremiah: Exile and Homecoming* (Grand Rapids: Eerdmans, 1998): God is "not dependent on what is in the world" (p. 105; see 463).

18. The New Testament also will speak of civil authorities as executors of the divine wrath (Rom 13:4). In a modern context, one might consider the allied armies in the defeat of Hitler in similar ways.

19. For discussion of these relational themes, see ch. 1.

20. See the references in n. 3.

21. The noun *rā'āh* occurs eighty-five times in Jeremiah and about three hundred times in the Old Testament; related forms of the word occur fifty-seven times in Jeremiah.

22. In view of these two senses of *rā'āh*, its translation varies somewhat in the versions. The RSV (following the KJV) tends to translate "evil" for both senses of the word (e.g., Jer 18:8). The NRSV, however, commonly changes the translation to "disaster" when it refers to the effects of human evil, though, strangely, not consistently (e.g., Jer 18:11; cf. 11:11, 23 with 11:17). Among other translations, the NIV translates "disaster" consistently (e.g., Jer 18:11). The NEB is nearly as consistent, and, in the two texts where it translates "evil" (Jer 18:8, 11), its successor (the REB) changes both to "disaster."

23. This understanding can be ascribed to the root *nqm*, commonly (and unhelpfully) translated "vengeance" and linked with wrath ("in anger and wrath I will execute vengeance," Mic 5:15; Isa 59:17; Ezek 25:14, 17). The root *nqm* also occurs within "act-consequence" contexts, for example, Jer 50:15, "take vengeance on her, / do to her as she has done" (see also Isa 59:17-18; Jer 50:28-29; 51:6).

24. God's role is not, in John Barton's words, "simply to oil the works and check the switches," ("Natural Law and Poetic Justice in the Old Testament," *JTS* 30 [1979]: 10); Barton's language of "poetic justice" is helpful, but it should be formulated in such a way that the created moral order is a genuine divine agent; God always acts through means.

25. This understanding of wrath is prominent in the New Testament (e.g., Rom 1:18). God's anger consists in the deliverance of humankind into the consequences of their own thinking and actions. External violence does not necessarily play a role (though, see Rom 12:19; 13:4). This conception grants full stature and respect to both the human action and the divine response. For similar formulations in Ezekiel, see 16:42-43*a*; 7:3-4, 8-9; 7:14, 27; 9:8-10; 24:13-14; 38:18-19, 21. There are over fifty such texts in the Old Testament that link divine wrath with such formulations (e.g., Ps 7:12-16; Isa 59:17-18; 64:5-9; Jer 6:11, 19; 7:18-20; 21:12-14; 44:7-8; 50:24-25; Lam 3:64-66).

26. The *practical* implications of the translation of *pāqad* can be seen in a comparison of RSV and NRSV in Exod 20:5*b*. The RSV translates "visiting the iniquity of the fathers upon the children"; the NRSV, however, changes that to read, "punishing children for the iniquity of parents." Strangely, the NRSV translates the same formulation in Exod 34:7 as "visiting the iniquity of the parents / upon the children."

27. Gerhard von Rad, *Old Testament Theology* (trans. D. M. G. Stalker; New York: Harper & Row, 1962), speaks of a "synthetic view of life" (1:265) in which the "retribution is not a new action which comes upon the person concerned from somewhere else; it is rather a last ripple of the act itself which attaches to its agent almost as something material. Hebrew in fact does not even have a word for punishment" (1:385).

28. Stefan Paas thinks that talk about a created moral order is unfortunate; rather, it is *God* who acts (*Creation and Judgement: Creation Texts in Some Eighth Century Prophets* [Leiden: Brill, 2003], 432-36). The disasters are the punishments of God (p. 435). The interpreter, however, does not have to choose between God and the moral order; both are involved in every move from sin to consequence. The moral order is a divine agent, and God is genuinely active in and through that agent.

29. See Terence E. Fretheim, *The Suffering of God: An Old Testament Perspective* (Overtures to Biblical Theology, ed. Walter Brueggemann and John R. Donahue; Minneapolis: Augsburg Fortress, 1984), 77.

30. For details on this point, see ch. 5.

31. For an earlier discussion of these oracles, see ch. 5. For a basic survey of the issues relating to the oracles against the nations (OAN), see Fretheim, *Jeremiah*, 575-649 and the introductions to chs. 46–51 in the commentaries.

32. This common designation is somewhat of a misnomer, for these oracles are not simply "against" the nations, even if this is predominantly the case. Several texts speak of God as one who "restores the fortunes" of some of these nations (e.g., 46:26; 48:47; 49:6; 49:39), is engaged passionately in their lives (e.g., 48:31-32, 36), and uses them as agents for God's purposes (e.g., 46:26).

33. Notably, God's anger is never directed against the Canaanites in holy war texts in Joshua or Judges.

34. Remarkably, unlike the judgment on Israel, idolatry is not a focus in these oracles (e.g., Jer 46:15, 25). Two reasons for the experience of *rāʿāh* come into play: their own evil (Jer 46:8, 17), or the disaster that spills over into their lives not because of their own evil but because of the wide-ranging effects of the judgment being visited on others (Jeremiah 47). Arrogance is the form of human sinfulness most commonly indicted in these oracles (Jer 48:26, 29-30, 35, 42; 50:24-27, 31-32; 51:6, 11, 25-26, 56).

35. A related purpose of these oracles (at least those in Jeremiah 46–49), depending on the historical context, may have been to alert Israel that appealing to such nations for help would be a vain exercise. Yet, the texts are remarkably silent about such a purpose.

36. Contrary to Brueggemann, *Jeremiah*, 222.

37. See John Sanders, *The God Who Risks* (Downer's Grove, Ill.: InterVarsity, 1998).

38. On the place of the nations in prophetic eschatology, see Donald E. Gowan, *Eschatology in the Old Testament* (2nd ed.; Edinburgh: T&T Clark, 2000), 42-58.

39. For brief surveys of the difficult issues related to these texts and bibliographies, see Jörg Jeremias, *The Book of Amos: A Commentary* (Louisville: Westminster/John Knox, 1998), 76-80; Shalom M. Paul, *Amos* (Hermeneia; Minneapolis: Fortress, 1991), 152-53. The issues include the nature of their setting in life and the purpose therein, whether they were original to Amos, and

whether they were from a single source. Paul's judgment about these matters remains intact: "Scholarly disagreement still abounds." This brief exposition seeks to interpret them in their present context; as disjunctive as the oracles appear to be, they reveal the close link between judgment and creation we have observed in other texts. For the most thorough treatment of these texts, see Paas, *Creation and Judgement*, 183-326; for an earlier study, see James L. Crenshaw, *Hymnic Affirmations of Divine Justice: The Doxologies of Amos and Related Texts in the Old Testament* (SBLDS 24; Missoula, Mont.: Scholars, 1975). See also Hans Walter Wolff, *Joel and Amos* (Hermeneia; Philadelphia: Fortress, 1977), 215-17; Bruce Birch, *Hosea, Joel, and Amos* (Louisville: Westminster/John Knox, 1997), 209-10.

40. Crenshaw dates the texts after the fall of Jerusalem; in a time that "seemed to indicate Yahweh's impotence, the doxologies were an expression of faith in Yahweh" (*Hymnic Affirmations*, 143).

41. Walter Brueggemann, "Amos 4:4-13 and Israel's Covenant Worship," *VT* 15 (1965): 11. See also his *Theology of the Old Testament: Testimony, Dispute, Advocacy* (Minneapolis: Fortress, 1997), 152-53.

42. Paul, *Amos*, 143. So also Francis I. Andersen and David Noel Freedman, *Amos* (vol. 24A of the Anchor Bible; New York: Doubleday, 1989), 89-90; James Luther Mays, *Amos: A Commentary* (The Old Testament Library; Philadelphia: Westminster, 1969), 83-84; Paas stresses that creation themes lift up the freedom of God to enter into judgment and the "darker side of God's creative power" to "overturn the historical order of things and turn himself against his own people" (*Creation and Judgement*, 315, 323, 325, 434-36).

43. Jeremias, *Amos*, 79.

44. See the helpful comments by Frederick J. Gaiser, "Why Does It Rain? A Biblical Case Study in Divine Causality," *HBT* 25 (2003): esp. 3-10. The comment of Walter Brueggemann that "Yahweh may disrupt creation itself (famine, drought, blight and mildew, pestilence, and earthquake)" suggests no explicit linkage between Israel's disobedience and these effects in the natural order, only God's activity, no agent (*Theology*, 152).

45. See Paul, *Amos*, 167-70, for details.

46. See Jeremias, *Amos*, 91.

47. Parallels between this text and the doxologies are evident in the references to the rising and sinking of the Nile River in both 8:8 and 9:5 and the darkening of the daytime in 4:13; 5:8, and 8:10.

48. Paul cites evidence for solar eclipses in 784 and 763 B.C.E. (*Amos*, 262 n. 7).

49. See the end of this chapter.

50. Simkins, *Creator and Creation: Nature in the Worldview of Ancient Israel* (Peabody, Mass.: Hendrickson, 1994), 211.

51. See Fretheim, *Suffering of God*, 5-12.

52. A recent exception is Walter Brueggemann, "Jeremiah: Creatio in Extremis," in *God Who Creates: Essays in Honor of W. Sibley Towner* (ed. William P. Brown and S. Dean McBride Jr.; Grand Rapids: Eerdmans, 2000), 152-70.

53. These materials are drawn from two of my articles, "The Earth Story in Jeremiah 12," in *Readings from the Perspective of Earth* (ed. Norman C. Habel; Sheffield: Sheffield Academic Press, 2000), 96-110, and "The Character of God in Jeremiah." See also Brueggemann, *Jeremiah*; William Holladay, *Jeremiah 1* (Minneapolis: Fortress, 1986); William McKane, *A Critical and Exegetical Commentary on Jeremiah* (vol. 1; Edinburgh: T&T Clark, 1986); Jack R. Lundbom, *Jeremiah 1–20* (New York: Doubleday, 1999).

54. See ch. 8.

55. Brueggemann disputes the common claim that 4:23-26 is hyperbolic, for that "misses the cumulative intent of the rhetoric." The intent "is to imagine and invite the listener of the poem to host a scenario in which nothing reliable or life-sustaining is left. Creation theology here functions to voice a complete, unreserved, elemental negation of all that makes life livable" ("Creatio in Extremis," 156). Yet, while the text does voice the "real thing" about what will happen to the earth, it is not a literal description thereof, for 4:27 makes clear that Yahweh will not bring a full end.

56. See Abraham J. Heschel, *The Prophets* (New York: Harper & Row, 1982); Fretheim, *Suffering of God*; and Fretheim, "I Was Only a Little Angry."

57. For introductory matters relating to Jeremiah 12, see Fretheim, *Jeremiah*, 191-92. Scholars usually do not treat Jeremiah 12 as either a unit or a unity. Working with the present form of the book of Jeremiah, I consider the chapter as a whole as the unit with which to work. From the perspective of the speaker, Jeremiah 12 consists of two parts, Jeremiah's lament (vv. 1-4) and the divine response (vv. 5-17). I keep vv. 7-17 linked to vv. 1-6 and interpret them as a continuation of God's response to Jeremiah's lament, begun in v. 5. One good reason for this linkage pertains to the land; the concern for a land that mourns (vv. 4, 11) and for the land as heritage (vv. 7-9, 14-15) are interlocking themes. Jeremiah brings his lament to a climax in v. 4, not with a concern about himself (though that concern remains) but with an appeal on behalf of the land and its creatures ("How long?"). If v. 4 is the climactic point of Jeremiah's lament, focused finally on a concern about the land, the verse fits well with vv. 1-3 (it is, of course, quite possible for the wealthy to thrive in a time of drought). Comparably, God does not respond simply to Jeremiah's more personal issues (vv. 5-6); God also engages his concern about the present situation of the *land* (vv. 7-13) and its future (vv. 14-17). When vv. 7-17, with their focus on the land, are included in God's response to Jeremiah's lament, God does provide something of an "answer" to him in a way that vv. 5-6 alone do not.

58. Jeremiah's confessions/laments have spawned a considerable literature; how they are to be interpreted is much debated and the options cannot be considered here. For details, see A. R. Diamond, *The Confessions of Jeremiah in Context: Scenes of a Prophetic Drama* (Sheffield: Sheffield Academic Press, 1987); Kathleen M. O'Connor, *The Confessions of Jeremiah: Their Interpretation and Role in Chapters 1–25* (Atlanta: Scholars Press, 1988); Fretheim, *Jeremiah*, 187-89.

59. For a survey of prophetic texts that speak of the adverse effect of human sin on the land, see Carol J. Dempsey, *Hope Amid the Ruins: The Ethics of Israel's Prophets* (St. Louis: Chalice, 2000), 74-88. The texts she selects are: Isa 6:8-13; 13:9-13; 24; 33:7-9; 34:8-12; Jer 7:16-20; 12:4; 23:9-11; Hos 4:1-3; Joel 1:15-18; Amos 4:6-10; 8:4-8; Zeph 1:2-6. There is "a systemic connection between the oppression of people and the oppression of this land" (p. 87).

60. On this text, see Fretheim, *Suffering of God*, 66, 133-34, 157.

61. On this theme, see Norman C. Habel, *This Land Is Mine: Six Biblical Land Theologies* (Minneapolis: Fortress, 1995), 33-35, 75-96.

62. *House* refers to temple in 11:15, used with "beloved"; see also 23:11; 13:11.

63. So Brueggemann, *Jeremiah*, 122.

64. Ibid., 121.

65. They are called "shepherds" in 6:3; Israel's own shepherds/kings may also be in view (10:21; 23:1).

66. Heschel, *Prophets*, 112.

67. See the concluding section of this chapter.

68. Studies of creation in Second Isaiah include: Carroll Stuhlmueller, *Creative Redemption in Deutero-Isaiah* (Rome: Pontifical Biblical Institute, 1970); S. Lee, *Creation and Redemption in Isaiah 40–55* (Hong Kong: Alliance Bible Seminary, 1995); Richard J. Clifford, *Creation Accounts in the Ancient Near East and in the Bible* (Washington: Catholic Biblical Association, 1994); Ben C. Ollenburger, "Isaiah's Creation Theology," *ExAud* 3 (1987): 54-71; P. B. Harner, "Creating Faith in Deutero-Isaiah," *VT* 17 (1967): 298-306; Thomas W. Mann, "Stars, Sprouts, and Streams: The Creative Redeemer of Second Isaiah," in Brown and McBride, *God Who Creates*, 135-51; Millard C. Lind, "Monotheism, Power, and Justice: A Study in Isaiah 40–55," *CBQ* 46 (1984): 432-46.

69. The verbs, used nearly eighty times, are: *bārā'* (create, 16x); *'āsāh* (make, 24x); *yatsar* (form, 15x); *pā'al* (make, 3x); *nāṭah* (stretch out, 5x); *yāsad* (establish, 5x); *rāqa'* (spread out, 2x); *sāmah* (sprout, 5x); *kûn* (establish, 2x); *nāta'* (plant, 1x); *tāpah* (spread out, 48:13). See Goldingay's convenient listing of the uses of *bārā'* in Second Isaiah (*Israel's Gospel*, 78).

70. Mann, "Stars, Sprouts, and Streams," 136.

71. On the birthing imagery in Second Isaiah, see Leila Leah Bronner, "Gynomorphic Imagery in Exilic Isaiah (40–66)," *Dor le Dor* 12 (1983–1984): 70; M. I. Gruber, "The Motherhood of God in Second Isaiah," *Revue Biblique* 90 (1983): 351-59; K. P. Darr, "Like Warrior, Like Woman: Destruction and Deliverance in Isaiah 42:10-17," *CBQ* 49 (1987): 560-71. Given the explicit references to God as a mother birthing children, the texts which speak of God forming Israel in the womb are probably also to be so understood; that is, only God could be the mother of Israel in a *corporate* sense (44:2, 24). The reference to the servant being formed by God in the womb (49:5) seems to have an explicit earthly mother in mind (49:1); yet, God's act of forming in the womb would still have God involved in what would normally be a motherly activity.

72. Harner, "Creating Faith," 301.

73. On this point in Jeremiah, see Fretheim, *Jeremiah*, 444-46.

74. My colleague, Frederick Gaiser, pointed out to me that the bracketing verses (44:23 and 45:8) are both creation hymns.

75. Generally speaking, people may experience God without realizing it or being able to name the experience in proper ways.

76. Ben C. Ollenburger, *Zion, the City of the Great King: a Theological Symbol of the Jerusalem Cult* (Sheffield: JSOT Press, 1987), 156.

77. On issues of power in Second Isaiah as related to issues of agency, see Gaiser, "To Whom Then Will You Compare Me?" Yahweh in Isaiah 40–55 is "both warrior and shepherd. . . . It is not that sometimes God is strong and sometimes God is tender; God's strength is also God's tenderness, God's tenderness is also God's strength. In bringing these images together, the warrior image especially is sharply redefined" (p. 144; also p. 150). On images of God qualifying one another, see also my "Suffering God and Sovereign God in Exodus," *HBT* 1 (1989): 31-56.

78. Mann, "Stars, Sprouts, and Streams," in Brown and McBride, *God Who Creates*, 141.

79. Brevard S. Childs, *Biblical Theology of the Old and New Testaments: Theological Reflection on the Christian Bible* (London: SCM, 1992), 388 (emphasis mine).

80. See also Brueggemann's formulation: "The purpose of this testimony concerning the Creator is to assert (and so to establish) that Yahweh is the only God who has demonstrated power as Creator, and therefore the other gods merit no obedience or deference" (*Theology of the Old Testament*, 150).

81. Ibid., 159.

82. Lind, "Monotheism, Power, and Justice," 434-36.

83. See Mann, "Stars, Sprouts, and Streams," in Brown and McBride, *God Who Creates*, 140.

84. The specific language of power is relatively infrequent in Isaiah 40–55 (see 40:10; 42:13; 44:12; 49:26; 50:2). Frederick J. Gaiser ("To Whom Then Will You Compare Me?") helpfully points out the many striking images of God in Second Isaiah that qualify the usual understandings of power (e.g., mother, shepherd, servant, helper, friend, etc.). To this may be added that, while God works through powerful agents such as Cyrus, agents such as servant and herald, even Jerusalem, qualify the nature of that power.

85. This is especially emphasized by Lind, "Monotheism, Power and Justice." See the critique of Lind in William P. Brown, *The Ethos of the Cosmos: The Genesis of Moral Imagination in the Bible* (Grand Rapids: Eerdmans, 1999), 257-58.

86. Oftentimes *redemption* and *salvation* are simply considered synonyms, but the evidence (see below) suggests that *salvation* is a broader term within which *redemption* refers to God's specific actions on behalf of Israel.

87. Harner, "Creating Faith," 298.

88. Gerhard von Rad, *The Problem of the Hexateuch and Other Essays* (trans. E. W. Trueman Dicken; Edinburgh: Oliver & Boyd, 1965), 56, 63.

89. Von Rad's perspective has been seconded by Carroll Stuhlmueller, "The Theology of Creation in Second Isaias," CBQ 21(1959): 429-67.

90. At the same time, the issue is not whether Israel's creation faith is independent and self-contained; no article of Israel's faith can be so understood, nor can creation be made ancillary to history (contrary to Harner, "Creating Faith," 305).

91. Rolf Rendtorff, *Canon and Theology: Overtures to an Old Testament Theology* (ed. and trans. Margaret Kohl; Overtures to Biblical Theology, ed. Walter Brueggemann, et al.; Minneapolis: Fortress, 1993), 107-8. See Claus Westermann, *Elements of Old Testament Theology* (Atlanta: John Knox, 1982), 101-2; *Isaiah 40–66: A Commentary* (The Old Testament Library, ed. Peter Ackroyd, et al.; Philadelphia: Westminster, 1969), 25.

92. Mann, "Stars, Sprouts, and Streams," in Brown and McBride, *God Who Creates*, 142.

93. Ibid., 137; so also Brown, *Ethos*, 264. Cf. Westermann: Creation and redemption are "very closely connected: however, this must never be taken as meaning that, in whole or in part, the two merge. . . . He used this polarity to make his hearers remember that God's saving action upon his chosen people . . . was . . . an island within the mighty universe of God's work as creator" (*Isaiah 40–66*, 25).

94. For a discussion of Isa 45:7 as a reference to historical rather than cosmic events, see my "Divine Dependence" (pp. 6-7):

> The language of darkness and woe *(ra')* is not cosmic in orientation, but language typical in the prophets for *specific* (historical) divine judgments, whether against non-Israelites (perhaps especially in this context, see 47:5, 11) or Israel itself (commonly; e.g., Jer 32:42; see Isa 42:7). Israel's God is often the subject of verbs of judgment; "there is no other" god who is responsible. Yet, God's "creating" here is no *ex nihilo*, but action that gives specific shape to a situation of historical judgment (for other historical uses of *br'* in Isaiah 40–55, see Isa 41:20; 43:1, 7; 45:8; 48:7; 54:16).

On the *real power* of agents other than God in Isaiah 40–55, see Gaiser, "To Whom Then Will You Compare Me?"

95. Temporal distinctions in the use of creation language for Israel seem to be present in, say, 43:1, where the God "who created you" and "formed you" has now redeemed Israel.

96. Simkins, *Creator and Creation*, 110; he cites my "Reclamation of Creation," 357-59. See the discussion in ch. 4.

97. Ibid., 110 (emphasis mine).

98. Terence E. Fretheim, *Exodus* (Interpretation: A Biblical Commentary for Teaching and Preaching, ed. James Luther Mays; Louisville: Westminster John Knox, 1991), 168. A comparable use of creation language linked with (potentially) key historical events is also present in Pss 74:12-17; 77:11-20; 89:8-13; 135:5-11 (cf. Pss 80:8-18; 136).

99. Harner, "Creating Faith," 304; so also E. Haag, "Gott als Schopfer und Erloser in der Prophetie des Deuterojesaja," *Trierer Theologische Zeitschrift* 85 (1976): 193-213.

100. Hans-Jürgen Hermisson, *Studien zu Prophetie und Weisheit: Gesammelte Aufsatze* (ed. Jorg Barthel, Hanalore Jauss, and Klaus Koenen; Tubingen: Mohr Siebeck, 1998), 117-31, esp. 125-31.

101. For the discussion of identity of the "former things," see Frederick J. Gaiser, "'Remember the Former Things of Old': A New Look at Isaiah 46:3-13," in *All Things New: Essays in Honor of Roy A. Harrisville* (ed. Arland J. Hultgren, Donald H. Juel, and Jack Dean Kingsbury; Word and World Supplement Series 1; St. Paul: Word and World, 1992), 53-63. Ralph W. Klein plausibly suggests that at least some of these "former things" refer to past events more generally, including the fall of Jerusalem (*Israel in Exile: A Theological Interpretation* [Philadelphia: Fortress, 1979], 101). This is likely the case in Isa 46:8-9, where "former things" *are* to be remembered.

102. Childs, *Biblical Theology*, 109 (emphasis mine). In this same paragraph Childs makes explicit his approval of von Rad's perspective regarding the relationship of creation and redemption.

103. James K. Bruckner, *Implied Law in the Abraham Narrative: A Literary and Theological Analysis* (Sheffield: Sheffield Academic Press, 2001), 40-41. Bruckner also notes: "That the development of the idea or 'tradition' of creation and the composition of its texts came later as the result of a crisis in Israel's redemption history does not mitigate its role as the context, premise and firmament of the whole biblical text" (p. 41).

104. The word *soteriological*, though linguistically related to *salvation*, should be reserved for specific acts of redemption (or forgiveness). It is notable that the language of *salvation*, in both Testaments, is rarely used with sin as the object (see Matt 1:21); in such contexts *sin* is best understood as referring to the *effects* of sin.

105. Contrary to some commentators (e.g., Gowan, *Eschatology*, 97; Frank Moore Cross, "The Redemption of Nature," *PSB* 10 [1989]: 94-104), the language of "redemption" is used only for Israel, not for the natural order (cf. phrases such as "cosmic redemption" or "redemption of the natural world").

106. It is possible that a new heaven and new earth is included in God's purposes from the beginning, quite apart from sin. Such a perspective has been common among theologians through the centuries but seems not to have any explicit grounding in Old Testament texts.

107. Among the studies of eschatology and the natural order, see Simkins, *Creator and Creation*, 207-51; Gowan, *Eschatology*, 97-120. Gowan's entire

discussion is pertinent to the relationship of creation and eschatology; he also includes chapters on the transformation of human society and the human person.

108. See Gowan: "An element of threat to all that is stable and ordered (the 'chaotic') which can be felt lurking just beyond the edges of the normally dependable world that God has created" (*Eschatology*, 97).

109. Brown, *Ethos*, 232.

110. See Cross, "The Redemption of Nature," 97. See Gen 1:11-13 for calls to the creation to bring forth new life.

111. The concern for the earthy and tangible is also evident in the restoration of cities and their buildings (Isa 44:24-28; 45:13; 54:11-12; see 61:1-4; 65:21-22; Jer 30:18; 31:38-40; Ezek 36:10, 33-36).

112. See Gowan's discussion of the transformation of the human.

113. The Noachic covenant was a promise of God to "all flesh," but, given Gen 9:2-5, this does not entail a covenant of peace between human beings and the animals. While the "covenant of peace" refers to the God-Israel relationship in Ezek 37:26 (see Isa 54:10), and may do so here, the immediate references to various elements of the natural order (34:25-29) suggest a more comprehensive understanding. For discussion of the covenant of peace, see Simkins, *Creator and Creation*, 235-36.

114. Note that the covenant in Hos 2:18 does not include domestic animals, suggesting that the covenant is a kind of truce that will characterize the relationship between Israel and this animal world in such a way that violence between them is excluded, but not that violence among the animals is.

115. For a study of Isaiah 11 and its implications for creation theology, see Karl Löning and Erich Zenger, *To Begin with, God Created . . . : Biblical Theologies of Creation* (trans. Omar Kaste; Collegeville, Minn.: Liturgical Press, 2000), 173-81; Gene M. Tucker, "The Peaceable Kingdom and a Covenant with the Wild Animals," in Brown and McBride, *God Who Creates*, 215-25; W. Sibley Towner, "The Future of Nature," *Int* 50 (1996): 27-35. Whether 11:9 carries a universal perspective or only a local one ("holy mountain" refers to Zion or Israel) is uncertain, but the "earth" as a whole seems to be in view, with Zion as a microcosm for that world.

116. One unlikely suggestion is an allegorical interpretation, namely, that the animals are actually nations (Christopher R. Seitz, *Isaiah 1–39* [Louisville: Westminster John Knox, 1993], 106-7). For a critique, see Gene M. Tucker, "The Book of Isaiah 1–39" (vol. 6 of *The New Interpreter's Bible*; Nashville: Abingdon, 2001), 142-43.

117. Simkins, *Creator and Creation*, 226.

118. Gowan, *Eschatology*, 104.

119. Löning and Zenger suggest this interpretation when they speak of "a creation-theological utopia . . . how life in harmony with creation ought to look" (*To Begin with*, 176).

120. Brevard S. Childs correctly calls this a "new act of creation," but he

underestimates the links between this text and Gen 1:29-31; 3:15; and 9:2-5 (*Isaiah* [Louisville: Westminster, 2001], 104). These links do not have to be downplayed in order to speak of significant discontinuities between original and new creation.

7. *Wisdom and Creation*

1. We do not intend to introduce Wisdom literature here. For helpfully gathered introductions to Wisdom literature, see James L. Crenshaw, *Old Testament Wisdom: An Introduction* (rev. ed.; Louisville: Westminster/John Knox, 1998); Dianne Bergant, *Israel's Wisdom Literature: A Liberation-Critical Reading* (Minneapolis: Fortress, 1987); Athalya Brenner, *A Feminist Companion to Wisdom Literature* (Sheffield: Sheffield Academic Press, 1995); more briefly, see Leo G. Perdue, *Proverbs* (Louisville: Westminster/John Knox, 2000), 1-53 (in effect, summarizing his many works on wisdom). For an older, classic treatment of wisdom, see Gerhard von Rad, *Wisdom in Israel* (Nashville: Abingdon, 1972). For a specific treatment of wisdom and creation, see Leo G. Perdue, *Wisdom and Creation: The Theology of Wisdom Literature* (Nashville: Abingdon, 1994).

2. Brevard S. Childs overstates the matter when he says that wisdom "cannot be found through reason or by human cleverness. The way to wisdom is in the fear of the Lord" (*Old Testament Theology in a Canonical Context* [Philadelphia: Fortress, 1985], 35).

3. James L. Crenshaw, "Studies in Ancient Israelite Wisdom: Prolegomenon," in *Studies in Ancient Israelite Wisdom* (ed. James L. Crenshaw; New York: KTAV, 1976), 23.

4. For this distinction, see James K. Bruckner, *Implied Law in the Abraham Narrative: A Literary and Theological Analysis* (Sheffield: Sheffield Academic Press, 2001), 34-35.

5. Ibid., 35-36. Bruckner here follows the distinction of Childs between the "ontic" dimension of creation faith and the "noetic" dimension (*Biblical Theology in Crisis* [Philadelphia: Westminster, 1970], 110).

6. Crenshaw, for example, subordinates creation to theodicy as the centering issue for wisdom, especially in view of threats to life and well-being; "creation belongs under the rubric of justice. The function of creation theology . . . is to undergird the belief in divine justice" ("Ancient Israelite Wisdom," 34). To this Bruckner responds appropriately: creation is the "fundamental presupposition . . . the context and ground of the belief in divine justice presented in the wisdom texts" (*Implied Law*, 38).

7. Walther Zimmerli, "The Place and Limit of the Wisdom in the Framework of the Old Testament Theology," *SJT* 17 (1964): 148.

8. Roland E. Murphy, "Wisdom and Creation," *JBL* 104 (1985): 4.

9. Perdue, *Wisdom and Creation*, 35, 326, 340.

10. Perdue, *Proverbs*, 48. Having recognized that creation is the basic premise

and theological framework of the wisdom writers, the question arises as to what particular issue(s) within that framework center wisdom's reflections on creation. Perdue reviews several options: anthropology, cosmology, theodicy, and anthropology/cosmology; he identifies with the last noted in dialectical fashion (*Wisdom and Creation*, 35-46; idem, *The Collapse of History: Reconstructing Old Testament Theology* [Minneapolis: Fortress, 1994], 113-50). I think these "centers" or approaches are not as separable as Perdue suggests, not least because they are often closely linked and, more important, the distinction is not especially fruitful in the analysis of specific texts. The wisdom writers range widely across various dimensions of the topic of creation and the texts are best studied in recognition of their thematic interdependence.

11. Crenshaw, "Ancient Israelite Wisdom," 23. On the issue of "order," see discussion below.

12. This is an important theme stressed by Walter Brueggemann, *In Man We Trust* (Richmond: John Knox, 1972).

13. See the brief discussion in Perdue, *Proverbs*, 199.

14. Von Rad, *Wisdom in Israel*, 299.

15. Colin E. Gunton, "Christ, the Wisdom of God: A Study in Divine and Human Action," in *Where Shall Wisdom Be Found? Wisdom in the Bible, the Church and the Contemporary World* (ed. Stephen C. Barton; Old Testament Studies; Edinburgh: T&T Clark, 1999), 250.

16. Von Rad, *Wisdom in Israel*, 317.

17. Ibid., 301 (emphasis mine).

18. Ibid., 315 (emphasis mine).

19. Ibid., 313.

20. Hans-Jürgen Hermisson: "Creation is the basis not only of regularity, but of a meaningful and satisfactory order of events in the world, a purposefulness of created beings and things" ("Observations on the Creation Theology in Wisdom," in *Creation in the Old Testament* [ed. Bernard W. Anderson; Issues in Religion and Theology 6, ed. Douglas Knight and Robert Morgan; Philadelphia: Fortress, 1984], 121).

21. Perdue, *Proverbs*, 41.

22. Cf. Ps 19:1-6; God's voice is not spoken aloud but, nonetheless, is heard. See ch. 6.

23. Hermisson, "Creation Theology in Wisdom," in Anderson, *Creation in the Old Testament*, 119.

24. Albert Wolters, *Creation Regained: A Transforming View of the World* (Grand Rapids: Eerdmans, 1985), 28.

25. I owe this translation to my colleague Diane Jacobson.

26. Wolters, *Creation Regained*, 27 (emphasis mine).

27. The first-person address parallels divine speech in God's appearances in theophany (e.g., Gen 17:1-8).

28. Roland E. Murphy, "The Personification of Wisdom," in *Wisdom in Ancient*

Israel: Essays in Honor of J.A. Emerton (ed. John Day, et al.; Cambridge: Cambridge University Press, 1995), 226; see also in the same volume the essay by Judith Hadley, "Wisdom and the Goddess" (pp. 234-43).

29. On the importance of relationship in creation texts, see ch. 1.

30. The origins of the image of Woman Wisdom are unclear; see especially the discussion of Claudia V. Camp, *Wisdom and the Feminine in the Book of Proverbs* (Decatur: Almond Press, 1985); Michael V. Fox, *Proverbs 1–9: A New Translation with Introduction and Commentary* (vol. 18A of the Anchor Bible; New York: Doubleday, 2000), 331-45. Among the proposed models for wisdom are: prophet, messenger, angel, human women, wisdom teacher, the Egyptian *ma'at* (the world order), or no single view. Roots in goddess worship (such as Isis) have also been suggested, with a possible polemical edge.

31. Historical-cultural factors that occasioned speaking of wisdom in these terms are uncertain. The idea may have emerged at a time when emphasis on the transcendence of God led to the development of intermediaries (e.g., angels). Or, at a time when wisdom was suspect in theological circles, it was used to enhance wisdom's close relationship with God. For a review, see R. Norman Whybray, *Proverbs* (Grand Rapids: Eerdmans, 1994), 27-28.

32. To claim with Perdue that "Woman Wisdom intends to present the wisdom tradition as a metaphorical personification of a divine attribute" (*Proverbs*, 146) insufficiently recognizes the creatureliness of wisdom. Moreover, the God who birthed her could not be said to have been in need of wisdom and hence birthed more wisdom. The same critique would apply to the even stronger view of Murphy: Wisdom "is to be somehow identified with the Lord, as indicated by her very origins and her authority. . . . The call of Lady Wisdom is the voice of the Lord. She is, then, the revelation of God, not merely the self-revelation of creation" ("Wisdom and Creation," 9-10).

33. See Fox, *Proverbs 1–9*. Fox argues that, inasmuch as wisdom was created by God, "she did not exist from eternity. Wisdom is therefore an accidental attribute of godhead, not an essential or inherent one" (p. 279). But would this not mean that God is not eternally wise? A better direction to take is to find a way between wisdom as a divine attribute and wisdom as simply a creature.

34. Von Rad, *Wisdom in Israel*, 161-62.

35. See the discussion in Karl Löning and Erich Zenger, *To Begin with, God Created . . . : Biblical Theologies of Creation* (trans. Omar Kaste; Collegeville, Minn.: Liturgical Press, 2000), 62-63, 75.

36. For links with the Holy Spirit, see Acts 6:3, 10. The work of the Spirit moving over the face of the uncreated world in Gen 1:2 may be another way of speaking of Wisdom. For a study of later Jewish reflection on Wisdom and *Logos* in the Gospel of John, see Löning and Zenger, *To Begin with*, 65-95. For some of the complexities of these developments, see the discussion by Diane Jacobson, "Jesus as Wisdom in the New Testament," in *The Quest for Jesus and the Christian Faith* (ed. Frederick J. Gaiser; St. Paul: Luther Seminary, 1997).

37. Claudia V. Camp, "Woman Wisdom as Root Metaphor: A Theological Consideration," in *A Listening Heart: Essays in Wisdom and the Psalms in Honor of Roland E. Murphy* (ed. K. Hoglund; Sheffield: JSOT Press, 1987), 45. Camp speaks here of the woman, but her language is more generally applicable to human beings.

38. See Camp: "The transcendent otherness to which the metaphor Woman Wisdom refers is life in all of its relationality, with people, nature and God" ("Woman Wisdom," 65).

39. Among others, see Perdue, *Wisdom and Creation*, 46-47. Perdue stresses God's freedom as a factor that militates against a "legalistic" understanding of "order." Yet, God's freedom must be qualified in view of God's commitment to established relationships. Von Rad, while recognizing that the personal dimension of wisdom is indispensable, overstresses the theme of order: "great all-embracing order"; "ordering power"; "Wise orderliness"; "world order"; "primeval world order" (*Wisdom in Israel*, 154-56).

40. Camp, "Woman Wisdom," 65 (in agreement with Murphy, "Wisdom and Creation," 9).

41. See Murphy, "Personification of Wisdom," 226. But to say that wisdom "has assumed the burden of the covenant, fidelity to the Lord" is to overstate the links to Israel's historical traditions.

42. See Perdue, *Wisdom and Creation*, 48.

43. This theme relates to the elements of "disorder" that we have seen in Genesis 1–2, not least in the command to "subdue the earth" (Gen 1:28).

44. William P. Brown claims that "unlike the Priestly account of creation, Wisdom's litany does not depict an altogether perfect creation" (*The Ethos of the Cosmos: The Genesis of Moral Imagination in the Bible* [Grand Rapids: Eerdmans, 1999], 275). As we have sought to show, the priestly account does not depict a "perfect" creation, so the continuities with Proverbs 8 may be greater than Brown allows.

45. It is possible that the female form is particularly in mind; see Löning and Zenger: "The vivacious, wonderfully beautiful Lady Wisdom is in a certain sense a personified idea of creation that makes YHWH one who creates out of fascination—with the goal of copying her form in the artistic work of the creation" (*To Begin with*, 60). This feature may also be present in order to appeal to male readers.

46. Among the many who have worked with this issue, see Camp, "Woman Wisdom"; Silvia Schroer, *Wisdom Has Built Her House: Studies on the Figure of Sophia in the Bible* (Collegeville, Minn.: Liturgical Press, 2000), 17; Gale A. Yee, "The Theology of Creation in Proverbs 8:22-31," in *Creation in the Biblical Traditions* (ed. Richard J. Clifford and John J. Collins; Catholic Biblical Quarterly Monograph Series 24; Washington: Catholic Biblical Association, 1992), 85-96.

47. Camp, "Woman Wisdom," 45.

48. For a careful look at translation possibilities of Prov 8:22-31, see Brown, *Ethos*, 272-74.

49. The image of divine acquisition could be said to beg the question: from whom would God acquire such a figure? But birthing is an acquisition in its own right.

50. Helmer Ringgren, *Word and Wisdom: Studies in the Hypostatization of Divine Qualities and Functions in the Ancient Near East* (Lund: Ohlssons, 1947), 101.

51. See Yee, "Theology of Creation," in Clifford and Collins, *Creation in the Biblical Traditions*, 85-96; Brown, *Ethos*, 273. The most common meaning of this verb is "pour out" (a libation, Gen 35:14), which could be an indirect reference to the breaking of the water in birthing. See Perdue, *Proverbs*, 144. The sense of "set up" is rare (only Ps 2:6).

52. The link to these texts may be made closer if the verb in v. 23 is *skk*, "cover, weave."

53. See Yee, "Theology of Creation," 85, 90.

54. The claim is sometimes made that, inasmuch as God created her, Woman Wisdom is not a reference to divine immanence. See Camp, "Woman Wisdom," 58-59; Yee, "Theology of Creation," 90. But if Woman Wisdom is both creature and divine, both transcendence and immanence language is appropriate. Wisdom transcends creation but actively calls human beings from *within* creation. See Brown, *Ethos*, 278; Perdue, *Proverbs*, 9. Generally, God is present in and through creaturely means; one thinks of God's assuming human form in theophanic appearances (e.g., Exod 3:1-6).

55. Transcendence speaks of the otherness, not the distance of God, as Perdue tends to do; for him, transcendence refers to God "existing beyond time and space" (*Proverbs*, 37). See Fretheim: "The God who is present is *both* immanent and transcendent; both are appropriate words for a constant divine state of affairs. God is 'transcendent in relationship.' 'God remains transcendent in his immanence, and related in his transcendence'" (*Suffering of God*, 71). The phrases are from Paul R. Sponheim, "Transcendence in Relationship," *Di* 12 (1973): 264-71, and Abraham J. Heschel, *The Prophets* (New York: Harper & Row, 1982), 486.

56. The pervasiveness of the theme of life in Proverbs is remarkable.

57. Walter Brueggemann, *Theology of the Old Testament: Testimony, Dispute, Advocacy* (Minneapolis: Fortress, 1997), 346.

58. See ch. 2 for discussion of this passage.

59. See the discussion of relationship in ch. 1.

60. These images are combined with the image of God as lawmaker (v. 29), so that law is an integral dimension of God's creation (see Genesis 1–2). If the marking of boundaries for the sea has a mythological reference to primeval chaos (so Perdue, *Proverbs*, 144), it lies in the deep background of the passage.

61. Helpful connections between Proverbs 8 and Job (e.g., 15:7; 38:4-11, 21) have been drawn. Queries to Job, "where were you," are here contrasted with Woman Wisdom, "I was there." See, e.g., Dexter E. Callender Jr., *Adam in Myth and History: Ancient Israelite Perspectives on the Primal Human* (Winona Lake,

Ind.: Eisenbrauns, 2000), 191-200; Lennart Bostrom, *The God of the Sages: The Portrayal of God in the Book of Proverbs* (Stockholm: Almqvist and Wiksell, 1990), 54 n. 34.

62. R. C. Van Leeuwen, "The Book of Proverbs" (vol. 5 of *The New Interpreter's Bible*; Nashville: Abingdon, 1997), 92-93. But Van Leeuwen's further statement needs qualification: "Wisdom's knowledge of the cosmos . . . provides a stable point of reference by which to judge the new things that occur in human history and behavior." The word *stable* should not be understood in the sense of an immutable natural law. The liveliness of wisdom means an openness to the "new" that may cut against the grain of the old. See ch. 5 on law.

63. Cf. Num 11:12, a nursing child. Alternatively, Brown, *Ethos*, 274, translates it as a verb meaning "growing up," with further bibliography.

64. Ibid., 274 n. 14.

65. Ibid., 281-82.

66. So Van Leeuwen, "Proverbs," 94.

67. If "little child" be preferred, would this not entail changing the common nomenclature to Child Wisdom rather than Woman Wisdom? From some formulations, it does not appear that wisdom ever "grows up" in this text, even with the inhabited world (v. 31). See Brown, *Ethos*, 277-80; on p. 297, he speaks of wisdom having matured by 9:1. I would need a more explicit marker in the text to accept the suggestion that a double entendre is intended.

68. See Fox, *Proverbs*, 286-87.

69. See Brown, *Ethos*, 277-80.

70. The word *first* has reference to both first action (v. 22) and to temporal sequence: "at the first, before the beginning" (v. 23). The word *daily* (v. 30) assumes some passing of time, but the length is unclear (like the days of Genesis 1?). Verse 31, with its introduction to an inhabited world and the human race, assumes an even further passage of time. Both originating and continuing creation are in view, but the length of that time is uncertain. See Yee ("Theology of Creation," 93), who cites Hermisson ("Observations on the Creation," in Anderson, *Creation in the Old Testament*, 46-47) for support. Interpreters must be careful not to read modern understandings of the age of the earth into the text.

71. Brown, *Ethos*, 277.

72. Wolters works more fully with the architectural imagery of the passage, and thinks of the *'āmôn* as a blueprint or scale model which serves as a standard for God the builder (*Creation Regained*, 27). See also Fox, *Proverbs*, 286; Perdue thinks of wisdom as an imaginative architect, an "instrument of divine creativity" (*Proverbs*, 8-9).

73. So also Löning and Zenger, *To Begin with*, 57-64.

74. This interpretation would link up with the created cocreator theme in Genesis 1–2.

75. See ch. 2 for details.

76. On the relational model of creation, see ch. 1 and the Conclusion.

77. Gale Yee speaks helpfully on this point: through "the mediation of Woman Wisdom . . . God and humanity become co-creators in the ongoing task of keeping the created world order stable" ("Theology of Creation," 94). It would be important not to understand *stable* in unchanging terms. Human beings are involved by God in the kind of stability that entails change and the continuing becoming of the world.

78. Allen P. Ross, "Proverbs," in *Psalms, Proverbs, Ecclesiastes, Song of Songs* (vol. 5 of *The Expositor's Bible Commentary*, ed. Frank E. Gaebelein; Grand Rapids: Zondervan, 1991), 5:946. See Callender, *Adam in Myth and History*, 198 n. 393.

79. Yee, "Theology of Creation," 94.

80. See the section on God as Evaluator in ch. 2.

81. It is often noted that a widespread pattern in both ancient and modern cultures is an expression of joy at the completion of a construction project. So, e.g., van Leeuwen, "Proverbs," 95. But this text reports a rejoicing that does not wait for completion; it is expressed all along the way (so also Job 38:7).

82. See Fox, *Proverbs*, 288-89. Fox's emphasis that "Wisdom's play expresses the joy of intellect: exploring, thinking, learning" should not be stressed at the expense of other dimensions of a genuine relationship. Note also the importance that delight/pleasure has in Ps 119:14, 16, 24, 70, 77, 92, 143, 174. The psalmist takes pleasure in the law because of the way it gives shape to a life of joy and gladness.

83. Löning and Zenger speak helpfully of the image of God as an artist who forms the world "in a kind of euphoric creative 'high'" (*To Begin with*, 62).

84. Ringgren, *Word and Wisdom*, 55.

85. Von Rad, *Wisdom in Israel*, 156.

86. Ellen F. Davis, *Proverbs, Ecclesiastes, and the Song of Songs* (Louisville: Westminster/John Knox, 2000), 68.

87. Hermisson, "Observations on the Creation," in Anderson, *Creation in the Old Testament*, 122.

88. Von Rad, *Wisdom in Israel*, 311.

89. For a discussion of law and natural theology, as well as reflections on Psalm 19, see ch. 5.

90. Richard J. Clifford, *Creation Accounts in the Ancient Near East and in the Bible* (Catholic Biblical Quarterly Series 26; Washington, D.C.: Catholic Biblical Association of America, 1994), 184.

91. Perdue, *Wisdom and Creation*, 93.

92. Von Rad, *Wisdom in Israel*, 298.

93. Ibid., 165.

94. Ibid., 304.

95. See Camp, "Woman Wisdom," 60.

96. J. Gerald Janzen, "The Place of Job in the History of Israel's Religion," in *Ancient Israelite Religion: Essays in Honor of Frank Moore Cross* (ed. Patrick D. Miller, et al.; Philadelphia: Fortress, 1987), 528.

97. Crenshaw, "Ancient Israelite Wisdom," 31.

98. Among the many studies of Job, I have found these especially helpful in pursuing issues of God and creation: William P. Brown, *Character in Crisis: A Fresh Approach to the Wisdom Literature of the Old Testament* (Grand Rapids: Eerdmans, 1996); idem, *Ethos of the Cosmos*, 317-80; David J. A. Clines, *Job 1–20* (Dallas: Word, 1989); James L. Crenshaw, *Urgent Advice and Probing Questions: Collected Writings on Old Testament Wisdom* (Macon: Mercer, 1995); Norman C. Habel, *The Book of Job: A Commentary* (Philadelphia: Westminster, 1985); J. Gerald Janzen, *Job* (Atlanta: John Knox, 1987); Carol A. Newsom, "The Book of Job" (vol. 4 of *The New Interpreter's Bible*; Nashville: Abingdon, 1996); idem, *The Book of Job: A Contest of Moral Imaginations* (Oxford: Oxford University Press, 2003); Leo G. Perdue, *Wisdom in Revolt: Metaphorical Theology in the Book of Job* (Sheffield: Almond, 1991); Leo G. Perdue and W. Clark Gilpin, eds., *The Voice from the Whirlwind: Interpreting the Book of Job* (Nashville: Abingdon, 1992), especially the essay by Norman C. Habel, "In Defense of God the Sage" (pp. 21-38); Daniel J. Simundson, *The Message of Job* (Minneapolis: Augsburg, 1986); see also the essays in Norman C. Habel and Shirley Wurst, eds., *The Earth Story in Wisdom Traditions* (Sheffield: Sheffield Academic Press, 2001).

99. This section is a significantly revised version of my article, "God in the Book of Job," *CurTM* (1999): 85-93. This discussion is not a thoroughgoing treatment of all the issues raised by the book of Job; the focus is on issues raised regarding God and Creation. I read the book as a literary whole, recognizing that various portions of the book (prologue; ch. 28; the Elihu speeches; the epilogue) may not have been an original part of the book. The present form of the book is the only certain form of the book of which we are aware; all other proposed forms are speculation.

100. For discussion, see Newsom, *Book of Job*, 38-41.

101. Ibid., 234 (see also 17-31, 260-64). Newsom recognizes that the God speeches constitute a problem for this perspective. I would claim that readers need not understand that the God speeches "finalize what has gone before" (p. 235) to argue that they constitute the most decisive word on the subject, though not a word that recognizes no value in the other perspectives presented. To simply level the God speeches and, say, the speeches of Job's friends or the latter with Job's speeches, would be to claim too much ambiguity, especially given the amount of evaluation in the book. Newsom does not seem to do this, but is "without privilege" then fully accurate (pp. 19-20)? Newsom is to be commended for seeking the "good" in the speeches of the friends and Elihu.

102. Cf. Newsom, *Book of Job*, 20-21. Recognizing the ambiguity, God's word about the "rightness" of Job's speaking would stand *against* God's earlier judgment of Job's speaking ("words without knowledge," 38:2) only if there were a one-to-one correspondence in the content of the references, about which we are not informed one way or the other.

103. Habel, "In Defense of God," 33.

104. I find that many laypersons know the story in Job 1–2 best and, unfortunately, understand it in historical terms. The use made of Job in personal suffering situations is often drawn directly from such a historical interpretation of the prologue. Most commonly, for all too many people, this means that their suffering is due to a direct divine decision.

105. So Brown, *Character in Crisis*, 54-58.

106. To say that Job 2:3 reveals a divine pathos or remorse (Brown, *Character in Crisis*, 56) is not grounded in any specific textual reference (unlike the text Brown cites, namely, Gen 6:6).

107. A lack of textual grounding also holds for the claim that Job's (and Abraham's, Gen 22:1) testing is efficacious for the subsequent community of faith (so Brown, *Character in Crisis*, 57-58; similarly, Clines, *Job 1–20*). Such a view necessitates some historical basis for the test and, in addition, one wonders why Abraham's testing was not efficacious for Job!

108. See Newsom, "Book of Job," 360; Habel, "In Defense of God," 26.

109. The most convincing work on this point is that of Janzen, *Job*, 51-55.

110. Texts such as Deut 32:39 and Isa 45:7, where the "evil" refers to *judgment*, are not strictly parallel. On Isa 45:7, see my comments in ch. 6.

111. For details, see Janzen, *Job*, 51-55.

112. Cf. the narrator's strong claim regarding Job in 1:22; note also Job's concern about the state of his sons' "hearts" in 1:5.

113. Habel, "In Defense of God," 27 (emphasis mine).

114. James L. Crenshaw, "When Form and Content Clash: The Theology of Job 38:1–40:5," in Clifford and Collins, *Creation in the Biblical Traditions*, 71.

115. A fuller treatment of the dialogue and these creational texts and themes within it is called for.

116. Clifford, *Creation Accounts*, 185. Clifford's comments on the dialogue are brief but helpful.

117. Ibid., 186.

118. Ibid., 185.

119. For this and related texts, see William P. Brown, "*Creatio Corporis* and the Rhetoric of Defense in Job 10 and Psalm 139," in *God Who Creates: Essays in Honor of W. Sibley Towner* (ed. William P. Brown and S. Dean McBride Jr.; Grand Rapids: Eerdmans, 2000).

120. The text assigns this chapter to Job, but many interpreters think it continues the speech of Bildad (or is possibly the missing speech of Zophar). The outline is similar to Psalm 104.

121. On the significance of Job's prayers for both friends and God, see Samuel E. Balentine, "My Servant Job Shall Pray for You," *ThTo* 58 (2002): 502-18.

122. Some closure has been achieved in view of Dale Patrick's article, "The Translation of Job 42:6," *VT* 26 (1976): 369-71. See also the review of current translations of 42:6 in Carol A. Newsom, "Considering Job," *Currents in Research: Biblical Studies* 1 (1993): 111-12.

123. Jeremiah 8:6 may be an exception, but see NEB. For a full discussion of the use of this verb, see Terence E. Fretheim, "The Repentance of God: A Key to Evaluating Old Testament God-Talk," *HBT* 10 (1988): 47-70.

124. Janzen, *Job*, 251.

125. Especially to be noted is the imaginative discussion of Newsom, *Book of Job*, 234-58.

126. For detail on theophany, see Fretheim, *Suffering of God*, 79-106. Two types of theophanies are commonly recognized, "Theophanies of God as Warrior" and "Theophanies of God as Bearer of the Word." Inasmuch as God speaks no word in the former type of theophany, this appearance to Job needs to be linked to the latter. Hence, and including other factors, God does not appear here as a warrior, contrary to Leo G. Perdue, *Wisdom in Revolt: Metaphorical Theology in the Book of Job* (Sheffield: Almond, 1991), 232.

127. Contrary to Athalya Brenner, "God's Answer to Job," *VT* 31 (1981): 132; Perdue, *Wisdom in Revolt*, 202.

128. See Crenshaw, "When Form and Content Clash," 81.

129. Ibid., 71

130. Von Rad, *Wisdom in Israel*, 225.

131. Crenshaw, "When Form and Content Clash," 76.

132. Cf. ibid., 75.

133. NRSV "counsel" is better translated "design." The most basic issue addressed in these speeches is the divine design of the created order of things and its implications for the interpretation of suffering.

134. A helpful analysis of "suffering as becoming," that recognizes that suffering is commonly a human experience quite apart from sin and evil, is that of Douglas John Hall, *God and Human Suffering* (Minneapolis: Augsburg, 1986), 49-71.

135. My interpretation of this text has been helpfully informed by a course paper by student Abigail Pelham, "The Best of All Possible Worlds Is Not a Harmless World: Yahweh's Order of Creation in Job 38–41." Newsom thinks the second speech "says nothing new. Since Job appears to be hard of hearing, God simply repeats the message, louder and more slowly" (*Book of Job*, 248).

136. Crenshaw, "When Form and Content Clash," 76.

137. E. Good, "Job and the Literary Task: A Response," *Soundings* 56 (1973): 481.

138. See discussion in ch. 2.

139. Janzen, *Job*, 244.

140. Contrary to Habel, *Book of Job*, 558-61.

141. Contrary to Perdue, *Wisdom and Creation*, 179.

142. Newsom offers another translation of v. 19*b*, "made to dominate his companions" (*Book of Job*, 250). Yet, with my interpretation, a more traditional translation (NRSV) can be maintained without speaking against her overall understanding of the Behemoth text.

143. Contrary to Perdue, *Wisdom in Creation*, 174. I agree with Newsom (*Book of Job*, 243-44, 248-52) that there "is little or no reference to enmity or hostility between God and these creatures" (p. 249). Comparably, Kathleen M. O'Connor: "If the ancient combat myth of creation lurks here, it has been seriously defanged. . . . this text is not about battle, nor conflict, nor hostility with God, nor primarily about Job's inability to conquer these creatures. It is about God's pleasure in their beautiful wildness" ("Wild, Raging Creativity: The Scene in the Whirlwind (Job 38–41)," in *A God So Near: Essays on Old Testament Theology in Honor of Patrick D. Miller* [ed. Brent A. Strawn and Nancy R. Bowen; Winona Lake, Ind.: Eisenbrauns, 2003], 176-77).

144. Cf. the formulation of Newsom: "God's identification with the chaotic is as strong as with the symbols of order" (*Book of Job*, 252).

145. See discussion in ch. 2.

146. Newsom speaks of Job's lack of perspective regarding the divine design as due to the "human rage for order" and, somewhat differently, "the human passion for rendering the world rationally transparent" (*Book of Job*, 252-53). It should be noted that a "rage for order" can be profoundly irrational. Her perspective seems to interpret the God speeches as primarily a criticism of Job, with no significant positive word about the creational perspective presented by God for Job's understanding of his suffering. Newsom seems to me not to recognize sufficiently that the God speeches do address themselves to the question *why* (see p. 256); the "aesthetic experience," however important for Job, does not overwhelm an appropriate role for "rational judgment" (pp. 19-20) or, in Job's words, "knowing" and "understanding" (42:2-3). Some very important things can be said—and God does say them—about the "whence" of (innocent) suffering, but not in such a way that arrives at an "explanation," where no questions remain. We can agree that "the final word can never be spoken" (p. 30), that the book insists that the questions not be closed down (see below), but an important advance in understanding can be made short of finalization or "the truth" (p. 26). See my "To Say Something—About God, Suffering, and Evil," *WW* 19 (1999): 339, 346-50.

147. Crenshaw, "When Form and Content Clash," 72.

148. Ibid., 76.

149. Clifford, *Creation Accounts*, 197.

150. Crenshaw, "When Form and Content Clash," 77.

151. Ellen F. Davis, *Getting Involved with God: Rediscovering the Old Testament* (Cambridge, Mass.: Cowley, 2001), 139. The word *aesthetic*, while helpful, may not sufficiently get to the heart of things if it entails only a point about beauty and diversity. Such a divine creational preference also has implications regarding the importance for God that such diverse creatures be given the freedom to be what they were created to be and not tightly controlled within a creational "system."

152. Annie Dillard, *Pilgrim at Tinker Creek* (New York: Harper & Row, 1974), 136-37.

153. Crenshaw, "When Form and Content Clash," 74.

154. Crenshaw suggests that the speeches may reflect an educational setting in which belittling and nagging were a part of the educational process (Ibid., 78-79).

155. Crenshaw suggests that one vision of the animal world presented is that "might makes right," as the stronger prey on the weak (e.g., lion, hawk, vulture). He asks whether readers are being invited to think in similar terms about the human world when faced with divine power.

156. Crenshaw, "When Form and Content Clash," 74-75.

157. Ibid., 84.

158. That 42:7 does not simply refer to the words of Job in 42:1-6 but to all of his words is shown by God's negative evaluation of the friends' speeches that reaches back to ch. 25, their last word, and earlier. It might be said that the positive evaluation of 42:7, in effect, declares the rightness of the lament tradition in which Job stands.

159. See Brown, *Ethos of the Cosmos*, 338-41.

160. Samuel E. Balentine, "'What Are Human Beings, That You Make So Much of Them?' Divine Disclosure from the Whirlwind: 'Look at Behemoth,'" in *God in the Fray: A Tribute to Walter Brueggemann* (ed. Tod Linafelt and Timothy K. Beal; Minneapolis: Fortress, 1998), 265.

161. Brown, *Ethos of the Cosmos*, 341. Brown's use of the phrase "blustery discharge" in this context is unfortunate for "bluster" often carries the sense of pomposity and given to making empty charges or threats.

162. Brown, *Character in Crisis*, 103.

163. See Janzen, *Job*, 225-30; Habel, "In Defense of God," 33.

164. Janzen, "Place of Job," 529. He draws links with Second Isaiah regarding mortal human beings who are given a vocation in and through suffering (Isa 40:6-8; 41:14; 55:1-5; 52:13–53:12). See Mark 10:35-45.

165. Ibid., 534. Janzen's use of the language of royalty needs to be understood in terms of what a king *does* and who a king *is* (see the discussion in ch. 2).

166. So Janzen, "Creation and the Human Predicament in Job 1:9-11 and 38–41," *ExAud* 3 (1987): 52-53. Such a view stands in sharp contrast to that of Crenshaw: the absence of reference to the human is a "shattering of every human illusion of occupying a special place in God's sight" ("When Form and Content Clash," 70) and "gives resounding testimony to Job's littleness" (p. 74). Finally, it seems to me that Job 38–41 stands with Psalm 8 in its recognition of the special place of the human.

167. Habel, "In Defense of God," 38.

168. O'Connor suggests that interpreters shift from a focus on the interrogative aspects of God's questions to Job to "the *content* of the questions, the *subject* about which Job is ignorant" ("Wild, Raging Creativity," 174).

169. This dimension of the God speeches is insufficiently recognized in Newsom's claim that the God speeches "lift up the theme of human incapacity in the face of an overwhelming divine capacity" (*Book of Job*, 241). Her repeated

use of the language of the "unknowable" (and human "powerlessness") is better stated in the phrase "ultimately unknowable" (pp. 242-43). O'Connor shows that, in the questions regarding the animals (38:39–40:30), God is not saying to Job: "I can do this, but you cannot." The basic point is that the animals are free to be what they were created to be apart from *both* human and divine control ("Wild, Raging Creativity," 175).

170. For a brief and succinct statement, see John Polkinghorne, *Quarks, Chaos, and Christianity: Questions to Science and Religion* (New York: Crossroad, 1994), 40-47. See also the clear and direct statement by Philip Clayton, "Emerging God: Theology for a Complex Universe," CC 121 (2004): 26-30.

171. See the helpful question asked by Frederick J. Gaiser: If it "darkens counsel" to ask seriously about the rain (and other natural events, such as occasioned Job's suffering), "whence all the various insights that mark God's own speech in Job 38? . . . even the 'primitive' notions betray an interest in the aetiology or mechanism(s) of rain, and the chapter also makes relatively 'enlightened' observations about the wondrous relation between water and ice (38:29-30) and clouds and rain (38:34)" ("Why Does It Rain? A Biblical Case Study in Divine Causality," *HBT* 25 [2003], 2).

172. See Habel, "In Defense of God," 35.

173. Janzen, "Creation and the Human Predicament," 53.

174. Newsom lifts up this dimension of the God speeches ("Book of Job").

8. *Nature's Praise of God*

1. Of the many studies of creation in the Psalms, see Patrick D. Miller, "The Poetry of Creation: Psalm 104," in *God Who Creates: Essays in Honor of W. Sibley Towner* (ed. William P. Brown and S. Dean McBride Jr.; Grand Rapids: Eerdmans, 2000), 87-103; Jon D. Levenson, *Creation and the Persistence of Evil: The Jewish Drama of Divine Omnipotence* (San Francisco: Harper & Row, 1988), 53-65; Karl Löning and Erich Zenger, *To Begin with, God Created . . . : Biblical Theologies of Creation* (trans. Omar Kaste; Collegeville, Minn.: Liturgical Press, 2000), 32-44; Odil Hannes Steck, *World and Environment* (Nashville: Abingdon, 1980), 78-89; Richard J. Clifford, "The Hebrew Scriptures and the Theology of Creation," *TS* 46 (1985): 512-16; James L. Mays, " 'Maker of Heaven and Earth': Creation in the Psalms," in Brown and McBride, *God Who Creates*, 75-86; John Goldingay, *Israel's Gospel* (vol. 1 of *Old Testament Theology*; Downer's Grove, Ill.: InterVarsity, 2003), throughout pp. 42-192; James Limburg, "Who Cares for the Earth? Psalm Eight and the Environment," in *All Things New: Essays in Honor of Roy A. Harrisville* (ed. Arland J. Hultgren, Donald H. Juel, and Jack Dean Kingsbury; Word and World Supplement Series 1; St. Paul: Word and World, 1992); idem, "Down to Earth Theology: Psalm 104 and the Environment," *CurTM* 21 (1994): 340-46; idem, "Quoth the Raven: Psalm 147 and the Environment," in *A God So Near: Essays on Old Testament Theology in Honor of Patrick D. Miller* (ed. Brent A.

Strawn and Nancy R. Bowen; Winona Lake, Ind.: Eisenbrauns, 2003), 101-11. See also the several psalm studies in Norman C. Habel, *The Earth Story in the Psalms and the Prophets* (Sheffield: Sheffield Academic Press, 2001).

2. Psalm 104:31*b*, "may the LORD rejoice in his works," may witness to God entering into the praise as well.

3. References to creation are frequent and occur in many types of psalms; among the more extensive texts are Pss 65:6-13; 74:12-17; 77:11-21; 89:5-13; 93:1-4; 136:1-9.

4. See the chart at the end of this chapter; almost all the texts are in Psalms or Second Isaiah. This chapter is an adaptation of my article, "Nature's Praise of God in the Psalms," *ExAud* 3 (1987): 16-30; in this chapter I use the word *nature* to refer to the nonhuman world.

5. H. Paul Santmire *The Travail of Nature: The Ambiguous Ecological Promise of Christian Theology* (Philadelphia: Fortress, 1985), 198-99. Regarding the theme of nature more generally, see the monographs of Ronald A. Simkins, *Creator and Creation: Nature in the Worldview of Ancient Israel* (Peabody, Mass.: Hendrickson, 1994); Luis I. J. Stadelmann, *The Hebrew Conception of the World: A Philological and Literary Study* (Rome: Pontifical Biblical Institute, 1970); Theodore Hiebert, *The Yahwist's Landscape: Nature and Religion in Early Israel* (New York: Oxford University Press, 1996). A number of articles have been published, e.g., Theodore Hiebert, "Re-Imagining Nature: Shifts in Biblical Interpretation," *Int* 50 (1996); Gene M. Tucker, "Creation and the Limits of the World," *HBT* 15 (1993): 105-18; idem, "Rain on a Land Where No One Lives: The Hebrew Bible on the Environment," *JBL* 116 (1997): 3-17; J. Rogerson, "The OT View of Nature: Some Preliminary Questions," *OtSt* 20 (1977): 67-84; Klaus Koch, "The Old Testament View of Nature," in *Anticipation* 25 (1979): 47-52; Jeanne Kay, "Concepts of Nature in the Hebrew Bible," *Environmental Ethics* 10 (1988): 309-27.

6. Emil Brunner, *Revelation and Reason* (Philadelphia: Westminster, 1946), 33n.

7. Cf. S. M. Daecke, "Profane and Sacramental Views of Nature," in *The Sciences and Theology in the Twentieth Century* (ed. Arthur R. Peacocke; Notre Dame, Ind.: University of Notre Dame Press, 1981).

8. As a consequence, biblical-theological study has tended to abandon the study of nature to the sciences.

9. See discussion of relationships in ch. 1. Cf. Steck, *World and Environment*, 18-23.

10. Cf. the comment of Thomas F. Torrance: In approaching the world of nature "we have to think in a dimension of ontological depth in which the surface of things is coordinated with a deep, invisible, intelligible structure. . . . Really to know is to be in touch with a depth of reality, which has the capacity for disclosure beyond what we can anticipate or imagine" (*Transformation and Convergence in the Frame of Knowledge* [Grand Rapids: Eerdmans, 1984], 253). Cf. also Arthur R. Peacocke, *Creation and the World of Science* (Oxford: Oxford University Press, 1979), vii-viii and passim.

11. For the history of Christian thought, see Santmire, *Travail of Nature*. See also his "Toward a New Theology of Nature," *Di 25* (1986): 43-50; Claude Y. Stewart Jr., *Nature in Grace: A Study in the Theology of Nature* (Macon: Mercer University Press, 1983).

12. Quoted in Warren Lewis, *Witnesses to the Holy Spirit* (Valley Forge: Judson Press, 1978), 156-57.

13. Quoted in Santmire, *Travail of Nature*, 129-30.

14. E.g., Albertus Magnus and Hugh of St. Victor. Cf. J. M. Neale, *A Commentary on the Psalms* (vol. 4; London: Joseph Masters, 1883), 427.

15. W. O. E. Oesterley, *The Psalms* (London: SPCK, 1939), 584.

16. J. Christiaan Beker considers this psalm to be central in Paul's theology (*Paul the Apostle: The Triumph of God in Life and Thought* [Philadelphia: Fortress, 1980]).

17. Neale, *Commentary on the Psalms*, 427.

18. Cf. P. Craigie, *Psalms 1–50* (Waco: Word, 1983), 181.

19. James Barr, "Man and Nature: The Ecological Controversy and the Old Testament," *BJRL* 55 (1972), citing W. G. Lambert, *Babylonian Wisdom Literature* (Oxford: Oxford University Press, 1960), 1-20.

20. Stadelmann, *Hebrew Conception of the World*, 94.

21. Ibid., 7.

22. Hermann Gunkel, *Die Psalmen* (5th ed.; Göttingen: Vandenhoeck & Ruprecht, 1968), 618. This is quoted with approval by Delbert Hillers, "Study of Psalm 148," *CBQ* 40 (1978): 334.

23. H. Wheeler Robinson, *Inspiration and Revelation in the Old Testament* (Oxford: Clarendon, 1946). Eric Charles Rust follows Robinson on these matters (*Nature and Man in Biblical Thought* [London: Lutterworth, 1953]). See also C. Bonifazi, "Biblical Roots of an Ecologic Conscience," in *This Little Planet* (ed. Michael Hamilton; New York: Scribner, 1970), 203-33.

24. Robinson, *Inspiration and Revelation*, 12, 15-16, 47. It is probable that Robinson is somewhat dependent on Johannes Pedersen's *Israel: Its Life and Culture* (vol. 2; London: Oxford University Press, 1926) for some of these perspectives (see p. 479).

25. Henri Frankfort, et al., *The Intellectual Adventure of Ancient Man: An Essay on Speculative Thought in the Ancient Near East* (Chicago: University of Chicago Press, 1946).

26. Ibid., 4.

27. Ibid., 5. Cf. J. Rogerson, *Myth in OT Interpretation* (Berlin: de Gruyter, 1974), 96.

28. Thorkild Jacobsen, "Mesopotamia," in Frankfort, *Intellectual Adventure of Ancient Man*, 130-34.

29. Ibid, 134. Rogerson shows that the Frankforts are dependent upon the work of Ernst Cassirer and questions some of their methods. He notes particularly some of the differences between Jacobsen and the Frankforts, especially the former's distinction between the force in and behind the reality and the reality

itself. Finally, though, Rogerson does not consider himself in a position to judge the validity of Jacobsen's material (*Myth*, 86, 94), nor am I.

30. G. Ernest Wright, *The Old Testament against Its Environment* (London: SCM, 1950), 36; cf. p. 17; Walther Eichrodt, *Theology of the Old Testament* (vol. 2; Philadelphia: Westminster, 1958), 152. Israel did make important distinctions among the elements of the natural order. There is no suggestion, e.g., that rocks and animals were considered equally imbued with energies. Yet, the use of *nepeš* ("life," "living being") only for animals and human beings does not imply that nothing else in creation was considered alive. The land *('ădāmāh)* is understood to be alive, with plants reproducing according to their kind and the waters bringing forth living creatures (cf. Genesis 1). The natural order is not understood to be passive; it shares in God's creative activity (see Gen 1:11-13).

31. Artur Weiser, *Psalms: A Commentary* (Philadelphia: Westminster, 1962), 639; Eichrodt, *Theology of the Old Testament*, 2:153.

32. Leslie C. Allen, *Psalms 101–150* (Word Biblical Commentary 21, ed. David A. Hubbard and Glenn W. Barker; Waco: Word, 1983), 316.

33. Kenneth Schmitz, "World and Word in Theophany," in *Faith and Philosophy* 1 (1984): 56.

34. For a discussion of metaphor, see Terence E. Fretheim, *The Suffering of God: An Old Testament Perspective* (Overtures to Biblical Theology, ed. Walter Brueggemann, et al.; Philadelphia: Fortress, 1984), 5-12.

35. Cf. Allen, *Psalms 101–150*, 316.

36. Cf. A. A. Anderson, *The Book of Psalms* (vol. 2; London: Oliphants, 1972), 950.

37. This is consonant with Patrick D. Miller's understanding of hymns as both expressing and evoking praise, as language to God and about God; see his *Interpreting the Psalms* (Philadelphia: Fortress, 1986), 64, 69.

38. Ibid., 66.

39. S. Mowinckel, *The Psalms in Israel's Worship* (vol. 1; New York: Abingdon, 1962), 88; cf. p. 81.

40. Hillers, "Study of Psalm 148," 323-34.

41. Gerhard von Rad, *The Problem of the Hexateuch and Other Essays* (Edinburgh: Oliver & Boyd, 1966), 281-91.

42. Hillers, "Study of Psalm 148," 333.

43. Walter Beyerlin, *Near Eastern Religious Texts Relating to the Old Testament* (The Old Testament Library, ed. Peter Ackroyd, et al.; Philadelphia: Westminster, 1978), 20, 22.

44. Note that the reference to "his majesty" (i.e., the pharaoh) may well parallel the concluding reference to Israel in Ps 148:14.

45. See the discussion of theophany in Fretheim, *Suffering of God*, 79-106; Simkins, *Creator and Creation*, 128-52.

46. Fundamental continuities with the Christian understanding of Incarnation and the Sacraments might also be explored here.

47. See ch. 2 for discussion.

48. See H. Paul Santmire, "The Liberation of Nature: Lynn White's Challenge Anew," CC 102 (1985): 530-33. Cf. George M. Landes, "Creation and Liberation," *USQR* 33 (1978): 80.

49. C. Bruce Malchow, "Nature from God's Perspective: Job 38–39," *Di* 21 (1982): 130-33.

50. Koch, "Old Testament View of Nature," 47-49.

51. Martin Buber, *I and Thou* (Edinburgh: T&T Clark, 1937), 7-8.

52. On the importance of a relational ontology, see Douglas John Hall, *Imaging God: Dominion as Stewardship* (Grand Rapids: Eerdmans, 1986), 134 and passim. Cf. Joseph Sittler, "Ecological Commitment as Theological Responsibility," *Zygon* 5 (1970): 174; J. Cobb, "Process Theology and Environmental Issues," *JR* 60 (1980): 440-58.

53. At the same time it is clear that Israel was not so ignorant of "scientific" causes that they attributed natural activity to God alone while we today would express the same in more "natural" terms. Cf. J. Rogerson, "OT View of Nature"; P. Addinall, "Walter Eichrodt and the Old Testament View of Nature," *ExpTim* 92 (1981): 174-78. Because of the infancy in Israel's understanding of the natural world, it is probable that it understood certain natural events (e.g., eclipses) as more God-related than we would. Yet, Genesis 1, Jer. 8:7, etc., indicate that Israel had considerable practical knowledge about the regularities of the life of nature (cf. Gen 8:22). See Frederick J. Gaiser, "Why Does It Rain? A Biblical Case Study in Divine Causality," *HBT* 25 (2003): 1-18.

54. On creation in Second Isaiah, see ch. 6. Cf. Claus Westermann, *Isaiah 40–66: A Commentary* (Philadelphia: Westminster, 1969), 103, 144.

55. It is uncertain whether one should include in this tradition the talking snake in paradise, Balaam's ass, Jotham's trees, Elijah's ravens, and Jonah's repentant animals.

56. One text may witness to a different perspective (Isa 24:20). For a general discussion of the issue, see H. Paul Santmire, *Brother Earth: Nature, God, and Ecology in Time of Crisis* (New York: Thomas Nelson, 1970). Bruce Malchow believes that two contradictory views of nature are present in the Old Testament ("Contrasting Views of Nature in the Hebrew Bible," *Di* 25 [1986]: 40-43). One sees nature as "having been corrupted through human sin so that redemption is possible only in the eschaton. The other point of view sees nature as not having been decisively perverted by sin but as remaining good." It is not made clear wherein the "contradiction" lies, however. It seems to me that both perspectives have been integrated with one another into one understanding of nature as good and valuable and yet adversely affected by human sinfulness and in need of redemption.

57. On these texts and the issue of natural law, see ch. 5.

58. See "Let All Things Now Living," *Lutheran Book of Worship* (Minneapolis: Augsburg, 1978), no. 557. It is striking the extent to which nature's praise of God has been incorporated into the hymnody of the people of God. For a striking

paraphrase of Psalm 148, see *Lutheran Book of Worship*, no. 558, "Earth and All Stars!"

59. See Daniel W. Hardy and David F. Ford, *Praising and Knowing God* (Philadelphia: Westminster, 1985), 82.

60. This prominent theme should probably be related to nature's praise. All of God's creatures witness to God's love and faithfulness. See especially Ps 136:5-9, 25; Job 38–41; Jer 31:35-37; 33:19-26.

61. Cf. Allen, *Psalms, 101–50*, 312-13.

62. Gerard Manley Hopkins, "God's Grandeur," in *The Oxford Book of Christian Verse* (ed. Lord David Cecil; Oxford: Oxford University Press, 1940). For a discussion of Hopkins's earthy theology, see N. Scott Jr., "The Poetry and Theology of Earth: Reflections on the Testimony of Gerard Manley Hopkins and Joseph Sittler," *JR* 54 (1975): 102-23.

Conclusion: Implications of a Relational Theology of Creation

1. For clear reflections on this issue, see especially H. Paul Santmire, "Partnership with Nature according to the Scriptures: Beyond the Theology of Stewardship," *CSR* 32 (2003): 381-412, esp. 400-412.

2. For example, Bernhard W. Anderson states that a "doctrine of creation . . . is preeminently an affirmation about the sovereignty of God and the absolute dependence of all creatures" (*From Creation to New Creation: Old Testament Perspectives* [Overtures to Biblical Theology, ed. Walter Brueggemann, et al.; Minneapolis: Fortress, 1994], 28). Such a "radical" dependence suggests that creatures are not given sufficient gifts to care for themselves, to be what they were created to be.

3. For an earlier version of these initial reflections, see Terence E. Fretheim, "Creator, Creature, and Co-Creator in Genesis 1–2," in *All Things New: Essays in Honor of Roy A. Harrisville* (ed. Arland J. Hultgren, Donald H. Juel, and Jack Dean Kingsbury; Word and World Supplement Series 1; St. Paul: Word and World, 1992); on these themes, see Michael Welker, "What Is Creation? Rereading Genesis 1 and 2," *ThTo* 47 (1991): 56-71.

4. One could caricature the language of dependence by speaking of "codependence," but that understanding is not a necessary move from the use of this language. See my "Divine Dependence upon the Human: An Old Testment Perspective," *ExAud* 13 (1997).

5. Welker, "What Is Creation?" 64.

6. On God's use of agents, see Frederick J. Gaiser, "To Whom Then Will You Compare Me? Agency in Second Isaiah," *WW* 19 (1999): 141-52.

7. On the importance of balancing images of sovereignty with other images of God, see my "Suffering God and Sovereign God in Exodus," *HBT* 11 (1989): 31-56.

8. See John Sanders, *The God Who Risks* (Downer's Grove, Ill.: InterVarsity Press, 1998).

9. Vocation obviously involves relationships among human beings as well as among nonhuman creatures, but that would entail a larger project.

10. Douglas John Hall, *The Steward: A Biblical Symbol Come of Age* (Grand Rapids: Eerdmans, 1990) remains the best theological work on this topic.

11. For example, Norman C. Habel, "Stewardship, Partnership and Kinship," in *Lutheran World Federation Studies: A Just Asia* (ed. Viggo Mortensen; Geneva: Lutheran World Federation, 1998), 45-74; idem, *Readings from the Perspective of Earth* (Sheffield: Sheffield Academic Press, 2000), 50-51; Kathryn Tanner, "Creation, Environmental Crisis, and Ecological Justice," in *Reconstructing Christian Theology* (ed. R. Chopp and M. Taylor; Minneapolis: Fortress, 1994), 99-123; Santmire, "Partnership with Nature." Santmire suggests that the parable of the unjust steward in Luke 16 has shaped a "default meaning of stewardship in the popular mind of the Church, baptized, as it were, with the authority of Jesus: *we are called [to] do whatever it takes to manage the absent owner's resources as productively as we can*" (p. 384 n. 5). He notes that the NRSV translators changed the RSV "steward" to "manager" in this text. He also notes (p. 385 n. 6) that the word *partner* as used by Habel in *Readings from the Perspective of Earth* is closely associated with the word *custodianship*, which though defined as "mutual partnership," carries too much of the freight of stewardship.

12. See ch. 8.

13. It should also be noted that for Walter Brueggemann the word *partner* is an important construct and frames a major section of his *Theology*, with chapters that speak of Israel, the human person, the nations, and creation as Yahweh's partners (*Theology of the Olf Testament: Testimony, Dispute, Advocacy* [Minneapolis: Fortress, 1997], 407-564). As far as I can tell, he does not use the word to refer to the relationship between human beings and nonhuman creatures.

14. Santmire, "Partnership with Nature," 385.

15. Ibid., 411.

16. Steck, *World and Environment*, 199. Steck goes on to say, "*even less is man the partner of Yahweh the creator*," because he is created and (only?) dependent. Might one say "created partner"?

17. Ellen F. Davis, *Getting Involved with God: Rediscovering the Old Testament* (Cambridge, Mass.: Cowley, 2001), 192.

18. Ibid., 193.

19. Ibid., 194. Davis also points out that the verb *keep* is related to the care of the less fortunate and the vulnerable in the sense of "watch over" (see Pss 16:1; 17:8; 86:2). And so, the charge in 2:15 "can be heard as an extension of that prophetic concern for the vulnerable, expanding the sphere of covenant obligation to include the soil itself."

20. It should be remembered that servant language is also used for God (e.g., Isa 43:24, "burden," NRSV) and, of course, for Jesus Christ.

21. Steck, *World and Environment*, 198; Tanner speaks of a common "Creaturehood" ("Creation," 116-18).

22. See ch. 2 for a discussion of Gen 1:28 and related verses.

23. Tanner, "Creation," 119.

24. See William P. Brown: "God creates not by brute force, but with great care. The human task of subduing the earth does not pit humanity against nature, but reflects a working *with* nature through cultivation and occupation, through promoting and harnessing creation's integrity" (*The Ethos of the Cosmos: The Genesis of Moral Imagination in the Bible* [Grand Rapids: Eerdmans, 1999], 126).

25. For detail and texts, see ch. 8.

26. For detail and texts, see ch. 2.

27. Notably, in the ancient Near Eastern creation stories the gods alone are given these functions; hence, the role given to the creatures in Genesis 1 is an apparent point of uniqueness.

28. For detail, see Terence E. Fretheim, *Exodus* (ed. James Luther Mays; Interpretation: A Bible Commentary for Teaching and Preaching; Louisville: Westminster John Knox, 1991), 177, 181-82, 191.

29. Issues of historicity should not obscure the understanding of the role of the nonhuman in these texts.

30. See ch. 6 for human agency; Gaiser, "To Whom Then Will You Compare Me?"; see also Terence E. Fretheim, *The Suffering of God: An Old Testament Perspective* (Overtures to Biblical Theology, ed. Walter Brueggemann, et al.; Philadelphia: Fortress, 1984), 73-74; "Divine Judgment and the Warming of the World: An Old Testament Perspective," in *God, Evil, and Suffering: Essays in Honor of Paul R. Sponheim* (ed. Terence E. Fretheim and Curtis L. Thompson; Word and World Supplement Series 4; St. Paul: Word and World, 2000); for a thoughtful discussion of many pertinent biblical texts, see Frederick J. Gaiser, "Why Does It Rain? A Biblical Case Study in Divine Causality," *HBT* 25 (2003).

31. See the list of related texts in Gaiser, "Why Does It Rain?" 15.

32. One might observe in view of nature's praise of God (see ch. 8) that if God is the sole causative factor in the workings of the natural order, then nature's praise is actually God's praise of God!

33. One could profitably compare doxological language, ancient and contemporary, where the activity of God typically, and rightly, fills the scene; but, if pressed, one would not be saying that God is the sole causative factor in a whole range of things for which God is being praised.

34. See ch. 7 for details on the God speeches. Carol A. Newsom lifts up these dimensions of the God speeches ("The Book of Job" [vol. 4 of *The New Interpreter's Bible*; Nashville: Abingdon, 1996]).

35. Andrea Dorfman, "Potions from Poisons," *Time Magazine* 157, no. 2 (January 15, 2001).

36. It is even reported that people who own pets have 11 percent fewer visits to the doctor.

37. See ch. 8 for details and texts.

Author Index

Scripture Index

Genesis

Exodus

Leviticus

Joshua

1 Samuel

2 Samuel

1 Kings

2 Kings

1 Chronicles

2 Chronicles

Ezra

Nehemiah

Job

Psalms

Proverbs

Ecclesiastes

Song of Solomon

Isaiah

Jeremiah

Lamentations

Ezekiel

Daniel

Hosea

Joel